THE BATTLE OF LÜTZEN 1632

A Reassessment

André Schürger

'This is the Century of the Soldier', Fulvio Testi, Poet, 1641

Helion & Company

The editor wishes to thank Michał Paradowski for his assistance in procuring the greyscale images for this book.

Helion & Company Limited
Unit 8 Amherst Business Centre
Budbrooke Road
Warwick
CV34 5WE
England
Tel. 01926 499 619
Email: info@helion.co.uk
Website: www.helion.co.uk
Twitter: @helionbooks
Visit our blog http://blog.helion.co.uk/

Published by Helion & Company 2023
Designed and typeset by Serena Jones
Cover designed by Paul Hewitt, Battlefield Design (www.battlefield-design.co.uk)

ISBN 978-1-915113-96-2

British Library Cataloguing-in-Publication Data.
A catalogue record for this book is available from the British Library.

Contents

Note: The archaeology data and colour battle maps which accompany this work are available as a supplementary PDF download from the Helion website.

List of Tables

Tables are placed at the end of the relevant chapter

Foreword

The Battle of Lützen 1632: A Reassessment represents several things at once. Most obviously, it is the story of a 1632 battle in which a King was killed. While the death of Gustav II Adolph shocked a Continent because the mystery of how he died was lost in the literal fog of war, it did not end the war. The mystery fascinated people and added embellishment to historical accounts, and when it was examined there were problems in interpretation, which probably began the night after the battle ended. These questions continue to push interest in the Battle of Lützen even today. Curiosity about the battle, and what actually happened on 16 November 1632, drove historical research and then the battlefield artefact recovery. This is the story as understood today.

Even before the artefact recovery, the relic hunting, commenced, there had to be a clearly stated plan based on understanding of what the historical sources said about the battle. The plan came about because the documentary materials were in conflict; even when they provided the same details, their location within the battle's chronology and physical landscape was often confused. Unravelling the issue of who obtained information and how was a key to seeing the Battle of Lützen in a new way. It was of key importance to show that even eyewitnesses had to be crosschecked and verified because where they stood on the field, what they could see from there, and what activity they engaged in affected an eyewitness's oral and written battle reports.

A written report was important in this undertaking but if an eyewitness told someone who was not present what happened immediately after the battle and that person wrote it down, some credibility had to be given the post-battle report. Then, there were many others who took the initial reports and oral accounts and embellished them, passing them off as factual accounts after adding a particular bias to the history. This required tracing the written material back to an original source, then explaining what was added, interpreting why it might have been added, and how that affected later accounts. It was complicated.

The textual study was made more complicated by a lack of standardisation of terminology, not only across linguistic boundaries, but also within a single language. The specific meaning of an important word could have an impact on understanding a crucial battle episode. Any new interpretation of what a word meant had to be crosschecked in period literature, and then against what was found on the battlefield. At a time of tactical and weaponry evolution, it was important to know, for example that a weapon's terminology related to a certain range of bullet sizes, but it was not enough to say the term meant one thing; the precise terminology could, in many cases, be checked against what was found, and where, on the battlefield.

This sort of understanding could not be obtained without knowing the weapons and the methods they required for effective tactics in an engagement. Realising this, André went about the dual process of learning how units were equipped with certain weapons, how they could manoeuvre across the landscape, when the fighting began, and how they utilised their weapons within those formations. As this study progressed, he also learned how the weapons operated, how far a reach they had, and what problems they likely had during a battle. Together, the weapons and groups of men dictated the tactics of the battle in an evolving sequence that might be described as an arms race with black powder and long spears.

Then, once the documentary sources had been analysed, the landscape inspected, the weapons and tactics evaluated, a series of questions were drawn up that represented inconsistencies about battle events and their sequence. These questions were ones that, having exhausted the documentary and other historical sources, could only be answered by archaeology. In effect, non-field research created a wish list of what André wanted to know about Lützen. This led to organising the land available for research into manageable sections that could be systematically collected.

That field shows one very good example of how archaeology should be conducted on a battlefield. It is not a rapid process. It took five years with steady, often boring, work to retrieve pieces of metal lost almost 400 years ago. The field research was systematic, fully covering all zones available for collecting. It was the first metal detector collection on such a large scale with such closely ordered collecting lanes. It provided the solid evidence that is essential for creating meaningful artefact distribution maps. The fieldwork was time-consuming, labour-intensive and frustrating when nothing was turning up and when areas that the documents said nothing about, or indicated had not been involved, also had to be checked because areas where nothing was found could be as important as those where artefacts were recovered. It could also be exhilarating when numerous artefacts were found in places where nothing was supposed to have happened. Such metal detecting episodes required updating the research plan because an assumption driving the fieldwork had been proven wrong. It was possible because every battle relic was located in real space that could be shown on a scaled map.

Fieldwork ended when all available areas had been searched. This point needs clarification because some battle episodes took place where a parking lot or building complex exists today, and the field crew was denied access to other areas for a variety of reasons. Outdoor work is more enjoyable but once analysis started, new understanding of the Lützen engagement began. Putting all the artefacts, by type, on maps tied to the landscape clearly showed particular battle events that could be related to the historical sources.

Once a final report was submitted to the proper authority, thinking about the battle did not stop even when working on something else. Subsequently André embarked on university courses leading to his doctorate. At university, everything he had said was put under a new and intense scrutiny to see if it held up. Where interpretations were shaky, they were subjected to a rigorous academic testing to see if they were right. Ultimately, for each interpretation, he had to answer one question, 'What would it take to disprove my conclusion?' If there was a possibility of disproving something, then that had to be refined using his field and documentary information. Answering THE questions for specific events made the totality of his work stand out. There were elements that could not be answered given all the information at hand; these became the basis of research work that will hopefully be conducted in the future.

While the book answers a great many questions about the battle, refutes many 'truths', questions long-held views, and provides hard data, there is always more to be done. *The Battle of Lützen 1632: A Reassessment* reflects our understanding of the battle at the present time. This text also issues a challenge and will hopefully serve as an exemplar for how other battlefields should be examined in the future.

Dr Lawrence E. Babits
Author, *A Devil of a Whipping: The Battle of Cowpens*

Acknowledgements

First and foremost, I would like to thank my good friend retired Professor Lawrence E. Babits of East Carolina University for his ideas, advice, proofreading and moral support during the last 12 years, making this book possible.

The Parliamentary Secretary of the Saxony-Anhalt Ministry of Culture Ingo Mund initiated the Lützen research project, envisioning its potentials.

Within the Lützen Project I would like to thank Sonja Quente and Peter Berger for logistical support, my metal detecting team Annemarie Schmiedel, Peter Lohner, Ernst Brusberg, Ursula Stollberg, Ingolf Prellwitz and Detlef Krumpholz, the local historian Rainer Münzberg, and Christoph Foth from the ADG-Agricultural LLC Starsiedel for giving me access to their fields.

I would like to thank Dr Bo Knarrström (Heritage Board Lund) and Tim Sutherland (University of York) for coming to Lützen and sharing their knowledge of battlefield archaeology, metal detecting and geophysics. Special thanks to Peter Engerisser for sharing his time and insight on firearms and to Dr Glenn Foard for sharing his knowledge of battlefield archaeology and the data from his Edgehill project. Many thanks to Marlies Konze, Renate Samariter and Dr Heiko Schäfer from the Stralsund Heritage Board and Dr Fred Hocker from the Stockholm *Vasa* Museum for access to particular collections of bullets, and to Pavel Hrncirík for his data on bullet calibres from Czech Republic battlefields.

Thomas Richter and Dr Ralf Schwarz (Heritage Board Saxony-Anhalt) helped a great deal with computer logistics and general support. Katrin Twiehaus from the ESRI Company was so kind in providing me with a student version of the ArcGIS 10 computer program.

Within the archaeology department, University of Glasgow, I would like to thank the members of my panel Professor Bill Hanson, Dr Chris Dalglish and Dr Matthew Strickland, my supervisors Professor Tony Pollard and Dr Iain Banks, and Dr Natasha Ferguson (National Museum Scotland) who helped me with their insight and experience.

I am most grateful for all the productive discussions with the 'Fields of Conflict Conference' community, particularly Dr Douglas Scott (National Park Service), Dr Achim Rost and Dr Susanne Wilbers-Rost (Museum Kalkriese), Dr Adrian Mandzy (Morehead State University), Dr Lajos Nagyesy (Military Museum Budapest), and Dan Sivilich. Thanks for discussing my ideas and providing support go to Professor emeritus Herbert Langer, Professor Nils Erik Villstrand (University of Turku),

Professor Olaf Mörke (University of Kiel), Professor Vaclav Matousek (University of Prague), Professor Harald Stadler (University of Innsbruck), Professor Steve Murdock (University St. Andrews), Dr Ann Grönhammar (Livrustkammaren Stockholm), Dr Regina Erbentraut (Museum Güstrow), Dr Sabine Eickhoff (Heritage Board Brandenburg) and Dr Andreas Stahl (Heritage Board Saxony-Anhalt); for workshops on battlefield-related finds Dr Stefan Krabath (Heritage Board Saxony), Jochim Weise, Polgár Balázs (Military Museum Budapest) and Kathrin Misterek provided commentary and their thoughts on battlefields.

My thanks also go to the group of US Army company officers and NCOs, who visited the Lützen battlefield in 2011 on their way to Afghanistan; their excellent training and knowledge on strategy and tactics led me to see the battle in a different light; I hope they returned home safely.

Professor Jens Olesen (University of Greifswald) helped translating Danish documents and Dr Inger Schuberth (Lützen foundation) translated Swedish documents and provided me with contacts at several museums in Stockholm, making my research in the *Vasa* Museum possible.

Finally, I would like to thank Eva Carmen Szabó, my wife, who organised the Lützen Project and worked alongside me at the very beginning when metal detecting surveys on battlefields were unknown in Germany. We metal detected on the battlefield together and she helped establish the field methodology, she then worked on numerous aspects of research that provided data used in this book. It was Eva Carmen who translated the Italian documents, discussed many aspects of my research, and thus spent years on the Lützen Project, which would not be what it is now without her.

If I have omitted or forgotten some of you, I apologise and, again, say thank you. All of these people contributed to this project in so many ways. Without your assistance, it would not have been possible to see it completed. Any errors are, of course, my own.

Introduction

The Battle of Lützen has long been seen as the battle where the Swedish King, Gustav II Adolph, died in a thick fog, while his army was slaughtered assaulting Wallenstein's fortifications. The Swedes were fighting an enemy at least equal in strength, and whose front was covered by a two-kilometre-long double trench filled with musketeers, and only the wrath of the Swedish soldiers taking revenge for their slain King saved the day. This repeats, in brief, the myth of the Battle of Lützen as it is recounted in hundreds of books, articles and films – and is entirely wrong.

How could 388 years of such extensive research be so mistaken?

This book is the result of a five-year research project on the Lützen battlefield, where 1.1 km^2 were systematically surveyed with metal detectors and thousands of objects collected, measured and evaluated, followed by a five-year PhD programme at the Department of Battlefield Archaeology of the University of Glasgow.

By examining the battle's military material culture, historical accounts, the landscape and physical evidence, such as artefacts from the battlefield, new insights into the battle's events are generated. The study of battlefield artefact distributions requires a methodology that allows a comparison between two very different sources: the eyewitness account and the 'lead bullet'. To achieve this aim, the development of seventeenth-century firearms is highlighted through an assessment of historical sources and existing weapons and by an evaluation of the bullets from Lützen, providing a baseline for interpreting bullet distribution patterns on the battlefield.

The validity of bullet distribution patterns is also dependant on the deposition process during the battle and the metal detector survey methodologies that also provide vital information for future battlefield surveys. As an overarching methodology, statements from eyewitnesses of the battle are evaluated and compared to bullet distribution patterns, in conjunction with the historic landscape, equipment and tactics. Together, these ultimately lead to a better understanding of the battle and its historical narrative, by asking why reported events actually did not happen at Lützen. This last element is also important to understand the reliability of early modern battle accounts in general. Overall, a more general aim of this case study has been to provide a better insight into the wider potential of early modern battle research in Europe.

This book is the end of 14 years research on the Battle of Lützen and is the end of a long journey I undertook to understand the battle. The political situation of the Thirty Years' War itself is very complex, let alone the development in the military system and weaponry. Together with a combination of historical and archaeological sources, it was not always possible to provide all information needed to explain the Battle of Lützen within the context of the Thirty Years' War and, since battlefield archaeology is a relatively new source of additional detail, the work presented here offers insights into better evaluating any battlefield. To accomplish the best understanding of how historical and archaeological analyses aid our understanding of a battle's events, some basic knowledge of the period and archaeology before reading this book might be beneficial.

1

The 1632 Campaign

Gustav II Adolph

When the Thirty Years' War broke out in 1618, Catholics of the Holy Roman Empire fielded two mighty armies. *Generalleutnant* Johann Tserclaes *Graf von* Tilly commanded the Army of the Catholic League, an alliance of German Catholic states led by the Elector Maximilian of Bavaria. *Generalleutnant* Albrecht Eusebius Wenzel *Graf* von Waldstein, called Wallenstein, commanded the Imperial army of the Emperor Ferdinand II. Although technically on the same side, there was always some rivalry between the two armies and their commanders.

In 1626,[1] Wallenstein and Tilly defeated the Protestants and their Danish allies in Germany and the war seemed to be over. Following occupation of Danish Jutland, Wallenstein planned to build a fleet to finally defeat Denmark. However, when this plan became known, it brought two old enemies, the Danish King Christian IV and the Swedish King Gustav II Adolph,[2] closer together because both feared Imperial domination of the Baltic Sea.[3]

The first opportunity for a joint operation occurred in 1628, when Wallenstein besieged the Hanseatic city of Stralsund. Christian IV and Gustav II Adolph send troops, commanded by the Danish Colonel Heinrich Holk, who successfully relieved the city.[4] At the time, Sweden and Poland were at war (1626–1629) and Gustav II Adolph was not able to intervene more actively in the conflict. That changed in 1629 after diplomatic intervention by France when Cardinal Richelieu negotiated a peace treaty between Sweden and Poland. In December 1630, Gustav II Adolph landed

1 The Gregorian Calendar is used throughout this book.

2 Although often known as Gustavus Adolphus, the King should more correctly be called Gustav II Adolph – as he is called in Sweden – and that convention has been followed throughout in this book. [Ed.]

3 Jens E. Olesen, 'Dänische und Schwedische Zusammenarbeit gegen Wallenstein und den Kaiser 1626–1629', Jens E. Olesen (ed.), *Terra Felix Mecklenburg – Wallenstein in Nordeuropa* (Greifswald: Druckhaus Panzig, 2010), p.46.

4 Olesen, 'Dänische und schwedische Zusammenarbeit', p.54.

Gustav II Adolph Vasa, King of Sweden, commander of the Swedish Army

with a small army of 13,000 men in Germany, on the island Usedom.

In the meantime, Wallenstein fell victim to an intrigue at the Imperial Court and was relieved from service by the Emperor Ferdinand II. Tilly, now commanding both the League and Imperial armies, was unable to handle or supply his combined forces or to stop Gustav II Adolph's advance. After *Feldmarschall* Gottfried Heinrich *Graf* von Pappenheim conquered Magdeburg, one of the largest and most important Protestant cities in the Holy Roman Empire, on 20 May, Tilly's soldiers slipped his control and ran amok. They looted the city and burnt it to the ground, killing 20,000 people. Tilly's logistical problems then became so pressing that he invaded the Protestant but neutral Electorate of Saxony in order to feed his army. These incidents convinced the Electors Georg Wilhelm of Brandenburg and Johann Georg of Saxony to join in an alliance with the Swedish King, although they had kept their neutrality during the war. Gustav II Adolph had avoided battle against the experienced and combined Catholic armies, but now reinforced by a Saxon army he felt strong enough for an open confrontation.

Gustav II Adolph's Strategic Situation in Winter 1631/32

The decisive victory at Breitenfeld on 17 September 1631 enabled Gustav II Adolph and his main army to pursue Tilly through central Germany into Franconia without meeting any noteworthy resistance. After capturing Würzburg on 18 October, he consolidated his position by installing a Franconian government and garrisoning the surrounding cities.[5] He left *Överste* Hastver with 2,000 men in Königshofen to secure his eastern flank.[6] In the west, he captured Frankfurt/Main and Mainz with 13,000 men, thus freeing the Palatinate from Spain. *Fältmarskalk* Gustav Horn with 8,000 men was posted in Würzburg and therefore dispersing the main army for winter but retaining the ability for local attacks while ensuring adequate supplies could be drawn from each area.[7] From these operational bases, he would be able to resume his campaign against the Elector Maximilian of Bavaria in the spring.

5 Peter Engerisser, *Von Kronach nach Nördlingen. Der Dreissigjährige Krieg in Franken, Schwaben und der Oberpfalz 1631–1635* (Weissenstadt: Heinz Späthling, 2007), p.22.

6 Engerisser, *Von Kronach nach Nördlingen*, p.27.

7 Robert Monro, *His Expedition with the Worthy Scots Regiment levied in August 1626 by Sr. Donald Mac-Key* (London: William Jones, 1637) part II, p.108.

Generalissimus Albrecht Eusebius Wenzel Graf von Waldstein, Herzog von Friedland, called Wallenstein, commander of the Imperial–League army

In the east, *Feldmarschall* Hans Georg von Arnim successfully commanded a small Saxon army of 10,000 men against Imperial forces under *Oberst* Tiefenbach.[8] After capturing Bautzen and Görlitz, Arnim turned south to Bohemia and entered Prague on 5 November without any resistance. The Imperial commandant of Prague *Oberst* Marradas had retreated with his garrison to Tabor. A small-scale battle at Nimburg on 23 November against Tiefenbach, who had followed Arnim into Bohemia, revealed the weakness of the still inexperienced Saxon army, which was almost routed at the first sign of any fighting.[9] Even worse, massive supply problems started to damage the morale of Arnim's army and many soldiers died of dysentery or disease.[10] Arnim had lost his offensive capability.

Additionally, Gustav II Adolph had to send *Fältmarskalk* Johan Banér with an army of 8,000 men to recapture Magdeburg.[11] This strong fortress had an Imperial garrison of 2,300 men. Situated north of Gustav II Adolph's position, the Magdeburg garrison threatened the Swedish supply line and blocked Swedish use of the Elbe River for transport. The situation became serious when Pappenheim relieved the city with an additional 4,700 men from Wolfenbüttel. Banér had thought Pappenheim's forces to be much larger and retreated to Osterwied.

Wilhelm *von Sachsen-Weimar* was reinstated as *Herzog* by Gustav II Adolph during his advance south in October 1631. Wilhelm was building up a small army of 8,000 in the Saxon Duchies (Thuringia) to close the gap between Gustav II Adolph and Arnim and discourage any Imperial incursion into West Saxony. When Wilhelm learned about Pappenheim's arrival at Magdeburg, he immediately marched north to support Banér and joined him on the 18 January.[12] A strong Imperial force in Magdeburg could have a disastrous effect on Swedish supply by jeopardising the entire Swedish-Protestant campaign in Bavaria and Bohemia.

Moritz *von Hessen-Kassel* had also just been reinstated as *Landgraf* after his county was freed by Gustav II Adolph and was in the process of recruiting

8 Roland Sennewald, *Das Kursächsische Heer im Dreissigjährigen Krieg* (Berlin: Zeughaus Verlag, 2013), p.88.

9 Sennewald, *Das Kursächsische Heer*, p.92.

10 Sennewald, *Das Kursächsische Heer*, p.96.

11 Sascha Lunyakov and Alexander Querengässer, *Feldmarschall Pappenheim und das Kaiserlich-ligistische Heerwesen in der ersten Hälfte des Dreissigjährigen Krieges* (Berlin, Zeughaus Verlag, 2010), p.46.

12 Lunyakov/Querengässer, *Feldmarschall Pappenheim*, p.48.

Pamphlet describing the arrival of Gustav II Adolf and his army in Germany in 1630. (Sjöhistoriskamuseet, Stockholm)

regiments that would be ready in early 1632 with a total strength of around 8,000 men.[13]

In the north-west in Schleswig and Lower Saxony, *Generalmajor* Alexander Leslie commanded an army of 13,000 that protected Gustav II Adolph's long western flank against Pappenheim's force and the Spanish army in the Netherlands.

A corps of 4,000, commanded by *Fältmarskalk* Ake Henriksson Todd, was based in Mecklenburg, positioned to move against the remaining Imperial and League garrisons in the north.[14]

In early 1632, Gustav II Adolph's military situation seemed to have consolidated after the triumphal march south. He had freed most German Protestant states and cities from Imperial–League occupation and he had brought the Protestant, but previously neutral, Electorates of Saxony and Brandenburg into an alliance. On his march south, Gustav II Adolph had captured huge amounts of weaponry, artillery, and military equipment from various armouries and also from the Breitenfeld battlefield. His allies, including the *Herzog* Wilhelm and the *Landgraf* Moritz, were recruiting armies in the newly freed states. In addition, the Swedish main army spent

13 C. V. Wedgwood, *Der Dreissigjährige Krieg* (Hamburg: Nikol Verlagsgesellschaft, 2011), p.268.

14 Monro, *His Expedition*, part II, p.102.

the winter in Catholic territory, which made it easier and cheaper to supply and maintain them. The new territory provided the necessary manpower and economic power to carry a future offensive into the centre of the League and the Empire. In January 1632, the Swedish/Protestant alliance had a total strength of approximately 70,000 in the field and probably the same amount in garrisons distributed across Germany.

However, Gustav II Adoph's rapid advance into Franconia with his main army had an adverse side effect that would haunt him in 1632. By entering middle-south Germany to supply his army at low cost, Gustav II Adolph had brought all Catholic, but neutral, bishoprics and archbishoprics into the war on the Catholic side, thus making the same mistake that Tilly had when he invaded Saxony. In addition, his offensive into middle-south Germany had left Arnim without Swedish support.[15] As early as November 1631, it became clear that the Saxon army alone did not have the capability to maintain an offensive into Bohemia. Saxon soldiers still lacked experience, which negatively affected their confidence, discipline, and morale. With the supply system failing, they were in no shape to win a battle. Even though stuck in Prague only a small part of Bohemia was actually occupied by Saxon troops, who numbered perhaps no more than 10,000 men, and so the Imperial side began to recover. When Wallenstein received a commission to rebuild the Imperial army in December, he had Silesia and most of Bohemia at his disposal. Adding to the Saxon problems was Arnim's past. He had made his reputation under Wallenstein and that fact made him a target for intrigues at the Saxon court.[16] Failing to conquer the economically strong Bohemia and Silesia in 1631, when it could have been achieved easily, had a disastrous effect on Gustav II Adolph's campaign in 1632.

In the west, Gustav II Adolph had deployed four armies with capable commanders, for example Alexander Leslie and Johann Banér, with a total strength of around 40,000 men, half of them veterans. They outnumbered Pappenheim's army by at least two to one and could have defeated him easily. However, Gustav II Adolph failed to appoint an overall commander in the west, as he seemed, as a rule, to want to avoid giving one commander too much military power. The result was an uncoordinated advance aiming for enemy cities instead of defeating the opposing army first. Pappenheim evaded the main Protestant armies, concealed his actual low strength and conducted surprise attacks against isolated Protestant forces. His tactics of using economy of force while achieving mass against the dispersed Protestants were so effective that he delayed their advance until Gustav II Adolph ordered *Herzog* Wilhelm and Banér to join him in Franconia for his campaign against Bavaria in April 1632. That gave Pappenheim time to reorganise his forces; he remained a constant threat to Gustav II Adolph's western flank throughout the whole of the year.

15 Sverker Oredsson, 'Gustav II. Adolf und Wallenstein – ein Vergleich', Jens E. Olesen (ed.), *Terra Felix Mecklenburg – Wallenstein in Nordeuropa* (Greifswald, Druckhaus Panzig, 2010), p.96. Alternatively, the total absence of Swedish troops in Bohemia might have been the result of the Elector Johann Georg of Saxony refusing to accept help because he feared the Swedish influence.

16 Sennewald, *Das kursächsische Heer*, pp.90 and 102.

King Gustav II Adolf. Portrait by Michiel Jansz van Mierevelt, *c.* 1633. (Rijksmuseum)

Gustav II Adolph's Bavarian Campaign

After the failure of a brief diplomatic intervention from Cardinal Richelieu, being an attempt to drive a wedge between Habsburg and Bavaria and create an anti-Habsburg coalition,[17] the Swedes began their military action in February 1632, with *Fältmarskalk* Gustav Horn attacking the lands of the Prince-Bishop of Bamberg with 14,000 men. The city of Bamberg surrendered on 11 February after offering little resistance.[18] At the time, Tilly's once mighty League army consisted of only 12,000 men and 8,000 unreliable militia. Nevertheless, he commenced a counteroffensive against Horn. The Battle of Bamberg on 9 March would be Tilly's last victory. An error in communication led to an attack by one of Horn's regiments, which was ambushed and routed. Although the fight went on until two o'clock in the afternoon, Horn was forced to retreat – the retreat became a rout, which in turn became a slaughter.[19] It was the first Swedish defeat in Germany.

Meanwhile, *Herzog* Wilhelm and *Fältmarskalk* Banér reached Bavaria and joined Gustav II Adolph. With Horn's remaining troops, the Swedish King fielded an army of 36,600 men.[20] The objective of this massive troop concentration was the occupation of Bavaria and an offensive against Austria, which seemed the correct strategy at that time. Tilly had no other choice than to retreat, and a last attempt to stop the King's advance at the river Lech failed. Tilly was mortally wounded during the Battle of Rain on 15 April, when his army was routed, and the commander of the League army died in Ingolstadt on 30 April from osteomyelitis.[21]

Gustav II Adolph did not pursue Tilly, but marched to Augsburg, an economically and symbolically important city, which surrendered on 20 April. A few days later, he turned towards Ingolstadt.

While the Elector Maximilian retreated from Ingolstadt to Regensburg with the remnants of the League army, following the advice of his dying *Generalleutnant*, Gustav II Adolph began the siege of the city on 29 April. Ingolstadt was the strongest fortress in Bavaria with an important strategic

17 Wedgwood, *Der Dreissigjährige Krieg*, p.271, Monro, *His Expedition*, part II, p.103.

18 Engerisser, *Von Kronach nach Nördlingen*, p.39.

19 Engerisser, *Von Kronach nach Nördlingen*, p.47.

20 Engerisser, *Von Kronach nach Nördlingen*, p.57.

21 Marcus Junkelmann, 'Tilly. Eine Karriere im Zeitalter der *Religionskriege* und der Militärischen Revolution', in Marcus Junkelmann (ed.), *Heiliger oder Kriegsverbrecher* (Altötting: Gebr. Geiselberger, 2007), p.38. Monro, *His Expedition*, part II, p.117.

position on the Danube. It was well defended with a garrison of 7,000 men and ample artillery. Nevertheless, by the second day, the Swedish army was able to take several small outer forts and a bridge although taking heavy casualties.[22] It is uncertain why Gustav II Adolph lifted the siege on 4 May, but it was an error in judgement and a strategic mistake. With the possession of Ingolstadt and Regensburg, the League army controlled the important Danube bridges. Maximilian could keep open communications to Wallenstein in Bohemia, while his League army could reform and recruit its strength north of the Danube.

Gustav II Adolph marched south to conquer a much easier and more lucrative city, Maximilian's residence – Munich. However, by turning away from Ingolstadt, the Swedish King lost momentum and subsequently, his campaign against Bavaria and Austria failed.

Wallenstein, the Generalissimus and the Bohemian Campaign

Graf von Wallenstein was in a comfortable position in Bohemia after the Battle of Breitenfeld. The Swedish main army moved to mid Germany away from his county. Although Arnim occupied some possessions in Prague, he protected the area from being looted by his men. Wallenstein and Arnim esteemed each other as colleagues and always maintained good relations. Wallenstein's territory was secure and on 29 November, he opened negotiations with Arnim to conclude a separate peace with Saxony but it was without having the official authority.[23]

Meanwhile, the Swedish army approaching Bavaria put Maximilian under pressure. He feared the loss of the Electorate to Gustav II Adolph and saw no alternative other than to ask Ferdinand II to reinstate Wallenstein as overall commander of the Imperial army, although he had been the leading figure behind Wallenstein's fall in 1630. Despite Ferdinand II's efforts, Wallenstein refused several times until, in December 1631, Maximilian and Ferdinand were so desperate that they allowed Wallenstein to dictate his own conditions. For the moment, Wallenstein agreed to build an army – if the Emperor paid it in full for three months without him taking command.[24]

Albrecht von Wallenstein. Portrait by Conrelis Danckerts (I). (Rijksmuseum)

22 Engerisser, *Von Kronach nach Nördlingen*, p.61.

23 Sennewald, *Das kursächsische Heer*, p.90.

24 Helmut Diwald, *Wallenstein* (München: Bechtle, 1969), p.476.

What followed was a strange campaign without an Imperial commander. Nevertheless, *Generalwachtmeister* Heinrich Holk and *Generalfeldzeugmeister* Matthias Gallas followed Wallenstein's 'advice' in mid December to march from Upper Palatinate and Pilsen towards Prague. Tiefenbach and Marradas, however, had already sent their troops into winter quarters and were not so eager to follow Wallenstein into the field.[25] While Holk and Gallas made a slow advance against the Saxon army in Bohemia, Wallenstein made careful preparations for war. Meanwhile, he continued negotiating with Arnim and released Saxon prisoners, but also increased pressure on the Elector, Johann Georg, by sending troops into Saxony.[26] In February, still without official command, Wallenstein closed the ring around Prague.[27]

In March, when the situation in Bavaria became critical, negotiations with Wallenstein were renewed and he finally agreed to take command in mid April.[28] Although the actual contract is lost Wallenstein's new rank is enlightening. Traditionally, the ruler of a state was the overall commander, at least in theory; his assistant was a lieutenant-general who, in reality, commanded the army. Wallenstein, however, demanded the rank of '*Generalissimus*', which meant that he commanded instead of Ferdinand II, and not as his second in command; it was an unprecedented situation. Additionally, he would now outrank every other commander, something that was particularly important with regard to the commander of the League army, who held the rank of *Generalleutnant*, and who had been his rival in the past.

After taking command in April, Wallenstein sent 5,000 men to Tilly for the defence of Bavaria, but was unwilling to send more. His army was not fully operational and the Saxons, although weakened through supply problems, were still a threat to Bohemia that could not be left unchallenged. Wallenstein's strategy was to avoid a war on two fronts and thus he first concentrated his forces against Saxony. On 25 May, he took Prague after a short bombardment.[29] With the fall of Eger 24 June, there were now no Saxon troops left in Bohemia and Wallenstein could concentrate his army against Gustav II Adolph.[30] He failed, however, in his attempt to get a separate peace with Johann Georg.

Nurnberg

In early June, Wallenstein approached Franconia, while Maximilian marched north to join him and Gustav II Adolph realised the danger coming from a combined Imperial–League army to his rear. He immediately hurried to Fürth (17 June) with the intention of separating the two opponents,

25 Sennewald, *Das kursächsische Heer*, pp.94–95.

26 Sennewald, *Das kursächsische Heer*, pp.95, 102.

27 Sennewald, *Das kursächsische Heer*, p.106.

28 Diwald, *Wallenstein*, p.480.

29 Sennewald, *Das kursächsische Heer*, p.106.

30 Sennewald, *Das kursächsische Heer*, p.110.

Senior officer in three-quarter armour, first half of the seventeenth century. Jan Martszen the Younger. (Rijksmuseum)

but arrived one day late.[31] With only 16,000 men against approximately double that number of Imperial–League soldiers, the King fell back to Nurnberg and fortified his position while calling for reinforcements from all theatres of war.[32] Retreat was not an option because Nurnberg was economically and symbolically important; the strategic key position for all Swedish operations in Bavaria and Austria. Strategically the King could not leave such a massive force, the combined Imperial–League army, free to operate in his rear. His actions aimed at assembling a large army, albeit weakening the other theatres in the process, illustrates his intention to force Wallenstein into a decisive battle.[33] Wallenstein, however, did not want to risk his army by attacking a fortified Swedish position even with a numerical superiority, so he fortified the high ground at Zirndorf in close proximity to Nurnberg, on 27 July.[34]

With such a concentration of forces, supply became a major problem for both sides. A total of approximately 50,000 soldiers and 30,000 horses for the cavalry, artillery and baggage train consumed 150 tons of food and 600 tons of forage per day, not counting the camp followers and reinforcements.[35] A war of logistics began. The Protestant *Oberst* Georg Chistoph von Taupadel captured the Imperial–League main depot in Freystadt 9 August and carried those supplies back to Nurnberg. An attempt to recapture the supplies ended in the defeat of an Imperial force under *Generalwachtmeister* Ernst Georg von Sparr at Burgthann on 10 August.[36] Although a major setback for Wallenstein, it remained only a single incident. The *Generalissimus* controlled the whole area because of his superiority in light cavalry, making foraging for the Swedish army extremely difficult.[37] In addition, his supply sources were nearby in Bamberg, Ansbach, the Upper Palatinate and Bavaria, while Gustav II Adolph had to transport his supplies through a small corridor to the north-west.[38] Although the loss of soldiers due to starvation, disease and desertion in both armies was immense and thousands of horses died, Wallenstein's actions suggest that his strategy of fighting a war of attrition was intended to force Gustav II Adolph to attack his fortified position.

31 Engerisser, *Von Kronach nach Nördlingen*, p.104.

32 The strength of the Imperial–League army in early July is uncertain. Monro, *His Expedition*, part II, p.133.

33 Sennewald, *Das kursächsische Heer*, p.120.

34 Monro, *His Expedition*, part II, p.134.

35 According to Donald W. Engels, *Alexander the Great and Logistics of the Macedonian army* (Berkeley, University of California Press, 1980), p.18, each man consumes three pounds of food per day, which was the same in the sixteenth century (Lazarus von Schwendi, *Kriegs Discurs. Von Bestellung dess gantzen Kriegswesens und von den Kriegsämptern* (Frankfurt am Main, 1594), p.172. Each horse needs 20 pounds of forage per day.

36 Monro, *His Expedition*, part II, pp.144–145.

37 Diwald, *Wallenstein*, p.492.

38 Sennewald, *Das kursächsische Heer*, p.120–121, Engerisser, *Von Kronach nach Nördlingen*, p.105.

Bernard of Saxe-Weimar. Michiel Jansz. Van Mierevelt. (Public domain)

The Swedish–German reinforcements with Banér, *Herzog* Wilhelm, *Herzog* Bernhard *von Sachsen-Weimar*, *Landgraf* Wilhelm V *von Hessen*, and the *Pfalzgraf* Christian of Birkenfeld, led by the Swedish Chancellor Axel Oxenstierna, assembled at Kitzingen 16 August and arrived at Bruck, one mile from Nurnberg, on 24 August. With these reinforcements, the strength of the Swedish–German army increased to 46,000 men.[39] The sole purpose of such a concentration of forces was either a decisive battle or, if that failed, an assault on Wallenstein's position, because Gustav II Adolph could not supply this army for long.[40] After a few days of rest from the long march, Oxenstierna's army began to advance.

The Battle of Zirndorf began on 31 August with skirmishing between Imperial outposts and Oxenstierna's advance guard. The next day, the combined Swedish–German army began an artillery bombardment on the Imperial main redoubts, but it was ineffective. After some manoeuvres caused by false reconnaissance reports on 2 September, Gustav II Adolph, believing Wallenstein had withdrawn his main army, ordered an assault on the strongest part of the Imperial fortifications 3 September. The fierce Imperial defence surprised the Swedish assault group. After taking heavy losses, by evening they had been able to take some outer fortifications, but had to retreat after Wallenstein's reinforcements arrived. Wallenstein now had 44,500 men at his disposal opposing Gustav II Adolph's 46,000.

Rain during the night soaked the ground and made it impossible to move the Swedish heavy artillery closer to the Imperial redoubts. A Swedish assault the next morning was bloody, futile and brief; Gustav II Adolph broke off the attack.[41] Wallenstein lost 600 dead and 655 wounded, Swedish casualties amounted to at least 1,200 dead and 2,000 wounded, although the losses through desertion and exhaustion were much higher.[42] More serious was the high loss of officers; *Oberst* Robert Monro was wounded by a sniper;[43] *Överste* Lennard Torstensson, who was taken prisoner, would be particularly greatly missed at Lützen, where his expertise with artillery could have changed the

39 Sennewald, *Das kursächsische Heer*, p.120, Engerisser, *Von Kronach nach Nördlingen*, p.109.

40 Diwald, *Wallenstein*, p.493.

41 Sennewald, *Das kursächsische Heer*, pp.125–129, Engerisser, *Von Kronach nach Nördlingen*, pp.109–110.

42 At Nurnberg the Swedish army lost approximately 10,000 soldiers, mostly from sickness and desertion, and 10,000–12,000 horses, primarily from starvation (Engerisser, *Von Kronach nach Nördlingen*, p.116).

43 Monro, *His Expedition*, part II, p.149.

outcome of the battle.[44] The Swedish retreat broke the myth of Gustav II Adolph's invincibility.[45]

Arnim's Silesian Campaign

When Wallenstein moved his main army to Nurnberg, Arnim gained the time to regroup and the space to manoeuvre. He started an offensive against Bohemia with approximately 10,000 men. It ended after only four days at Zittau when, on 24 July, Marradas sent a relief force to the besieged garrison. However, instead of retreating to Dresden to defend Saxony, Arnim marched north to Hoyerswerda on 3 August to open a new offensive against Silesia, avoiding the strong Imperial garrison of Bohemia in the process.[46]

The Imperial garrisons in Silesia were caught by surprise. Freistadt fell without a shot being fired on 4 August, Gross Glogau surrendered on 7 August and the same day Steinau with its important Oder bridge fell into Saxon hands, and Lübben fell the following day. As a direct consequence of this surprise attack the Silesian *Herzog von* Liegnitz declared neutrality on 10 August.[47]

Meanwhile, the Imperial commander in Silesia *Feldmarschall* Christian von Illow, gathered a small army of approximately 10,000 men and retook Steinau 18 August, having the element of surprise on his side. However, his counter-attack ended there; when he learned that Swedish-Brandenburg troops commanded by *Oberst* Jacob Mac Duwall was marching towards Silesia to support Arnim, he fortified his position. Duwall joined the Saxon army 26 August increasing its strength to 16,000 men. Arnim, having regained numerical superiority, continued his offensive.[48] He avoided a costly attack on the fortified Imperial positions by bypassing them, and then built a fort at the Oder River to block the supply line along the river.[49] This strategy worked and forced the Imperial army to retreat to Breslau 4 September.[50]

At Breslau, Arnim utilised the same tactics with success. This time he pursued the Imperial army, which was defeated on 11 September with heavy losses. Exploiting the victory, Arnim marched south and took Neisse on 22 September and Oppeln on 14 October, without encountering any resistance, all the while leaving Duwall at Breslau, which still refused to surrender. At Oppeln, Arnim consolidated his position by occupying the surrounding towns and villages; here he heard about Wallenstein conquering West Saxony and threatening the capital, Dresden. Arnim broke off the offensive and rushed back to Saxony

44 Engerisser, *Von Kronach nach Nördlingen*, p.111.

45 Diwald, *Wallenstein*, p.495; Sennewald, *Das kursächsische Heer*, p.144.

46 Sennewald, *Das kursächsische Heer*, pp.133–134.

47 Sennewald, *Das kursächsische Heer*, pp.136–137.

48 Sennewald, *Das kursächsische Heer*, p.137.

49 The importance of river transport for supply during the Thirty Years' War is mentioned by Monro, *His Expedition*, part II, p.50, in this case for the Swedish camp at Werben in 1631.

50 Sennewald, *Das kursächsische Heer*, p.140.

with his best regiments.[51] *Feldmarschall* Illow took advantage of the new situation and opened a counteroffensive, retaking Neisse and Braun on 12 November.[52]

Wallenstein's Saxon Campaign

Heinrich Holk, artist unknown. At some stage the portrait has been reversed, as Holk was missing his left eye, not his right. (Nationalmuseum, Stockholm)

In mid August, Arnim, by taking the Oder bridges at Steinau, threatened Breslau and south Silesia – Wallenstein could not afford to lose this important duchy. While he was still at Nurnberg, struggling with Gustav II Adolph with supply, he sent *Feldmarschall Leutnant* Heinrich Holk with a small force of 6,000 men, all he could spare at the time, to Saxony to relieve Illow in Silesia. Holk looted Plauen and took Zwickau on 28 August.[53] On 2 September, he arrived at Chemnitz, which was successfully defended by Löser with the only regular infantry regiment in Saxony, the rest of Saxony was defended only by unreliable militia. Although Holk's Corps was too small and lacked heavy artillery to take Chemnitz by assault, his cavalry devastated Saxony; *Oberst* Marcus Corpes with a Croat regiment even looted villages near Dresden, where they met and were defeated by a newly raised cavalry regiment.[54] At the same time, *Generalwachtmeister* Nicolas *Freiherr* von Desfour, the Imperial commander in Bohemia, gathered his forces at the Saxon border to maintain contact with Holk and increase the pressure on the Elector, Johann Georg.[55]

Having an Imperial corps under Holk devastating his country and Desfour threatening his southern border, Johann Georg's position became precarious. Despite his pleas to Arnim to return to Saxony, Arnim refused because he did not want to jeopardise the Silesia offensive. By returning to Saxony, he would lose too much time marching back, still have an insufficient number of troops to beat Holk, and would give Desfour the ability to operate with more freedom, because the threat of a Saxon offensive against Bohemia from Silesia, which held him in place, would have been removed.

After Gustav II Adolph's retreat from Nurnberg on 18 September, Wallenstein sent a force of 10,000 men under *Feldmarschall* Matthias *Graf*

51 Sennewald, *Das kursächsische Heer*, pp.144–145.

52 Sennewald, *Das kursächsische Heer*, p.150.

53 Monro, *His Expedition*, part II, p.156.

54 Engerisser, *Von Kronach nach Nördlingen*, p.119.

55 Sennewald, *Das kursächsische Heer*, pp.145–148.

Gottfried Heinrich Graf zu Pappenheim. Cornelis Danckerts I, 1603–1656. (Rijksmuseum)

Gallas into Saxony.[56] Gallas arrived at Altenburg on 9 October, the same day that Holk finally took Chemnitz. Maximilian separated from Wallenstein and marched with the League army to defend Bavaria against Gustav II Adolph. In the meantime, Wallenstein marched the Imperial army to Coburg on 10 October, the strongest Protestant fortress, but failed to take it.[57] Meanwhile, Holk and Gallas joined forces and took Freiburg on 13 October, Meissen on 20 October, and Lommatzsch and Oschatz on 21 October. At Leipzig, Holk and Gallas joined Wallenstein and together they took the city and the castle Pleissenburg on 1 November.[58]

When he began his offensive against Saxony, Wallenstein had sent for Pappenheim, who, after the expedition to Maastricht, was operating in Lower Saxony against Brunswick and Hannover. The *Feldmarschall* had already disobeyed Wallenstein's orders once to join him at Nurnberg, but this time he yielded to the Generalissimus' command. Pappenheim marched via Mühlhausen and Erfurt, and took the castle of Heldungen and the cities of Halle and Merseburg on 5 November.[59]

Wallenstein now occupied West Saxony with the strategically and economically important city of Leipzig as his base of operations. Such a concentration of forces illustrates Wallenstein's plan to force a separate peace on Elector Johann Georg and lure Gustav II Adolph into a decisive battle on his terms.

Wallenstein's strategy had an impact on all theatres of war. After his retreat from Nurnberg, Gustav II Adolph at first resumed his offensive against Bavaria. He was in the process of planning a siege of Ingolstadt to finally take this important Bavarian fortress when, on 18 October, he received information about Wallenstein's offensive in Saxony. Saxony was Gustav II Adolph's most important ally, but having been forced to enter the war by Tilly a year ago, the Elector Johann Georg was not eager to fight. Gustav II Adolph had no alternative but to relieve Saxony. He immediately sent Bernhard von Weimar, whom he had left at Würzburg, with his corps to Saxony and followed with his main army, this gave Maximilian the time to reorganise the defence of Bavaria and to strengthen the League army. Gustav

56 Gallas was promoted to Field Marshal on 13 October (Engerisser, *Von Kronach nach Nördlingen*, p.120). Robert Monro, *His Expedition*, part II, p.154.

57 Engerisser, *Von Kronach nach Nördlingen*, p.123.

58 Sennewald, *Das kursächsische Heer*, p.148, Monro, *His Expedition*, part II, pp.154–156.

59 Sennewald, *Das kursächsische Heer*, pp.149–150, Monro, *His Expedition*, part II, p.157.

II Adolph and Bernhard von Weimar joined forces at Erfurt on 2 November and then rested their forces for six days.[60]

Arnim had finally sent some troops back to Saxony to prevent Dresden from being taken by Holk and Gallas and the Life Regiments of Foot and Horse arrived at Dresden on 14 October. Arnim returned to Saxony on 7 November to assess the situation, which he found to be serious, and he had returned with several regiments from Silesia, something he had been trying to avoid for weeks. On route to Saxony however, Arnim had received a letter from Gustav II Adolph advising him to stay in Silesia. The result was that Arnim's Corps marched back and forth, seriously decreasing the strength of the Silesian army and losing the momentum for the offensive, just as he came too late to take part in the Battle of Lützen.[61] †

† See PDF download, Plate 1: Start of Wallenstein's Saxony campaign, 21 August–5 November

On the other hand, Wallenstein weakened the Catholic position in Lower Saxony and Westphalia by ordering Pappenheim to Saxony, thus giving *Herzog* Georg von Braunschweig-Lüneburg the freedom to operate without the threat of Pappenheim's army. *Herzog* Georg arrived in Wittenberg with a corps of 6,000 men during mid October and from there he marched to defend the Elbe bridges at Torgau and secure the Saxon northern flank.[62] Wallenstein's separation of the Imperial and League armies to defend Bavaria and attack Saxony at the same time, instead of operating together, would have consequences.[63]

Bernhard von Weimar's advance guard arrived at Naumburg on 8 November and fortified the position.[64] Four days later, the King advanced 11 km north towards Weissenfels where Wallenstein's army, reinforced by a League force under Pappenheim, waited in full battle array. Outnumbered, the Swedish army returned to Naumburg, while Wallenstein fortified his camp at Weissenfels.[65]

Wallenstein's army of around 13,000 foot and 7,500 horse, with an estimated 5,000 camp followers and 2,500 horses of the baggage train, artillery train and cavalry reserve horses, consumed approximately 125 tons of food and forage per day and the Swedish army probably needed not much less. After four days 1,000 tons of food and forage was used and the area was almost certainly devastated, creating a similar situation to that at Nurnberg.

This time it was Wallenstein who weakened another theatre of war by ordering Pappenheim to Saxony with the intention of defeating Gustav II Adolph in a decisive battle. While Arnim approached from the east, *Herzog* Georg from the north, and Gustav II Adolph waited in the south, in

60 Sennewald, *Das kursächsische Heer*, p.149, Monro, *His Expedition*, part II, p.160.

61 Sennewald, *Das kursächsische Heer*, pp.149–150.

62 Sennewald, *Das kursächsische Heer*, p.149, Richard Brzezinski, *Lützen 1632. Climax of the Thirty Years' War* (Oxford, 2001), p.29, Brigitte Holl, 'Wallensteins angebliche Skizze für die Schlacht bei Lützen', in *Schriften des Heeresgeschichtlichen Museums in Wien*, vol. 7: *Der Dreissigjährige Krieg, Wien*, p.67.

63 Monro, *His Expedition*, part II, p.154.

64 Sennewald, *Das kursächsische Heer*, p.149, Monro, *His Expedition*, part II, pp.160–161.

65 Relation from 1632 (Droysen, 'Gedruckte Relationen', p.6).

† See PDF download, Plate 2: Gustav II Adolph's approach to Naumburg, 5–14 November

the absence of Pappenheim Lower Saxony was about to be conquered by Protestant armies. Time was working for Gustav II Adolph.†

After receiving news that a Protestant army was about to take Cologne,[66] and considering the logistical difficulties at Weissenfels, Wallenstein dispersed his army in the morning of 14 November.[67] He sent Pappenheim and his brigade back to Lower Saxony and the Rhineland to prevent the loss of the whole region; on the way, and he was ordered to take the fortress of Giebichenstein in Halle to take control of the city. At the same time, the Regiment Suys was sent to Zwickau and the Regiment Mannsfeld to Eilenburg to support *Oberst* Melchior von Hatzfeld, who with the Regiments Trcka foot, Thun, and Hatzfeld, some 3,000 men, was facing *Herzog* Georg's 6,000 in Torgau.[68]

Later that day, Wallenstein sent 17 regiments to Chemitz, Zwickau, Altenburg, Eilenburg and Merseburg, most of them to protect his route back to Bohemia from Arnim and/or Gustav II Adolph. The Generalissimus himself retained 10 regiments as a rearguard. On his route to Leipzig, a central position where he could move to support any garrison, he made camp at Lützen, while the Croats at Rippach under Beygott screened his withdrawal.[69]

Wallenstein has often been criticised for dispersing his army at this time,[70] but once his regiments were entrenched, he would have been in a strong position for the winter with the garrisons able to support each other, cutting

66 Brzezinski, *Lützen*, p.32.

67 Brzezinski, *Lützen*, p.32. The connection between logistical problems and Wallenstein's retreat has not yet been the subject of serious research, but the underdeveloped nature of the early modern economy caused logistical problems throughout the Thirty Years' War in general (David A. Parrott, 'The Thirty Years' War, 1618–48', in John Andreas Olsen and Colin S. Gray (eds), *The Practice of Strategy: From Alexander the Great to the Present* (Oxford: Oxford University Press, 2011), p.133). Naumburg and Weissenfels are both located on the Saale, a small, navigable river. The importance of river transport during the Thirty Years' War is mentioned by Monro, *His Expedition*, part II, p.50, although in this case for the Swedish camp at Werben in 1631. However, Wallenstein's river supply route was blocked by the Swedish army to the south and a Saxon garrison at Halle to the north. Concentrations of large forces could not be supplied for more than a few days. As an example, in 1863, food began to run low in two days after the 75,000-strong Confederate army had concentrated at Gettysburg, despite more modern means of transportation (Engels, *Alexander the Great*, p.45).

68 The Regiments Mannsfeld, Suys, and most of Pappenheim's corps did not arrive in time, or not at all, for the Battle of Lützen, because they were furthest away and must have moved first thing in the morning of 14 November according to the Trauttmansdorff list (Barbara Stadler, *Pappenheim und die Zeit des Dreissigjährigen Krieges* (Winterthur, Gemsberg-Verlag, 1991), pp.891–892).

69 According to Wallenstein's disposition 14 November see Hermann Hallwich, *Briefe und Akten zur Geschichte Wallensteins 1630–1634*, vol. 3 (*Fontes rerum Austriacarum*. vol. 65) (Wien, A. Hölder, 1912), pp.482–483.

70 Geoffrey Parker, *The Thirty Years' War* (London, Routledge & Kegan Paul, 1984), p.131, Peter Englund, *Die Verwüstung Deutschlands. Eine Geschichte des Dreissigjährigen Krieges* (Stuttgart: Klett-Cotta, 1998), p.129, William P. Guthrie, *Battles of the Thirty Years' War. From White Mountain to Nordlingen 1618–1635* (Westport/Connecticut/London: Greenwood Press, 2002), p.196. See Josef Seidler, *Untersuchungen über die Schlacht bei Lützen* (Memmingen, self-

Soldiers pillaging a village, a common occurrence during the Thirty Years' War. Jan Martszen the Younger (1609–after 1647). (Rijksmuseum)

off Swedish supply lines to the Baltic Sea, dividing the Swedish and Saxon armies, and supplying his own army from enemy territory.

What ruined Wallenstein's plans was an intelligence report Gustav II Adolph received in the afternoon of 14 November about the retreat and dispersal. The next morning, Gustav II Adolph took his whole army to follow the *Generalissimus*, attempting to catch him by surprise. Gustav II Adoplh left the Regiment Dam Vizthum and the Saxon militia as a garrison in Naumburg to protect communications with the centre of operations at Erfurt.[71] In addition, he left most of his baggage train behind to speed up the pursuit.

At noon, the Swedish advance guard, of Stalhandske's Finnish cavalry, engaged Beygott's Croats, but the position at Rippach, on a crest with a boggy stream to their front, was formidable. In the afternoon, Eberstein's regiment arrived and they forced their way over the bridges and onto the crest using salvos of musketry with the support of their regimental guns. Beygott had, however, delayed Gustav II Adolph's advance until dawn and prevented a surprise attack.

The Swedish army crossed the Rippach and camped on the northern side of the stream, ready to attack Wallenstein at Lützen the next morning.[72]

publishing, 1954), p.28 for criticism of the dispersal and Karl Deuticke, *Die Schlacht bei Lützen. 1632* (PhD Thesis, Universität Giessen 1917), p.49.

71 Brzezinski, *Lützen*, p.34, Sennewald, *Das kursächsische Heer*, p.150.

72 Brzezinski, *Lützen*, pp. 34–38.

Tables

Table 1. Equivalent ranks of officers and NCOs in German, Swedish and English

During the sixteenth century, different terms for German officer ranks depending on their association to a particular military service branch were developed. The six highest ranks had an order of seniority (indicated by number in brackets) and there was only one rank of each in an army in the sixteenth century. The *Generalleutnant* was second in command after the Lord General. The commander of the cavalry and his second, the *Feldmarschall* and *FeldmarschallLeutnant*,[73] were considered senior to the commander of the artillery, the *Generalfeldzeugmeister*, who in turn was considered senior to the commander of infantry, the *Generalwachtmeister*. This seniority of ranks was retained during the seventeenth century, even though many changes were made.

	Herscher/Generalissimus (1) Lord General/Generalissimus	
	Generalleutnant (2) *Generalleutnant* Lieutenant-general	
Cavalry	**Artillery**	**Infantry**
Feldmarschall (3) *Fältmarskalk* Field Marshal	*Generalfeldzeugmeister* (5) *General för Artilleriet* General of Ordinance	*Generalwachtmeister* (6) *Generalmajor* Major-general
Feldmarschall Leutnant (4) *Fältmarskalk Löjtnant* Field Marshal Lieutenant		
Oberst *Överste* Colonel	*Oberst* *Överste* Colonel	*Oberst* *Överste* Colonel
Oberstleutnant *Överstelöjtnant* Lieutenant-colonel	*Oberstleutnant* *Överstelöjtnant* Lieutenant-colonel	*Oberstleutnant* *Överstelöjtnant* Lieutenant-colonel
Obristwachtmeister *Major* Major	*Obristwachtmeister* *Major* Major	*Obristwachtmeister* *Major* Major
Rittmeister *Ryttmästere* Captain (horse)	*Hauptmann* *Kapten* Captain	*Hauptmann* *Kapten* Captain
Kapitänleutnant ‡ *Kaptenlöjtnant* 1st Lieutenant	*Kapitänleutnant* *Kaptenlöjtnant* 1st Lieutenant	*Kapitänleutnant* *Kaptenlöjtnant* 1st Lieutenant
Leutnant *Löjtnant* 2nd Lieutenant	*Leutnant* *Löjtnant* 2nd Lieutenant	*Leutnant* *Löjtnant* 2nd Lieutenant
Cornet *Fändrik* Officer Cadet (horse)	*Fähnrich* *Fändrik* Officer Cadet	*Fähnrich* *Fändrik* Officer Cadet

73 Leonhardt Fronsperger, *Fünff Bücher, vonn Kriegs Regiment und Ordnung, wie sich ein jeder Kriegssmann inn seinem Ampt und Beuelch halten soll, was zu anfang eines Kriegs zuerwegen unnd zubetrachten sey* (Frankfurt: 1558), pp.83–84.

Wachtmeister *Sergeant för Kavalleriet* Sergeant (horse)	*Wachtmeister* *Sergeant för Artilleriet* Sergeant (artillery)	*Feldwebel* *Sergeant för Fotfolket* Sergeant (foot)
Corporal *Korpral* Corporal	*Corporal* *Korpral* Corporal	*Corporal* *Korpral* Corporal

‡ Each regiment had only one *Kapitänleutnant*.

2

Historical Sources and Historiography

The first methodical study of the Battle of Lützen was published by Gustav Droysen in 1865.[1] He distinguished between eyewitness accounts and unreliable secondary sources, a fundamental method of battlefield research, and made some observations that are still valid, particularly the lack of physical remains from the battle. Unfortunately, his pioneering results were dismissed because he came to the conclusion that the events of the battle could not be reconstructed with such a limited number of eyewitness accounts.

Two PhD theses about the battle were published by Hermann Diemar in 1890 and by Karl Deuticke in 1917.[2] They left the historical methodology aside by using mostly unreliable secondary sources. Research during the next century followed the path laid out by Diemar and Deuticke. Seidler's theses from the 1930s as well as the publication from the Swedish General Staff in 1939 were flawed because of the uncritical use of historical sources, while Wedgwood's results in 1938 were based mostly on English sources, ignoring the previous German and Swedish discussions.[3]

Almost all other publications about Lützen were based on those six theses until Richard Brzezinski published his work in 2001.[4] Marking a return to Droysen's more scientific method, he used mainly eyewitness accounts with great success and additionally discovered some new sources, in particular pictorial representations.

1 Gustav Droysen, 'Die Schlacht bei Lützen 1632', in *Forschungen zur Deutschen Geschichte* vol. 5 (Osnabrück: 1865), pp.69–235.

2 Karl Deuticke, *Die Schlacht bei Lützen. 1632* (Giessen: 1917), Helmut Diemar, *Untersuchungen über die Schlacht bei Lützen* (16. Nov. 1632) (Kassel: Döll, 1890).

3 Generalstaben, *Sveriges Krig*, vol. 6, *Fron Lech till Lützen* (Stockholm: 1939), Josef Seidler, *Untersuchungen über die Schlacht bei Lützen* (Memmingen: self-publishing, 1954), Wedgwood, *Der Dreissigjährige Krieg*.

4 Brzezinski, *Lützen*.

However, most publications about Lützen are still based on Seidler's and Generalstaben's flawed results. Therefore, it is necessary to re-evaluate the historical sources first and discuss their reliability, as well as the position an eyewitness had during the battle. In a second step, the archaeological sources from the survey will be assessed and evaluated to fill the gap in physical remains pointed out by Droysen in 1865.

Historical accounts of a battle are a very special and unique source. They are different from other historical sources in the sense that they report events that people experienced under enormous stress. This stress factor makes it likely that the events of a battle are not remembered accurately, particularly if the event was very violent, while observations from afar or from the beginning of the battle might be more accurate.

After the battle, soldiers were discussing their experience, which might have further influenced their memory. Soon after the battle, stories were being told and written by people who had not been there, thus creating a myth that is repeated and further embellished. These secondary sources are highly unreliable, which will be illustrated in this chapter.

Eyewitness Accounts and Official Documents: the Facts

Swedish–German Eyewitness Accounts

There are only 18 eyewitness accounts known at the time of writing, of which 11 are from the Swedish–German army. Some of the letters written soon after the battle, like those from *Generalleutnant* Bernhard von Weimar, *Generalmajor* Dodo von Inn-und zu Knyphausen, *Oberst* Caspar *Graf* von Eberstein, *Oberst* Friedrich von Rostein and *Rittmeister* Bodo von Bodenhausen, just state that the Swedish army was in good order despite the death of the King.[5] [†]

The first account, written the day of the battle, is a letter from an unknown author in the Swedish Headquarters.[6] As a non-combatant, he very likely remained with the baggage train at Meuchen and moved to the Swedish base of operations at Naumburg before the battle ended, because the baggage train was in danger of capture by Imperial cavalry.[7] His letter is a valuable source for the Imperial outflanking manoeuvre that threatened the Swedish rear.

5 Anonymous, *Nordalbingische Studien*, vol. 1. part 1 (Kiel, 1844), Helmut Diemar, 'Der Anteil der Hessen an der Schlacht von Lützen 1632', in *Zeitschrift des Vereins für hessische Geschichte und Landeskunde N.F. 18* (1893), pp.347–349, 351–352, A. F. Glafey, *De Gladio quo cum Gustavus Adolphus Rex sveciae in proelio Luzenensi occubuit* (Leipzig, 1749), pp.10–11, J. Mankell, *Arkiv till upplysning om Svenska krigens och krigsinrättningarnes historia* vol. II (Stockholm 1860), pp.643–644.

6 Söltl, *Religionskrieg in Deutschland*, vol. 3 (Hamburg, 1842), pp.346–347, Droysen, 'Lützen', pp.75–76.

7 Söltl, *Religionskriege*, p.347.

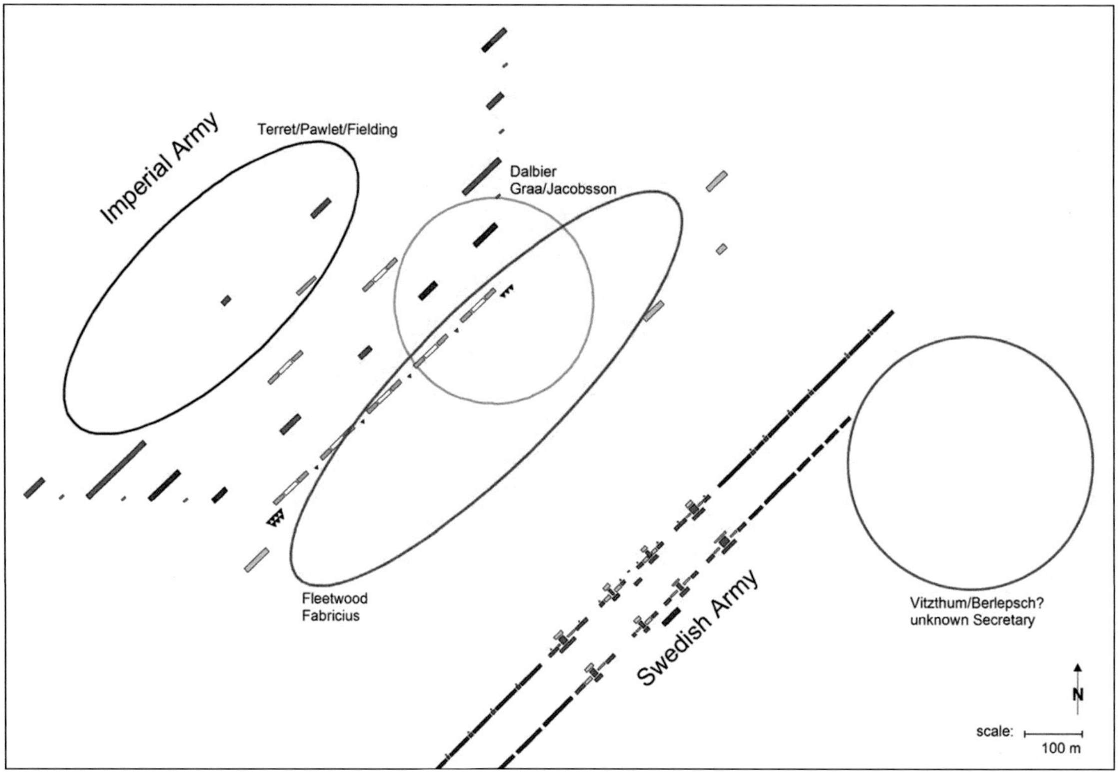

Circles indicate approximate positions of Protestant eyewitnesses. (Diagram: André Schürger)

The Elector *Herzog* Johann Georg of Saxony received a report of the battle[8] from Erich Volkmar Berlepsch, *Kriegskommissar*[9] in Erfurt, the Swedish Headquarters, and Johann Georg Vitzthum von Eckstedt, elder brother of *Oberst* Damian commander of the Saxon Regiment Dam Vitzthum and canon of Halberstadt and Naumburg Cathedrals.[10] As non-combatants, Vitzthum and Berlepsch are likely to have been with the baggage train at Meuchen. They give otherwise unreported details from the early stages of the battle such as the pre-battle skirmish, the early artillery fire and the first Swedish troop movements, all of which they could have seen from their position at the rear. Droysen believed that the letter was sent on 21 November 1632 together with one from Bodo von Bodenhausen.[11]

Oberst George Fleetwood wrote a letter to his father from Stettin on 2 December 1632.[12] His account is less influenced by others, because he left the army soon after the battle, except for his description of the King's death,

8 Glafey, *De Gladio*, pp.12–14.

9 'Commissary of War', a supply officer.

10 They are often incorrectly believed to have been Saxon officers (Diemar, *Untersuchungen*, p.30, Deuticke, *Lützen*, p.16).

11 Droysen, 'Lützen', pp.77–78, Glafey, *De Gladio*, pp.10–11.

12 George Fleetwood, Letter from George Fleetwood to his Father (Stettin: 1632).

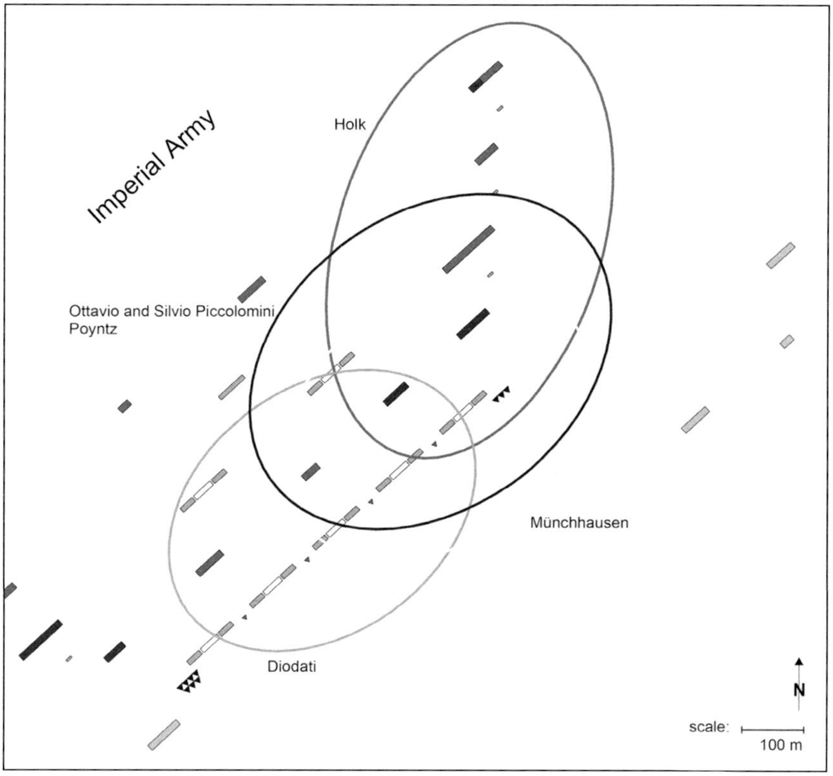

Circles indicate approximate positions of Imperial eyewitnesses. (Diagram: André Schürger)

which he may have copied from Truchsess.[13] Fleetwood had no command in battle[14] and was not with his fellow countrymen in Leslie's Scots Regiment, as Deuticke and Seidler believed,[15] because he would have outranked *Oberstleutnant* Ludovick Leslie. His detailed description of a pre-battle skirmish on the Swedish right wing suggests that he was initially on that wing, although later, Jacobus Fabricius saw him behind the centre.[16] Without a command, Fleetwood probably performed 'special duties' during the battle.

The King's Chaplain, Jacobus Fabricius, wrote an account of Gustav II Adolph's death 18 years after the battle.[17] Surprisingly, he did not repeat the circulating rumours, as everyone else did, but gave his own independent and very detailed account about the events after Gustav II Adolph vanished into the thick smoke of gunfire and the Swedish army almost routed.

Coincidently, in 1632 Gustav II Adolph's former Chaplain, Paul Stockmann, was vicar in Lützen. He did not witness the battle, but visited

13 Fleetwood quoted 'Truckes', which is Truchsess (Fleetwood, Letter, p.8). The account of Truchsess is lost, but was used occasionally by contemporary writers when describing the death of Gustav II Adolph, although Truchsess was not an eyewitness (Seidler, *Untersuchungen*, p.133, rem. 139).

14 Fleetwood, Letter, p.4 reported that his regiment was not with the army.

15 Deuticke, *Lützen*, p.23, Seidler, *Untersuchungen*, pp.49 and 135, rem. 146.

16 Georg Wittrock, 'Fyra relationer om slaget vid Lützen', in *Historisk tidskrift* 52 (1932), p.306.

17 Wittrock, 'Fyra relationer', pp.305–307.

Swedish army Generalmajor Dodo zu Innhausen und Knyphausen. Artist unknown; post 1620. (Rijksmuseum)

the battlefield the next day and described the scene in one of his sermons.[18]

Oberst Johann Dalbier's account of the battle was probably written soon after the battle.[19] He gave a detailed personal account of the second Swedish attack on the small Imperial battery in the afternoon. As a close associate of *Generalmajor* Dodo von Innhausen und zu Knyphausen, it is likely he was initially in the centre of the second line and then later sent with an infantry detachment to man the captured Imperial guns.[20] The events around the King's death he copied from the *Extrakt Schreiben aus Berlin*.[21]

There is an account from someone who claimed to be the father of August von Leubelfing, Gustav II Adolph's page, who was mortally wounded during the battle, writing the last words of his son.[22] This text is full of historical mistakes; one of them is that he confused Leubelfing's position in battle, something he should have remembered. These errors suggest the account did not originally derive from Leubelfing.[23]

Imperial Eyewitness Accounts

Wallenstein's 17 November letter to *Generalfeldzeugmeister* Johann *Graf* von Aldringen of the Court War Council is the earliest Imperial account. It does not provide any useful information and is misleading by incorrectly stating that Pappenheim arrived before the battle, to hush up his strategic mistake.[24] Wallenstein's official report to the Imperial Court was delivered later by *Oberst* Francesco Grana Marchese di Caretto.

18 Paul Stockmann, *Lamentatio Secunda Lützensium seu Epitaphium* (Leipzig, 1633).

19 Public Records Office (PRO): SP81/39: London: 'Johann Dalbier, Relation of the Battle of Lutzen (unknown, 1632)'. The account is in eighteenth-century handwriting in French and probably a copy or translation from the original.

20 Brzezinski, *Lützen*, p.75.

21 Mankell, *Arkiv-*, vol. II, pp.658–659.

22 Christoph Gottlieb von Murr, *Beyträge zur Geschichte des dreyssigjährigen Krieges* (Nürnberg, 1790), pp.121–124.

23 The unreliability of Leubelfing's account is proved in detail by Droysen, 'Lützen', pp.193–198 and Deuticke, *Lützen*, p.26 proved in detail that this account is not based on Leubelfing.

24 G. Lorenz, *Quellen zur Geschichte Wallensteins. Ausgewählte Quellen zur deutschen Geschichte der Neuzeit*, vol. 20 (Darmstadt: 1987), pp.255–256.

An anonymous author wrote a letter dated 19 November 1632.[25] He recorded that his regiment undertook a joint operation with the Infantry Regiment Baden; the commander of the Regiment Baden, *Oberstleutnant* Stolper, took command, because the author's *Oberst* was mortally wounded and his *Oberstleutnant* killed.[26] The letter must therefore have been written by an infantry officer. Two Imperial infantry officers, *Oberst* Berthold von Waldstein and *Oberst* Theodor Comargo, were mortally wounded during the battle, but the *Oberstleutnant* of Waldstein's Regiment was only wounded, while Comargo's *Oberstleutnant* was killed. In a second letter, written by Münchhausen to the Elector Maximilian of Bavaria on 6 December 1632, some sentences are virtually identical to the first, the anonymous, letter.[27] It is probable therefore that the author of the anonymous letter of 19 November 1632 letter is *Obristwachtmeister* Hans von Münchhausen of the Regiment Comargo.[28]

One of the most valuable accounts derives from *Oberstleutnant* Giulio Diodati. He was sent by Wallenstein to the Imperial Court in Vienna instead of *Oberst* Francesco Grana Marchese di Caretto who fell ill on the way. Diodati, Grana's second in command, reported to Ferdinand II on 29 November 1632.[29] The Regiment Grana was deployed as the central squadron in the centre of the first line, and Diodati reported largely those events that he had personally seen. Furthermore, Diodati's description of the Imperial deployments matches that of *FeldmarschallLeutnant* Heinrich Holk, providing vital information in the reconstruction of the Imperial battle line.[†]

Shortly after the battle, the Danish *Feldmarschall Leutnant* Heinrich Holk wrote an account of the events to King Christian IV of Denmark.[30] Holk commanded the Imperial left wing and, as Wallenstein's second in command in the absence of Pappenheim, he was responsible for deploying the army.[31] His position in the command structure is reflected in his account, which is short, but mostly honest and reliable, with the exception of the rout of Pappenheim's cavalry; Holk probably exaggerated the rout because he was responsible for the rallying of the wing and holding the ground, which made him look better.

25 Wittrock, 'Fyra relationer', pp.304–305.

26 Wittrock, 'Fyra relationer', p.305.

27 Bayerisches Hauptstaatsarchiv (BHStA) München, Kurbayern Äusseres Archiv, 2424t194 f. 158: Hans von Münchhausen to the Elector Maximilian of Bavaria, Zwickau 6 December 1632.

28 Brzezinski, *Lützen*, pp.67 and 80.

29 Josef Fiedler, 'Diodatis Bericht über die Schlacht bei Lützen', in *Forschungen zur Deutschen Geschichte IV* (Osnabrück: 1864) pp.555–568. According to Army List No. 18 (M. Toegel, 'Der Schwedische Krieg und Wallensteins Ende', in *Dokumenta Bohemica Bellum Tricennale Illustrantia* V (Prag, 1977), p.439) Diodati was promoted to Oberst after Lützen, where he served as Grana's second in command, and got his own regiment then.

30 Wittrock, 'Fyra relationer', pp.307–309.

31 Brzezinski, *Lützen*, p.38.

Two letters from Italian officers of the Arquebusier Regiment Piccolomini have survived. The commanding officer, *Oberst* Ottavio Piccolomini di Aragona, wrote the Emperor a boastful letter on 4 December 1632, informing him of his part in the events that led to Gustav II Adolph's death.[32] Leaving these embellishments aside, this account provides important details for the first Swedish attack on the Imperial left wing.

The 2 December 1632 letter from *Rittmeister* Silvio Piccolomini to the bishop of Siena Askanio Piccolomini contains some serious mistakes, such as the date of the battle, which is given as 15 November, and the arrival of Pappenheim before the battle, about which he should have known better.[33] Nevertheless, the description of wounds his fellow officers received is an important detail, which sheds light on the fighting.

Rittmeister Sydenham Poyntz wrote his *Relation* in 1636/37. His account about the Thirty Years' War is full of errors and is generally considered as being unreliable.[34] Even his account of the Battle of Lützen, which he witnessed, is a collection of anecdotes, such as the duel between Gustav II Adolph and Pappenheim.[35] Nevertheless, apart from these anecdotes there are some important details about the pre-battle manoeuvres and Wallenstein's skirmisher screen. According to Poyntz's *Relation*, he fought on horse and he gave a detailed account about the Regiment Piccolomini, which may have been the unit he served with.[36]

In addition to the 18 eyewitness accounts, there are 10 enquiry records. Nine of these concern the investigation into the desertion of entire Imperial regiments during the Battle of Lützen and the surrender of Chemnitz. These were based on sworn testimony involving the questioning of eyewitnesses.[37] Although based on subjective eyewitness accounts, the aim was to reveal facts. They represent important accounts of the Imperial cavalry's rout at Lützen. On 13 May 1633, a statement from the questioning of Pappenheim's trumpeter, Ehinger, was recorded about the death of the *Feldmarschall*.[38] Ehinger's statement about Pappenheim's cavalry disobeying orders is supported by the other testimonies.

Most eyewitnesses were positioned in either the centre or the Imperial left/Swedish right wing, and some witnessed the battle from the baggage train. However, there are no eyewitness accounts from the Imperial right wing, which makes it difficult to reconstruct this part of the battle.

32 Argang, 'Piccolominis bref om slaget vid Lützen', in *Historisk Tidskrift* 14 (1894), pp.89–90.

33 Anonymous, *Archivio Storico Italiano*. Serie terza. XIV (Firenze, 1871), pp.239–242.

34 Sydnam Poyntz, *The Relation of Sydnam Poyntz 1624–1636*, in Goodrick, A. T. S., Camden 3rd series, vol. 14 (London, 1908), pp.24–25, Brzezinski, *Lützen*, p.94.

35 Poyntz, *The Relation*, p.73.

36 Poyntz, *The Relation*, pp.72, 126.

37 Seidler, *Untersuchungen*, pp.141–148.

38 Hermann Hallwich, *Briefe und Akten zur Geschichte Wallensteins 1630–1634*, vol. 4 (*Fontes rerum Austriacarum*. vol. 66) (Wien: 1912), pp.133–136.

Official Documents

Several documents about troop strength and casualties have survived. There are eight Imperial army lists from 1631 to 1634 with all regiments and their companies and commanding officers listed.[39] These lists often give the number of 10 companies in a regiment, the official regimental organisation at that time,[40] but in reality, it seems unlikely that all regiments during the Thirty Years' War had this organisation. At least one list (no. 14) contradicts itself by officially listing Hagen's Regiment with 10 companies, then saying in a footnote that the regiment was disbanded and its 13 companies distributed among three other regiments.[41] Nevertheless, the lists provide useful information about Imperial regiments, their commanding officers and when they were raised.

The 'list of damaged'[42] is one of very few records with an exact and reliable number of Imperial soldiers, even though it only includes seven regiments.[43] Imperial commanders kept records of numbers of companies rather than men.[44] A 'reward list' names five regiments rewarded, probably for their service in Lützen.[45] Holk's 6 December 1632 list names 14 regiments, also named in the Trauttmansdorff list, suggesting that it is a list of the regiments present in Lützen.[46]

There are three reliable Swedish lists for regimental strength. Langman's of 14 November 1632 contains the actual number of foot and an approximate number of horse.[47] The second document is an undated casualty listing of wounded foot, written not long after the battle.[48] The last list is an unpublished and undated list of the strength of the regiments of foot after the battle.[49]

39 Toegel, 'Der Schwedische Krieg', pp.386–443.

40 Alphons Wrede, *Geschichte der K. und K. Wehrmacht. Die Regimenter, Corps, Branchen und Anstalten von 1618 bis Ende des 19. Jahrhunderts*, vol. 1 (Wien: L.W. Seidel 1898), p.29.

41 Toegel, 'Der Schwedische Krieg', pp.402 and 406.

42 In trying to give the meaning of seventeenth-century German or Italian, the author has usually favoured a literal over a 'correct' translation.

43 'Verzaichnuss der Beschädigten' (Hallwich, *Briefe und Akten*, vol. 3, pp.596–599). The record lists the wounded of the Regiments Desfour, Holk, Trcka, Götz, Bredau, Loyers and Goschütz. It does not include the killed, evidenced by the fact that the Oberstleutnant of Desfour's Regiment, who is recorded elsewhere as killed, is not listed.

44 Brzezinski, *Lützen*, p.26.

45 Hallwich, *Briefe und Akten*, vol. 3, pp.538–539.

46 Hallwich, *Briefe und Akten*, vol. 3, pp.577–578.

47 Langman, 'Ett par bref om slaget vid Lützen 1632', in *Historisk tidskrift* 12, 1892, p.162.

48 Mankell, *Arkiv* vol. III, pp.126–128.

49 Krigsarkivet i Stockholm (KiS): GAV u 121a Vol. 32d: Swedish Troop Strength 1628–1632, Brzezinski, *Lützen*, p.87.

Secondary Sources: the Creation of a Myth

Facing page, top: Encampment, with a trumpeter of a regiment of horse and other troops including a pikeman. Note the use of a drum as a card table, a common trope in period paintings and engravings. Jan Martszen the Younger (1609–after 1647). (Rijksmuseum)

Facing page, bottom: Combat between harquebusiers and cuirassiers. Jan Martszen the Younger (1609–after 1647). (Rijksmuseum)

As soon as the day after the battle, the falsification and mystification began. Misunderstandings, rumours and invented stories were copied and distributed in letters and printed accounts, and in particular the death of the King of Sweden generated a large number of letters, reports, printed relations and historic papers from non-eyewitnesses who tried to explain how he died.

Most of the early letters do not provide useful information:

> Secretary Heinrich Schwallenberg to *Fältmarskalk* Gustav Horn (17 November, 22 November).[50]
>
> An unknown author to the Chancellor of the Reich Axel Oxenstierna (probably 19 November).[51]
>
> The *Copia Verträulichen Schreibens from Pegau* (20 November).[52]
>
> The correspondent Lars Grubbe who was quoted as *Relation I from Grimma* (23 November).[53]
>
> Bernolf von Kreilsheim (approximately 23 November).[54]
>
> The *Extrakt Schreiben aus Berlin* (24 November).[55]
>
> *Feldmarschall* Matthias Gallas to Ferdinand King of Hungary (approximately 25 November).[56]
>
> The correspondent Lars Grubbe quoted as the *Relation II from Grimma* (28 November).[57]

50 Fiedler, 'Diodatis Bericht', p.569, Hallwich, *Briefe und Akten*, vol. 3, pp.522–523. Schwallenberg was Secretary in the Swedish Headquarters at Naumburg (Droysen, 'Lützen', p.77).

51 Mankell, *Arkiv* vol. II, pp.645–649, Droysen, 'Lützen', pp.78–79.

52 Söltl, *Religionskriege*, pp.340–341, Droysen, 'Lützen', pp.79.

53 Anonymous, *Studien*, pp.50–52. Grubbe was Gustav Adolph's correspondent in Torgau to report the movement of the allied Saxon army to him and prepare their joining with the Swedish army. He went to Grimma after the battle (Droysen, 'Lützen', pp.79–80).

54 Droysen, 'Lützen', p.80.

55 Mankell, *Arkiv* vol. II, pp.658–659.

56 Friedrich Förster, *Wallenstein's Prozess vor den Schranken des Weltgerichts und des K. K. Fiscus zu Prag* (Leipzig, 1844), pp.94–96, Diemar, *Untersuchungen*, pp.55–57.

57 Droysen, 'Lützen', pp.80–82.

The correspondent Johann Hallenus to the Swedish Council of the Reich (30 November).[58]

Three letters from unknown authors (26 November, 3 December, 7 December).[59]

Adam Heinrich Pentz probably to *Fältmarskalk* Horn (2 December).[60]

Letter from the Venetian Resident in Vienna Antonio Antelmi (4 December).[61]

Some letters, in particular Pentz's, contain many details about the battle and the circumstances of Gustav II Adolph's death, which entirely differ from the eyewitness accounts. These early letters rapidly began to influence each other, and this is most evident when comparing Kreilsheim's letter and *Relation I from Grimma*, where either one copied the other or both had access to a now unknown written account.[62] This one example demonstrates that some letters were copied and distributed by and to officials. Although their impact on the historic narrative was limited, they mark the beginning of the creation of the myth of Lützen.

An exception to those early letters and an example for the process of alteration of facts is the Hallenus account. On 29 November 1632, Hallenus received a report from two participants of the battle, *Löjtnant* Bengt Graa from Kyle's Regiment and *Fändrik* Ambrosius Jacobsson from Hastfehr's Regiment.[63] Both regiments mustered as part of the Swedish Old Blue Brigade and were thus deployed on the right centre.[64] According to Hallenus' account, *Generalmajor* Nils Brahe, *Greve till Visingborg* commanded the left wing; however, in fact he commanded the centre and the Yellow Brigade, something that Graa and Jacobsson should have known, because he was their wing commander. When Hallenus described Brahe's advance with his 'wing', he mentioned combat between a Swedish infantry brigade and an Imperial cuirassier regiment. From the casualty reports and from Diadati we know

58 Mankell, *Arkiv* vol. II, pp.661–664. Hallenus was correspondent in Stralsund to report the Council of the Reich. See also Droysen, 'Lützen', pp.82–83.

59 Söltl, *Religionskriege*, pp.349–356, Droysen, 'Lützen', pp.83–84.

60 Fiedler, 'Diodatis Bericht', pp.569–572.

61 Antelmi, 'Dispacci Nr. 23 des Residenten Antonio Antelmi an die Signoria in Venedig', in *Archiv für Kunde österreichischer Geschichtsquellen* XXVIII, pp.359–362. It is often claimed that this letter is excellent, based only on a statement of the German historian Ranke (Deuticke, *Lützen*, p.32) but, in fact, it is contradicted by most eyewitness accounts.

62 Droysen, 'Lützen', pp.137–138.

63 Mankell, *Arkiv* vol. II, pp.661–664.

64 Brzezinski, *Lützen*, p.22. As Swedish officers, they served in the Swedish Brigade and were not in Winckel's Old Blue Brigade, as Deuticke, *Lützen*, p.22 suggested.

The Swedish army in early 1632. Wenceslaus Hollar. (Krigsarkivet)

that Brahe's Yellow Brigade was almost wiped out.[65] Graa and Jacobsson certainly witnessed this incident, because the Yellow Brigade was positioned to the left to their unit. It is very likely, that the two officers correctly reported events that occurred to their left, but that Hallenus misunderstood, and thought Brahe commanded the 'left wing'.

Swedish–German Accounts: Development until *Inventarium Sueciae* and its influence

Printed accounts had a much bigger impact on the developing historical narrative than letters because of their high print run. The first printed account was published as early as 17 November 1632, the day after the battle, in the *58. Ordentliche Wochentliche Zeitung*,[66] a local newspaper from Naumburg. This short account, however, is full of mistakes – for example, it confuses the Rippach stream, the location of a skirmish the day before the battle, with the canal *Flossgraben*, an important feature on the battlefield, thus laying the foundation for creation of myths of the Battle of Lützen.

Two days later the *Bericht von der mächtigen Victoria* (*Relation from Torgau*)[67] was published, claiming to have had intelligence from an Imperial prisoner of war. However, this account is contradicted by all eyewitness accounts, which makes it unlikely to actually be based on eyewitness testimony. Particularly by describing a thick mist that influenced the battle, although, in fact, it did not exist, this account created a recurring cliché.

65 KiS: GAV u 121a Vol. 32d: Swedish Troop Strength 1628–1632, Fiedler, 'Diodatis Bericht', p.563, Brzezinski, *Lützen*, p.67.

66 Söltl, *Religionskriege*, pp.337–339, Droysen, 'Lützen', p.78.

67 Gustav Droysen, 'Gedruckte Relationen über die Schlacht bei Lützen', in *Materialien zur neueren Geschichte* vol. 1 (Halle: 1880), pp.13–15.

The 21 November 1632 *Extrakt Schreiben aus Erfurt*[68] (*Relation I from Erfurt*) is largely a touching story about Gustav II Adolph saying goodbye to his wife. Then to embellish the account, a speech to his soldiers in the middle of the battle was added, which became a cliché, repeated in almost every other account, but in very different ways.

The first printed account delivering an entire story of the battle was the '*Warhaffte und Eygentliche Relation, von der Blutigen Schlacht, Zwischen Königl. Mayest: zu Schweden, unnd der Kayserl: Armee den 5. und 6. Novemb dess Jahrs 1632. bey Lützen 2. Meilwege von Leipzig Vorgangen und Geschehen*' (*Relation II from Erfurt*), published 22 November 1632.[69] It is also the first 'relation' relying chiefly on the previously printed newspaper and the two accounts. The beginning of the battle, given as 9:00 a.m. in the *Relation I from Erfurt*,[70] and 10:00 a.m. in the newspaper,[71] is stated as 9:00 a.m. to 10:00 a.m.[72] The statement that Imperial forces would have been completely routed at Rippach if the Swedes had had more time before nightfall,[73] and a reference to the Imperial army's advantage in terrain,[74] is drawn from the newspaper, using similar phrases. The loss of all Imperial artillery, baggage, and ammunition is mentioned in all 'relations', while the Swedes taking advantage of a mist is probably from the *Relation from Torgau*.[75]

The concept of Gustav II Adolph giving a speech was borrowed from the *Relation I* from Erfurt. In addition to the compilation, the author invented new stories, such as an Imperial attack on the Swedish baggage train and he mistook the road ditches of the Via Regia for the Flossgraben (a canal), because he lacked knowledge of the battlefield. Trying to add to his credibility, the author claimed he was an eyewitness to the battle, when he was not, which seems to have become a figure of speech in printed accounts to give it weight.[76] Although the process of the mystification of the Battle of Lützen was not concluded, the *Relation II from Erfurt* played an important role in creating the myth as it had all elements that were used and embellished later by further 'relations' printed in 1633.

---

68 Söltl, *Religionskriege*, pp.342–344.

69 Droysen, 'Gedruckte Relationen', pp.16–23. There are seven almost identical versions published under different titles.

70 Söltl, *Religionskriege*, p.343.

71 Söltl, *Religionskriege*, p.338.

72 Droysen, 'Gedruckte Relationen', p.19.

73 Söltl, *Religionskriege*, p.338, Droysen, 'Gedruckte Relationen', p.18.

74 Söltl, *Religionskriege*, p.338, Droysen, 'Gedruckte Relationen', p.18.

75 Note that Droysen, 'Lützen', pp.151–166 has failed to realise the context between Relation II from Erfurt, *Ordentliche Wochentliche Zeitung* and Relation I from Erfurt.

76 Diemar, *Untersuchungen*, pp.18–23 believed this 'relation' to be the lost account from Schwallenberg based on the assumption that he was an eyewitness, both of which are incorrect (Seidler, *Untersuchungen*, p.10).

Swedish infantry and cavalry on the march, 1631. Note the artillery use of the fore wheels. Wenceslaus Hollar. (Rijksmuseum)

This applies to the *Relation from 1633*[77] and the *Declaration from 1633*,[78] which further increased the amount of details with embellishments and invented stories without having any sources from eyewitness testimonies.[79]

The *Inventarium Sueciae*,[80] published in 1633, continued this tradition by compiling from other printed accounts, particularly from the *Relation II from Erfurt* and the *Relation from 1633*.[81] However, it is the first publication with a copperplate, made by Friedrich van Hulsen, showing the initial Swedish and Imperial armies' deployment. It marks a shift to the developing historic narrative by adding this first pictorial representation of the Battle of Lützen, thus influencing almost all accounts for decades.

77 Droysen, 'Gedruckte Relationen', pp.24–35.

78 Droysen, 'Gedruckte Relationen', pp.36–46.

79 Droysen, 'Lützen', pp.166–188.

80 Johann Ludwig Gottfried, *Inventarium Sueciae*. Appendix *Andern Theil Inventarii Sueciae* (Frankfurt am Main, Wolfgang Hofmann, 1633).

81 Droysen, 'Lützen', pp.201–208.

The *Theatrum Europaeum*, first published in 1633,[82] not only copied almost verbatim the *Inventarium Sueciae* text and then added its own version of Gustav II Adolph's death, but also plagiarised van Hulsen's copperplate with slight differences while including a new copperplate from Matthaeus Merian, showing various battle events, based on the *Inventarium Sueciae* text.

Most later pamphlets, including the *Glaubwürdiger Bericht*[83] and *Wahrhaftige Beschreibung*,[84] then copied nearly the entire text from the *Inventarium Sueciae* and both copperplates; except for some minor alterations, there was no new information. However, the influence of the *Inventarium Sueciae* did not end with the publication of pamphlets.

Robert Monro's description of the Battle of Lützen in *Expedition with the Worthy Scots Regiment ...* is, in most respects, an exact translation of the *Inventarium Sueciae* with some minor alterations and translation errors.[85]

In 1648, Bogislaus Philipp Chemnitz[86] was the last author using the *Inventarium Sueciae* to such an extent, but he also used some earlier 'relations' which are known to us.[87]

Catholic Accounts: Development until Richelieu and Khevenhiller

The development of historical narrative until Chemnitz suggests that the Battle of Lützen was exclusively a Protestant German matter of interest. However, there are a few other 'relations' and historical papers. The first printed Catholic account, the *Particular from 1632*,[88] was published shortly after the battle and had some influence on the *Gründlicher und Aussführlicher Bericht* printed in 1632 (*Relation from 1632*).[89] Both pamphlets are contradicted by eyewitness accounts, but they created a story of their own, a different one from the Protestant accounts.

Seidler claimed, without providing any evidence, that Petrus Baptista Burgus was present at the battle.[90] Most of Burgus'[91] sources are unknown to us.

82 Johann Philipp Abelinum, *Theatrum Europaeum* (Frankfurt am Main, 1646).

83 Anonymous, *Glaubwürdiger Bericht und Erzehlung* (unknown, 1633).

84 Anonymous, *Eigendliche Abbildung und Warhafftige Beschreibung Der grossen und blutigen Schlacht so zwischen Königl. Maj. Zu Schweden und dem Keyserl. General von Wallenstein den 6. Novembris, Anno 1632. bey dem Städtlein Lützen 2. Meil von Leipzig vorgangen* (unknown, 1633)

85 Monro, *His Expedition*, part II, pp.162–165. The description of the results of the battle from page 165 on is different from *Inventarium Sueciae*.

86 Bogislaus Philipp Chemnitz, *Geschichte des Königlich Schwedischen in Teutschland geführten Krieges*, vol. I (Stettin, 1648), pp.463–467.

87 Droysen, 'Lützen', p.230.

88 Anonymous, *Vom 17. Novembris auss dem Kayserlichen Feldtlager bey Leipzig*, 1632.

89 Droysen, 'Gedruckte Relationen', pp.6–12.

90 Seidler, *Untersuchungen*, p.13.

91 Petrus Baptista Burgus, *Mars Sveco-Germanicus sive rerum a Gustavo Adolfo suecico rege gestarum libri tres* (Cologne: 1641), pp.316–334.

Although cuirassiers were far more common in the Imperial army, this illustration by Wenceslaus Hollar shows Swedish cuirassiers in 1631. (Rijksmuseum)

However, he copied the statement that Holk did not have enough musketeers to deploy some in the wood to his left from Holk's account. Moreover, his praise of Piccolomini's heroic deeds is identical to Diodati's account.[92] Apart from inventing a long speech of Gustav II Adolph, Burgus simply repeats the usual rumours and it is most unlikely that he was present in the battle. Nevertheless, he is probably the first historian who tried to be objective by using eyewitness accounts.

Galeazzo Gualdo Priorato[93] was the first historian to publish a complete list of those Imperial regiments he believed fought in the battle. However, since he listed every Imperial regiment whose name he knew, and many of them were not even close to Lützen, the listing is incorrect, as is his account of the battle.[94] Again, it is uncertain which sources Priorato used.

92 Burgus, *Mars Sveco-Germanicus*, p.325, Fiedler, 'Diodatis Bericht', p.563. For the similarity of Diodati's and Burgus' accounts see also Droysen, 'Lützen', pp.210–214 and Seidler's (*Untersuchungen*, p.14) counterargument that 'he could not find much of a conspicuous similarity [of Burgus and Diodati].'

93 Galeazzo Gualdo Priorato, *Historia dell Guerra di Ferdinando II e Ferdinando III Imperatori e del Re Filippo IV di Spagna contro Gustavo Adolfi Re Svetia e Luigi XIII Re di Francia Successe Dall'Anno 1630 fino all'Anno 1636*, vol. 1 (Vienna: 1672), pp.118–123.

94 Droysen, 'Lützen', p.230. Although Seidler (*Untersuchungen*, p.36) admitted the listing to be incorrect, he claimed that he would prove that Priorato's account 'is not as bad as usually suspected', but actually he did not even try (Seidler, *Untersuchungen*, p.14).

Above: Swedish cavalry and trumpeters, 1631. Whether cuirassiers were really as common in the Swedish Army as contemporary engravers like to show is unlikely. Matthäus Merian the elder (1593–1650). (Rijksmuseum)

Below: The Swedish Army on the march showing cavalry, and (probably) musketeers, 1631. The trooper at left appears to be wearing a cassock over his equipment. Matthäus Merian the elder (1593–1650). (Rijksmuseum)

In 1677, Vittorio Siri published *Memorie Recondite* with a section about the Battle of Lützen.[95] Siri claimed that he used an account from *Generalleutnant* Bernhard von Weimar, who had given it to the King of France and which is now lost.[96] However, Siri did not relate very much about the combat on the Swedish left wing, which he should have if he had actually drawn his information from Bernhard von Weimar, who commanded the left wing. Either Bernhard's account was not very informative about the battle or Siri lied about it to make his account appear to be more objective. It seems most likely that Siri used Burgus' account; in particular, his description of Wallenstein motivating his soldiers and Pappenheim arriving before the battle is similar to Burgus.[97]

It was often claimed by modern historians that Cardinal Richelieu's account was 'supplied by Bernhard's [von Weimar] chancellery' based on the fact that he was in French service and might have known Richelieu personally.[98] Richelieu's description about the Battle of Lützen, however, is a word-for-word translation of Vittorio Siri's account.[99] Therefore, Deuticke's and Seidler's assertion that Richelieu copied a letter from Truchsess, and that Truchsess made a personal report to Richelieu is incorrect.[100] In addition, Truchsess was not an eyewitness[101] and it is therefore unnecessary to speculate whether Siri used Truchsess. As long as there is no proof of the reliability of Siri's sources, his or Richelieu's accounts must be considered as unreliable.

Franz Christoph Khevenhiller was a member of the Imperial Court in Vienna and had access to the extensive chancellery of the court when he wrote his *Annales Ferdinandei*. Srbik claimed that Khevenhiller[102] used the now lost account of *Oberst* Nicolas Desfours, who fought on the Imperial right wing, for his chapter about the Battle of Lützen.[103] Srbik's presumption is based on a note in the 29 November 1632 expedition protocol of the

95 Vittorio Siri, *Memorie Recondite di Vittorio Siri dall'anno 1601. fino all' 1641*, vol. 7 (Parigi: Sebastiano Mabre-Cramoisy 1677).

96 Droysen, 'Lützen', p.231.

97 Burgus, *Mars Sveco-Germanicus*, pp.318–320, Friedrich Förster, *Albrechts von Wallenstein, des Herzogs von Friedland und Mecklenburg, Ungedruckte, Eigenhändige, Vertrauliche Briefe und Amtliche Schreiben aus den Jahren 1627 bis 1634*, vol. 2 (Berlin: 1829), p.337.

98 Brzezinski, *Lützen*, p.80, rem. 8, Armand-Jean du Plessis Richelieu, *Mémoires Du Cardinal De Richelieu, Sur la Régne De Louis XIII: depuis 1610 jusqu'à 1638. 7. Années, Livre XXIII, XIV, 1632, 1633* (Paris, 1823), pp.256–268.

99 Förster, *Wallensteins Briefe*, pp.336–341, Droysen, 'Lützen', p.231.

100 Deuticke, *Lützen*, p.24, Seidler, *Untersuchungen*, p.126, rem. 87.

101 Seidler, *Untersuchungen*, p.133, rem. 139.

102 Franz Christoph Khevenhiller, *Annales Ferdinandei*, vol. XII (Leipzig, 1726), pp.188–198.

103 Heinrich Ritter von Srbik, 'Zur Schlacht von Lützen und zu Gustav Adolfs Tod', in *Mitteilungen des Österreichischen Instituts für Geschichtsforschung* 41 (Innsbruck, 1926), p.246, Josef Seidler, 'Khlevenhüllers Bericht über die Schlacht bei Lützen 1632', in *Zeitschrift für sudetendeutsche Geschichte*. 3/II (Brünn, 1938), p.231.

War Council of the Court that '*Nicolaws des Four baro avisiert J. K. Mt. aus Leitmeritz vom 19. November des Schweden und von Pappenheim Tod*.'[104]

Srbik believed that Khevenhiller quoted Desfours' 'relation', which started with the headline '*Die Relation, so der Kayserl. Majestät dieses Todes halber in hoc passu überschickt worden, meldet*,'[105] followed by a bold printed text. That indicates that there was, in fact, an account by Desfours and that Khevenhiller used an account which is now lost, but not that he used the account of Desfours. The bold printed text describes the circumstances of Gustav II Adolph's death. Even if this part were from Desfours' 'relation', Desfours could not have seen it because the King of Sweden died on the Imperial left wing while he was serving on the right.[106] That makes Khevenhiller's account unreliable, although he endeavoured to a level of objectivity.

Independent English, French and Spanish Accounts

The development of historical narrative suggests that the Battle of Lützen is exclusively a German matter of interest. However, there are a few other 'relations', such as the account of the battle in William Watts' 1633 *Swedish Intelligencer*, the longest and most detailed 'relation' of the Battle of Lützen. Watts used different sources, such as the *Spanish Relation*,[107] which, in turn, utilised Diodati's eyewitness account. While Watts came to different conclusions, they are not necessarily more reliable. However, Watts claimed that he had reports from three English eyewitnesses, Francis Terret, John Pawlet, and Edward Fielding, who served in the Swedish army, were captured by Croats and saw the battle as prisoners of war from the Imperial army's baggage train, before they were freed.[108] Watts explicitly mentioned them twice as his source; once when noting that after Wallenstein sounded the alarm on evening 15 November, his regiments came in all night long.[109] The second event occurred when about 1,000–1,500 Imperial horse fled from the battle to the baggage train and frightened the women camp followers who, in turn, cut the wagon horses loose and rode off together with the cavalry.[110] It is almost certain that the English prisoners actually saw the two events,

104 'Nicolaus Desfour reports His Imperial Majesty from Leitmeritz the 19 November the death of the Swede [i.e. Gustavus Adolphus] and Pappenheim.'

105 Khevenhiller, *Annales Ferdinandei*, p.192. 'The 'relation' which was sent in hoc passu to the Imperial Majesty because of this death, reports ...'

106 Seidler ('Khlevenhüllers Bericht' and *Untersuchungen*) was eager to prove the reliability of Khevenhiller's account, because he tried to prove that Gustav II Adolph died on the left, rather than on the right wing, and his whole paper is based on that incorrect assumption (see also Brzezinski, *Lützen*, p.9).

107 The *Spanish Relation* seems to have been lost, but was translated and published by William Watts, *The Swedish Intelligencer*, vol. 3 (London, I. L. 1633), pp.160–164.

108 Watts, *Swedish Intelligencer*, vol. 3, p.118.

109 Watts, *Swedish Intelligencer*, vol. 3, p.125.

110 Watts, *Swedish Intelligencer*, vol. 3, p.142.

especially the second one. However, Watts did report a completely erroneous initial deployment and fortification of the Imperial army, which suggests that his eyewitnesses had not seen it and therefore probably had not seen anything else of importance about the battle itself either.[111] Watts' reliability is clearly restricted to the events mentioned by his eyewitnesses.

The *French Relation from 1633*, translated into English and published in London, provides a fictitious story about the Battle of Lützen.[112]

At this point, in 1633, some mystified stories about the Battle of Lützen had been developed that had little or nothing to do with the actual events known from eyewitness accounts, but continued an influence on research until the present.

Pictorial Representations

Copperplates and paintings are a different form of secondary source but with similar problems. The copperplates from van Hulsen in the *Inventarium Sueciae*, from Merian in the *Theatrum Europaeum*, and the copperplate published by Watts in *The Swedish Intelligencer*, were meant to illustrate their account of the battle, which had already altered the facts substantially.

However, there is one exception to this development. The painting *Die Schlacht bei Lützen* by Pieter Snayers, painted in 1642, shows the initial Imperial deployment with an unexpected accuracy but which is confirmed by eyewitness accounts, suggesting that Snayers had access to eyewitness testimony.[113] Giovanni Paolo Bianchi's copperplate of an equestrian portrait of Gustav II Adolph at Lützen shows a very similar Imperial deployment in the background and possibly used Snayers' painting as a model.[114]

Three hand-drawn maps that were believed to illustrate the Battle of Lützen did survive.

A sketch of the Imperial army, published by Förster in 1829, had long been misidentified as Wallenstein's battle plan for Lützen.[115] Brigitte Holl has since shown that it is a 12 November 1632 plan for a battle at Weissenfels, which did not happen.[116] However, it does provide clues leading to a better understanding of Wallenstein's battle tactics.

111 Watts, *Swedish Intelligencer*, vol. 3, p.130. It is a characteristic of the history of Lützen research that Deuticke, *Lützen*, p.31 claimed that the English prisoners had seen the whole battle without giving any argument.

112 Anonymous, *The Great and Famous Battel of Lutzen, Fought Between the Renowned King of Sweden, and Walstein* (London, 1633)

113 Pieter Snayers, *Die Schlacht bei Lützen, Kunsthistorisches Museum Wien*, Inv. Nr. GG1820.

114 Brzezinski, *Lützen*, p.47.

115 Förster, *Wallensteins Briefe*, pp.275–279.

116 Holl, 'Wallensteins angebliche Skizze', pp.71–72. See also Brzezinski, *Lützen*, p.48. The map is still misidentified as a battle plan for Lützen: Guthrie, *Battles of the Thirty Years' War*, p.202, Geoff Mortimer, *Wallenstein. The Enigma of the Thirty Years' War* (Houndmills, Basingstoke, Hampshire; New York, NY: Palgrave Macmillan, 2010), p.170.

Right: Imperial officer or NCO. Detail from *The Siege of Magdeburg*, 1631. Painted *c.* 1650. Pieter Meulener (1602–1654). (Nationalmuseum, Stockholm)

Below: Imperial artillery. Detail from *The Siege of Magdeburg*, 1631. Painted *c.* 1650. Pieter Meulener (1602–1654). (Nationalmuseum, Stockholm)

It is often claimed that the sketch of the Battle of Lützen from the Stockholm Krigsarkivet is from a Swedish soldier who fought in the battle.[117] However, the deployment of the Imperial army is incorrectly shown, while the Swedish centre and second line are missing. Particularly suspicious is that the illustration shows only four cavalry squadrons on each wing, which is stated incorrectly by the *Declaration from 1633* and Khevenhiller.[118] Although there are some remarkable details, such as the float-wood near the Flossgraben, where the baggage train was positioned, it seems more likely that someone who was studying accounts of the battle drew the sketch.

In 1991, Barbara Stadler published the Trauttmansdorff list, which shows an undated list of Imperial units marked with letters or signs.[119] It is dated to 1633 or later because there is an note included stating that the list is to be given to the Imperial Vice President of the War Council of the Court Löbl, who was not promoted to this position until 1633.[120] Although its origin cannot be proven without a date and the map itself, the Imperial units listed are known to have been at Lützen. There is a special mark noting the units of Pappenheim's force, so it is very likely that this legend belonged to a battle plan of Lützen, and is a vital source for the reconstruction of the Imperial order of battle.[121]

Interpretation of Historical Sources

As has been shown, all secondary sources are unreliable in general because either they are disproven by eyewitness accounts or they are telling stories for which there is no proof from more reliable sources. There are a few exceptions of authors using eyewitness testimony, such as Hallenus and Watts, but it is difficult to distinguish between facts and invented stories.

Eyewitness accounts, on the other hand, are mostly reliable, although they sometimes reproduce the common rumours about important events they have not seen, such as the death of Gustav II Adolph and they described only a very small portion of the battle. For this reason, most historians have relied too much on unreliable secondary sources to fill the gaps in our knowledge. In Lützen, however, the possibility of better understanding these short eyewitness testimonies and prove, or disprove, accounts of the battle came with the results of the archaeological survey.

117 Brzezinski, *Lützen*, p.52.

118 Droysen, 'Gedruckte Relationen', p.29, Khevenhiller, *Annales Ferdinandei*, p.189.

119 Stadler, *Pappenheim*, pp.891–892. She accidently omitted the Regiment Piccolomini (see Brzezinski, *Lützen*, p.48).

120 Löbl was Oberst in late 1632 (Letter from the Emperor to Wallenstein: Lorenz, *Quellen zur Geschichte Wallensteins*, p.256).

121 Brzezinski, *Lützen*, p.48.

Tables

Table 2: Eyewitness accounts of the battle in chronological order, with the author's approximate position during the battle

Name and rank	Date of Account	Position at the Battle
Unknown individual in the Swedish Headquarters	16 November 1632	Swedish baggage train
Generalissimus Albrecht von Wallenstein	17 November 1632	Imperial Army, right wing
Generalleutnant Bernhard von Weimar	18 November 1632	Swedish Army, left wing, 1st line
Generalmajor Dodo von Inn-und zu Knyphausen	18 November 1632	Swedish Army, centre, 2nd line
Obristwachtmeister Hans von Münchhausen	19 November 1632	Imperial Army, centre, 1st line
Rittmeister Bodo von Bodenhausen	21 November 1632	Swedish Army, position unknown
Kriegskommissar Erich Volkmar Berlepsch Canon Johann Georg Vitzthum	21 November 1632 (probably)	Swedish baggage train (probably)
Oberst Caspar Graf von Eberstein	28 November 1632	Swedish Army, right wing, 1st line
Oberstleutnant Giulio Diodati	29 November 1632	Imperial Army, centre, 1st line
FeldmarschallLeutnant Heinrich Holk	Date unknown Likely before 1633	Imperial Army, left wing
Oberst George Fleetwood	02 December 1632	Swedish Army, probably centre and right wing
Rittmeister Silvio Piccolomini	02 December 1632	Imperial Army, left wing and centre
Oberst Ottavio Piccolomini di Aragona	04 December 1632	Imperial Army, left wing and centre
Oberst Friedrich von Rostein	06 December 1632	Swedish Army, right wing, 2nd line
Obristwachtmeister Hans von Münchhausen	06 December 1632	Imperial Army, centre, 1st line
Oberst Johann Dalbier	date unknown, possibly late 1632	Swedish Army, centre, 2nd line
Rittmeister Sydnam Poyntz	date unknown, possibly 1636	Imperial Army, probably left-centre or left wing
King's chaplain Jacobus Fabricius	30 December 1650	Swedish Army, centre, 2nd line

3

Archaeological Sources

From 2006 to 2011, a metal detector survey was conducted on the Lützen battlefield. The goal was to produce an archaeological source by surveying the battlefield systematically and recording all finds by GPS. The georeferenced maps of small finds, particularly the lead bullets, are showing distribution patterns, which are helping to understand the historical accounts and to fill the gaps in the narrative of the Battle of Lützen. Such a survey and interpretation of small finds distribution patterns require an understanding of the deposit and looting process, the survey methodology, the firearms used and their ammunition.

The Creation of a Battlefield: Battle Preparations, Small Finds Deposit Process and the Clearing and Looting Process

The creation of the Lützen battlefield started a day before the battle when Wallenstein's camp was erected in the area where the battle would take place. Here, the first battle-related small finds were lost, although presumably far less than during the battle. Additionally, two artillery positions with earthworks were constructed.

Most finds were deposited during the battle. The total number of bullets fired might be from 100,000 to 200,000, if it is assumed that each musketeer fired six to eight times and each cavalryman two to five times during the six-hour engagement. This great number makes shot the most important archaeological source as their distribution defines the battlefield's extent, the location of wings, and even single units. Although the absence of bullets does not necessarily show the absence of troops, it demonstrates the absence of combat, as all independent units had firearms in the Thirty Years' War. In addition to lead bullets, artillery discharged hundreds rounds of round shot, grapeshot or caseshot. In hand-to-hand combat, many buttons, buckles and pieces of equipment (harness, gun parts, et cetera) would be lost, although these would not be nearly as numerous as firearms ammunition.[1]

It took several days after both armies had left the battlefield until 200 civilians from Weissenfels, led by Saxon officials, cleared the battlefield.[2] With vast amounts of weapons, ammunition and equipment lost and with all artillery pieces captured, the Lützen battlefield contained considerable riches, which were collected by the Saxon administration. In this process, they carried the bodies to the *Via Regia*, the major road running through the battlefield, to systematically remove their clothing and equipment. The weapons and armour were handed over to the Saxon *Oberst* Tauber before burying the bodies in mass graves along that road.[3]

After the officials left, the battlefield was open to be looted by the local population, a process that is still ongoing due to the availability of metal detectors. Although, many finds may have been removed from the battlefield, there is a natural limit when the effort is greater than the gain.[4] Considering the time-consuming process of collecting small finds from a battlefield even with a metal detector, it is assumed that many more small finds were removed from high density rather than from low density artefact scatters.[5]

Agriculture and development have an impact on the battlefield artefact scatter as well. The finds might have been moved a few metres after four centuries of ploughing and many are buried, but all finds remain in the plough zone in those areas that were not destroyed by development. Therefore, the unstratified artefact scatter in the topsoil is the most important archaeological

1 Glenn Foard, *Integrating Documentary and Archaeological Evidence in the Investigation of Battles: A Case Study from Seventeenth Century England* (PhD Thesis, University of East Anglia 2008), p.69.

2 Landeshauptarchiv Sachsen-Anhalt (LASA) Abteilung Magdeburg/Aussenstelle Wernigerode: Rep. D Lützen A XI Nr. 29: Lützen Battlefield clearing Record December 1632; Andreas Stahl, '… die Todten Cörper vf der Wahlstadt begraben' Das Amt Lützen und die Schlacht', in I. Schuberth, M. Reiche (eds), *Die blut'ge Affair' bei Lützen. Wallensteins Wende* (Wettin-Löbejün: Verlag Janos Stekovics 2012), pp.258–259. One of these mass graves was found in 2011 by the author: André Schürger, *The Archaeology of the Battle of Lützen: An examination of seventeenth-century military material culture* (PhD Thesis, University of Glasgow 2015), pp.357–363.

3 The clearing process is illustrated in a Saxon inventory from the Battle of Breitenfeld in 1631, which is an exact list of every item collected from the battlefield, mostly weapons, armour and artillery pieces, but also artillery ammunition and 357 kg of musket shot. Sächsisches Hauptstaatsarchiv Dresden (HSTAD): 11237, III. Abt. Loc. 10826/1 (Artilleriesachen), Bl. 17r: Breitenfeld battlefield clearing record October 1631: '7 rl.64 pf. Mussquetir Kugeln (7 hundredweight 64 pounds of musket bullets).'

4 André Schürger, '30 Jahre Schlachtfeldarchäologie: Von Little Big Horn bis Lützen', in I. Schuberth, M. Reichel (eds), *Die blut'ge Affair' bei Lützen. Wallensteins Wende* (Wettin-Löbejün: Verlag Janos Stekovics 2012), p.248. During the American Civil War, lead bullets were picked up on sight by the local population: Mary Ann Harris Gay, *Life in Dixie During the War: 1861–1862–1863–1864–1865* (Atlanta: C. P. Byrd 1897), p.256.

5 Achim Rost, 'Characteristics of Ancient Battlefields: Battle of Varus (9 AD)', in D. D. Scott, L. E. Babits, Ch. Haecker (eds), *Fields of Conflict. Battlefield Archaeology from the Roman Empire to the Korean War* (Washington: Potomac Books, 2009), p.54.

signature of a battle, and one that cannot be effectively recovered through conventional archaeological methods.[6] Mass graves, however, play a minor role in the interpretation of a battle, because the bodies have been moved before they were buried, which makes it difficult to connect them to an event, and, with usually only one mass grave of a battlefield available, it represents only a tiny portion of the battlefield.

The Survey: Methodology

The facts that almost all battle-related artefacts are located in the top soil, being partially removed due to clearing and looting, and being dislocated by ploughing has an impact on the archaeological methodology. At present, a metal detector survey is the only practical means of an archaeological investigation of a battlefield.[7]

A metal detector survey is very similar to the field walking developed in the 1970s to locate settlements and graveyards by systematically walking fields, collecting artefacts on sight and mapping all finds. Field walking produces valid data even if the survey was not conducted entirely systematically because a concentration of artefacts still indicates a settlement. In battlefield archaeology, however, unspecified concentrations of artefacts collected in an unsystematic or semi-systematic survey represents insufficient data for comparing and interpreting small finds distribution patterns, because the percentage number of finds collected needs to be similar on the entire battlefield. Otherwise, concentrations of small finds would be merely the result of an unsystematic survey and not the result of the battle.

There are several factors influencing the survey methodology and its interpretation, particularly the percentage of finds we are actually collecting compared to the finds deposited during the battle. During the clearing and looting process almost all larger artefacts, such as weapons, armour and artillery round shot, would almost certainly be collected, while most small finds, such as lead bullets and uniform pieces, initially remained on the battlefield, because they were too time-consuming to collect in large quantities. That changed with the availability of metal detectors in the 1980s. Since then, many battlefields have been severely looted; the Lützen battlefield, however, was not.[8]

The most important role determining the small finds recovery rate is the agriculture of the area. While ploughing does not generally move small finds horizontally over long distances, with few exceptions, it moves the items

6 Foard, *Integrating Documentary and Archaeological Evidence*, p.68; Achim Rost, 'Alesia, Kalkriese, Little Big Horn. Das neue Forschungsgebiet der Schlachtfeldarchäologie', in *Varusschlacht im Osnabrücker Land. Museum und Park Kalkriese* (Mainz: Verlag Philipp von Zabern, 2009), p.106; Schürger, '30 Jahre Schlachtfeldarchäologie', p.247.

7 For more detail see Schürger, *The Archaeology of the Battle of Lützen*, pp.116–119.

8 For more details on methodology and small finds recovery rate with all test results see Schürger, *The Archaeology of the Battle of Lützen*, pp.119–123.

Musketeer and pikeman, 1618, Sebastiaen Vrancx (1573–1647). The poses are clearly taken from *Wapenhandelinghe van Roers Musquetten ende Spiessen* (Den Hague 1607), Jacob de Gheyn II (1565–1629). (Staatliche Kunsthalle Karlsruhe)

vertically to a depth of the ploughing, i.e. 30 cm. The result is that we can only find about one-third of the remaining artefacts because the depth penetration of most available metal detectors is approximately 10cm for small finds.

The actual recovery rate is influenced further by the speed of the detectorist, the faster he moves the fewer finds he will make, with an average of 50 percent of small finds overlooked even when moving very slowly. In addition, dry soil has a negative impact on the recovery rate as well and although it affects the detection of thin material, such as coins and buttons, it does not affect the detection of lead bullets.

At Lützen, the metal detector survey was carried out as a systematic full coverage survey at low speed; that means the entire investigated area was surveyed once, and only once, in an attempt to cover the entire area with a metal detector coil. This methodology ensured a representative and statistically relevant sample of approximately 10 percent non-ferrous metal of what was supposingly deposited during the battle.[9] Iron, however, was not collected systematically because it would have severely slowed down the survey, while results had to be presented to keep the project running.

Early Modern Firearms

One of the main concerns within the field of seventeenth-century battlefield archaeology is matching firearms ammunition to weapon types and models, and their assignment to different service branches and armies. This issue is the key to understanding the distribution of firearms, as represented by

9 Foard, *Integrating Documentary and Archaeological Evidence*, p.73.

archaeological recovery of particular types of ammunition, and therefore being able to make interpretive assessments of gunfire combat and sequencing a battle's events.

Definition: Calibre and Weapon Types

Firearm calibres are mentioned occasionally by sixteenth- and seventeenth-century military handbooks, which specify the calibres of firearms as the number of bullets that can be produced from a pound of lead.[10] Therefore, calibres were measured in weight (i.e. pound) not width.[11] Unfortunately, calibres of sixteenth- and seventeenth-century firearms were calculated according to local weight systems, which could vary substantially; this was particularly problematic in the Holy Roman Empire, where most states had their own weight system.

Adding to the problem was that the silver pound was occasionally used instead of the regular pound, i.e. the pound Sterling (453 g) instead of the regular English pound (489 g).[12] That applied often to wheellock weapons, because fine motor skill specialists, such as clock makers, who used the silver pound, often produced the complicated lock.

In addition to the problem of using different weight systems for specifying calibres, the use of weight instead of width in early modern military handbooks has led to the misconception that they are always referring to the calibre of bullets. In fact, however, they refer to two different calibre specifications, which are often confused or misunderstood.

The calibre of the barrel is called 'bore', which defines the inside diameter of the barrel, and which is also the technical term in English sources: 'The Armes of a Musquetier offensive, are a Musquet, the barrel of a length of foure foote, the bore of 12 bullets to the pound …'[13]

English sources refer to bullet calibre by stating that the bullet is 'rolling [in]', as Cruso did:

> pistols … having the barrel of 18 inches long, and the bore of 20 bullets in the pound (or 24 rowling in).[14]

10 For calibre specifications see André Schürger, 'Theoretical calibre specifications of hackbuts and matchlock muskets in sixteenth and seventeenth century military handbooks', in Simon Sutherland, Tim Sutherland (eds), *Fields of Conflict Conference Proceedings* (online publication 2019) <http://fieldsofconflict.com/c_conf_papers.php?id=1>.

11 The 10-gauge shotgun is a holdover of early modern calibre specification.

12 Engerisser, *Von Kronach nach Nördlingen*, p.547. As leading weapon manufacturer, the Nurnberg pound became a standard measurement in the Holy Roman Empire in the early seventeenth century. Herbert Schwarz, *Gefechtsformen der Infanterie in Europa durch 800 Jahre* (München, Schwarz, 1977), p.207.

13 Thomas Kellie, *Pallas Armata* (Edinburgh: The Haires of Andre Hart 1627), p.3.

14 John Cruso, *Militarie Instructions for the Cavallrie* (Cambridge, University of Cambridge 1632), pp.30–31. For more examples see Foard, *Integrating Documentary and Archaeological Evidence*, pp.110–111.

Swedish officer and musketeer, from the engraving dated 1631. (Skokloster Castle)

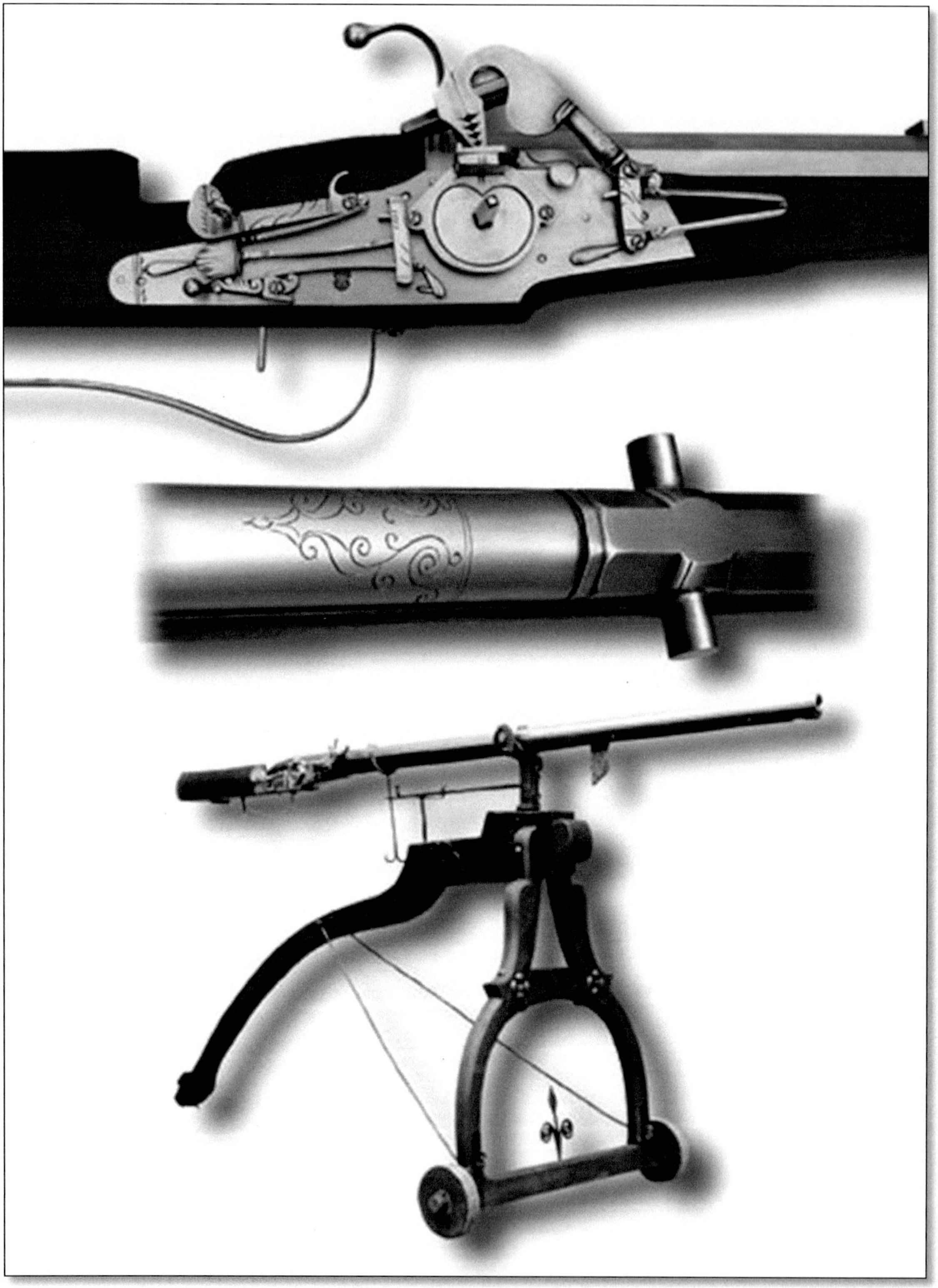

A 4-bore (27 mm) Doppelhaken from Suhl. (Armin König)

Most sources use the term either 'bore' or 'rolling in', few sources use both terms to specify the calibre of a weapon model.[15] This is additional evidence for the existence of two different terms, one for the barrel's diameter and one for the bullet's diameter.

In the Thirty Years' War, firearms were defined by the type of lock on the gun and the weapon type. There were three types of ignition systems, represented by different locks: matchlock, wheellock and snaphaunce. The matchlock required ignition using a burning fuse that had to be attached to the serpentine before each shot.[16] The wheellock had a spring-powered iron wheel with a roughened surface, which was wound up with a spanner. The wheel span when the trigger was pulled, running against a piece of marcasite or pyrites,[17] causing sparks that ignited the priming powder. The snaphaunce was a precursor of the flintlock with a flint striking a steel plate and the resultant sparks igniting the priming powder. The snaphaunce was considered more unreliable than the matchlock and was not common during the Thirty Years' War except in Sweden, although Gustav II Adolph made great efforts to replace his snaphaunce weapons with matchlock weapons.[18]

Infantry Weapons

Early modern military handbooks provide an overview of types of infantry firearm and their calibres during the sixteenth and seventeenth centuries. In the Holy Roman Empire, infantry used three different types of portable matchlock firearms, called *Hakenbüchse*, during the sixteenth century.[19] The Dutch term *haakbus*, having the same meaning as the German word *Hakenbüchse*, was the name given for the English term hackbut and for the French term *arquebus*.

The *Hakenbüchse* (hackbut) was a heavy long gun with a calibre of 10-bore or 8-bore, which had to be fired with a rest. The *Halbe Hakenbüchse* (half hackbut) was a light shoulder gun with a calibre of 20-bore. The *Doppelhaken* (rampart gun) was a 20 kg very heavy long gun with a calibre of 4-bore, and was operated by two soldiers.[20] These firearms got their name

15 Cruso, *Militarie Instructions*, pp.29–30. Anonymous, 'Ordre op de Wapeninghe 1599', in Johannes Bastiaan Kist and Jan Pieter Puype and Robert Balder Frank van de Sloot, *Musket, Roer ende Pistolet* (Den Haag : Gaade 1974), p.144.

16 See Daniel M. Sivilich, *Musket Ball and Small Shot Identification. A Guide* (Norman: University of Oklahoma Press, 2016), pp.6–7 for all types of gun locks.

17 Lawrence E. Babits, *The Evolution and Adoption of Firearm Ignition Systems in Eastern North America: An Ethno-Historical Approach* (Master Thesis, University of Maryland 1974), p.7. It was mostly marcasite, not pyrites, used in wheellocks; however, both look very similar and have only been listed as independent minerals since the mid nineteenth century.

18 Engerisser, *Von Kronach nach Nördlingen*, p.558, Richard Brzezinski and Richard Hook, *Die Armee Gustav Adolfs. Infanterie und Kavallerie* (Königswinter, Brandenburgisches Verlagshaus 2006), p.20.

19 For the development of infantry weapons see also Schürger, 'Theoretical calibre specifications'.

20 Engerisser, *Von Kronach nach Nördlingen*, p.544; Fronsperger, *Fünff Bücher*, p.44.

Haken (hook) from an iron pin beneath the barrel, which was hooked over the breastwork of a wall. However, these names were only generalised terms for portable firearms of which only the *Doppelhaken* was always equipped with the iron pin. The term *halb* (half) or *doppel* (double) refers to the calibre: a *Doppelhaken* had double the calibre of a *Hakenbüchse* and a *HalbeHakenbüchse* had half the calibre of a *Hakenbüchse*, similar to ordnance calibre specifications. All three weapon types continued to exist during the Thirty Years' War as arquebus or caliver, musket and rampart gun. A developmental continuation from *Hakenbüchse* to musket is reflected by the fact that German late sixteenth-century muskets are still referred to as *Hakenbüchse*, although it is clear that they were muskets; an inconsistency in sixteenth-century weapon terminology.[21]

Arquebuses and Calivers

The arquebus was developed in France in the sixteenth century from the German 20-bore *Halbe Hakenbüchse* (half hackbut).[22] This matchlock, smoothbore gun with a weight of less than 5 kg and a calibre of approximately 12 mm to 14 mm,[23] became the first standard infantry gunpowder weapon.[24] Its high military value, combining low weight with a simple lock mechanism that was easy to handle, was demonstrated in particular by the Spanish army during the first half of the sixteenth century[25] and from then on soon replaced longbows, crossbows and older gunpowder weapons in most European armies.[26]

While the arquebus kept its name in France and Spain (*arcabuz*), most European countries developed their own version under different names: caliver in England, *roer* in the Netherlands, *rör* in Sweden and *Rohr* or *Schützenrohr* in Germany; the latter thus replaced the *Halbe Hakenbüchse*.[27]

To complicate matters, the arquebus later became a term for a cavalry weapon in the second half of the sixteenth century and gave its name to the new light cavalryman, the 'harquebusier'.[28] In order to enable the cavalryman to have it ready to fire from horseback, the matchlock was replaced with

---

21 Schwendi, *Kriegs Discurs*, p.60.

22 Ignacio López and Iván Notario López, *The Spanish Tercios 1536–1704* (Oxford: Osprey 2012), p.34, Fronsperger, *Fünff Bücher*, p.44. The French word *arquebus* derived from the German word *Hakenbüchse*.

23 Arquebus bullets from the ship *La Trinidad Valencera*, sunk in 1588 as part of the Spanish Armada, had a calibre of 13 mm (Colin Martin, 'Before the battle: undeployed battlefield weaponry from the Spanish Armada, 1588', in Phil W. M. Freeman and Tony Pollard (eds), *Fields of Conflict: Progress and Prospect in Battlefield Archaeology. Proceedings of a conference held in the Department of Archaeology University of Glasgow, April 2000* (Oxford: Archaeopress, 2001), p.81).

24 López and López, *The Spanish Tercios*, p.35.

25 López and López, *The Spanish Tercios*, pp.6–7.

26 Keith Roberts, *Matchlock Musketeer* (Oxford: Osprey 2002), p.4.

27 Brzezinski/Hook, *Die Armee Gustav Adolfs*, p.19, Engerisser, *Von Kronach nach Nördlingen*, p.548, Foard, *Integrating Documentary and Archaeological Evidence*, p.81.

28 Engerisser, *Von Kronach nach Nördlingen*, p.559.

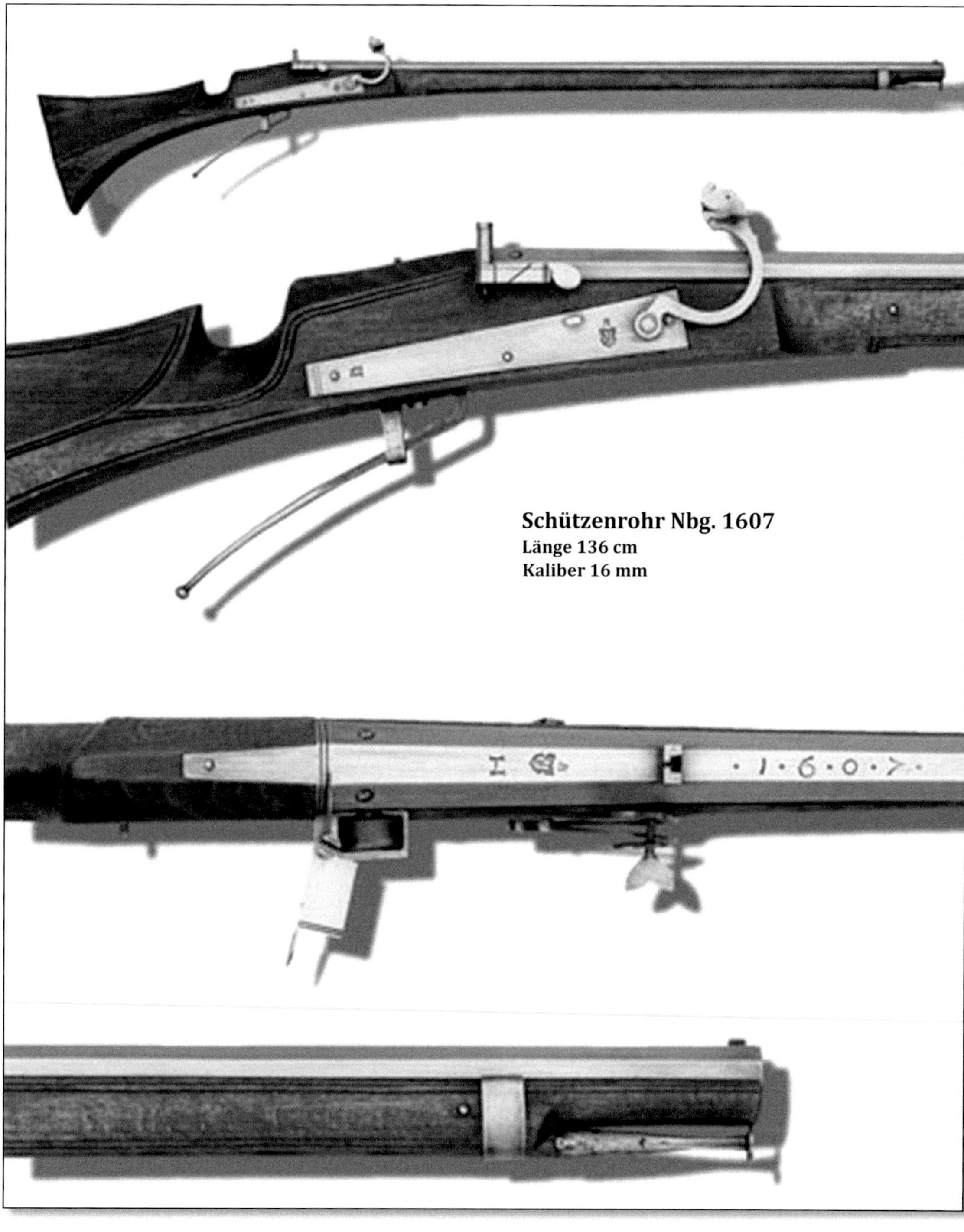

A 15.9 mm caliver. (Armin König)

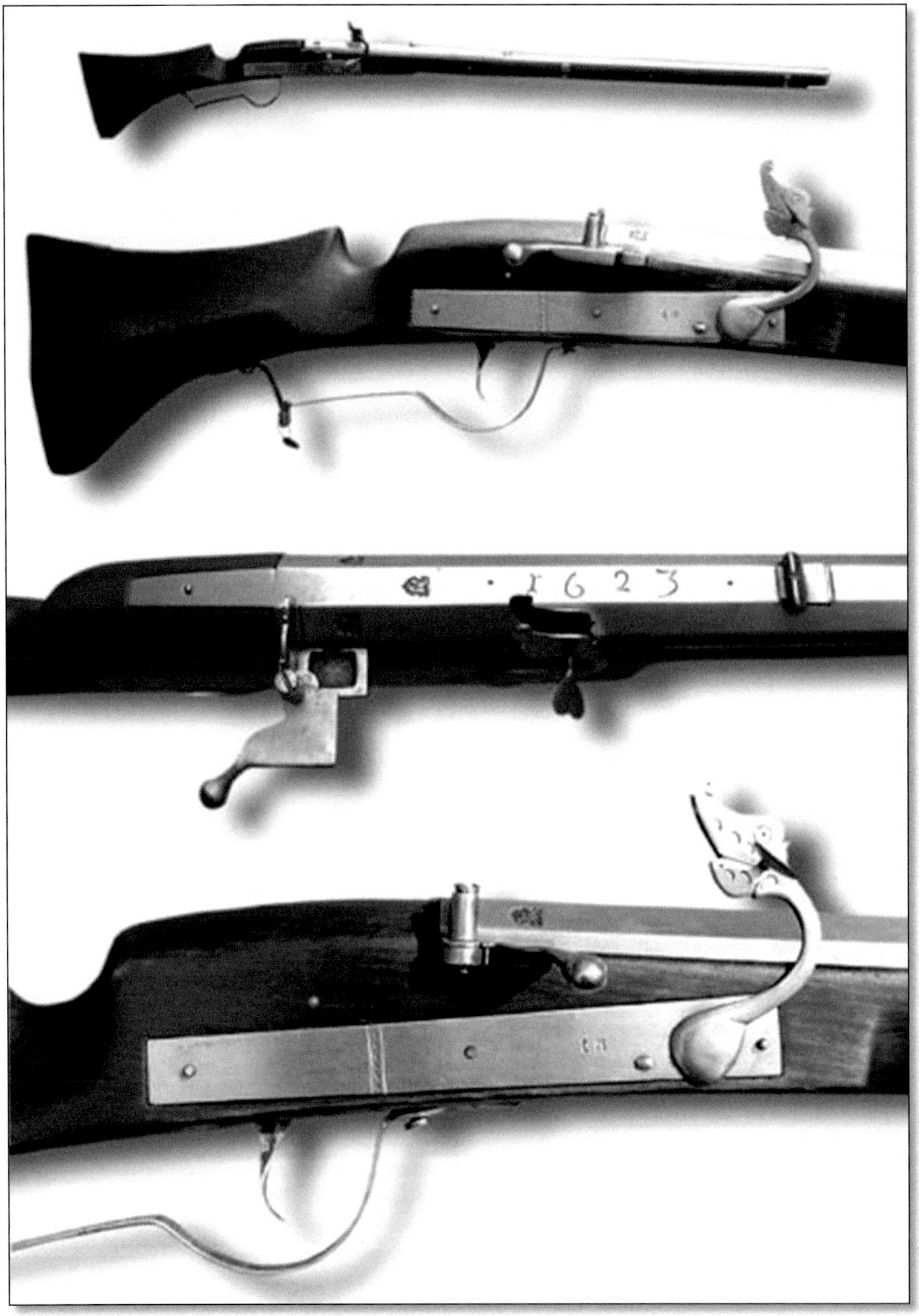

An 'older' 19.7 mm musket. (Armin König)

a wheellock. The barrel was constantly shortened during the seventeenth century and became a new weapon type, the carbine,[29] but even then, it was often still referred to as an arquebus. The use of infantry caliver/arquebuses in Europe is general evidence for the Spanish-style infantry formation except in Eastern European and Turkish armies.

Although by far the most common shot in sixteenth-century armies was the caliverman, this weapon lacked striking force. To counter this disadvantage, a small body of shot, usually about 10 percent, was equipped with the heavier *Hakenbüchse*, which was more able to hurt armoured troops.

Muskets[30]

In the early sixteenth century, the *mosquetta* (mosquito), a much longer, heavier and larger calibre weapon than the arquebus, which needed to be fired with a rest, was developed in Spain from the *Hakenbüchse*. In the late sixteenth century it became the dominant European heavy firearm and soon most European states had designed their own 'muskets', named after the Spanish *moschetta*.

There seemed to have been a kind of standardised calibres for hackbuts and muskets from the mid sixteenth to the early seventeenth century in the borders of the mid sixteenth century Habsburg Empire (i.e. Spain, Germany, Austria, the Netherlands), which also influenced England and Scandinavia, mostly due to the Dutch export of vast numbers of early muskets.[31] Initially, the calibre of hackbuts and early muskets was either 10-bore or 8-bore; also called '*rechte* [true]' or 'full' muskets.[32] Naturally, this standardisation of calibres was limited because many different local weight systems were used to define the calibre.

In the early seventeenth century, musket calibres became smaller and more diversified in the old Habsburg Empire. Saxony produced 16-bore muskets in Suhl, which were exported chiefly to southern Germany, Switzerland and Austria.[33] It is not certain if Augsburg was producing the 13-bore muskets in the very early seventeenth century, but if not it was probably not much later. Muskets from Nurnberg, and possibly Augsburg, had a calibre of 14-bore. Probably influenced by this development, England and later also Denmark developed 12-bore muskets. All these early muskets had a weight of approximately 7.2–7.7 kg.[34]

29 From French *carabine* (Engerisser, *Von Kronach nach Nördlingen*, p.559).

30 For all details on musket calibres see André Schürger, 'Theoretical Calibre Specifications'.

31 For all weapons and their specifications see tables at the end of the chapter.

32 Engerisser, *Von Kronach nach Nördlingen*, p.545; Gervase Markham, *The Souldiers Accidence* (London, W.I. and T.P. 1635), p.3; Anonymous, 'Ordre op de wapeninghe 1599', p.144; James Turner, *Pallas Armata* (London: M.W. 1683), p.175; Johann Jacob von Wallhausen, *Kriegskunst zu Fuss* (Oppenheim, Iohann Theodor de Bry 1615), p.32.

33 Engerisser, *Von Kronach nach Nördlingen*, p.545.

34 Engerisser, *Von Kronach nach Nördlingen*, p.545; Peter Engerisser <http://www.engerisser.de/Bewaffnung/Doublehackbut.html> (accessed 24 February 2018).

The production of larger calibres was generally abandoned between 1620 and 1630. In addition, muskets became lighter through the shortening of the barrel and developments in engineering which made it possible to produce thinner barrels.[35] The new muskets from Amsterdam and Suhl had a calibre of 15-bore and 16-bore with a reduced weight of approximately 5.5 kg.[36]

During the 1630s, there was a renaissance of large calibre muskets when Sweden entered the Thirty Years' War. In 1631, Gustav II Adolf ordered his manager of weapon manufacturing, Louis de Geer, to equip 32 regiments with a new design of a lighter musket that has caused some misunderstanding among researchers for over a century.[37] It was produced in Suhl, Amsterdam and Jönköping, had a calibre of 10-bore, a weight of 4.6 kg and it is said that it was the first musket that could be fired without a rest.[38]

Hans Delbrück, and many others after him, suggested a tactical superiority of the Swedish army because of this light musket.[39] This is partially based on an incorrectly quoted text from Sebastian Dehner who was said to have reported on 6 May 1632 that 'a Swedish company arrived at Rothenburg or der Tauber with musketeers carrying the new light musket without a rest' – which he did not.[40]

Archaeological evidence from the battlefield of Lützen (16 November 1632) proves that only a very few muskets of this new design were used by the Swedish main army in 1632.[41] In addition, the 1620s Dutch–German muskets were not much heavier than the sixteenth-century Spanish arquebuses that were specifically designed to be fired without a rest, and so the 1620s muskets could be used the same way.[42] Therefore, it was not Gustav II Adolf who suddenly came up with a new light musket, as often

35 Engerisser, *Von Kronach nach Nördlingen*, p.546. Brzezinski/Hook, *Die Armee Gustav Adolfs*, p.22.

36 Engerisser, *Von Kronach nach Nördlingen*, p.545; H. L. von Erlach, 'Project und Guttachten. Über die anstellung eines gemeinen Defensionalwercks, so er uff bevelch syner H. Loblichen Statt Bern, etlichen myner Herren allhie zu Jhrem bedencken überreicht, uft den 21. Januarij Anno 1629', in Frauenholz, Eugen von (ed.), *Das Heerwesen in der Zeit des Dreissigjährigen Krieges. Zweiter Teil. Die Landesdefension* (München, 1939), p.112; Hans Conrad Lavater, *Kriegs-Büchlein. Das ist grundtliche Anleitung zum Kriegswesen* (Zürich, 1644), pp.50–51. Although the models of musket produced in Suhl in 1600 and 1620 had the same calibre, they were completely different weapons with a weight difference of 2 kg.

37 Brzezinski/Hook, *Die Armee Gustav Adolfs*, p.20.

38 Brzezinski/Hook, *Die Armee Gustav Adolfs*, p.20. Engerisser, *Von Kronach nach Nördlingen*, pp.546–547.

39 Ernest Marsh Lloyd, *A Review of the History of Infantry* (London, Longmans, Green and Co 1908), p.112; Deuticke, *Lützen*, p.67; Hans Delbrück, *Geschichte der Kriegskunst im Rahmen der politischen Geschichte*, vol. 1. *Neuzeit* (Hamburg, Nikol, 2008), p.224; followed by Michael Roberts, 'Gustav Adolf and the Art of War', in Michael Roberts (ed.), *Essays in Swedish History* (London, Weidenfeld & Nicolson, 1967), p.69; Schwarz, *Gefechtsformen der Infanterie*, p.217.

40 Engerisser, *Von Kronach nach Nördlingen*, pp.546–547.

41 Schürger, *The Archaeology of the Battle of Lützen*, p.157.

42 Johann von Nassau proposed already in 1596 that muskets should be light enough to be fired without rest in emergencies (Engerisser, *Von Kronach nach Nördlingen*, p.547; Eugen

claimed;[43] he only continued a general development and it is not even clear if it was his idea. It took at least more two decades until the musket rest finally vanished. This development can be seen in the Stockholm Armoury records where the number of rests in store increased from 5,300 in 1626, to 12,126 in 1635, but decreased to 826 in 1645.[44] The rest was probably still produced until 1635, but not delivered to the Swedish field army in Germany, instead it was kept for the militia in Sweden. The massive drop in numbers between 1635 and 1645 might be seen as evidence for the final abandoning of the rest.

Both arquebus and musket coexisted alongside each other for at least half a century in different military types, the musketeers and the calivermen or *Rohrschützen* or *arcabuceros*.[45] However, after the difference in weight between musket and calivers became increasingly smaller, England, the Netherlands and Germany were the first countries to abandon the caliver and in the first years of the Thirty Years' War the musket, which had a better range, replaced it.[46] The last calivers produced in Germany and the Netherlands were manufactured in the early seventeenth century in Nurnberg, Amsterdam and Suhl. They had a larger calibre (20 bullets to the pound, or between 15.8 mm and 15.9 mm) than the Spanish version and a weight of approximately 3–3.5 kg.[47] Despite reorganisation of the infantry during the Thirty Years' War, some local militia (*Landesdefension*) and possibly some dragoons continued to use calivers throughout the war.[48]

Sweden missed the musket's development in the sixteenth century.[49] It was due to Gustav II Adolph's military reform that the Swedish *rör* and snaphaunce weapons were replaced with muskets before Sweden entered

von Frauenholz, *Das Heerwesen in der Zeit des Dreissigjährigen Krieges. Zweiter Teil. Die Landesdefension* (München: 1939), p.58).

43 Roberts, 'Gustav Adolf and the Art of War', pp.68–69.

44 Brzezinski/Hook, *Die Armee Gustav Adolfs*, p.20.

45 Engerisser, *Von Kronach nach Nördlingen*, p.548.

46 Engerisser, *Von Kronach nach Nördlingen*, p.548, Foard, *Integrating Documentary*, p.81. In 1608 Jan de Gheyn, *Waffenhandlung von den Röhren, Musquetten und Spiessen* (Gravenhagen, 1608), gave a detailed description of handling a caliver, while Wallhausen, *Kriegskunst zu Fuss*, p.42 recommended not using calivers. However, according to Pavel Hrncirík, 'Prispevek k nálezum munice do rucních palných zbraní v prostoru bojiste Rozvadov 1621', in Vaclav Matousek (ed.), *Zpráva o 1. sezóne systematického archeologického výzkumu bojiste z roku 1621 u Rozvatova, Sborn muzea Ceského lesa v Tachove* (Domazlice, 2011), pp.17–21, some League infantry still used calivers during the Battles of Rakovnik (1620) and Rozvadov (1621). See also Raimundo Montecuccoli, *Besondere und geheime Kriegs-Nachrichten des Fürsten Raymundi Montecuculi, Röm. Kays. Maj. Generalissimi, Worinnen die Anfangs-Gründe der Kriegs-Kunst sehr deutlich beschrieben sind* (Leipzig, 1736), p.11.

47 Engerisser, *Von Kronach nach Nördlingen*, p.548.

48 Engerisser, *Von Kronach nach Nördlingen*, p.548.

49 The first documented delivery of muskets arrived in Sweden in 1592 (Brzezinski/Hook, *Die Armee Gustav Adolfs*, p.19).

the Thirty Years' War in 1630.[50] Spain retained the arquebus[51] until the development of a light musket in the 1630s made them obsolete, because their infantry formations (*cuadro*) and tactics were based on both weapon types. It seems that a different version of the arquebus saw service until the second half of the seventeenth century in Turkey and Eastern Europe, which was particularly favoured by Janissaries, having a calibre of mostly 13–14 mm.[52]

Rifles

The inaccuracy of early modern firearms was not as much a military problem, it was solved by firing volleys, as it was a problem for huntsmen and marksmen who used crossbows in addition to firearms until the late sixteenth century.[53] To increase accuracy, rifled barrels were tested in the late fifteenth century.[54] Although probably invented for hunting and target shooting, the value of rifled weapons was soon discovered by the military. The Austrian army used them, particularly in border defence against the Ottoman Empire, where skirmishes against small groups of marauding Turks were common and to be able fire at an individual target of opportunity was more important than volley fire.[55] These weapons are documented physically in the firearms collection in the Armoury in Graz, where the oldest of 147 rifles from the sixteenth and seventeenth centuries is dated to 1520–1540.[56]

The rifles in the Graz Armoury have a calibre of 11.0 mm to 16.5 mm and were produced in Styria, Nurnberg and Augsburg, but no pattern of

50 Robert Allen Doughty and Ira D. Gruber, *Warfare in the Western World*, Vol. 1., *Military Operations from 1600 to 1871* (Lexington: Cengage Learning 1996), p.15.

51 The average composition of the Spanish infantry was 37 percent pikemen, 40 percent arquebusiers and 23 percent musketeers in 1601 (López and López, The Spanish Tercios, p.36), 37 percent pikemen, 42 percent arquebusiers and 21 percent musketeers in 1632 and 31 percent pikemen, 11 percent arquebusiers and 56 percent musketeers in 1636 (Peter Engerisser and Pavel Hrncirík, *Nördlingen 1634. Die Schlacht bei Nördlingen – Wendepunkt des Dreissigjährigen Krieges* (Weissenstadt: Heinz Späthling 2009), p.190). There is almost no change in the composition between 1601 and 1632. While the number of musketeers increased substantially between 1632 and 1636, very likely a result from the introduction of the new light musket, the number of pikemen was steady.

52 Some small calibre bullets found on the battlefield of Zboriv/Ukraine (1649) derive probably from a Turkish version of the arquebus. Gábor Ágoston, 'Firearms and Military Adaption: The Ottomans and the European Military Revolution, 1450–1800', in *Journal of World History*, Volume 25, Number 1 (2014), p.105; Adrian Mandzy, 'Tartars, Cossacks, and the Polish army: The Battle of Zboriv', in D. D. Scott et al., *Fields of Conflict*, pp.200–201; Montecuccoli, *Besondere und geheime Kriegs-Nachrichten*, p.149.

53 Vladimir Dolínek and Jan Durdík, *Historische Waffen* (Hanau: Dausien, 1996), pp.247 and 267.

54 Bo Knarrström and Stefan Larsson, *Hans Majestäts Friskyttar av Danmark* (Lund, Riksantikvarieämbetet 2008), p.107.

55 Robert Brooker, *Landeszeughaus Graz*, Austria. *Radschloss Sammlung* (Graz, Landesmuseum Joanneum, 2007), p.315.

56 Brooker, *Landeszeughaus Graz*, p.79.

calibre development can be determined. Swedish snaphaunce rifles of the second half of the seventeenth century have much smaller calibres – as low as 8.8 mm.[57] Although from a later period and an advanced weapon type, it seems that northern European rifles took a different developmental track. One snaphaunce musket, which is not rifled, but was probably used by a marksman, has a very small calibre of 6.0 mm.[58] There seems to have been a genuine military development of rifles, but it is often difficult to establish whether a rifle was produced for the military or as a civilian weapon.[59] †

† See PDF download, Plate 3: Calibre graph of rifles from the Styrian Armoury, Landeszeughaus, Graz

Cavalry Weapons

While the matchlock was a reliable weapon and perfectly suited for infantry, the burning fuse was a problem to handle on horseback. The wheellock could be easily prepared for firing in advance, although it was more complicated to reload and tended to malfunction after a few shots because of gunpowder residue. Nevertheless, the advantage of having a weapon ready to fire was more important when mounted than the disadvantages. The main firearms used by cavalry were pistols and carbines, but whereas nearly every cavalryman carried pistols, carbines were primarily used by harquebusiers.

Pistols

Pistols of the first half of the Thirty Years' War tended to be decorated and many of them were produced in pairs and in a number of different calibres rather than in large quantities.[60] Based on those in the Armoury Graz, German–Austrian pistols had a relatively small calibre of 10.0 mm to 12.7 mm in the early seventeenth century.[61] Slightly larger models with a calibre of 35 bullets to the pound (13.1–13.5 mm) were produced in Nurnberg and Suhl by 1620.[62] There were changes, probably due to the increased production of wartime, between 1630 and 1640 as decorative embellishments vanished and the calibre became much larger, up to 16.0 mm, although smaller calibres were still produced.[63] It is, however, unlikely that any large quantities of larger calibre pistols reached the Imperial or Swedish armies before the Battle of Lützen. John Cruso, who served in the Swedish army, stated in 1632 that the typical military pistol had a calibre of 20 bullets to the pound (15.6 mm).[64] If we compare pistol development to muskets and carbines, it seems likely that the Netherlands also produced pistols with a larger calibre in the early seventeenth century.†

† See PDF download, Plate 4: Calibre graph of pistols from the Styrian Armoury, Landeszeughaus, Graz

57 Knarrström/Larsson, *Hans Majestäts Friskyttar av Danmark*, pp.109–124.

58 Knarrström/Larsson, *Hans Majestäts Friskyttar av Danmark*, p.122.

59 Brooker, *Landeszeughaus Graz*, p.671.

60 Brooker, *Landeszeughaus Graz*, pp.60–61.

61 Brooker, *Landeszeughaus Graz*, pp.269–497.

62 Engerisser, *Von Kronach nach Nördlingen*, p.561.

63 Brooker, *Landeszeughaus Graz*, p.427.

64 Cruso, *Militarie Instructions*, p.30.

Cuirassier (Wallhausen)

Harquebusier. (Wallhausen)

Carbines

Not much is known about carbine evolution[65] but it seems that there was a development similar to muskets. In the early seventeenth century the Netherlands produced large calibre carbines of 14 bullets to the pound (18.1 mm), while carbines produced in Ferlach had a calibre of approximately 32–38 bullets to the pound (13.1–13.9 mm). That changed in the 1620s, when the calibre in the Netherlands was increased to 15 and 20 bullets to the pound (17.2 mm and 16.1 mm),[66] while Suhl produced the much-favoured 16 bullets to the pound (16.8 mm) carbine of the 1630s.[67] There were, nonetheless, still far too many exceptions to speak of a standard carbine. Unfortunately, carbines of late sixteenth and early seventeenth centuries were often remanufactured in the 1620s with new wheellocks using the old stocks and barrels, which certainly reflects on the calibre of carbines in service between 1620 and 1640.[68] Carbines used at Lützen, therefore, were of all and every calibre from 13.1 mm to 18.1 mm but with a tendency towards 16.8 mm.

Firearms Ammunition

The idea to locate battlefields by looking for firearms ammunition goes back to the nineteenth century, but historians failed to see the significance of this new information source.[69] With metal detectors readily available in the 1980s, many musket-era battlefields were subsequently worked on and produced huge collections of bullets. Many more large samples were found from shipwrecks.

Over the last two decades there has been an ongoing discussion about the interpretation of bullets and it therefore seems necessary to provide a short evaluation of recovered bullets, and in particular their calibre and weight.[70] Once archaeologically recovered bullets are statistically arranged, they can be applied to specific weapon types and models. This result in turn forms the basis for all further discussion of bullet distribution patterns.

Measuring Lead Bullets: Width or Weight?

There are two approaches to determine a bullet's calibre: measuring the diameter or measuring the weight. To be able to measure the diameter accurately, the bullet should have little or no impact damage or other deformation, which can often present a problem on stony or forested battlefields. While determining the calibre from weight by calculating the specific weight and converting it into the diameter seems to be a better

65 Most information about carbine calibres is from Peter Engerisser and is, as yet, unpublished.

66 Cruso, *Militarie Instructions*, pp.30–31.

67 Engerisser, *Von Kronach nach Nördlingen*, p.559.

68 Brooker, *Landeszeughaus Graz*, p.315.

69 Foard, *Integrating Documentary and Archaeological Evidence*, p.37.

70 For further details see Schürger, *The Archaeology of the Battle of Lützen*, pp.124–160.

solution at the first glance, it requires the bullet to have originally been spherical and to be made of pure lead.†

† See PDF download, Plate 5: Shape of bullets: divergence of width to depth

The accuracy of a bullet's weight and diameter is influenced by its shape. In theory, all unfired bullets should be spherical, but at Lützen only 1.2 percent of recovered ones actually are. While 8.7 percent are almost spherical with a divergence of width to depth of less than 0.15 mm, 90.1 percent of the bullets are more or less elliptical, as in the form of a cherry stone. Compared to other seventeenth-century bullet collections, the elliptical shape of the Lützen bullets is a commonly occurring inaccuracy for the period, but one that seems to have mostly been overcome by the revolutionary era of the late eighteenth century.[71]

The consequence of this divergence in width and depth is that calculating weight into calibre gives inaccurate results.†

† See PDF download, Plate 6: Bullets: Material, corrosion, casting sprues

The weight is further influenced by bullets with their casting sprue still attached. At Lützen 162 bullets (5 percent) recovered have sprues at least 2 mm in length still attached, these have a weight of around 1.5 g to 2.5 g. Another problem is that 51 bullets (2 percent) have had their casting sprues removed by cutting off parts of the bullet as well, which reduced their overall weight.

Another influence on the weight is the bullet's material. Although the bullets from Lützen have not been fully analysed, some general observations can be made according to the colour of corrosion and their specific weight. 182 (7 percent) are dark grey tin bullets.[72] As tin has a specific weight of 7.28 g/cm^3, while lead is 11.34 g/cm^3, tin bullets are substantially lighter than lead bullets. We must also consider the possibility that tin and lead was mixed on different scales. Small amounts of tin in a lead bullet might not create a different patina.[73] This consideration can be demonstrated with five lead bullets from Lützen. These bullets are spherical, as exactly as can be measured with a digital calliper rule, are only slightly corroded, and have no sprues. They are between 2.5 percent to 10.0 percent lighter than a pure lead bullet should be and likely have small portions of tin mixed into them. In addition, corrosion and firing a bullet reduces the weight.[74] In summary, shape, different material, corrosion, and firing all reduce the weight of bullets at differing rates. A conclusion is that there are too many inaccuracies and variables to simply calculate a bullet's weight to find the bore.

At Lützen, 2,019 bullets out of 2,756 were not or only slightly deformed due to firing or impact and therefore eligible for measuring their calibre in 1/10 millimetre.

71 See Schürger, *The Archaeology of the Battle of Lützen*, pp.127–128 for more evidence from Edgehill and Stralsund. Bullets from the American Revolution (Sivilich, *Musket Ball and Small Shot Identification*, pp.16–35) and the Napoleonic era (ongoing project at Leipzig) are more regular.

72 See Daniel M. Sivilich's comment on tin and pewter bullets, in *Musket Ball and Small Shot Identification*, p.116.

73 Sivilich, *Musket Ball and Small Shot Identification*, p.116.

74 Foard, *Integrating Documentary and Archaeological Evidence*, p.118.

Cuirassier in close helmet, 1618. Sebastiaen Vrancx (1573–1647). (Staatliche Kunsthalle Karlsruhe)

The *Vasa*: the Accuracy of Seventeenth-Century Lead Bullet Production

Another important aspect in interpreting lead bullets and allocating them to particular weapons is the accuracy of their calibre. While modern firearms ammunition is accurate down to 1/100th millimetre, seventeenth-century ammunition is far from that precise.

The bullets from the Swedish warship *Vasa*, which capsized in 1628, provide evidence for seventeenth-century calibre accuracy. The ship carried several barrels of lead bullets – no tin bullets were among them – probably stored to be used as case shot. Their diameter varies from 17.5 mm to 18.7 mm.

While most *Vasa* bullets (87 percent) have a calibre of 18.0 mm to 18.3 mm, the distributional curve of the calibre graph drops steeply at 18.4 mm and 17.9 mm and is phased out at both ends. Although the calibre of the bullets has a divergence of 1.3 mm, the form of this curve suggests that one specific calibre was intended and the bullets were produced for one specific model of musket before they were set aside to be used as case shot. The bullets were most likely produced originally for a 10-bore musket, possibly the heavy Dutch musket with a calibre of 20.2 mm. This presumption is consistent with a 1626 eyewitness account, which stated that the Swedish army used heavy muskets, and with the fact that Sweden imported most firearms from the Netherlands until the late 1620s.[75] However, it might have been a different English, German or Swedish version with a calibre of 19.3 mm to 20.5 mm. The windage can be only roughly deduced from this data to be between 0.6 mm and 3.0 mm.

There is similar data for the French Charleville musket used by American troops during the American Revolutionary War. This musket had a calibre of 17.5 mm, while the bullets had a diameter of 15.2 mm to 16.8 mm with most bullets at 16.0 mm.[76] That means a windage of 0.7 mm to 2.3 mm and a bullet calibre divergence of 1.6 mm. Currently it appears that the calibre values did not change substantially over time in the musket era.[†]

† See PDF download, Plate 7: Calibre graph of musket bullets from the *Vasa*

Lützen: Interpretation of Calibres

The standardisation of muskets for infantry had only begun during the Thirty Years' War, while most cavalry used numerous models of pistols and carbine. Firearms thus had a variety of calibres, ranging from 8.4 mm to 21.8 mm. Considering the inaccurate calibre of barrels and bullets of approximately 1.3 mm, the majority of bullets can be allocated only to broad groups of weapon models. The weapon type can, however, be deduced more accurately from

75 Engerisser, *Von Kronach nach Nördlingen*, p.547, Brzezinski/Hook, *Die Armee Gustav Adolfs*, pp.9 and 54.

76 Sivilich, *Musket Ball and Small Shot Identification*, p.32.

† See PDF download, Plate 8: Lützen calibre graph with models of firearms

the bullet calibre.[77] Bullet diameters for the three broad weapon classes are 17.6 mm to 19.9 mm for musket shot, 15.3 mm to 15.8 mm for carbine shot and 8.4 mm to 11.7 mm for pistol shot, although it is possible the latter might also include rifle bullets.†

At Lützen only the largest bullets (18.9–19.9 mm) can be allocated to a weapon model with a certain degree of probability; the heavy 8-bore musket, either the 22.0 mm German or the 21.8 mm Dutch version. Only a very few of those bullets where found at Lützen. This does not come as a surprise, as this weapon had already been out-of-date for two decades. Weighing 7.5 kg, it was relatively heavy, of particular relevance on long campaigns.

The bullets on a somewhat unclear curve of the calibre graph between 17.9 mm and 18.8 mm represent several different 10-bore weapon models. Most of them belong either to one of the old early seventeenth-century Dutch (20.2 mm) or German (20.5 mm) models, which were comparatively heavy, or the newer Saxon (19.8 mm), Dutch (20.2 mm) or Swedish (19.3 mm) lighter models. The low number of bullets used by the out-of-date models and the newer models is one key for understanding the calibre graph. According to the Lützen bullet distributions, older weapons were still in use in the Thirty Years' War, but in significantly lower numbers. As the army upgraded its weaponry, it still took some years until everyone was equipped with a newer model.

Another unclear, flat calibre graph curve at 17.3 mm to 17.8 mm derives mostly from two musket models, the 13-bore and the 14-bore (18.8 mm and 18.3 mm) muskets from Augsburg and Nurnberg. However, in this calibre range are also several other musket models and one large calibre carbine model.

The most conspicuous concentration (1,200 bullets, 59.4 percent) on the calibre graph occurs in the range between 15.9 mm and 17.2 mm with a peak (202 bullets) at 16.4 mm. It has the typical bell-shaped curve expected from a single weapon model, but the bullets actually represent nine different models: five muskets and four carbines. Although it is impossible to allocate these bullets to any specific weapon, it is the typical curve of one weapon model that must be considered.

The curve suggests most of this bullet group derives from a single model or similar models with a similar calibre. These are the 15-bore musket (17.7 mm) from Amsterdam and the German 16-bore musket (17.0 mm to 17.5 mm). The large number of bullets that would fit these muskets suggests that they were the main musket for both armies at Lützen. It seems likely that the Swedish army acquired many Suhl-manufactured 17.5 mm muskets during 1631 and 1632, when Saxony became an ally and a number of new regiments were recruited. There are also carbines that are known to have a calibre in the 15.9 mm to 17.2 mm range: the Dutch 15-bore (17.2 mm) and German 16-bore (16.8 mm) models. Normally there are far fewer carbine bullets than musket bullets on the 'usual' seventeenth-century battlefield, so most of these bullets are probably from muskets. That changes in the lower

77 See Schürger, *The Archaeology of the Battle of Lützen*, pp.137–150 for more details on the Lützen bullets.

calibre range at 16.0 mm and less, where musket bullet calibres are at their lower end. In particular the small peak at 16.0 mm represents a carbine's primary calibre and might indicate carbine bullets predominate at 15.9 mm and 16.0 mm.

Bullets with a calibre of 15.0 mm to 15.8 mm are exclusively carbine shot, with the larger calibre carbines mentioned above plus the Dutch 20-bore carbine, which creates a small concentration on the calibre graph at 15.1 mm to 15.2 mm. Although Gustav II Adolph had disbanded his harquebusier regiments, the Swedish army certainly had some carbines in service, in particular with his German cavalry. Nevertheless, most carbine bullets probably derive from the Imperial army, which fielded 11 harquebusier regiments at Lützen.

The bullets between 14.0 mm and 14.9 mm derive mostly from large calibre pistols, particularly the 20-bore pistol, and perhaps a from few carbines at 14.6 mm to 14.9 mm. Most important at this calibre range is the fact that there is no clearly visible concentration between 14.4 mm and 14.8 mm, where German calivers have their primary calibre. Only 12 years before Lützen, during the Bohemian war, the caliver was still a principal firearm of the infantry alongside the musket. By the time of Lützen, however, it appears that the caliver had been abandoned completely.

Caution is essential when interpreting the smaller calibres because there were very likely many more small calibre pistol and carbine models in service than suggested by the calibre distribution graph. Bullets with calibres between 11.8 mm to 13.9 mm can be allocated to various 42-bore to 28-bore pistol models and some smaller calibre carbines produced in Ferlach. Although these carbines were obsolete at the time of Lützen, many were remanufactured and still in service in the Imperial army.[78]

There are only 75 bullets (3.7 percent) with a calibre between 8.4 mm and 11.7 mm. They can be allocated almost exclusively to pistols with the exception of possibly a few rifle bullets. Small calibre pistols from Germany and Austria are thought to have been used more regularly by Imperial cavalry in the early 1630s. However, 11 mm bullets from the Swedish ships *Vasa* and *Solen* suggest that the Swedish army also used them and not just the larger calibre Dutch pistols that one might have expected because of the good trade relations between Sweden and the Netherlands.[79]

There are no standard military weapons known which could have fired bullets with a calibre of 8.3 mm or below. This is reflected in the fact that only four bullets (0.2 percent) with a calibre of 6.6 mm to 7.9 mm were found at Lützen. They might not even relate to the battle, because small shot usually derive from hunting weapons.[80] If they are battle-related, these bullets most likely derive from Swedish hunting rifles used by Gustav II Adolph's *djurskyttar*.

78 Schürger, *The Archaeology of the Battle of Lützen*, p.83, Brooker, *Landeszeughaus Graz*, p.315.

79 Schürger, *The Archaeology of the Battle of Lützen*, p.152.

80 Sivilich, *Musket Ball and Small Shot Identification*, p.145.

The low number of these small calibre bullets makes it unlikely that buckshot, which ranges in size from 6.1 mm to 9.1 mm, was used at Lützen.[81]

Firearms Ammunition and Distribution Patterns

While the calibre of firearms ammunition provides for an understanding of weapon types and models used in a battle, firearm ammunition features can add valuable interpretive information to the battlefield distribution patterns. Lead and tin are soft metals leaving many imprints on their surface, but some imprints, such as bite marks and others not entirely understood, are too infrequent to provide any clear distribution pattern.[82] The most important features supporting interpretation of bullet distributions on the calibre graph or the battlefield are firing evidence, intact casting sprues and modified ammunition.

Lead bullet distribution patterns: an introduction

When evaluating small finds distribution patterns in general, the recovery rate, in comparison to initially deposited artefacts, must be considered. At Lützen the archaeological recovery rate was approximately 10 percent and a little higher for large calibre bullets. Another important fact is that Lützen was a static battle, which led to small finds concentrations from overlapping but different events. This makes small groups of finds almost undetectable because a concentration of less than 20 initially deposited artefacts is reduced to perhaps two actually found by the archaeologist. In addition, a low density artefact scatter is often mixed with artefacts from other events, not all of which are related to the battle, making it difficult or impossible to detect.

The goal of interpreting bullet distribution patterns is to identify combat zones of single units or groups of units and compare them to historical accounts. However, with so many different weapon models in use, and their overlapping calibres, it is extremely difficult to create clear ammunition patterning ascribed to a single weapon model or even a single weapon type. Distribution patterns will be illustrated in two different maps according to musket and rifle bullets used by infantry and pistol and carbine bullets used by cavalry.[†]

† See PDF download, Plates 9 and 10: Bullet distributions in specific fields

81 Sivilich, *Musket Ball and Small Shot Identification*, p.170.

82 Bite marks might come from bullets chewed by animals, especially pigs after the battle, or by soldiers holding the bullet in the mouth ready for loading. Lavater, *Kriegs-Büchlein*, pp.85–86 wrote in 1644 that experienced musketeers filled their mouths full of bullets before battle; they took the gunpowder with their hands out of a pocket, poured it into the barrel, spat the bullet from their mouth directly into the barrel, tamped the musket butt twice on the ground, attached the match, and fired the musket without a rest (Engerisser, *Von Kronach nach Nördlingen*, p.555). It is also suggested that some soldiers chewed bullets to promote salivation (Foard, *Integrating Documentary and Archaeological Evidence*, p.152, Sivilich, *Musket Ball and Small Shot Identification*, pp.102–105).

Infantry

Considering the small finds recovery rate, the long duration of the battle, and the fact that Lützen was a static battle, it is not surprising that musket bullet distribution does not create a clearly visible pattern. However, some general observations can be made. The highest bullet density representing the main Imperial battle line is in the southern part of field VII and the western part of field I. The area west and north of this line consists of high and low density areas that are in the Imperial army's rear. The low density areas in fields II and III, and in the eastern part of field I, are skirmishing zones in front of the Imperial army. The musket bullets in the south-west half of field VII form linear patterns parallel to the Via Regia and thus represent infantry battle lines, although they are somewhat obscured by intersecting events.

Cavalry

Surprisingly, the densest pistol and carbine bullet concentration is in the southern part of field VII, the same area as the densest musket bullet concentration at the windmills, suggesting that the most intense action took place there in the middle of infantry combat. Another surprise is the moderate pistol/carbine bullet concentration on field IX, south of the Via Regia, where no cavalry action was thought to have happened. The few pistol/carbine bullets on fields II and III support the interpretation of a skirmishing area here due to the low density musket bullet concentration. Altogether, the pistol/carbine bullet concentrations appear to be less linear than musket bullets; if they are linear, then they follow a direction at a 90° angle to the Via Regia. Since this orientation is also at a right angle to the Imperial battle line, the bullets very likely represents a cavalry charge.

Firing Evidence

There are two groups of firing evidence: markings caused by the firing process and impact damage. There are no markings from ramrods on the Lützen bullets because the ramrods in use during the Thirty Years' War were usually wooden.[83]

Experiments conducted in the USA and the UK while attempting to understand markings caused by the firing process revealed banding is the most significant feature. A flattened band forms around the circumference of the bullet by compression caused by the gunpowder explosion.[84] The degree of banding ranges from very distinct around the whole bullet, to barely visible on one side. At Lützen 545 bullets (20 percent) show a flattened band. There seems to be a slight increase of 'banded' bullets towards the larger calibres, but groups of fewer than 30 bullets appear not to be representative.

286 bullets (10 percent) have markings from the powder combustion when the main charge detonated and propelled the bullet out the barrel.

83 Engerisser, *Von Kronach nach Nördlingen*, p.551, Foard, *Integrating Documentary and Archaeological Evidence*, pp.88 and 155. This is confirmed by the absence of ramrod marks on bullets from Edgehill (Foard, *Integrating Documentary and Archaeological Evidence*, p.158).

84 Foard, *Integrating Documentary and Archaeological Evidence*, p.157.

Above: Firing evidence: flattened band. (Photo: Eva Carmen Szabó)

These marks are not as distinctive as banding and it is possible that some examples have already eroded away.[85] A higher percentage of larger calibre bullets have markings from burning gunpowder explosion; this can be explained by the larger amount of gunpowder used in larger calibre firearms and the broader surface that was impacted.[86]

Lead and tin bullets deform when impacting against hard materials such as stone, metal, bone, or wood. The degree and nature of impact damage depends on many different factors, including bullet velocity, angle of impact, the shape and hardness of the material and its ability to bend, compress, or flatten, as when iron is struck; or break, as when bone or wood is hit. Unlike firing evidence, there is little known with any degree of precision about the degree and nature of impact damage and for interpreting what object a bullet may have hit. A great deal more analytical experimentation and data from different battlefields would be required to enable accurate interpretation of impact damage.[87] Even if comparable data from numerous battlefields were available, it is likely that every battlefield would have its own signature of impact damage according to the nature of battle, ground condition, vegetation et cetera.[88] It is the intention here, therefore, to provide a general analysis of the degrees of impact damage to aid in interpreting of bullet distributions on the battlefield. This is particularly important where a volley may have hit a battle line.

The ratio of the number of impacted to non-impacted bullets depends partially on ground condition, vegetation and the existence of houses and walls. For the Lützen battlefield, there are no contemporary reports mentioning walls, trees, or other vegetation such as hedges within the surveyed areas. In November 1632, the crops in the fields had already been harvested, leaving almost no vegetation on the battlefield. The only structures near the surveyed area that could have been responsible for causing bullet impact damage were three windmills, the mud walls around the gardens, and the field fortifications erected around Wallenstein's two batteries.†

† See PDF download, Plate 11: Distribution of firing evidence in percent

85 Foard, *Integrating Documentary and Archaeological Evidence*, pp.160–161.

86 If the quality of the gunpowder was high enough, an amount of half the bullet's weight was used; on lower quality gunpowder, the amount was up to ⅔ the bullet's weight (Engerisser, *Von Kronach nach Nördlingen*, p.553).

87 Foard, *Integrating Documentary and Archaeological Evidence*, pp.164–169.

88 For impact damage see also Sivilich, *Musket Ball and Small Shot Identification*, pp.47–57. The Sivilich sample bullets are from a very different kind of battle with more trees and the absence of body armour.

Today the soil on the battlefield is not particularly stony and there was no significant difference between surveyed areas. The field conditions could have changed over time as all surveyed areas have been in agricultural use from the Thirty Years' War until the present day. Stone removal from fields is a common practice, in particular with twentieth-century mechanisation. Six m^2 of soil were sieved to a depth of 0.6 metres in the park at Lützen – an area created in the late nineteenth century that never been ploughed by heavy machinery. All stones were smaller than 1 cm and these could not have caused massive impact damage on lead projectiles.

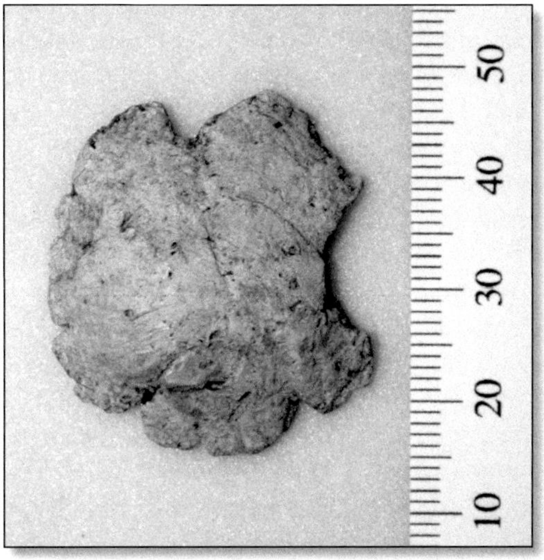

Bullet with severe impact damage caused by striking a hard, flat surface. (Glenn Foard)

In 2011, a 340 m long and 4 m wide trial trench was dug on the battlefield to a depth of 0.5 metres to 1.0 m. It revealed three large stones of approximately 0.5 metres diameter and a few stones of approximately 0.1 metres to 0.2 metres diameter, slightly more than could be seen on the surface and which probably reflects the situation in 1632. Stones cover less than two percent of the ground, which, theoretically, should also be the percentage of bullets hitting stones. Therefore, it may be assumed that the battlefield was not much stonier in 1632 than it is at present and that most impact damage on shot is battle-related i.e. bullets hit men, their weapons, armour, equipment, etc.

Presently, there is no practical objective method to classify impact damage in a way that would show any significant distribution pattern on a battlefield. Impact damage was subjectively classified according to the degree of deformation in 10 percent steps from 10 percent (impact damage barely visible) to 90 percent (flattened ball showing no sign of its former shape); at 50 percent the shape of half the bullet is still intact. It was hoped that this classification would show any distribution patterns, such as a battle line. This notion presumed that most heavily impacted bullets hit soldiers at point-blank range, in particular the armour of pikemen and cuirassiers.

At Lützen 921 bullets (33.5 percent) show various degrees of impact damage. Because of the subjective classification, and because most groups contain too few bullets to show any significant distribution patterns, distribution will be discussed according to three main groupings: light, moderate and severe impact damage. Many bullets have either a type of firing evidence or impact damage, but some have a combination of both features, demonstrating that the firing process does not necessarily create firing evidence. Likewise a bullet landing on soft ground, or after it has lost all velocity, can show no sign of impact damage. Therefore, impact damage or firing evidence demonstrates only that a bullet was fired, but their absence does not prove that it was not.[89]

The distribution patterns of bullets with impact damage can help to understand their significance. Musket balls with severe or moderate impact damage seem concentrated in the area of the Imperial centre's infantry line; they appear to have hit the armour of pikemen at point-blank range. Bullets with light impact damage are distributed more widely on the battlefield. The probable reason so few bullets with heavy or moderate impact damage are on the Imperial left wing, where they might be expected to have hit cuirassier armour, may be that musketeers tended to fire on charging cavalry at longer distances to prevent being overrun before they could deliver at least one volley; or that they were trying to aim at the horses to dismount the riders. Pistol and carbine shot with severe impact damage are distributed over the whole battlefield with some even found in the skirmish area on field III. The distribution patterns of bullets with and without impact damage are shown and interpreted in two separate maps.†

In general, there is a much higher percentage of pistol and carbine shot than of musket balls with heavy impact damage as compared to bullets with moderate or light impact damage. It is possible that smaller bullets tended to deform more severely than larger bullets, but another reasonable explanation may be that, in particular, pistols were used more often at point-blank range, or in hand-to-hand combat.†

Pistol and carbine bullets with heavy impact damage tend to be distributed more widely over the battlefield, creating fewer concentrations. The exception is the southern part of field VII near the windmills, where the densest shot distribution of all weapon types has been identified. This confirms that the most serious action took place near the windmills.

† See PDF download, Plate 12: Firing evidence: impact damage, gunpowder markings, and flattened band

† See PDF download, Plates 13 and 14: Interpretation of distribution patterns of bullets with and without impact damage

Casting Sprues, Paper Cartridges and Bandoliers

Casting sprues were the by-product of bullet manufacture and normally cut off after casting. However, balls with sprues still attached are found on seventeenth-century battlefields. At Lützen 162 bullets (5 percent) were found with intact casting sprues. It is sometimes argued that bullets with sprues found on battlefields are unfinished or unfired bullets; however, 28 bullets with sprues show impact damage and 50 show firing evidence, suggesting that there must be another reason for leaving sprues on bullets.[90]

89 Foard, *Integrating Documentary and Archaeological Evidence*, p.156.

90 Foard, *Integrating Documentary and Archaeological Evidence*, p.145 suggests also that intact sprues are no indicator for unfinished or unfired bullets.

Bullet with casting sprue. (Eva Carmen Szabó)

Battlefield archaeologists and historians alike agree that the sprue was sometimes left on bullets to attach a paper cartridge containing gunpowder, from at least the early seventeenth century to the late eighteenth century. There is no historical evidence before 1707, when Pierre Surirey de Saint Remy claimed that this had been done 'previously'.[91] There are two approaches known to have been used to connect the bullet to a paper cartridge, either by wrapping the whole bullet into the paper or by tying the paper to the sprue. Any advantage of tying bullets by the sprue over wrapping the bullet into the paper is unknown. It is possible that if the paper cartridge was tied onto the sprue and the ball was exposed, then the cartridge paper and ball could be loaded together after tearing the paper because the paper around the sprue would not interfere with the ball going down since the sprue was narrower than the bore.

The origins of paper cartridges are almost as mythical as Gustav II Adolph's leather cannons and it is still believed that he was also responsible for their development,[92] in particular for musketeers, based on a misunderstanding by Reverend Walter Harte in 1759.[93] Although it is possible that paper cartridges were invented in the late sixteenth century,[94] neither Lodovico Melzo in 1611,[95] nor Giorgio Basta in 1612,[96] mentioned paper cartridges in their military handbooks.[97] The earliest European reference to paper cartridges in a military context is from Wallhausen in 1616, who claimed that harquebusiers should either use powder flasks and bullets from a bag or, alternatively, paper cartridges.[98] Cruso in 1632[99] and Vernon in 1644[100] already knew only paper cartridges were used as ammunition for cavalry, cuirassiers and harquebusiers alike.[101] Those sources

91 Jürgen Pirkl, 'Die Handfeuerwaffenmunition des österreichischen Soldaten', in Peter Krenn (ed.), *Die Handfeuerwaffen des österreichischen Soldaten* (Graz, Akademische Druck und Verlags-Anstalt, 1985), p.27. Foard, *Integrating Documentary and Archaeological Evidence*, p.145, Mandzy, 'Tartars', p.201.

92 Weigley, 'Auf der Suche nach der Entscheidungsschlacht', p.143.

93 Brzezinski/Hook, *Die Armee Gustav Adolfs*, p.87, Mandzy, 'Tartars', p.202.

94 Pirkl, 'Die Handfeuerwaffenmunition', p.27, Dolínek/Durdík, *Historische Waffen*, p.295, Mandzy, 'Tartars', p.202.

95 Lodovico Melzo, *Kriegs-Regeln von der Reitereij* (Jena, 1625).

96 Giorgio Basta, *Il Governo della cavalleria leggiera. Das ist Bericht von Anführung der leichten Pferde* (Frankfurt, Iohann Theodor de Bry 1614).

97 Engerisser, *Von Kronach nach Nördlingen*, p.560.

98 Engerisser, *Von Kronach nach Nördlingen*, p.560, Johann Jacob von Wallhausen, *Kriegskunst zu Pferdt* (Frankfurt am Main, Iohann Theodor de Bry 1616), p.35.

99 Cruso, *Militarie Instructions*, pp.37–42.

100 John Vernon, *The young Horse-man* (London, 1644), p.8. See also Turner, *Pallas Armata*, p.173.

101 Engerisser, *Von Kronach nach Nördlingen*, pp.560 and 563.

appear to confirm that paper cartridges were adopted by the military over a very short period between the mid 1610s to the late 1620s, but exclusively for cavalry, evidently because the loading process on horseback was more difficult than on foot. It can be assumed, therefore, that some cavalry troopers probably used cartridges at Lützen.

During the Thirty Years' War, musketeers, but not calivermen, usually used a bandolier; 11 to 15 flasks, each holding a single charge of gunpowder, hanging from a leather belt, and with a bag for bullets. In 1683 James Turner, who served in the Swedish army during the Thirty Years' War, wrote in *Pallas Armata* that 'it is thirty years ago since I saw these (bandoliers) laid aside in some German armies', because they were exchanged for paper cartridges.[102] Although there is no reason to disbelieve his account, there are no other historical sources stating that musketeers used cartridges in the Thirty Years' War and it is not even certain if he was referring to that or a later period. The Stockholm Armoury issued bandoliers until 1670.[103] So it seems more likely that Turner relates to just one incident he saw and that probably a few musketeers were using cartridges towards the end of the Thirty Years' War. However, it was not until 1670 that bandoliers were generally replaced by paper cartridges in the Swedish army, and not much earlier in other European armies.[104]

Another explanation for leaving sprues on bullets is suggested by Mandzy and concerns the extra damage inflicted by the sprue when using low muzzle-velocity weapons.[105] Some ballistic testing has been conducted in which the sprue was sometimes parted from the bullet when fired, which did extra damage, but it is not certain if sprues were deliberately left on bullets for that purpose.[106]

In evaluating the archaeological evidence from Lützen, the percentage of bullets with sprues according to weight shows a very distinct concentration at 5.25 g to 17.50 g on the graph. These are almost exclusively pistol and carbine bullets, while there are comparatively few musket bullets with sprues. The calibres from 15.0 mm to 15.9 mm, which are almost exclusively carbine bullets, have a weight of 16.5 g to 23.0 g. and very few of these bullets have sprues, which suggest that at Lützen carbine bullets tend to have no sprues.

It is unclear why many, but not the majority, of pistol bullets had sprues, while carbine bullets tend to have no sprues. If intact sprues are an indicator for paper cartridges, a higher ratio of carbine bullets from Lützen should be expected to have sprues, because cavalry is reported to have used paper cartridges in the 1630s. It is also possible that for an unknown reason cartridges were attached to pistol bullet sprues, while carbine bullets were wrapped into the cartridge paper.

102 Turner, *Pallas Armata*, p.176, Brzezinski/Hook, *Die Armee Gustav Adolfs*, p.22.

103 Brzezinski/Hook, *Die Armee Gustav Adolfs*, p.22.

104 Engerisser, *Von Kronach nach Nördlingen*, p.546, Brzezinski/Hook, *Die Armee Gustav Adolfs*, p.22.

105 Mandzy, 'Tartars', p.203.

106 According to a paper held by Sivilich on the Fields of Conflict Conference in Osnabrück.

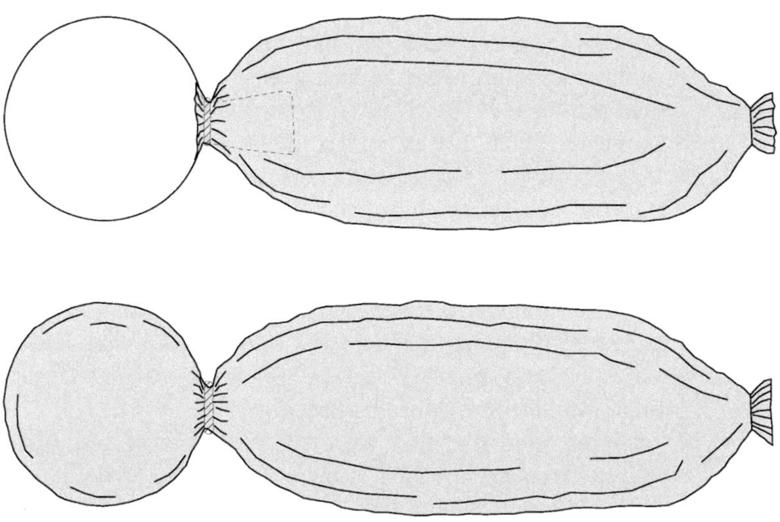

Paper cartridges. Top: Paper attached to casting sprue. Bottom: Bullet wrapped into paper. (A. Schürger)

Intact casting sprues on bullets must probably be seen in a context of the intended purpose of pistols, either their use at distances shorter than 5 m, or because they were used more often by cavalry against other cavalry rather than against infantry. Currently there is not enough historical or archaeological evidence for a reasonable interpretation of sprues left on bullets. To demonstrate the connection between sprue and cartridge, comparative data from a sixteenth-century battlefield, where no cartridges are expected to have been used, is required. Musket bullets with casting sprues are known from battlefields dating after the Thirty Years' War. They have been found at 1649 Zboriv, Ukraine, 1677 Landskrona, Sweden, and at several 1655–1675 Seneca village sites in upstate New York.[107] However, no bullets found from 1634–1695 at St. Mary's City, Maryland, had sprues.[108]

Modified Ammunition

The most common type of seventeenth-century firearm ammunition is round balls, but there are occasional bullets modified by individual soldiers prior to battle. These include parted bullets, slugs and nailed bullets.

Parted Bullets

Parted bullets are ordinary round balls cut into two, four or eight parts leaving a crosspiece at one end so that they split when fired, creating a spray pattern.[109] They are known from seventeenth- and eighteenth-century battlefields, but it is possible that they have a longer tradition and have not been discovered

107 Sivilich, *Musket Ball and Small Shot Identification*, pp.42–45.

108 Sivilich, *Musket Ball and Small Shot Identification*, p.46.

109 Foard, *Integrating Documentary and Archaeological Evidence*, p.127, Sivilich, *Musket Ball and Small Shot Identification*, pp.73–76.

Parted bullet.
(Photo: Eva Carmen Szabó)

yet on earlier or later battlefields. In the seventeenth century, parted bullets are known to have been used as fragments in ceramic hand grenades, probably in sieges, but their use in a field battle cannot be dismissed completely.[110]

Pieces of 25 parted bullets (0.9 percent) were found at Lützen – five halves, twelve quarters and eight eighths. It is difficult to measure their exact calibre, because they are not symmetrically divided, but most seem originally to have been musket or possibly large carbine bullets. A similar percentage of parted bullets (0.7 percent) with a similar distribution of halves (two), quarters (three) and eighths (two) were found at Edgehill, suggesting that this is a typical ratio of parted bullets on a seventeenth-century battlefield.

Other than that they were certainly fired at point-blank range, there is not much known about them. A letter from the British General Lord Howe written in 1777 to General Washington complaining about the use of parted bullets suggests that they were used unofficially by soldiers, but not in what situation, as any found have only been found on campsites.[111]

At Lützen, the majority (18) of parted shot are in the pistol bullet concentrations on the Imperial left wing, while only six were found in the centre; none were recovered from the cavalry skirmish area in front of the Imperial left wing or behind the Imperial centre. This suggests that they were used by musketeers against cavalry where infantry–cavalry interaction was to be expected and thus probably by the interlined Swedish or Imperial musketeer companies on the wings.

Slugs

Slugs were originally round bullets altered by hammering them into cube-shaped, elongated cube-shaped, or cylindrical bullets to be used as pistol and carbine shot by cavalry.[112] Because most slugs are altered to a large extent, their calibre often cannot be identified with any certainty.

Thirty-six possible slugs (1.3 percent) of different shapes with a calibre of 11.3 mm to 16.2 mm and 8.5 g to 33.5 g were found in Lützen. Most are elongated, cube-shaped or cylindrical, but some are short cube-shaped, or cylindrical. The length depends on the former size of the bullet and the final size of the slug, and there seem to be no obvious purpose for the different lengths.[113] It is more difficult to alter a bullet into a cylindrical form than into a cube-shaped slug, but cylindrical slugs seal the barrel more tightly and therefore have a higher velocity, and possibly greater accuracy. Five bullets with casting sprues look as if they were severely banded and are similar to

110 Foard, *Integrating Documentary and Archaeological Evidence*, p.127.

111 Sivilich, *Musket Ball and Small Shot Identification*, p.77.

112 Foard, *Integrating Documentary and Archaeological Evidence*, pp.121–122, Sivilich, *Musket Ball and Small Shot Identification*, pp.78–79.

113 Foard, *Integrating Documentary and Archaeological Evidence*, p.123.

those from the battles of Zboriv in 1649 or Monmouth in 1778, but they appear to be altered into a cylindrical shape for use as slugs.[114]

The asymmetrical shape caused a slug to tumble in the air, but it is unclear for what reason. Sivilich suggests that they were used because they caused more severe wounds than round bullets, but they are probably less likely to penetrate armour.[115] They may also have made a noise that might instil some uneasiness among the soldiers who were being shot at. At Lützen they were found almost everywhere on the battlefield except in the skirmish area to the front of the Imperial left wing suggesting that they were not fired by cavalry against cavalry. Their distribution pattern concentrates more on the outer centre, where cavalry–infantry combat took place, suggesting that slugs were used in particular by cavalry against dense infantry formations, something also suggested by Foard for the Battle of Edgehill, where 34 slugs (3.5 percent), a significantly higher percentage than at Lützen, were found.[116] The densest concentration of slugs is near the windmills in the southern part of field VII.

The origins of slugs are unknown. Seventeenth-century Turkish musketeers seem to have used slugs that they cut from lead bars in large quantities.[117] A mould for elongated cube-shaped firearms ammunition and a hunting musket with a square-shaped inner barrel from the eighteenth-century Schwerin weapon collection suggest that slugs might originally have been used in hunting.[118]

Nailed Bullets

Two carbine calibre bullets, and possibly a third (0.1 percent), have an iron pin or nail driven through their axis. This is also reported from the American War of Independence, and one example was recently discovered on the 1644 battlefield of Tywardreath.[119] If this low ratio of 0.1 percent is representative for seventeenth-century battles, they would be almost invisible

Top and centre: Elongated and cylindrical slugs. (Photos: Glenn Foard)

Bottom: Bullet with iron pin. (Photo: Eva Carmen Szabó)

114 Mandzy, 'Tartars', p.201, Sivilich, *Musket Ball and Small Shot Identification*, p.79.

115 Sivilich, *Musket Ball and Small Shot Identification*, p.79.

116 Glenn Foard, 'The investigation of early modern battlefields in England', in Harald Meller (ed.), *Schlachtfeldarchäologie* (Battlefield Archaeology). *1. Mitteldeutscher Archäologentag vom 09. bis 11. Oktober 2008 in Halle (Saale)* (Halle Saale: 2009), p.124.

117 Polgár Balázs, 'Egy török ólomlövedék-típus régészeti perspektívaja', in Hausner Gábor (ed.), *Zrínyi-Újvár emlékezete* (Budapest, 2012), pp.104–107.

118 Anonymous, *Die Schweriner Waffensammlung: 50 Jahre Verlust und Rückgabe* (Schwerin: Staatliches Museum, 2008), pp.68 and 147.

119 Sivilich, *Musket Ball and Small Shot Identification*, pp.76–78, Natasha Ferguson, *An assessment of the positive contribution and negative impact of hobbyist metal detecting to sites of conflict in the UK* (PhD Thesis, University of Glasgow 2013), p.171.

in archaeological collections. They probably served the same purpose as slugs to inflict extra damage against unarmoured soldiers. However, two of these bullets might be spring shot, two bullets wired together.[120]

The low number of modified bullets suggests that they were unofficially produced and fired by individual soldiers, rather than in official ammunition issues, and that the effect they achieved was not important enough to produce this ammunition in large quantity.

Artillery Ammunition

Approximately 80 to 100 cannon were deployed in the Battle of Lützen. These should have left substantial evidence after six hours of fighting, but only a few small finds can be classified as artillery ammunition. One reason for the lack of artillery evidence might be that the surveyed area was limited largely to the initial Imperial deployment. This means that the areas that the Imperial artillery fired into have not yet been surveyed. Another reason is certainly the type of ammunition used in the Battle of Lützen.

A variety of types of artillery ammunition were used in the seventeenth century depending on the nature of engagement, but they can be subsumed into four categories: round shot, grapeshot, case or canister shot and shells.

Round Shot

Iron round shot was used at long distance, but was usually not very effective in terms of hitting soldiers.[121] As the rate of fire of seventeenth-century heavy artillery pieces was low, only a few would be deposited during a battle. Because of their considerable size most were picked up during the clearing and looting process and none were found during surveys on the battlefields of either Lützen or Edgehill.

One lead round shot (116.8 g) was discovered on the Lützen battlefield. The bullet was almost certainly fired from a 4-bore *Doppelhaken*, possibly from Suhl as the bullet's weight is a perfect match to a ¼ pound Saxon.[122] The 17–19 kg, 2.3 metre-long *Doppelhaken* were very heavy wheellock muskets, sometimes combined with a matchlock, and usually used during sieges against artillery crews. They were able to fire through earthworks and wooden planks, but it is not unlikely that they were also deployed in a linear battle, possibly on a mount and utilised together with regimental artillery, although there is no historic evidence. Some *Doppelhaken* are known to have had rifled barrels, which makes them excellent, long range, sniper rifles with a high striking impact.[123] *Generalleutnant* Tserclaes *Graf* von Tilly was killed

---

120 Sivilich, *Musket Ball and Small Shot Identification*, p.89.

121 Foard, *Integrating Documentary and Archaeological Evidence*, p.129.

122 Engerisser <http://www.engerisser.de/Bewaffnung/Doublehackbut.html> (accessed 24 February 2018).

123 Brooker, *Landeszeughaus Graz*, p.92.

by a *Doppelhaken* at the Battle of Rain am Lech,[124] which suggests that they may sometimes have been deployed in battle to fire at officers.

Grapeshot

Grapeshot was a projectile with a number of iron balls of approximately 2–5 cm size, which was very effective at medium range. Initially developed for naval warfare, possibly as early as the fifteenth century, it is not entirely certain when it found its way into European land warfare, but it seems likely that the Swedish army used grapeshot during the Thirty Years' War,[125] as some were found on the battlefield of 1677 Landskrona.[126] Chemnitz reported that Gustav II Adolph's 3-pounders fired mostly 'Kartätschen' and 'Schrot' instead of round shot, which seems to have the meaning of 'grapeshot' and 'case shot'.[127]

Five iron bullets with a diameter of 24 mm to 30 mm, which could have been grapeshot, were found on the Lützen battlefield. Grapeshot should produce a pattern similar to case shot, but grapeshot projectiles are bigger and easier to find during the post-battle clearing and looting processes. Another factor is that iron objects were not specifically searched for at Lützen and thus most grapeshot might have been overlooked during the archaeological survey because of the use of the discrimination function on the metal detectors. Finally, without any distribution pattern or material analysis, the iron balls cannot be classified as grapeshot or even be allocated with certainty to the battle. Another possibility is that the iron balls are round shot from falconet type artillery pieces, which have a calibre of approximately 32 mm to 55 mm.

Case Shot

A type similar to grapeshot, case shot or canister was multiple ball artillery ammunition, but with smaller bullets fired at close quarters that produced devastating effects against dense formations.[128] In the seventeenth century, one case usually consisted of around 70 or more musket bullets which, when fired, formed a long triangular distribution pattern on the battlefield, as can be seen at Edgehill.[129] Bullets from case shot have very distinctive hexagonal

124 Junkelmann, 'Tilly', p.38.

125 Brzezinski, *Lützen*, p.23. Grape shot was present on the *Vasa* (Foard, *Integrating Documentary and Archaeological Evidence*, p.131).

126 Bo Knarrström, 'Battlefield Research in Scania, Southern Sweden. Epic battles and small-scale skirmishes in the scope of battlefield archaeology', in Harald Meller (ed.), *Schlachtfeldarchäologie* (Battlefield Archaeology). *1. Mitteldeutscher Archäologentag vom 09. bis 11. Oktober 2008 in Halle (Saale)* (Halle/Saale, 2009), p.189.

127 Engerisser, *Von Kronach nach Nördlingen*, pp.584 and 590. The German word 'Kartätsche' is a general description of any multiple load ammunition, while today 'Schrot' has the meaning of small shot used by huntsmen. As there are no adequate German terms for 'grapeshot' or 'case shot', Chemnitz possibly tried to describe this type of ammunition.

128 Foard, *Integrating Documentary and Archaeological Evidence*, p.129.

129 Foard, *Integrating Documentary and Archaeological Evidence*, p.132, Foard, 'The investigation of early modern battlefields in England', p.124.

Case shot.
(Photo: Glenn Foard)

facets, which distinguish them from firearm ammunition.[130] Since case shot projectiles were not standardised in the seventeenth century, it could contain a variety of projectiles, including non-metal material such as pebbles or cast off iron fragments.[131]

At Lützen, only one bullet with hexagonal facets was found. Since the battlefield was surveyed to 100 percent coverage, it is extremely unlikely that any further case shot balls were overlooked, if they were part of an all lead bullet case shot. Although the Imperial artillery probably fired mostly into an area that has not yet been surveyed, the 40 Swedish regimental guns, which almost certainly fired case, were distributed along the whole Swedish front line and must have deposited case projectiles in the surveyed area. The only reasonable explanation is that either small iron or non-metal projectiles (langrage) were used as case at Lützen. It is uncertain how only a single bullet from case shot could have been deposited on the battlefield.

Artillery Shells or Hand Grenades

Nineteen fragments of spherical cast iron shells, two of them with part of a fuse hole, were found at Lützen. Their form is not entirely spherical, which complicated measuring their diameter. Only two fragments were large enough to determine a fairly accurate calibre, while nine smaller fragments provided at least an approximate calibre, ranging from 50 mm to 200 mm. Spherical cast iron shells are rarely found on seventeenth-century battlefields, as at Landskrona,[132] so these derive either from artillery shells or hand grenades.

Shells were usually fired by mortars during sieges. Their short range made them unsuitable for open field battles and there is no historical reference of their use in that way in the seventeenth century, although it is not impossible. Shells could also be fired by normal field artillery pieces of any calibre; although there is no account of their use in battle, it is more likely that they were used against the enemy's heavy artillery. As the Imperial artillery positions in Lützen were fortified, which would have made a bombardment with round shot ineffective, the Swedish heavy artillery possibly fired shells against them.

Initially hand grenades had been used in siege warfare during the sixteenth century, and they were recommended for battle as early as 1590 although their use in battle became more common during the seventeenth century.[133] It is not known whether hand grenades were used at Lützen.

130 Foard, *Integrating Documentary and Archaeological Evidence*, figs 65 and 66.

131 Foard, *Integrating Documentary and Archaeological Evidence*, p.130.

132 Knarrström, 'Battlefield Research', p.189.

133 Foard, *Integrating Documentary and Archaeological Evidence*, p.139.

Currently, it is not possible to distinguish cast iron shells from hand grenades from those shells fired by artillery and both seem possible for Lützen. The very different calibres suggest that they were fired by artillery; moreover, two large-calibre cast iron shells were found on the Imperial left wing, and these were obviously too heavy to be thrown as hand grenades. These two shell fragments very likely derive from a Swedish 24-pounder firing at the Imperial artillery. The author has recently found several fragments of cast iron shells on the battlefield of Breitenfeld (1631), suggesting that this type of artillery ammunition was used more regularly during Thirty Years' War battles than previously believed.

Tables

Table 3: Sixteenth- and seventeenth-century hackbuts and matchlock muskets

Prod. site/ country	Weapon calibre – bullets/ pound (bore)	Bullet calibre – bullets/ pound (rolling in)	Pound (mostly uncertain, with a '?' speculative)	Weapon calibre (mm)	Bullet calibre	Appr. date	(a) Historical or archaeological source (b) Actual musket
Spain	8	10	Madrid 460 g	21.3	19.8	1580–1610	Martin, 'Before the battle', p.81 (a)
Holland	8	10	Amsterdam 494 g	21.8	20.2	1590–1615	Turner, *Pallas Armata*, p.175
Germany	8	10	Nurnberg 510 g	22.0	20.5	1590–1615	Wallhausen, *Kriegskunst zu Fuss*, p.32
England	9	11	England 489 g	20.9	19.5	1630–1650	William Eldred, *The Gunners Glasse* (London: T. Forcet 1646), p.96
Germany	10	12	Nurnberg? 510 g	20.5	19.3	1530–1560	Fronsperger, *Fünff Bücher*, p.44
Holland	10	12	Amsterdam 494 g	20.2	19.1	1590–1620	Anonymous, 'Ordre op de wapeninghe 1599', p.144
Germany	10	12	Nurnberg 510 g	20.5	19.3	1600–1620	Wallhausen, *Kriegskunst zu Fuss*, p.32
England+	10	12	England 489 g	20.3	19.0	1585–1620	Turner, *Pallas Armata*, p.175; 1589*
Suhl	10	12	Saxony 467 g	19.8	18.7	1630–1640	** (b)
Holland	10	12	Amsterdam 494 g	20.2	19.1	1630–1640	** (b)
Jönköping	10	12	Sweden 425 g	19.3	18.1	1630–1640	** (b)
England	10	12	England 489 g	20.3	19.0	1630–1640	Council of War 1630* Anon 1638*

England	12	14	England 489 g	19.0	18.0	1610–1630	Kellie, *Pallas Armata*, p.3
Denmark	12	14	Copenhagen 500 g	19.1	18.2	1620–1660	Turner, *Pallas Armata*, p.175
Augsburg	13	15	Nurnberg 510 g	18.8	17.9	1600–1620	Erlach, 'Project und Guttachten', pp.112
Augsburg/ Nurnberg	14	16	Nurnberg 510 g	18.3	17.5	1600–1620	Erlach, 'Project und Guttachten', pp.112
Amsterdam	15	17	Amsterdam 494 g	17.7	17.0	1620–1630	Engerisser, *Von Kronach nach Nördlingen*, p.545
Suhl	16	18	Nurnberg 510 g	17.5	16.8	1600–1620	Engerisser, *Von Kronach nach Nördlingen*, p.545
Suhl	16	18	Saxony 467 g	17.0	16.3	1620–1630	Lavater, *Kriegs-Büchlein*, pp.50–51

Bore Actual calibre mentioned in the historical source
\+ and other countries
* Foard, *Integrating Documentary and Archaeological Evidence*, pp.110–111
** Engerisser, *Von Kronach nach Nördlingen*, pp.546–547; Brzezinski/Hook, *Die Armee Gustavus Adolphus*, p.20

Table 4: Pistol specifications

Production location	**Weapon calibre, bullets/ pound**	**Bullet calibre, bullets/ pound**	**Pound**	**Weapon calibre (mm)**	**Bullet calibre (mm)**	**Approx. date**
Amsterdam	20	24	England 489 g	15.6	14.7	1620–1630
Suhl/Nurnberg/ Ferlach	28	32	England 489 g	14.0	13.4	1625–1650
Suhl/Nurnberg	35	42	Nurnberg 510 g	13.5	12.7	1620–1635
Suhl	35	42	Saxony 467 g	13.1	12.3	1620–1630
Nurnberg	38	45	Nurnberg 510 g	13.1	12.4	1625–1635
Nurnberg	42	50	Nurnberg 510 g			1620–1625
Nurnberg/ Ferlach	50	60	Nurnberg silver 477 g			1625–1630
Nurnberg/ Augsburg	70	90	Nurnberg silver 477 g			1625–1630
Nurnberg	80	100	Nurnberg silver 477 g			1620–1625
Nurnberg/ Augsburg	80		Nurnberg silver 477g			1600–1630

Table 5. Carbine specifications

Production Location	Weapon calibre, bullets/ pound	Bullet calibre, bullets/ pound	Pound	Weapon calibre (mm)	Bullet calibre (mm)	Approx. Date
The Netherlands	14	16	Amsterdam 494 g	18.1	17.3	1600–1620
The Netherlands	15	17	England 489 g	17.2	16.5	1620–1630
Nurnberg/ Amsterdam	16	18	England 489 g	16.8	16.2	1630–1640
Suhl	16	18	England 489 g	16.8	16.2	1620–1630
The Netherlands	20	22	Amsterdam 494 g	16.1	15.5	1620–1630
Ferlach	32	35	Nurnberg 510 g	13.9	13.5	1600–1620
Ferlach	38	42	Nurnberg 510 g	13.1	12.7	1600–1620

Table 6. Number of bullets with impact damage according to their degree of deformation

	Light impact damage			Moderate impact damage			Severe impact damage		
Percent	10	20	30	40	50	60	70	80	90
Number	93	141	150	146	98	73	68	71	81

Table 7. Calibre of spherical cast iron shells

Calibre (mm)	Gauge (mm)	Artillery piece
164–180 f	17–20	24-pounder
164–170	16–20	24-pounder
140–180*	15–17	24-pounder
120–200*	15–16	24-pounder or 12-pounder
120–160*	16–20	24-pounder or 12-pounder
104–120*	14–15	12-pounder or 6-pounder
90–100*	9–19	12-pounder or 6-pounder
80–100*	11–14	12-pounder, 6-pounder or 3-pounder
70–100 f*	14–17	12-pounder, 6-pounder or 3-pounder
60–70*	12–16	3-pounder
50–70*	11–14	3-pounder

f = fuse hole
* = small fragment, approximate calibre

4

Order of Battle

Research on the participating Imperial army regiments and their strength at Lützen was conducted by German historians influenced largely by Seidler on one side, and by Swedish and English historians influenced by the Swedish General Staff on the other, with both groups coming to erroneous conclusions.[1] Even for the well-documented Swedish army, it is not entirely certain which regiments actually were at Lützen. This can only be understood by looking at both armies and their movements during the week before the battle.

The Armies at Weissenfels and Naumburg

On 8 and 10 November 1632 Gustav II Adolph and Wallenstein entrenched their armies only 11 km apart at Naumburg and Weissenfels.[2] On 12 November Gustav II Adolph undertook a reconnaissance in force to Weissenfels, where Wallenstein, reinforced by a League force under Pappenheim, waited for him with the army in full battle array. Since this important battle plan of the Imperial army survived, we know what regiments of Wallenstein's army were present on that day.[3]

Gustav II Adolph must have been impressed by the Imperial forces as he made no attempt to attack. With winter drawing near, both commanders knew they could not supply their armies in these positions indefinitely. To avoid a disaster comparable to that suffered by the Swedish army at Nurnberg two month before, Wallenstein made the first move. On the morning of 14 November he dispersed his army and sent it to winter quarters. His order survives but lists seven regiments that are not mentioned in the Weissenfels'

1 Seidler, *Untersuchungen*, pp.37–39. Generalstaben, *Sveriges Krig*, pp.413–414. Guthrie, *Battles of the Thirty Years' War*, pp.223–224.

2 Brzezinski, *Lützen*, p.31.

3 Holl, 'Wallensteins angebliche Skizze', p.59 and Fig. 3.

battle plan nor in the Trauttmansdorff list.[4] The order is very likely not only a plan for Wallenstein's army at Weissenfels, but also the order for the army's winter quarters in Saxony, including the regiments already in garrison.[5]

On the same day, 14 November, the Swedish army was mustered, and a record of this survives providing the exact number of infantry and approximate number of cavalry for each regiment on that day.[6] When Gustav II Adolph learned Wallenstein was dispersing his army he followed him the next day, but left a garrison in Naumburg hoping he could catch Wallenstein by surprise.[7] Gustav II Adolph's advance was delayed at Rippach by a small group of Croats and dragoons, who held the high ground on the eastern side of the small stream just long enough to give Wallenstein time to gather his forces.[8]

Wallenstein was then on his way to Leipzig and, at the time, 6 km north-east of Rippach in Lützen with a force of only 10 regiments, approximately 6,000 men, when he was informed of Gustav II Adolph's approach around midday.[9] With the Swedish army on his heels, he could not move without risking being chased out of Saxony and perhaps losing his slow moving artillery train. Wallenstein opted to stay at Lützen and prepared for battle. His other bodies of troops were already a day and a half further on from Weissenfels towards their winter quarters but he hoped to be able to concentrate enough troops to face the Swedish army the next day.[†]

† See PDF download, Plate 15: Wallenstein's 14 November dispersal plan

The Imperial Army at Lützen

Until Barbara Stadler published the Trauttmansdorff list in 1991[10] there was an ongoing debate about which regiments managed to return in time for the battle. According to that list, all regiments of the Weissenfels army returned to Lützen in time except the Mannsfeld's[11] and Suys' Regiments and most of Pappenheim's brigade, of which only the Bredau and Tontinelli Regiments arrived before the battle. The arrival of these two of Pappenheim's regiments before the battle may be the reason why some secondary sources, but only

4 Hallwich, *Briefe und Akten*, vol. 3, pp.480–484. Regiments: Hatzfeld, Trcka Foot, Thun, Contreras, Mohr vorm Wald, Scharffenberg and Czernin.

5 Priorato's list is incorrect (Priorato, *Historia dell Guerra*, p.119).

6 Langman, 'Lützen', p.162.

7 Brzezinski, *Lützen*, p.34.

8 Brzezinski, *Lützen*, pp.34–38.

9 The Regiments Waldstein, Chiesa, Altsachsen, Baden, Holk, Hagen, Lohe, Westfalen, Drost and Beygott (Hallwich, *Briefe und Akten*, vol. 3, pp.482–483). It is not entirely certain if Wallenstein had only his corps at Lützen at midday on 15 November or if there were also parts of the rearguard of other units.

10 Stadler, *Pappenheim*, pp.891–892. See also Brzezinski, *Lützen*, p.48. The list is often overlooked in modern publications (Guthrie, *Battles of the Thirty Years' War*, pp.223–224).

11 Mannsfeld's Regiment was on his way to Eilenburg to support the Regiments Trcka Foot, Thun and Hatzfeld against the 6,000 strong Saxon corps of Herzog Georg von Braunschweig-Lüneburg at Torgau (Holl, 'Wallensteins angebliche Skizze', p.67. Brzezinski, *Lützen*, p.29).

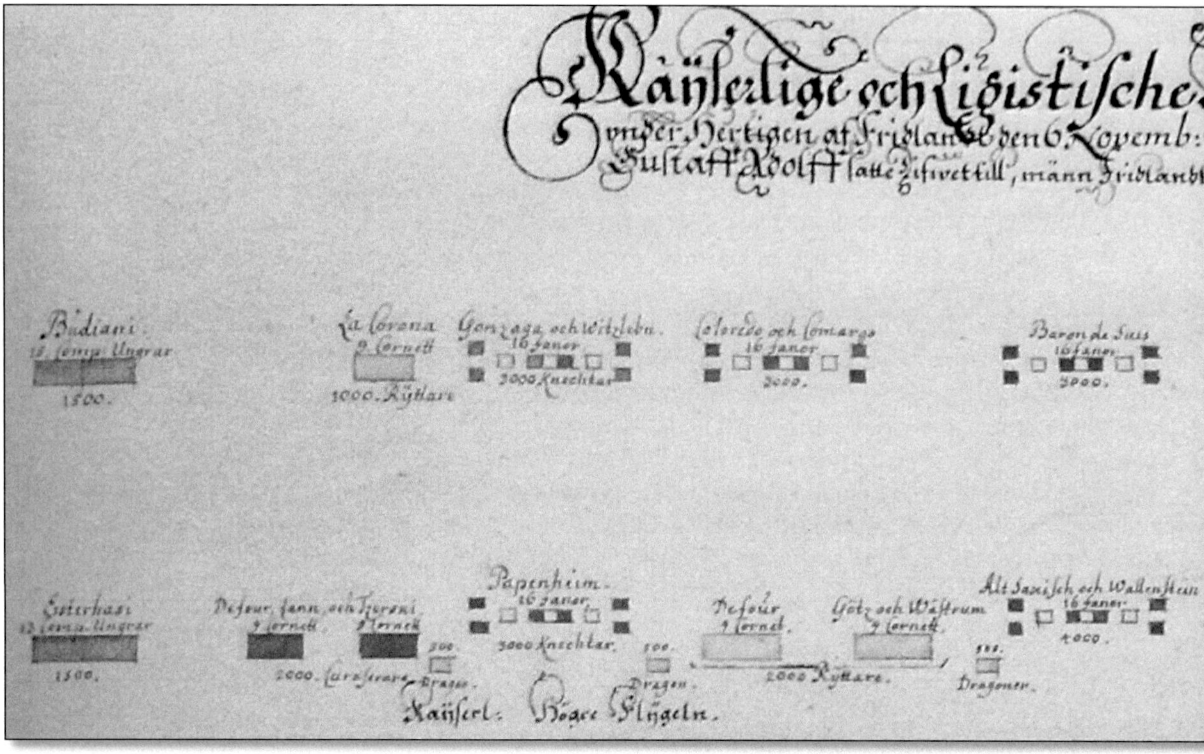

The Imperial army (above) and Swedish army (below) at Lützen. Erik Dahlbergh, *Ordres de Bataille 1600–1679*. (Krigsarkivet)

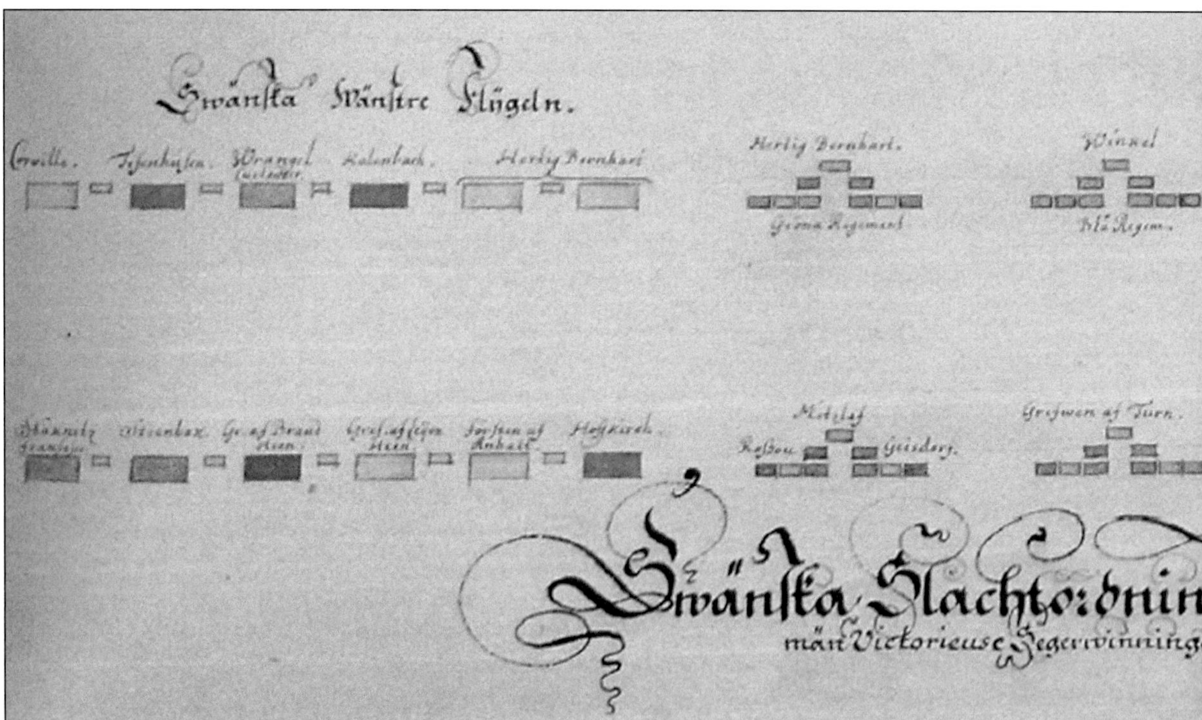

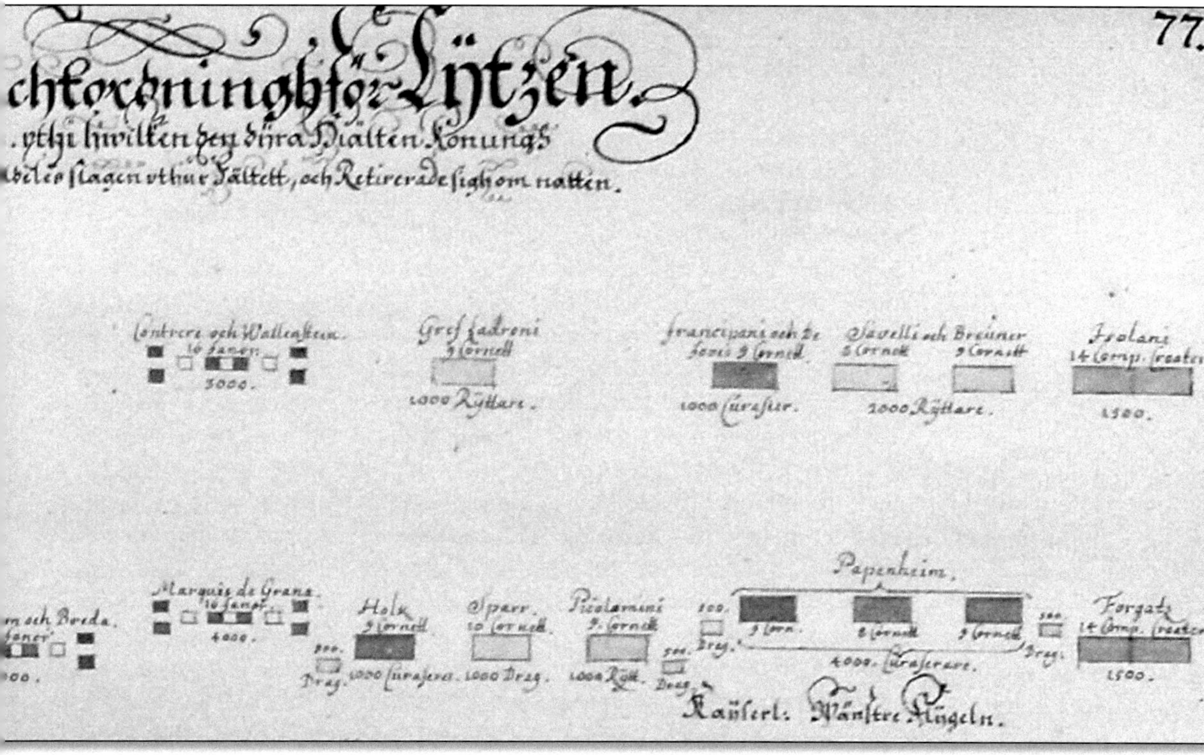
77.
Contrere och Wallenstein.
16 fanor.
3000.
1000 Ryttare.
1000 Curasier.
2000 Ryttare.
1500.
Marquis de Grana
4000.
Holk
Sparr
Picolomini
Papenheim.
4000 Curaserare.
Forgatz
1500.
1000 Curaserer.
1000 Drag.
Drag.
Kayserl: Wänstre Flygeln.

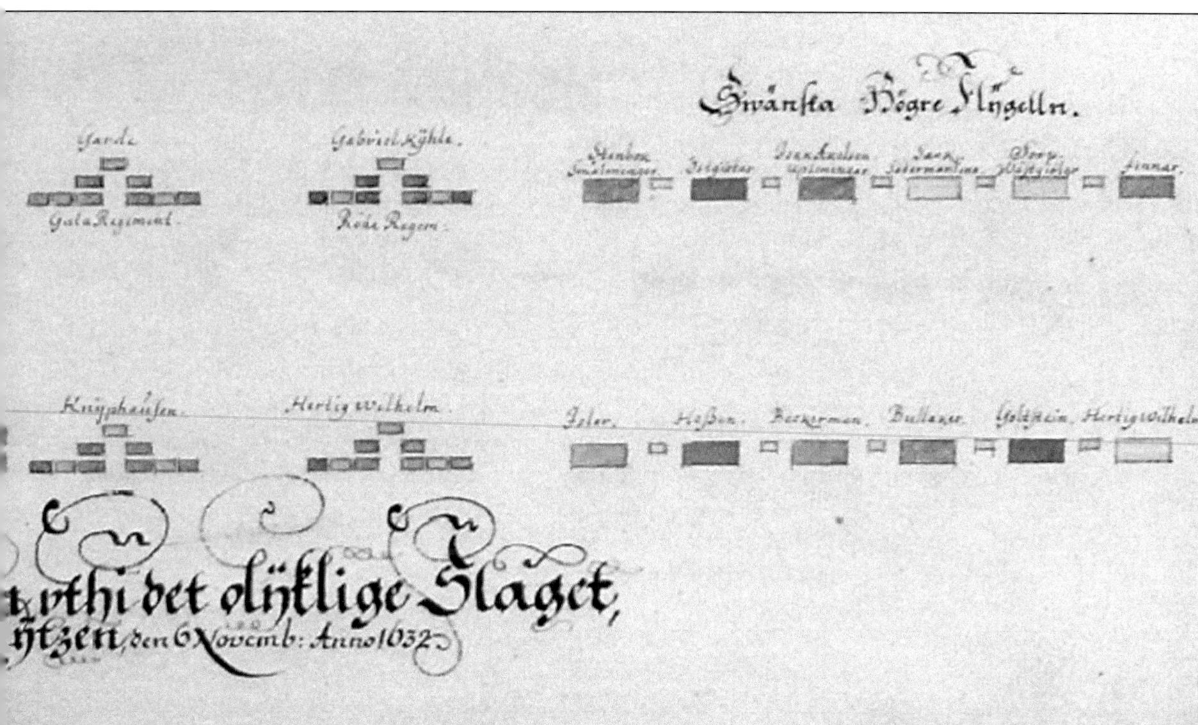
Swänska Högre Flygeln.
Garde
Gula Regiment.
Gabriel Kyhle.
Röde Regem.
Finnar.
Knyphausen.
Hertig Wilhelm.
Hessen.
vthi det olyklige Slaget,
Lützen, den 6 Novemb: Anno 1632

two eyewitnesses, reported incorrectly that Pappenheim arrived with all his cavalry regiments before the battle started.

Some units that probably were at Lützen are not mentioned in the Trauttmansdorff list. It lists only one Croat[12] unit, that of Isolani, but the Croats are mentioned on the Weissenfels battle plan, not by the name of their regiment but simply as 'Croats'.[13] Since Wallenstein had the Croat Regiment of Beygott in his corps at Lützen and Isolani was General of all Croats it is very likely that 'Isolani' in the Trauttmansdorff list means any number of Croat regiments including his own. There was at least one Croat regiment on the rImperial wing. Fleetwood mentioned a fierce combat between Stalhandske's 500 Finns and the Croats on the Imperial left wing at the beginning of the battle, which would not have been worth mentioning, if it were only one Croat regiment.[14] It is therefore likely, that Wallenstein had more than two Croat regiments, possibly in addition to Isolani and Beygott, he had the Regiments of Corpes[15] and Révay that are listed in Brzezinski's order of battle.[16] A company of Reinach's Regiment of Pappenheim's brigade was in garrison at Weissenfels and reached Lützen, closely pursued by the Swedish army.[17] The Harquebusier Regiment Leutersheim is mentioned in the Trauttmansdorff list and on Wallenstein's dispersal plan, but not on the Weissenfels battle plan. On 12 November it may have been on patrol, or in a nearby garrison, but it arrived in time for the fighting at Lützen on 16 November.

In theory, most Imperial regiments consisted of 10 companies as the Imperial Army Lists suggest, but those lists are not entirely reliable. Many companies were detached from their regiments, and furthermore, the strength of companies varied considerably so the number of companies in a regiment does not reveal much about a regiment's overall strength. The only reliable source mentioning the total number of companies at Lützen is Holk's letter to Christian IV, and he stated that there were 36 cavalry companies on each Imperial wing, a figure that is very close to Brzezinski's calculations.[18]

Excursus: Wallenstein's Musketeer Reserve

One of the few uncertainties in Holk's account is his statement, 'och sidst stode udcommenderet 5 Fahner à 500 Mand til foedz'[19] about the Imperial

12 Irregular light cavalry recruited in Hungary.

13 Holl, 'Wallensteins angebliche Skizze', p.64a, Fig. 3.

14 Fleetwood, Letter, p.7, André Schürger, 'Die ersten Minuten der Schlacht von Lützen (16.11.1632): Isolanis Kroaten und Stalhandskes finnische Reiter aus archäologischer Sicht', in M. Reichel, I. Schubert (eds), *Leben und Sterben auf dem Schlachtfeld von Lützen* (Lützen/Göteborg, 2011), pp.103–120.

15 Mentioned by Holk's payment list (Hallwich, *Briefe und Akten*, vol. 3, pp.577–578).

16 Brzezinski, *Lützen*, p.25.

17 Brzezinski, *Lützen*, p.25.

18 Wittrock, 'Fyra relationer', p.308. Brzezinski, *Lützen*, p.25 assumes 37 companies on the left and 36 on the right wing. All other calculations, such as those of Generalstaben, *Sveriges Krig*, pp.413–414 (29 and 50 companies) and Guthrie, *Battles of the Thirty Years' War*, p.223 (38 and 41 companies), are highly inaccurate.

19 'And last stood a detachment of five colours of 500 men on foot each.'

reserve.[20] Holk himself admitted that he would have liked to deploy 1,000 musketeers in the town of Lützen and the wood to his left if he had had them. Given this circumstance, it seems very unlikely that he held 2,500 musketeers in reserve. The term 'Fahner' means infantry colour, in the context of a unit it usually means a company. The theoretical full strength of an Imperial company was 343 men; the actual field strength was much less. In Gallas' force on 7 November 1632, each company had an average strength of 68 men.[21] It is therefore much more likely that Holk meant 'five companies with a total of 500 men', something confirmed by Diodati, who stated that the infantry reserve consisted of one squadron, which together with the 7,000 men in seven brigades and 700 detached musketeers, yields a total of 8,200 infantrymen.[22]

Troop Strength

There are three accounts by Imperial eyewitnesses giving the Imperial army's strength. Both Diodati[23] and Münchhausen[24] give a total number of 12,000 men, 6,000 infantry and 6,000 cavalry, while Holk states the infantry was 8,200 strong. Holk's statement seems reliable, because his number would give each of the 10 Imperial infantry regiments a strength of approximately 820 men. This can be compared to the average strength of 725 men in Gallas' seven Imperial regiments on 7 November 1632, which appears a more reasonable field strength.[25] The total army strength of 12,000 in Diodati's and Münchhausen's accounts seems too low. However, it is unlikely Diodati would

---

20 Wittrock, 'Fyra relationer', p.308.

21 Hallwich, *Briefe und Akten*, vol. 3, p.448. Number of companies according to Toegel, 'Der Schwedische Krieg', pp.397–399. Note, average troop strengths give only a clue to the strength of other units and they are in no way a guide to calculating the actual field strength of an entire army, because they can vary so considerably. See also below.

22 Fiedler, 'Diodatis Bericht', p.561. See also Seidler, *Untersuchungen*, p.125, ref. 79 and 82, Brzezinski, *Lützen*, p.39 and Sennewald, *Das kursächsische Heer*, p.169. According to Brzezinski, *Lützen*, p.25 there were 8,550 infantrymen, but he admitted that those numbers were highly speculative. Generalstaben, *Sveriges Krig*, p.413 and Guthrie, *Battles of the Thirty Years' War*, p.223 gave a number of 9,870, which is too high (see also Bo Eriksson, *Lützen 1632* (Stockholm: 2006), p.235, Göran Larsson and Nils Erik Villstrand and Lars Ericson Wolke, *Trettioariga kriget. Europa i brand 1618–1648* (Värnamo: 2006), p.128, Lars Ericson Wolke, 'Die Schlacht bei Lützen', in Mike Reichel, Inger Schuberth (eds), *Gustav Adolf. König von Schweden. Die Kraft der Erinnerung 1632–2007* (Dössel: Verlag Janos Stekovics, 2006), p.64.

23 Fiedler, 'Diodatis Bericht', p.562. There is no hint in Diodati's account that the Imperial army had 8,000 infantry and 4,000 cavalry, as Deuticke, *Lützen*, p.55 claimed.

24 Wittrock, 'Fyra relationer', p.304.

25 Letter from Gallas to Wallenstein (Hallwich, *Briefe und Akten*, vol. 3, p.448). The theoretical full strength of a regiment was 2,000, but this was only a commission, given by the Emperor or the Generalissimus to a colonel, allowing him to raise a regiment of 2,000 men (Wrede, *Geschichte der K. und K. Wehrmacht*, p.33). There was probably not a single regiment in the Imperial army that had this strength, but the historical sources do not give any valuable information. The actual full strength of a regiment was more likely nearer 1,500 and the actual field strength after a few months of campaigning would have been far less.

have substantially changed the army's strength in his report to the Emperor because some eyewitnesses of the battle would have noticed the change. He certainly rounded the numbers down slightly in order that Wallenstein's retreat from Lützen would look more acceptable. It is also possible that he did not include the Croats or the cavalry regiments that arrived on the battlefield at the last minute. We can thus assume a total strength of around 13,000–14,000, but certainly no more than 15,000.[26] That figure would have left Wallenstein with approximately 4,800–5,800 cavalry: 1,000 as a reserve in the centre and 1,900–2,400 on each wing.[27] Together with 150 musketeers, each wing would thus have had 2,050–2,550 men against approximately 2,400 Swedes of the first line, a reasonable figure that accounts for the eyewitness accounts that reported a long and fierce combat on both wings.

Artillery

The number of Imperial artillery pieces and their calibre is not entirely certain, as virtually no Imperial eyewitnesses mentioned any numbers of guns. The Swedes captured the entire Imperial artillery at Lützen, and according to Schwallenberg, nine 24-pounders and 12 other guns were taken, but it is uncertain whether or not these were all the guns or only the intact ones.[28] A document of 18 April 1633 states that when the captured Imperial artillery from Lützen arrived in Mecklenburg, it comprised of nine 24-pounders, two 16-pounders, two 14-pounders, four 12-pounders, one 10-pounder and six 7-pounders.[29] The nine

26 Most modern historians come to the conclusion that the Imperial army's strength was 16,000 or higher. Their arguments derive either from presuming that regiments fought at Lützen but which were actually somewhere else or in garrison (Generalstaben, *Sveriges Krig*, pp.413–414, Guthrie, *Battles of the Thirty Years' War*, p.223), or they calculate the Imperial army's strength at Lützen by estimating the average company strengths of the Imperial army (Seidler, *Untersuchungen*, p.42). As long as there is no reason to doubt the eyewitnesses Diodati (Fiedler, 'Diodatis Bericht', p.562) or Holk (Wittrock, 'Fyra relationer', p.308), the numbers they give must be considered seriously (See Wedgwood, *Der Dreissigjährige Krieg*, p.325, Sennewald, *Das kursächsische Heer*, p.168).

27 Brzezinski, *Lützen*, pp.25–26 gave a number of 5,350 cavalry, which fits within the limit of 14,000 men total. Also Marcus Junkelmann, *Gustav Adolf. Schwedens Aufstieg zur Grossmacht* (Regensburg: Pustet, 1993), p.453 calculated 6,000 cavalry, including Croats, and 8,000 to 9,000 infantry. Generalstaben, *Sveriges Krig*, p.414) gave a number of 6,700 cavalry; Guthrie, *Battles of the Thirty Years' War*, p.223 (followed by Larsson, Villstrand, Wolke, *Trettioariga kriget*, p.128, Wolke, 'Die Schlacht bei Lützen', p.64) claimed 6,900 and M. Pfaffenbichler, 'Waldstein als Kriegsunternehmer', in Fuciková, Eliška, Cepicka, Ladislav (eds), *Albrecht von Waldstein. Inter arma silent musae?* (Prague, Academia, 2007), p.269) 7,500; all three are too high.

28 Hallwich, *Briefe und Akten*, vol. 3, p.523. Watts, *Swedish Intelligencer*, vol. 3, p.152) gives almost the same number – nine 24-pounders and 11 or 12 field pieces. A total number of 21 guns is mentioned in the *Relation from 1633* (Droysen, 'Gedruckte Relationen', p.32) and Gottfried, *Inventarium Sueciae*, pp.25–26, copied by the anonymous *Glaubwürdiger Bericht*, Monro, *His Expedition*, part II, p.164, Abelinum, *Theatrum Europaeum*, p.750 and Chemnitz, *Geschichte*, p.464.

29 Landesamt für Kultur und Denkmalpflege Landeshauptarchiv Schwerin (LaKD), Feindliche Invasion, vol. XVI, 2.12–2/19 (unknown, 1633), Generalstaben, *Sveriges Krig*, p.414. The strange calibres are probably due to the use of different weight systems in the various countries. Specifications in the

24-pounders are consistent with Schwallenberg's and Knyphausen's statement; the latter also mentioned six 12-pounders and four 6-pounders.[30]

Only two Swedish eyewitnesses give specific numbers of Imperial guns at Lützen. The most reliable source is *Oberst* Dalbier, who probably commanded the small captured Imperial battery, which lost four 24-pounders and two 12-pounders. Again, it is not certain if this number is the total or only the small Imperial battery guns not destroyed.[31] This is confirmed by Silvio Piccolomini, who incorrectly says that the Imperial army lost six pieces, in reality this seems to have been the guns only of the small Imperial battery, near which he had fought.[32] The other 'Swedish' eyewitness, who gives a specific number of Imperial artillery, 21 in total, in common with most other sources, is Fleetwood.[33] He stated that the windmill battery had nine guns, and 12 guns were in two or three other batteries, a statement that contradicts almost all other sources. Fleetwood probably never went close to the front line and therefore could not see individual guns, which might explain the low total he gives for the windmill battery, although he could certainly see whole batteries firing. Since we know that the Imperial army had only two main batteries, the other one or two batteries mentioned by Fleetwood are possibly regimental guns. This suggestion is supported by a sketch in the Stockholm Krigsarkivet that shows a total of three batteries; the copperplate published in *The Swedish Intelligencer* shows two smaller batteries between the main batteries.[34] The painting by Snayer shows the Imperial artillery deployed in 10 batteries flanking each of the five infantry squadrons in the first line centre; two large batteries are on the flanks and eight small batteries, probably regimental guns, are posted between the infantry squadrons.[35]

No historical source makes an explicit mention of any Imperial regimental guns at Lützen, which does not mean that there were not any.[36] When Wallenstein was reinstated as Generalissimus in December 1631[37] and reassembled his army, he asked his colonels on 14 May 1632 if they had their regimental guns on hand or if they were obtainable.[38] Additional evidence might be the 1632 army lists numbers 14 and 15 that give two light pieces

Schwerin document are probably calculated according to the Swedish pound. A 14-pounder in Swedish pounds is a 12-pounder in Saxon pounds and a 7-pounder would be a 6-pounder.

30 Anonymous, *Studien*, p.50.

31 PRO: SP81/39: London: Dalbier, *Lutzen*, p.252.

32 Anonymous, *Archivio*, p.240.

33 Fleetwood, Letter, p.7.

34 Brzezinski, *Lützen*, pp.50 and 52.

35 Snayers, *Lützen*.

36 As Seidler, *Untersuchungen*, p.35 claimed. It is most unlikely that all regimental guns of Wallenstein's army were detached to Gallas' Corps, as Stadler suggested, *Pappenheim*, p.729.

37 The exact date is unknown, but possibly mid December (O. Kortus, 'Albrecht von Wallenstein zu der Zeit des sächsischen Feldzugs in Böhmen 1631/1632', in Jens E. Olesen (ed.), *Terra felix Mecklenburg – Wallenstein in Nordeuropa* (Greifswald: Druckhaus Panzig, 2010), pp.117–118).

38 Anonymous, 'Aus dem dreissigjährigen Kriege', Mittheilungen des k. k. Kriegs-Archivs 41 (Wien: 1882), p.346.

for every regiment, but this seems more likely a theoretical figure than the actual number.[39] Nevertheless, these documents suggest that Wallenstein had regimental guns at Lützen, although certainly not as many as were mentioned in the sources, and that there were two to eight batteries each with two or four guns, but probably adding up to not more than 16 in total.[40]

The Swedish Army at Lützen

Gustav II Adolph's tactical plan was to force parts of Wallenstein's dispersed army to engage on 15 November. Most of the Swedish baggage train was left with the garrison in Naumburg; this likely consisted of one brigade, probably that of Vitzthum. The main sources for the Swedish army at Lützen are Langmann's 14 November list of the army at Naumburg and the incomplete Swedish casualty list with the number of foot killed at Lützen.[41] There are secondary sources, most are based on the *Inventarium Sueciae* that lists Swedish cavalry regiments at Lützen and corresponds with Langmann's list, and these are accepted by modern historians. Gustav II Adolph's plan to launch a surprise attack suggests that he took all his regiments except the Naumburg garrison with him. However, it should be noted that there is no first-hand evidence for the Swedish cavalry at Lützen.[42]

The six infantry regiments in Naumburg on 14 November are missing from the casualty list. These six were Hard, Hastfer, Brandenstein, Erbach, Uslar and Vitzthum, but since the casualty list is incomplete, absence is not proof that these regiments did not fight at Lützen. When historical sources mention any Swedish infantry, they usually refer to brigades instead of regiments, so it is not entirely certain if a brigade had all of its component regiments present at Lützen. Nevertheless, it appears that the 10 brigades of Gustav II Adolph's main army in Saxony remained intact as brigades without single regiments being detached to different places. One missing regiment is mentioned by Johann Hallenus, who wrote that two officers were sent to him to provide information about the battle. One of these officers was Fändrik Ambrosius Jacobsson, an officer in Hastfer's Regiment.[43] Hard's Regiment was part of the Swedish Brigade and therefore very likely in Lützen, as was Brandenstein's Regiment, a part of the '9th Brigade'.[44] Erbach's and Uslar's

39 Toegel, 'Der Schwedische Krieg', pp.404 and 417.

40 Brzezinski, *Lützen*, p.25 suggests two regimental guns per front line battalion, or 10 in total.

41 Langman, 'Lützen', p.162, Mankell, *Arkiv* vol. III, pp.126–128.

42 Brzezinski, *Lützen*, p.50. Watts, *Swedish Intelligencer*, vol. 3, p.128 and Gottfried, *Inventarium Sueciae*, pp.27–28, copied by Anonymous, *Wahrhaftige Beschreibung*, Anonymous, *Glaubwürdiger Bericht*, Abelinum, *Theatrum Europaeum*, pp.751–752 and Chemnitz, *Geschichte*, pp.463–464. According to Khevenhiller, *Annales Ferdinandei*, p.189, the *Relation from 1633* (Droysen, 'Gedruckte Relationen', p.29) and the sketch in Stockholm Krigsarkivet (Brzezinski, *Lützen*, p.52) there were only four squadrons per line on each wing, which is incorrect.

43 Mankell, *Arkiv*, vol. II, p.661.

44 A '9th Brigade' is mentioned by Hülshorst (Wittrock, 'Fyra relationer', p.303).

Regiments were likely part of 'Vitzthum's Brigade' and therefore probably guarding the camp at Naumburg.[45] This 850 strong garrison had to protect the supply base and was a last defence if the Battle of Lützen ended in a defeat. A *djurskyttar* company of 48 mounted riflemen accompanied Gustav II Adolph to Germany in 1630 as part of his personal entourage.[46] Although this unit is not mentioned in any Swedish troop lists of the Battle of Lützen, it is likely that they participated as they were not customarily mentioned in muster rolls. In total the Swedish army at Lützen fielded about 19,272 men, 13,032 infantry and approximately 6,240 cavalry.

Artillery

There are no eyewitness accounts or documents giving a total number of Swedish artillery pieces. The eyewitness Vitzthum/Berlepsch was alone in stating that the battle was opened by three Swedish 24-pounders. Almost all research, contemporary and modern, is based on the *Inventarium Sueciae*, according to which the Swedes had 20 larger cannon and 40 regimental guns.[47] Although the numbers from the *Inventarium Sueciae* seem reasonable when compared to the 42 regimental guns the Swedish army had at Breitenfeld on 17 September 1631, doubts must remain until we have more reliable sources.[48] Gustav II Adolph experimented with 'leather guns' as regimental pieces during the Swedish–Polish War of 1621–1629, but they tended to explode if fired continuously in rapid succession.[49] In Germany the Swedish army usually used cast iron 3-pounder guns instead of leather guns,[50] but probably they had also some small-calibre German falconet pieces; although common in Germany, they are not usually mentioned in historical sources.[51]

45 According to Watts, *Swedish Intelligencer*, vol. 3, p.121, Oberst Damian Vitzthum was left as commander of the garrison of Naumburg (Brzezinski, *Lützen*, p.22), but he remained unclear about the units under his command. However, Swedish infantry was usually grouped into brigades and it is therefore likely that the Regiments Vitzthum, Uslar and Erbach formed a brigade.

46 Richard Brzezinski, Richard Hook, *Die Armee Gustav Adolfs. Infanterie und Kavallerie* (Königswinter: Brandenburgisches Verlagshaus 2006), pp.67–68.

47 Gottfried, *Inventarium Sueciae*, p.27, copied by Anonymous, *Wahrhaftige Beschreibung*, Anonymous, *Glaubwürdiger Bericht*, Abelinum, *Theatrum Europaeum*, pp.751–752 and Chemnitz, *Geschichte*, p.464. Watts, *Swedish Intelligencer*, vol. 3, p.128, notes 24 larger cannons and 40 regimental guns.

48 Brzezinski, Hook, *Die Armee Gustav Adolfs*, p.70.

49 Brzezinski, Hook, *Die Armee Gustav Adolfs*, p.70.

50 Brzezinski, Hook, *Die Armee Gustav Adolfs*, p.70. Nevertheless, leather guns were still used by the Scottish army at Newburn in 1640 (Peter Edwards, 'Arming and Equipping the Covenanting Armies, 1638–1652', Steve Murdoch, Andrew Mackillop (eds), *Fighting for Identity. Scottish Military Experience c. 1550–1900* (Leiden, Boston, Cologne: Brill, 2002), p.243).

51 Engerisser, *Von Kronach nach Nördlingen*, p.580. The German falconet-type artillery pieces have a slightly smaller calibre of 3.8 cm to 5.5 cm than the English falconet's 7 cm. Pappenheim was reported to have been shot by a 'Falkonett', but the reliability of this statement is not entirely certain.

Tables

Table 8: The Imperial army at Lützen according to the Trauttmansdorff list

Cuirassiers	Commander	Coy	Str.	Year	Destination
Desfours (b, c, f)	*Oberst* Nicolas Desfours	6	300	1628	Chemnitz
Götz (c, d, f)	*Oberstleutnant* Moritz von Falkenberg	9	400	1626	Zwickau
Holk (b, e, f, j)	*Oberstleutnant* Frantz von Uhlefeld	8	250	1630	Leipzig
Lohe (a, b, c, e)	*Oberst* von der Lohe	5	150	1632	Leipzig
Trcka (b, c, f, g)	*Oberst* Adam Erdmann *Graf* von Trcka	4	250	1629	Altenburg
Bredau (a, f) *	*Oberst* Hans Rudolf von Bredau	6	300	1631	Aschersleben
Harquebusiers					
Drost (e)	*Oberst* Wilhelm von Westfalen, Landdrost und Dringenberg	5	250	1632	Leipzig
Goschütz (f, g)	*Oberst* Benedikt Goschütz	5	250	1632	Merseburg
Hagen (e, g)	*Oberst* Johann Nicolaus Hagen von Sauwenbein	13	800	1631	Leipzig
Leutersheim	*Oberst* Johann *Freiherr* von Leutersheim	6	200	1632	Eilenburg
Loyers (f)	*Oberst* Gottfried *Freiherr* von Loyers	5	200	1632	Merseburg
Piccolomini (b, c, d, j)	*Oberst* Ottavio Piccolomini di Aragona	12	500	1629	Altenburg
Tontinelli ‡*	*Oberstleutnant* Anton Tontinelli	6	250	1619	Merseburg
Westfalen (e)	*Oberst* Heinrich Leo von Westfalen	3	150	1632	Leipzig
Westrumb (a)	*Oberst* Johann von Westrumb	3	100	1632	
Dragoons					
Trcka		5	100	1632	Merseburg
Croats					
Isolani (j)	*General* Ludwig Johann Hector *Graf* von Isolani	5	250	1625	Merseburg
Beygott (e)	*Oberst* Daniel Beygott	5	100	1632	Leipzig
Corpes (j)	*Oberst* Marcus Corpes	10	300	1631	Eileburg
Révay	*Oberst* Paul *Freiherr* von Révay	5	250	1632	
Infantry					
Baden (a, e, j)	*Oberstleutnant* Stopler	6	**	1630	Leipzig
Friedrich Breuner (h, j)	*Oberst* Philipp Friedrich von Breuner	10	**	1632	Zwickau
GFZM Breuner (b, c, h, j)	*Generalfeldzeugmeister* Hans Philipp von Breuner	13	**	1618	Chemnitz

Jung-Breuner (c, j)	*Oberst* Hans Gottfried von Breuner	5	**	1630	Zwickau
Colloredo (c, h)	*Generalwachtmeister* Rudolf von Colloredo	7	**	1625	Zwickau
Comargo ‡ (b, h, j)	*Oberst* Theodor Comargo	10	**	1619	Altenburg
Grana (c, h)	*Oberst* Francesco Grana, Marchese di Caretto	8	**	1627	Altenburg
Chiesa[52] (e, j)	*Oberstleutnant* Matias Lasky or *Oberst* Andreas Matthias Kehraus	12	**	1618	Leipzig
Reinach (detachment) ‡		1	**	1620	Weissenfels
Alt-Sachsen (c, e)	*Oberstleutnant* Bernhard Hämmerle	8	**	1618	Leipzig
Waldstein (b, c, e)	*Oberst* Berthold von Waldstein	11	**	1628	Leipzig

italic: Units not mentioned in the Trauttmansdorff list, but probably at Lützen.
* Regiments of Pappenheim's brigade arriving before battle
** A total of 8,200 infantry
‡ League regiment
Coy: Number of Companies
Year: Year of Raising
Str.: Strength according to Brzezinski, *Lützen*, pp.25–26 (highly speculative)
Destination: Destination of units according to Wallenstein's dispersal plan
(a, b ...): see below

Regiments at Lützen mentioned by eyewitnesses (a-d) or documents (e-j):
a: Münchhausen (Wittrock, 'Fyra relationer', p.305)
b: Holk (Wittrock, 'Fyra relationer', p.309)
c: Diodati (Fiedler, 'Diodatis Bericht', pp.563–567)
d: Piccolomini (Argang, 'Piccolominis bref', p.88)
e: Wallenstein's Corps according to the disposition of 14 November 1632 (Hallwich, *Briefe und Akten*, vol. 3, pp.482–483)
f: Verzeichnis der Beschädigten (Hallwich, *Briefe und Akten*, vol. 3, pp.596–598)
g: Protocols of the court-martial at Prague (Seidler, *Untersuchungen*, pp.141–148)
h: Wallenstein's letter to Falchetti, 22 November 1632, Chemnitz (Hallwich, *Briefe und Akten*, vol. 3, pp.538–539)
j: Holk's payment list, 6 December 1632 (Hallwich, *Briefe und Akten*, vol. 3, pp.577–578)

52 Chiesa himself was in Frauenstein on 16 November (Hallwich, *Briefe und Akten*, vol. 3, p.505). *Oberstleutnant* Kehraus commanded the Regiment Dohna in 1632 (Toegel, 'Der Schwedische Krieg', pp.397 and 409), but was promoted to *Oberst* and put in charge of Chiesa's Regiment in late 1632. However, it is uncertain whether before or after the battle (See also Brzezinski, *Lützen*, pp.25 and 48).

Table 9. Imperial artillery at Lützen according to the Schwerin 1633 document (Generalstaben, *Sveriges Krig*, p.414)

Artillery
Nine 24-pounders, two 16-pounders, six 12-pounders, one 10-pounder, six 6-pounders

Table 10. Pappenheim's cavalry that arrived midday at Lützen

Cuirassiers	Commander	Coy	Str.	Year	Destination
Sparr (g)	*Oberstleutnant* Albrecht von Hofkirchen	10	300	1629	Halle
Harquebusiers					
Bönninghausen (g)	*Oberst* Lothar von Bönninghausen	11	500	1630	Aschersleben
Lamboy (c, j)	*Oberst* Wilhelm von Lamboy	6	250	1632	Halle
Dragoons/Guard					
Merode's 'Obwacht' Lifeguard		1	40		Halle
Pappenheim's 'Rennfahne'[53] Lifeguard ‡		1	40		Halle
Merode (j)	*Oberstleutnant* Robert Borneval d'Arlin	5	160	1625	Halle
Pappenheim (j) ‡		4	140	1632	Halle
Croats					
Batthyanyi	*Oberst* Franz *Graf* Batthyanyi	9	200	1632	Halle
Forgacs (c)	*Oberst* Nicolas Forgacs de Gymes	2	100	1630	
Orossy	*Oberst* Paulus Orossy	9	450	1631	Halle
Cossacks					
Poles (j)		3	250	1631	Querfurt

53 'Rennfahne' was the general term for a sixteenth century elite cavalry advance guard (Fronsperger, *Fünff Bücher*, p, 84, Schwendi, *Kriegs Discurs*, p.72).

Table 11. Pappenheim's infantry that arrived in the evening at Lützen

Infantry	Commander	Coy	Str.	Year	Destination
Gil de Haes	*Oberst* Gil de Haes	6	500	1632	Halle
Goltz	*Oberst* Martin Maximilian *Freiherr* von der Goltz	10	700	1626	Halle
Moriamez-Pallant	*Oberst* Karl Dietrich Pallant, Baron de Moriamez	8	500	1632	Aschersleben
Pallant	*Oberst* Rudolf *Freiherr* von Pallant	10	500	1632	Halle
Reinach ‡	*Oberstleutnant* Gabriel *Freiherr* Comargo	9	650	1620	Halle
Würzburg ‡	*Hauptmann* Willich		75	1631	Halle

Table 12. Regiments on Weissenfels' battle plan and Wallenstein's dispersal plan that were not at Lützen

Infantry	Commander	Coy	Str.	Year	Destination
Mannsfeld	*Oberstleutnant* Niderum	10		1625	Eilenburg
Suys	*OberstFreiherr* Ernest Rolland von Suys	10		1631	Zwickau

Table 13. Regiments on Wallenstein's dispersal plan that were probably already in winter quarters on 14 November

Infantry	Commander	Coy	Str.	YoR	Garrison
Trcka Foot	*Oberstleutnant* Adrian Enckhevoert	7		1631	Eilenburg
Thun	*OberstGraf* Rudolf Thun	7		1631	Eilenburg
Contreras	*Oberst* Andreas von Contreras	5		1628	Altenburg
Mohr vorm Wald	*Oberst* Franz Wilhelm Mohr vorm Wald	10		1628	Freiberg
Scharffenberg	*Oberst* Gotthard von Scharffenberg	10		1630	Freiberg
Cuirassiers					
Hatzfeld	*Oberst* Mechior von Hatzfeld	6		1625	Eilenburg
Harquebusiers					
Czernin	*OberstGraf* Czernin	10		1632	Freiberg

Table 14. Swedish cavalry at Lützen according to Langmann's list and Swedish casualty list

Regiment	Commander	Coy	Str	Year
Smaland ‡	*Överste* Fredrik Stenbock	8	400	1627
Östgöta ‡	*Överstelöjtnant* Lennart Nilsson Baat	4	100	1627
Uppland ‡	*Överstelöjtnant* Isaak Axelsson	4	250	1627
Södermanland ‡	*Överste* Otto Sack	4	200	1627
Västgöta ‡	*Överste* Knut Soop	8	400	1627

Finland ‡	*Överste* Torsten Stalhandske	8	500	1627
Georg von Uslar †	*Oberst* Georg von Uslar	8	160	1630
Hessian squadron §				
Rostein §	*Oberst* Friedrich Rostein	5	180	
Kurt von Dalwigk §	*Oberstleutnant* Kurt von Dalwigk		100	
Franz von Dalwigk §	*Oberst* Franz von Dalwigk		50	
Thilo Albrecht von Uslar §	*Rittmeister* Birckenfeld		50	
Beckermann †	*Oberst* Eberhard Beckermann	4	150	
Bulach †	*Oberst* Klaus Konrad Zorn von Bulach	8	120	1631
Goldstein †	*Oberstleutnant* Marx Conrad von Rehlinger	8	150	1632
Duke Wilhelm †	*OberstHerzog* Wilhelm von Sachsen-Weimar	12	120	1631
Bernhard's Life Regiment †	*Oberstleutnant* Bouillon	12	500	1631
Carberg †	*Oberst* Carl Joachim Carberg	8	220	1630
Kurland †	*Oberst* Hans Wrangel	4	230	1630
Livland †	*Oberstleutnant* Karl von Tiesenhausen	8	300	1630
Courville †	*Oberst* Nicholas de Courville	5	300	1628
Hofkirchen ¶	*Oberstleutnant* Henning von Geisto	12	350	
Ernst von Anhalt ¶	*Oberst* Ernst von Anhalt-Bernburg	8	300	
Löwenstein†	*Oberst* Georg Ludwig *Graf* von Löwenstein	6	200	
Brandenstein†	*Oberst* Brandenstein	4	300	
Steinbach†	*Oberst* Jaroslav Wolf von Steinbach	4	200	
Stechnitz†	*Oberstleutnant* Georg Matthias von Stechnitz	4	80	
Öhm†	*Oberst* Johann Bernhard von Öhm	8	300	1626
Krak's *Djurskyttar* (b)‡	*Kapten* Nils Krak	1	30	1611

a: Infantry regiments not listed in the Swedish casualty list.
b: Not listed in any source, but probably took part in the battle as part of Gustavus Adolphus' entourage.
c: Regimental commander *Oberst* Caspar *Graf* von Eberstein commanded the right wing musketeer detachment.
d: Regimental commander *Oberst* Hans Abraham *Graf* von Gersdorf commanded the left wing musketeer detachment.

m: musketeers
p: pikemen
offs: officers

Key to Tables 14, 15, 16:
‡ Swedish army, national Swedish regiments
† Swedish army, foreign regiments
§ Hessian allies
¶ Saxon allies

Table 15: Swedish infantry at Lützen according to Langman's list and Swedish casualty list

Regiment	Commander	Coy	Str	Year
Swedish or New Blue Brigade: ‡	*Överstelöjtnant* Gabriel Kyle		1,575	
Eric Hand's New Blue Regiment ‡	*Överstelöjtnant* Gabriel Kyle	8	465m, 267p, 96offs	1628
Karl Hard (a) ‡		8	447m, 96offs	
Klas Hastfer (a) ‡		4	156m, 48offs	
Yellow Brigade: †	*Generalmajor* Nils Brahe, *Greve* till Visingborg		1,221	
Royal Lifeguard †	*Kaptenlöjtnant* Erik Stenbock	1	45m, 38p, 12offs	
Yellow Guard Regiment †	*Generalmajor* Nils Brahe, *Greve* till Visingborg	16	610m, 324p, 192offs	1624
Old Blue Brigade: †	*Oberst* Hans Georg aus dem Winckel		1,110	
Winckel's Old Blue Regiment †	*Oberst* Hans Georg aus dem Winckel	16	486m, 432p, 192offs	1624
Green Brigade: †	*Oberst* Georg Wulf von Wildenstein		2,036	
Bernhard's Green Life Regiment†	*Oberstleutnant* Johann Winckler	12	396m, 210p, 142offs	1627
Wildenstein's Black Regiment	*Oberst* Georg Wulf von Wildenstein	12	468m, 102p, 142offs	1629
Leslie's Scotts †	*Oberstleutnant* Ludovick Leslie	16	360m, 24p, 192offs	
Duke Wilhelm's Brigade: ¶	*Oberst* Carl Bose		1,726	
Duke Wilhelm's Life Regiment †	*Oberstleutnant* Georg Philip von Zehm	12	276m, 78p, 142offs	
Carl Bose ¶	*Oberst* Carl Bose	8	540m, 156p, 96offs	
Pforte ¶	*Oberst* Hans von der Pforte	4	306m, 84p, 48offs	
White Brigade: †	*Generalmajor* Dodo von Innhausen und zu Knyphausen		1,120	
Knyphausen's White Regiment †	*Generalmajor* Dodo von Innhausen und zu Knyphausen	12	708m, 270p, 142offs	1630
Thurn's Brigade: †	*Oberst* Hans Jacob *Graf* vonThurn		1,252	
Thurn's Black Regiment †	*Oberst* Hans Jacob *Graf* von Thurn	8	240m, 144p, 96offs	1629
Isenburg †	*Oberst* Wolfgang Heinrich *Graf* von Isenburg-Büdingen	8	120m, 54p, 96offs	
Hessen-Kassel's Green Life Regiment §	*Oberstleutnant* Hans Heinrich von Güntherode (c)	12	216m, 144p, 142offs	
Mitzlaff's Brigade: †	*Oberst* Joachim Mitzlaff		1,834	
Gersdorf †	*Oberstleutnant* (d)	8	330m, 96p, 96offs	
Mitzlaff †	*Oberst* Joachim Mitzlaff	12	342m, 198p, 142offs	
Rossow †	*Oberst* Friedrich von Rossow	8	366m, 168p, 96offs	

'9th Brigade': †			1,158	
Brandenstein (a) †	*Oberst* Brandenstein	4	198m, 48offs	
Löwenstein †	*Oberst* Georg Ludwig *Graf* von Löwenstein	7	600m, 84offs	
Henderson †	*Oberst* John Henderson	4	180m, 48offs	

Table 16. Probable Naumburg garrison regiments

Regiment	Commander	Coy	Str	Year
'Vitzthum's Brigade': †	*Oberst* Damien Vitzthum von Eckstädt		*850*	
Dam Vitzthum (a) ¶	*Oberst* Damien Vitzthum von Eckstädt	8	150m, 24p, 96offs	
Erbach (a) †	*Oberst* Georg Friedrich *Graf* von Erbach	8	144m, 18p, 96offs	
Thilo Albrecht von Uslar Guard (a) §	*Oberstleutnant* Alexander von Östringer	12	144m, 36p, 142offs	

5

The Battlefield

Geography: Reconstruction of the Historical Battlefield

In 1632 Lützen, located between Weissenfels, 13 km south-west, and Leipzig, 19 km north-east, belonged to the Electorate of Saxony. The town itself was unimportant but it was sited on the Via Regia, one of Germany's most important medieval/early modern roads, running from Paris through Mainz, Erfurt, Leipzig, Görlitz, and on to Kiev. This road saw the movement of millions of soldiers and eight major battles were fought near it in the region of Leipzig alone: Auerstädt (1806), Rossbach (1756), Grossgörschen (1813), Lützen (1632), Leipzig (1813), Breitenfeld (1631 and 1642) and Torgau (1760).

The Landscape in General

The battlefield is located on a flat plain, 115.1 metres to 126.3 metres above sea level, with a maximum gradient below 1 percent and almost no visible heights. Holk mentioned that Gustav II Adolph had the advantage of a wood and small hill on his right wing, one 'musket shot from the battaglia.'[1] There is only one barely visible elevation, Hill 126; this is 1,200 metres south of the Imperial first line. As no Swedish eyewitness mentioned any hill, we can assume that Hill 126 played no major role in the battle, however, it does block the line of sight from the Imperial battle line to the Flossgraben. This obstruction might have had an impact on early Imperial artillery fire against the deploying Swedish army. It is not entirely certain, which 'wood' Holk meant in his account.

The main source for understanding the battlefield landscape is a 1710 field boundary map.[2] Although this map was drawn almost 80 years after the battle, the landscape did not generally change very much during this period and it very likely shows the battlefield as it was during the battle. There are no hills or woods on the map, but a few green areas, that are not farmland, are present.[†]

† See PDF download, Plates 16 and 17: Approximate military situation 15 November 1632; the battlefield according to a 1710 field boundary map

1 Wittrock, 'Fyra relationer', p.308.

2 Museum in the Castle of Lützen.

The Canals: Mühlgraben, Flossgraben and their bridges

The Flossgraben ('Floss' = raft, 'Graben' = ditch) is an artificial canal dug in 1578 for transporting wood to the Saxony salt mines.[3] Although very narrow, it has a steep embankment, making it a serious obstacle to movement and, considering the fact that the water was cold in November, it would have been difficult to cross, except on the few bridges.[4] The Flossgraben has not often been recognised as an obstacle by historians,[5] probably because the water level has dropped because of extensive brown coal mining operations in recent decades.[6] The canal, however, presented a serious obstacle in the 1813 Napoleonic Battle of Grossgörschen, 2 km south of Lützen.[7]

The bridges and fords are best known from an 1809 map.[8] It is assumed that the road system has not changed substantially since 1632 and most 1809 crossings probably existed during the 1632 battle. Since the bridges were only three metres wide, units were forced to break formation before crossing with time then lost in reforming on the other side. The major problem for Gustav II Adolph caused by the Flossgraben and its narrow bridges was how to cross it with his heavy artillery pieces, in particular his 24-pounders weighing approximately 3.5 tons that needed 20 to 25 horses to pull them.[9] As Gustav II Adolph had only two bridges available for his army to cross the Flossgraben, the Meuchen and Sckölpitz, he put effort into building additional makeshift bridges from float-wood, as the sketch from Stockholm suggests.[10]

A more serious obstacle was the Mühlgraben, an artificial canal or millrace, for the water mills in Lützen. It had the same steep embankments as the Flossgraben, but no bridges crossed it outside of the town. In addition, to the west of Lützen the Mühlgraben's banks were marshland and thus impossible for cavalry or artillery to cross. Gustav II Adolph had little choice but to move south of Lützen and cross the Flossgraben twice.

The Woods: Grossgöttern Orchard and Skölzig Wood

Trees did not play a role as obstacles in the Battle of Lützen as there were very few. Nevertheless, there is a misunderstanding among historians regarding a small wood called 'Skölziger Holz' located 300 metres east of the

---

3 Svetoslav Andronov, *Der Elsterflossgraben. Geschichte und Gestalt eines technischen Denkmals* (Leipzig: Verlag Pro Leipzig, 2006), p.22.

4 Brzezinski, *Lützen*, p.43, Sennewald, *Das kursächsische Heer*, p.168. See also Richelieu, *Mémoires*, p.258.

5 Guthrie, *Battles of the Thirty Years' War*, p.202. Mortimer, *Wallenstein*, p.173.

6 Andronov, *Der Elsterflossgraben*, p.94.

7 Hartmut Bücker and Dieter Härtig, *Das Gefecht bei Rippach am 1. Mai 1813, Die Schlacht bei Grossgörschen am 2. Mai 1813 und der Überfall auf das Lützow'sche Freikorps bei Kitzen am 17. Juni 1813* (Vellberg: 2004), pp.35–40.

8 Andronov, *Der Elsterflossgraben*, p.29.

9 Engerisser, *Von Kronach nach Nördlingen*, p.579.

10 Float-wood was stored along the entire length of the Flossgraben to ensure a constant supply for the salt production in Halle (Andronov, *Der Elsterflossgraben*, pp.28–29, Brzezinski, *Lützen*, pp.47 and 52, Sennewald, *Das kursächsische Heer*, p.168).

Flossgraben.[11] This wood has often been misidentified as the wood on the far left Imperial wing, where Holk wanted to deploy the 1,000 musketeers, if he had had a sufficient numbers.[12] Although Holk did not name this wood, it has been suggested that he meant the Skölziger Holz,[13] which is mentioned three times, in the *Relation from 1633*, *Theatrum Europaeum* and Khevenhiller, as an emplacement for the Swedish artillery.[14]

This wood was located 1,200 metres south-east of the Imperial battle line on the east side of the Flossgraben. It was, therefore, some distance from the battlefield, which makes the wood neither an ideal position for Swedish artillery[15] nor for Imperial musketeers, as the distance would have left them cut off from their own lines and with no targets to fire at. However, Holk mentioned another wood on the Swedish right wing 'one musket shot from the battaglia'.[16] This wooded area could have been the 'Skölziger Holz'.

William Watts wrote that:

> the King advanced, till he came with the end of the Right wing, within Musket shot of a little wood: having all the way a full view of the Imperiall army.[17]

This suggested a wheeling manoeuvre by the Swedish right wing towards its left. This left wheel is confirmed by Vitzthum/Berlepsch.[18] From the little wood Gustav II Adolph would have had a full view of Wallenstein's army's left wing. Although Watts was not an eyewitness, this is the only source mentioning a wooded location. If Watts is credible, then this 'little wood' could only have been Grossgöttern, a village abandoned in the fifteenth century. The village pond still exists and the deserted village is marked on the 1710 field boundary map as a small green area, which at the time, meant any vegetation other than farmland. It is possible that the site of the village was a small wood or an orchard in 1632. This location would have been an ideal location for Holk's musketeers, positioned on his left wing's extremity where they could give flanking fire from a covered position as the right wing musketeers did from the gardens of Lützen.

---

11 The 'Skölziger Holz' has completely gone today and is localised according to a map of 1:25,000 map from 1903.

12 Wittrock, 'Fyra relationer', p.308.

13 Guthrie, *Battles of the Thirty Years' War*, p.202. Seidler, *Untersuchungen*, p.34. Deuticke, *Lützen*, p.66. Generalstaben, *Sveriges Krig*, p.419. Golo Mann, *Wallenstein* (Frankfurt am Main: Fischer, 1971), p.849.

14 Abelinum, *Theatrum Europaeum*, p.745 and Khevenhiller, *Annales Ferdinandei*, p.190 copied this part from the *Relation from 1633* (Droysen, 'Gedruckte Relationen', p.30).

15 Incorrectly suggested by Mann, *Wallenstein*, p.851.

16 Wittrock, 'Fyra relationer', p.308.

17 Watts, *Swedish Intelligencer*, vol. 3, p.132.

18 Glafey, *De Gladio*, p.13.

The Structures: City walls, enclosures, windmills and miller's house

When the Swedish army approached Lützen, they were fired on from the city walls and the castle of Lützen.[19] According to Holk the Imperial army had placed 400 detached musketeers in Lützen, but he estimated that 1,000 would have been needed to defend the town.[20] To prevent the Swedish army from using the town, the musketeers set it alight and necessarily abandoned it.[21] The only source mentioning what happened to the musketeers after firing the town is William Watts:

> Between the Mills and the towne, were there divers gardens with mudd-walls round about them…[22] and … he [Bernhard von Weimar] must with the end of his wing, even touch (as it were) the very walls with Muskettiers; they must needs have so sorely galled his Horsemen, that there had beene no coming neere: nor could horse and Pistols, have done any service against walls and Muskettiers.[23]

The 1710 field boundary map does not show any walls around the gardens, but since it does not show the city walls, it is possible, that there was an enclosure defended by musketeers as Watts claimed.

Wallenstein's key defensive point was the fortified large battery on the windmill hills.[24]

Today there are no hills left; the last picture of the windmills made in the early twentieth century show the hills were slight inclines of a metre or less. Even if slightly higher in 1632, they would not have been much of a rise. There was possibly enough space to give three guns a slightly better field of fire. Although Fleetwood and Watts claimed the hills were an advantage for the Imperial army, Holk does not mention them[25] and they were certainly not a decisive factor in the battle. There was also a miller's house near the mills, which is mentioned by *Inventarium Sueciae*.[26] The van Hulsen and Merian copperplates (see previous two pages) show it south or on [*sic*] the Via Regia, while the more reliable 1710 field boundary map (left) shows it north of the Via Regia.

---

19 Vitzthum/Berlepsch (Glafey, *De Gladio*, p.13). The castle is one of the two still-existing seventeenth-century structures.

20 Wittrock, 'Fyra relationer', p.308.

21 Fleetwood, Letter, p.7.

22 Watts, *Swedish Intelligencer*, vol. 3, p.131.

23 Watts, *Swedish Intelligencer*, vol. 3, p.147.

24 Vitzthum/Berlepsch (Glafey, *De Gladio*, p.13).

25 Fleetwood, Letter, p.6. Watts, *Swedish Intelligencer*, vol. 3, p.131. See also Declaration from 1633 (Droysen, 'Gedruckte Relationen', p.39) and Poyntz, *The Relation*, p.72.

26 Gottfried, *Inventarium Sueciae*, p.25, copied by Anonymous, *Wahrhaftige Beschreibung*. Anonymous, *Glaubwürdiger Bericht*. Monro, *His Expedition*, part II, p.164. Abelinum, *Theatrum Europaeum*, p.750 and Chemnitz, *Geschichte*, p.465.

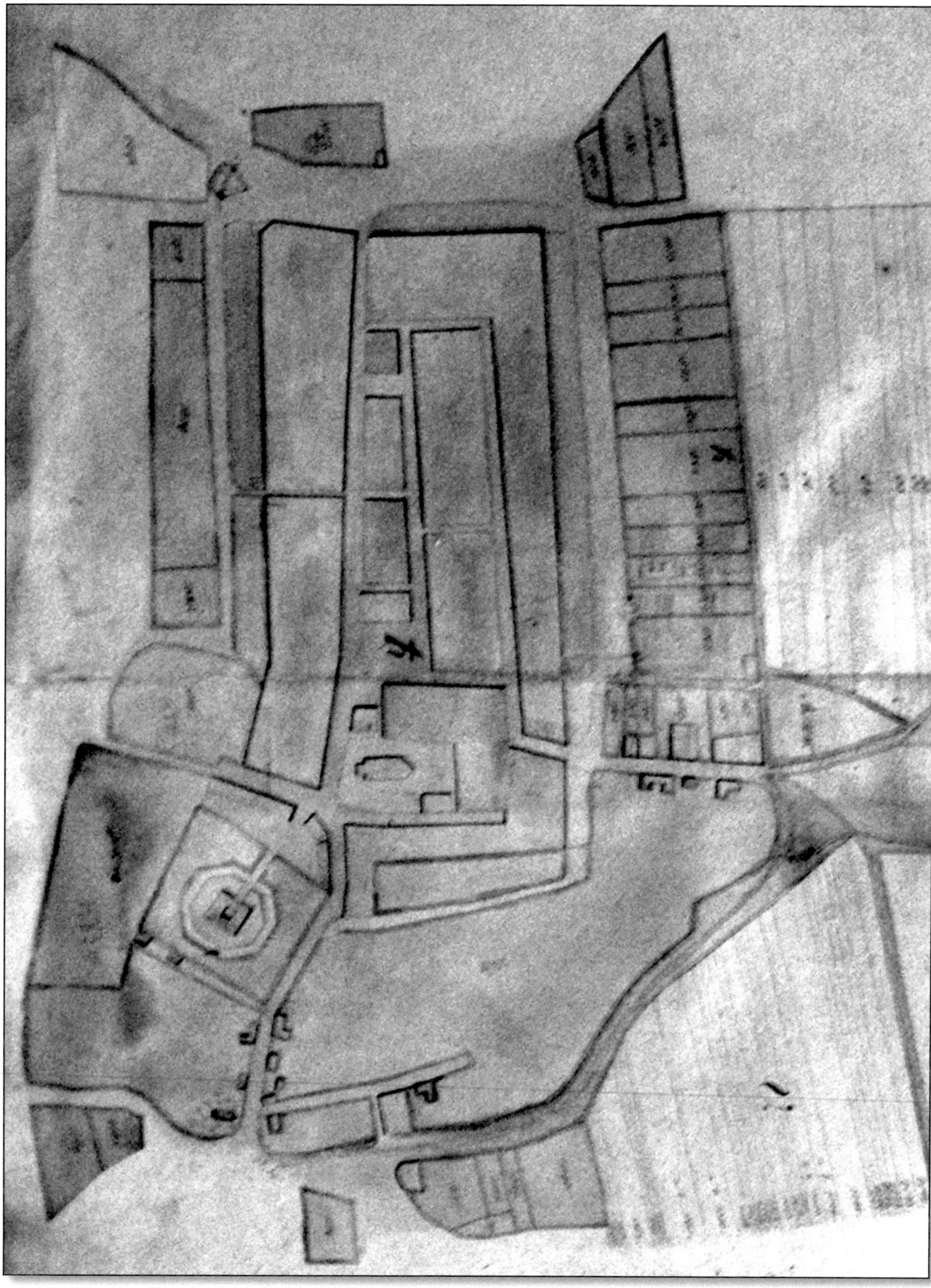

Lützen on 1710 field boundary map.

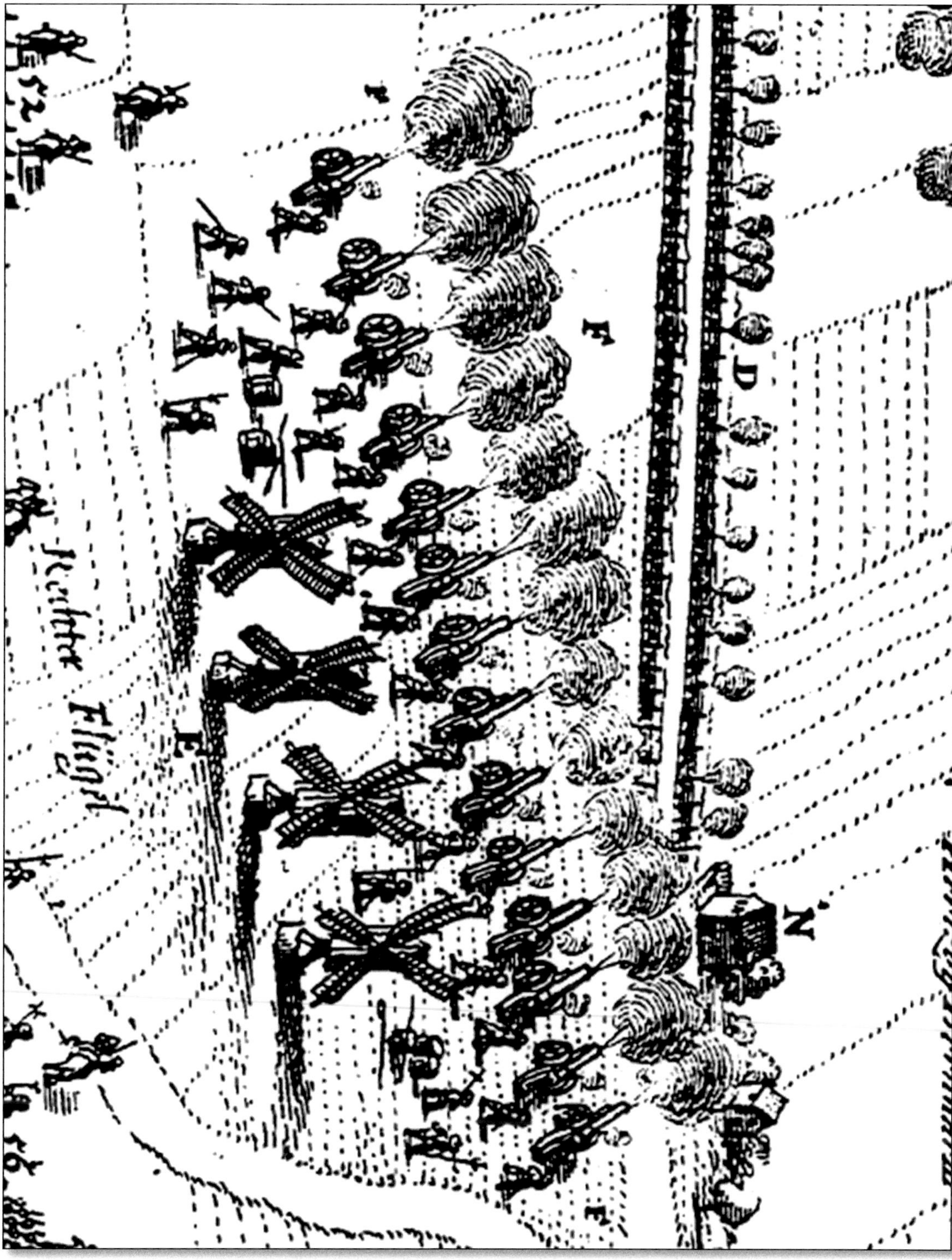

Above: Miller's house (N) on van Hulsen's copperplate.
Below: Miller's house (N, top-centre) on Merian's copperplate

Windmills and miller's house on 1710 field boundary map.

The Via Regia and Wallenstein's Trenches

According to the 1710 field boundary map, the Via Regia extended north-east a distance of 1,350 m in a straight line from Lützen. It was not curved, as Deuticke believed, and this was demonstrated by trial trench 4 (see below).[27] Only after 1,350 metres did it turn, first east, and then north, where it crossed the Flossgraben, as shown by trial trenches 1–3 (see below). The road had drainage ditches on either side of which Wallenstein took advantage. He deployed his infantry centre and artillery behind those ditches. If there is one thing most historians[28] agree on, it is Wallenstein's fortification, a 2.5 km long double trench system covering the whole Imperial battle line, dug into the road ditches of the Via Regia during the night of 15/16 November. It is believed that this position served detached musketeers as a first defensive line and caused a fierce engagement, while the trench posed a severe obstacle hindering Swedish troop movements.[29] Over the last 150 years this double trench system has not been questioned by historians, although its construction meant digging 5 km of trench in one night, which, although it seems possible, would have exhausted the Imperial army before an important battle. As such a fortification would have had a major impact on the course of the battle, it is important to discuss it in detail.

Historical Sources

In the historical sources there seems little doubt about the existence of an Imperial trench system. Most contemporary non-eyewitness accounts agree that there was such a fortification and all copperplates show some kind of artificial trenches (see below). This picture changes if we look to the eyewitness accounts however.

Swedish-German Eyewitnesses

Vitzthum/Berlepsch and Fabricius did not mention any trenches or musketeers at the road.[30] Vitzthum/Berlepsch described Gustav II Adolph's manoeuvre before the battle as wheeling around with his right wing against the refused Imperial left wing and having no difficulty in getting over the

27 Deuticke, *Lützen*, p.58.

28 Droysen, 'Lützen', p.102 and Wedgwood, *Der Dreissigjährige Krieg*, p.326 are exceptions. However, the latter is still suggesting heavy combat at the ditches of the Via Regia.

29 Deuticke, *Lützen*, p.65, Generalstaben, *Sveriges Krig*, pp.420 and 431, Seidler, *Untersuchungen*, pp.32, 45 and 47, Mann, *Wallenstein*, p.850, Brzezinski, *Lützen*, pp.39 and 54, Guthrie, *Battles of the Thirty Years' War*, p.203, Eriksson, *Lützen*, p.255, Mortimer, *Wallenstein*, p.171 and Sennewald, *Das kursächsische Heer*, p.169 are only a few out of a long list assuming trenches in Lützen.

30 Glafey, *De Gladio*, pp.12–14. Wittrock, 'Fyra relationer', pp.305–307.

Via Regia.[31] The only fortification Vitzthum/Berlepsch mentioned is an entrenchment of the Imperial right battery at the windmills.[32] Similar to Vitzthum/Berlepsch, Fabricius wrote that 'Gustav II Adolph advanced over a ditch and attacked the enemy' without suggesting any delay or combat at the Via Regia.[33]

Dalbier stated that the enemy waited for the Swedes in a fortified and advantageous position behind a great ditch where they had placed their guns.[34] This great ditch could be one of the road ditches or even the Via Regia itself, which was a sunken road (see below), but Dalbier described neither trenches nor any other problems the Swedish army had in passing the Via Regia, so the fortified position is very likely the Imperial batteries.

Fleetwood's comment on Imperial fortifications is difficult to understand. When he described the Imperial deployment, he wrote, 'the enimie had the advantage of Lypsicke highwaye, on either side of which a grafte.'[35] And in discussing a skirmish just before the battle, 'upon which the enimies they retyred again behinde the dike, where they had cast upp a kind of a brestworke.'[36]

The 'grafts' are very likely simple road ditches[37] and have nothing to do with the 'breastwork'. At least Gustav II Adolph did not seem to have any difficulty when 'he leaped over the graft and charged the enimie.'[38] The 'brestworke' was probably the fortified artillery position, as Vitzthum/Berlepsch and Dalbier described it.

The key to understanding the nature of the Imperial fortifications is the letter from Swedish Headquarters, which states, '... they [the Imperial army] moved on a hill, with three windmills on top, digging a trench and a redoubt ...'[39] It seems obvious that this describes the fortified artillery position at the windmills. Although it should be noted that this eyewitness was with the Swedish baggage train and had probably not seen the fortification himself, at least not from a close distance.

Imperial Eyewitnesses

The Imperial eyewitnesses Münchhausen and Diodati did not mention any trenches or road ditches nor any musketeers on the Via Regia, important evidence given the particular details in Diodati's substantial account.[40] Ottavio

31 Glafey, *De Gladio*, p.13.

32 Glafey, *De Gladio*, p.13.

33 Wittrock, 'Fyra relationer', p.306.

34 The National Archives, London: SP81/39. Dalbier, *Lutzen*, p.251.

35 Fleetwood, Letter, p.6.

36 Fleetwood, Letter, p.7.

37 According to Christian Kay and Jane Roberts and Michael Samuel and Irené Wotherspoon (eds), *Historical Thesaurus of the Oxford English Dictionary* (Oxford: University Press, 2009), p.382, 'graft' is known to have been used from 1644 to 1737 as a term for 'field drain ditch.'

38 Fleetwood, Letter, p.7.

39 Söltl, *Religionskriege*, p.346.

40 Wittrock, 'Fyra relationer', pp.304–305. Fiedler, 'Diodatis Bericht', pp.557–568.

Piccolomini reported the Swedes crossed a ditch and road and closed on them, without having any difficulties. Later he charged the Swedes to a ditch and road, but he could not pursue them because of the 'bad condition of the road'.[41] Cavalry could not charge across the road because it was a hollow with road ditches, but it was not impossible to cross. Silvio Piccolomini, who served in his uncle's regiment, described an entirely different event when he wrote, 'we advanced to a small ditch and there we waited,' by which he meant the whole army before the battle and not his regiment alone.[42] It is important that neither Piccolomini mentioned any trenches nor any fighting at the Via Regia.

Sydenham Poyntz wrote, 'In the front of his [Wallenstein's] Camp lay a long dry ditche which hee filled full of Musketiers.'[43] Poyntz is the only eyewitness, who mentioned Imperial musketeers in ditches, but he does not mention an entrenchment. His meaning by 'in front of his camp' is uncertain, although it seems possible that he meant the Imperial centre.

Holk, who was responsible for deploying the Imperial army, and therefore must have known the battlefield best, wrote that the Imperial army had a hollow road to their front, which served neither side as advantage once they stood together with the enemy at push of pike.[44] At this point Holk should have mentioned trenches if there were any. Even more important is that he listed the detached musketeers deployed in the town of Lützen and in front of the wings, but did not mention any on the road and it is highly unlikely that he forgot them. In this circumstance, a reasonable explanation could be that Holk noted only independent units, while the musketeers in the road ditches were not an independent unit. The men in the ditches were likely detached musketeers from the front line infantry sent forward as skirmishers, but who otherwise fought as part of their squadron.

Secondary Sources

It is certainly not coincidental that no eyewitness to the Battle of Lützen mentioned artificial trenches made by the Imperial army,[45] nor did the early non-eyewitness accounts. Neither a short account from 19 November[46] nor *Relation I from Grimma* of 23 November[47] mention ditches or trenches; the 24 November *Extrakt Schreiben aus Berlin* stated, 'the enemy had the advantage of the pass and several ditches, which were occupied by musketeers.'[48]

41 Argang, 'Piccolominis bref', p.89.

42 Anonymous, *Archivio*, p.240.

43 Poyntz, *The Relation*, p.72.

44 Wittrock, 'Fyra relationer', p.308.

45 With the exception of Leubelfing's account (Murr, *Beyträge*, p.122), which proves again that this account did not derive from an eyewitness and is almost certainly a forgery.

46 Droysen, 'Gedruckte Relationen', p.14.

47 Anonymous, *Studien*, pp.50–52.

48 Mankell, *Arkiv*, vol. II, p.658.

Plate A

Imperial Cuirassier

(Illustration by Sergey Shamenkov © Helion & Company 2023)

See Colour Plate Commentaries for further information

Plate B

Imperial Croat

(Illustration by Sergey Shamenkov © Helion & Company 2023)

See Colour Plate Commentaries for further information

Plate C

Imperial Dragoon

(Illustration by Sergey Shamenkov © Helion & Company 2023)

See Colour Plate Commentaries for further information

Plate D

Imperial Harquebusier

(Illustration by Sergey Shamenkov © Helion & Company 2023)

See Colour Plate Commentaries for further information

Plate E

Imperial Pikeman

(Illustration by Sergey Shamenkov © Helion & Company 2023)

See Colour Plate Commentaries for further information

Plate F

Imperial Musketeer

(Illustration by Sergey Shamenkov © Helion & Company 2023)

See Colour Plate Commentaries for further information

Plate G

Finnish Cavalry Trooper

(Illustration by Sergey Shamenkov © Helion & Company 2023)

See Colour Plate Commentaries for further information

Plate H

Swedish Yellow Brigade Pikeman

(Illustration by Sergey Shamenkov © Helion & Company 2023)

See Colour Plate Commentaries for further information

Plate I

Swedish Blue Brigade Musketeer

(Illustration by Sergey Shamenkov © Helion & Company 2023)

See Colour Plate Commentaries for further information

Scottish Pikeman

(Illustration by Sergey Shamenkov © Helion & Company 2023)

See Colour Plate Commentaries for further information

Plate K

Swedish Cavalry Trooper

(Illustration by Sergey Shamenkov © Helion & Company 2023)

See Colour Plate Commentaries for further information

Plate L

Saxon Musketeer

(Illustration by Sergey Shamenkov © Helion & Company 2023)

See Colour Plate Commentaries for further information

Plate M

Gustav II Adolph

(Illustration by Sergey Shamenkov © Helion & Company 2023)

See Colour Plate Commentaries for further information

Plate N

1

2

Imperial Cavalry Cornets

1. **Cornet of a cuirassier regiment**

2. **Guidon of a dragoon regiment**

3. **Cavalry cornet**

(Illustrations by Sergey Shamenkov © Helion & Company 2023)

See Colour Plate Commentaries for further information

3

Plate O

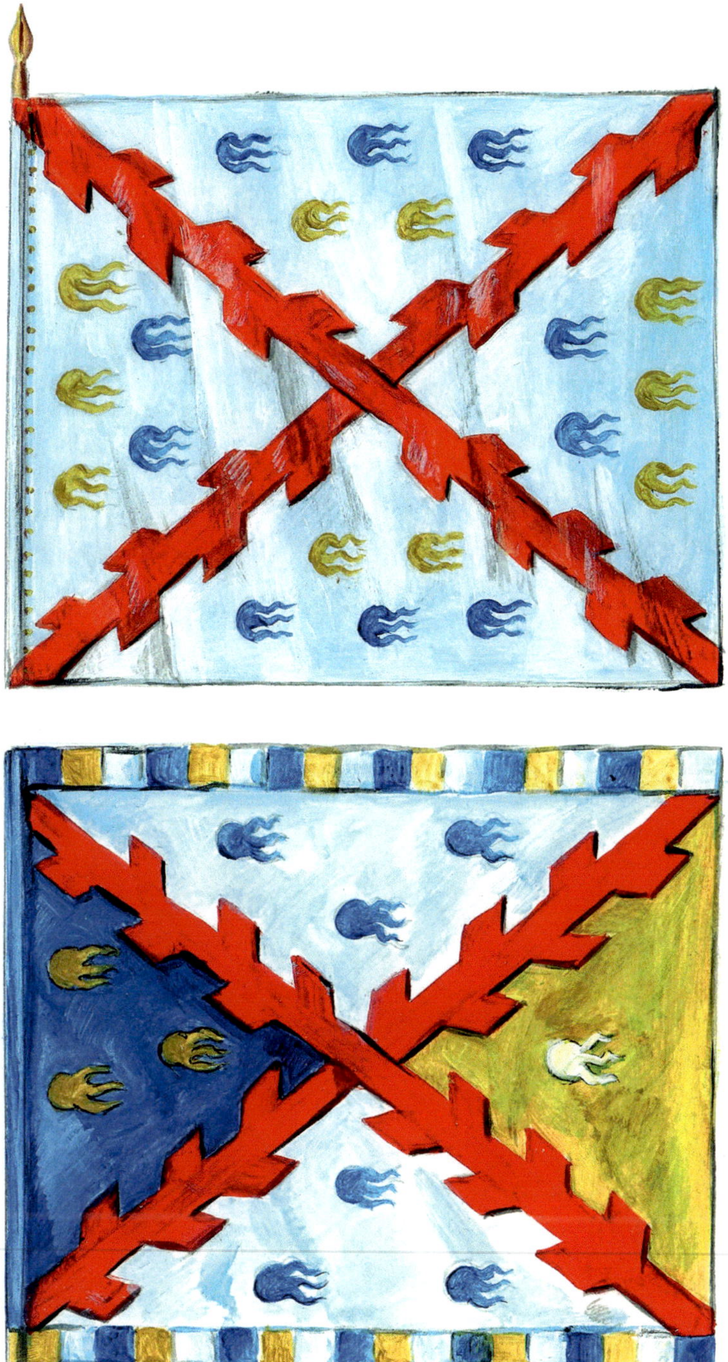

Imperial Infantry Colours

(Illustrations by Sergey Shamenkov © Helion & Company 2023)

See Colour Plate Commentaries for further information

1

3

2

4

Swedish/Saxon Cavalry Cornets

1. Cornet of Prince Ernst of Anhalt's Regiment (Saxon)
2. Uppland Cavalry Regiment, troop cornet
3. Lorenz von Hofkirchen's Regiment (Saxon) troop cornet
4. Finnish cavalry company, troop cornet

(Illustrations by Sergey Shamenkov © Helion & Company 2023)

See Colour Plate Commentaries for further information

Swedish/Saxon Infantry Colours

1–3, Duke Wilhelm's Brigade, Regiment Pfordte, company colours; 4. Company colour of the Swedish 'Blue' Infantry Regiment, Blue Brigade; 5. Company colour of the Swedish 'Green' Infantry Regiment, Duke Bernhard's (Green) Brigade; 6. Company colour of the Swedish 'Yellow' Infantry Regiment, Yellow Brigade

(Illustration by Sergey Shamenkov © Helion & Company 2023)

See Colour Plate Commentaries for further information

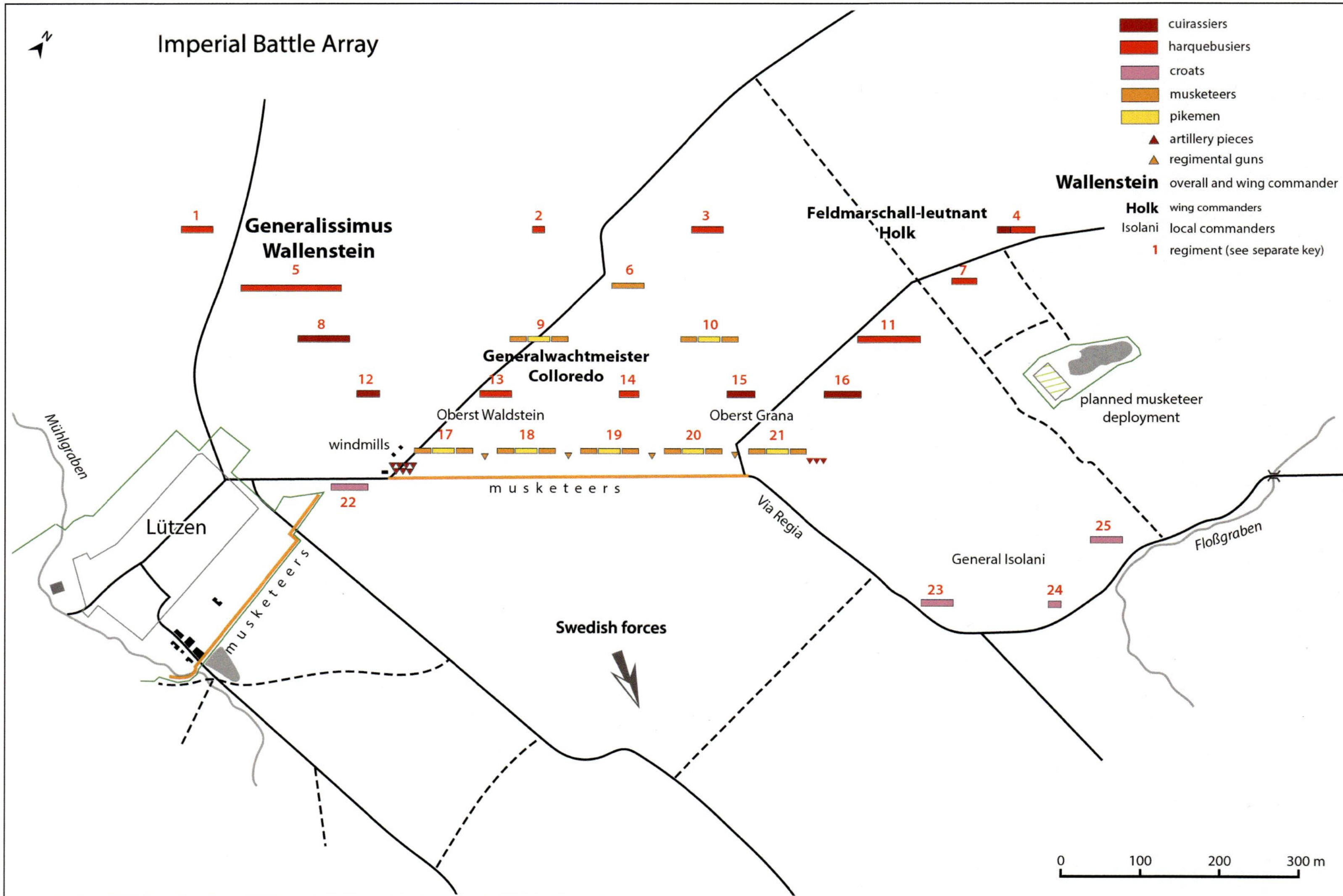

Imperial battle array (see Chapter 6)

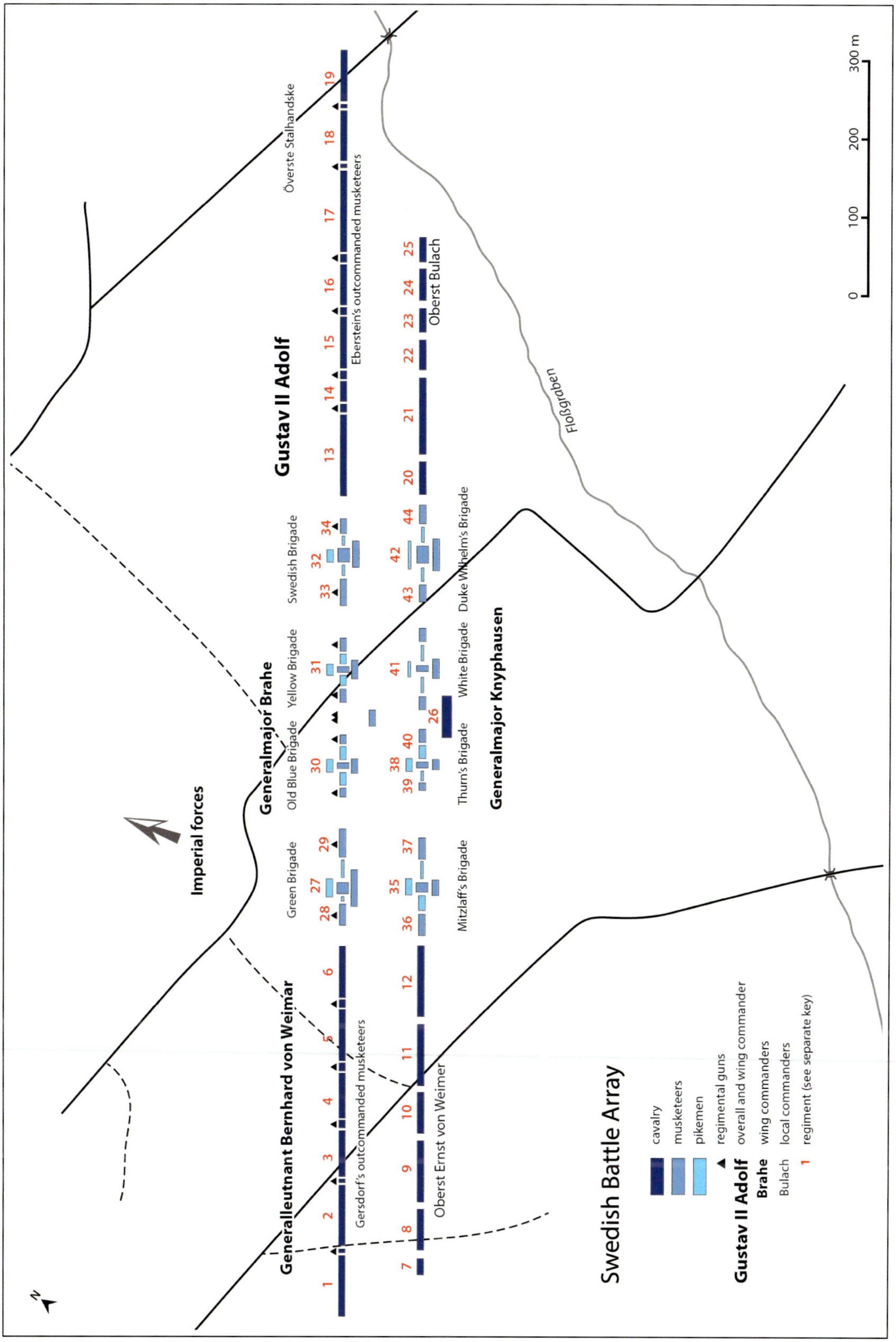

Swedish battle array (see Chapter 6)

Map Keys

Swedish Regiments

1. Courville
2. Livland
3. Kurland
4. Carberg
5. Bernhard's Leibregiment
6. Bernhard's Leibregiment

7. Stochnitz
8. Steinbach
9. Brandstein
10. Löwenstein
11. Ernst von Anhalt
12. Hofkirchen

13. Smaland
14. Östgöta
15. Uppland
16. Södermanland
17. Västgöta
18. Finland
19. Finland

20. Uslar
21. Hessian
22. Bockermann
23. Bulach
24. Goldstein
25. Duke Wilhelm

26. Öhm

27. Green Regiment
28. Leslie's Scots
29. Black Regiment

30. Old Blue Regiment

31. Yellow Regiment

32. Östergötland
33. Västergötland
34. Finland

35. Mitzlaff
36. Rossow
37. Gersdorf

38. Thurn
39. Isenburg
40. Hessen Kassel

41. White Regiment

42. Bose
43. Wilhelm von Weimar
44. Pforte

Imperial Regiments

1. Drost
2. Westrumb
3. Goschütz
4. Lohe & Loyers

5. Hagen
6. Musketeer reserve
7. Leutersheim

8. Trcka & Desfour
9. Jung-Breuner
10. Baden
11. Piccolomini

12. Holk
13. Tontinelli
14. Westfalen
15. Bredau
16. Götz

17. Waldstein & Alt-Sachsen
18. Colloredo & Chiesa
19. F. Breuner & Grana
20. GFZM Breuner
21. Comargo

22. Corpes

23. Révay
24. Beygott
25. Isolani

Hallenus' 30 November account is one of the earliest mentioning some kind of artificial trenches (löpgrafvar) occupied by Imperial soldiers in context with the small Imperial battery, but was otherwise not specific about them, nor did he suggest that they were tactically important.[49] It is possible that his eyewitnesses actually reported trenches to him, but they had seen them in front of the small Imperial battery very close to their unit.

The turning point in the historic narrative concerning the road ditches was the 22 November *Relation II from Erfurt*, 'the enemy had built a breastwork at the Flossgraben during the night and occupied it to his advantage.'[50]

Shortly after, Adam Heinrich Pentz wrote a letter to Gustav Horn, describing two long ditches that were impassable for cavalry except on a narrow 'grass trail', where Gustav II Adolph could cross with his right wing only in road march formation. Pentz suggested that the Swedes had to go from a line of battle to a column, get over the ditches, then reform line of battle line once they had crossed, which it took some time to do,[51] an incident repeated by Watts.[52] For the first time, the impassability of two ditches and a fortification at a ditch is emphasised. The key to understanding what had changed and was falsified, is found in the *Declaration from 1633*, which stated, 'Gustavus Adolphus reached the Flossgraben occupied by Imperial musketeers, forced them out and used it to harass Wallenstein's troops with his own musketeers.'[53]

The Flossgraben was certainly not occupied by Imperial musketeers, because it was filled with water and at a distance of 1.4 km to 1.8 km was too distant from the main Imperial line of battle line for a skirmish line and thus was certainly not fortified. These non-eyewitness accounts simply confused the Flossgraben, which was indeed an obstacle, with the road ditches, which were held by the musketeers; in German both are called *Graben*.

The Swedish army had to cross the Flossgraben twice. Gustav II Adolph and the advance guard crossed on a narrow bridge to reach the battlefield and it seems likely that Pentz misunderstood an eyewitness, believing that this event was at the beginning of the battle and that Gustav II Adolph had to get over an near-impassable ditch on a narrow 'grass trail'. If the road ditches were truly impassable, they would contradict Fleetwood's eyewitness statement that Gustav II Adolph 'leaped over the graft'.

Unfortunately, almost all later accounts[54] follow this newly created, erroneous historic narrative that gave a false impression of Wallenstein's

49 Mankell, *Arkiv*, vol. II, p.662.

50 Droysen, 'Gedruckte Relationen', p.18.

51 Fiedler, 'Diodatis Bericht', p.570.

52 Watts, *Swedish Intelligencer*, vol. 3, pp.131 and 134.

53 Droysen, 'Gedruckte Relationen', pp.39–40.

54 Except for the Spanish Relation from 16 February 1633 (Watts, *Swedish Intelligencer*, vol. 3, p.160).

fortifications. Khevenhiller,[55] Chemnitz[56] and *Inventarium Sueciae*[57] were very specific about artificial trenches made by the Imperial army. Watts, in particular, mentioned them:

> All night and next morning, his Dragooners and Pioners, wrought with their Spades about the High-way; and to make the Ditches, or Draine by it, serve them for a Breast-worke, to lodge their Muskettiers in.[58]

According to Watts, the trenches were man high and the Swedes had considerable problems getting over them.[59] Watts also described a trench erected around the artillery batteries.[60] This second trench, at the windmills, is probably what Watts' eyewitnesses saw, and was possibly one source for introducing the misunderstanding that there was some sort of entrenchment along the Imperial army's front.

Although Priorato and Richelieu did not mention any artificial trenches, their accounts suggest there was some obstacle, describing either the difficulty of the Swedish army getting over the ditches[61] or heavy fighting at the ditches.[62] Of the non-eyewitness accounts only Burgus more specifically describes the fortification as one trench, and only in front of the infantry centre and not on the cavalry wings.[63]

Pictorial Representations: Copperplates and paintings

Most copperplates follow the most copied plan from Friedrich van Hulsen, continuing the later tradition of historic narrative by showing a double trench system running from Lützen across the whole battlefield in front of the Imperial army to the Flossgraben. Merian's copperplate combined the trenches with a fierce combat.

A slightly different trench system is illustrated by The *Swedish Intelligencer*. It shows a single trench in one road ditch on the Imperial battle line's eastern half and a double trench south of the Via Regia in the western half. This configuration is even more unlikely, because it would have meant digging a new double trench instead of modifying existing road ditches. There is no historical evidence supporting such a fortification.

The only pictorial representation illustrating a completely different situation is the painting by Snayers, showing no trenches and no musketeers on the Via

55 Khevenhiller, *Annales Ferdinandei*, p.188.

56 Chemnitz, *Geschichte*, p.464.

57 Gottfried, *Inventarium Sueciae*, p.25, copied by Anonymous, *Wahrhaftige Beschreibung*, Anonymous, *Glaubwürdiger Bericht*, Monro, *His Expedition*, part II, p.163 and Abelinum, *Theatrum Europaeum*, p.749.

58 Watts, *Swedish Intelligencer*, vol. 3, pp.125–126, 131.

59 Watts, *Swedish Intelligencer*, vol. 3, p.131.

60 Watts, *Swedish Intelligencer*, vol. 3, p.125.

61 Priorato, *Historia dell Guerra*, p.120.

62 Richelieu, *Mémoires*, pp.258–259.

63 Burgus, *Mars Sveco-Germanicus*, p.317.

Regia, which is shown as a hollow road. The painting shows the situation of the Imperial army more accurately than of the other copperplates or paintings.

Archaeological Sources: Excavations

Because the historical sources are not entirely conclusive, four trial trenches were excavated where the Via Regia was located according to the 1710 field boundary map. Trenches 1 to 3 were positioned on the Imperial left wing.[64] Only trench 1 covered the road entirely. Wheel tracks in two areas over a distance of 19.9 metres between the outer tracks at maximum depth of 1.02 metres from the topsoil's surface[65] confirmed that the Via Regia was a shallow hollow dirt road, as Holk and Ottavio Piccolomini described it, and a typical medieval/early modern major road in Germany.[66]

A modern drain destroyed all archaeological evidence on the southern side, where the old road ditch was expected. The northern road ditch was used until the mid twentieth century, the bottom of the old ditch was still intact. This indicates a total width of 24 metres from road ditch to modern drain. The northern ditch is 1.8 metres wide and has a depth of 0.32 metres below the old road (the Via Regia) and 0.99 metres below the current ground surface. In order to date the ditch, 10 metres of its filling was sieved, producing 67 pieces of monochrome lead-glazed pottery, dating to the sixteenth and seventeenth centuries. Since no more recent or older pottery was found, the bottom of the road ditch very likely represents the original seventeenth-century ditch. The northern road ditch showed no traces of any attempt to reshape it into a trench. The shape of the northern drain was confirmed in trenches 2 and 3, where it looked like the road ditch in trench 1.

In the Imperial centre, the Via Regia was built over by a modern road for most of its length and the southern road ditch was destroyed by a gas pipeline. Trial trench 4 revealed 15 metres of the northern road ditch and a very small part of the hollow roadway. It confirms that the Via Regia went in a straight line from Lützen to the Gustav II Adolph Memorial, where it made a turn to the south, as shown on the 1710 field boundary map. In trench 4, the road ditch is 1.6 metres wide and has a depth of 0.64 metres below the old road and 1.42 metres to the modern ground surface. It is therefore 0.43 metres deeper than in trench 1, but it still did not show any sign of entrenchment. No battle-related artefact was found anywhere in the road ditch.

64 André Schürger, 'Die Schlacht von Lützen 1632: Archäologische Untersuchungen auf dem linken kaiserlichen Flügel', in Harald Meller (ed.), *Schlachtfeldarchäologie* (Battlefield Archaeology). *1. Mitteldeutscher Archäologentag vom 09. bis 11. Oktober 2008 in Halle* (Saale) (Halle Saale: 2009), pp.138–141.

65 Depths from the topsoil's surface means from the modern and 1632 surface, which were almost identical.

66 André Schürger, *Die Entstehung des mittelalterlichen Strassennetzes im Nordharzvorland*, in Harald Meller (ed.), *Archäologie in Sachsen-Anhalt. Sonderband 4. Archäologie XXL. Archäologie an der B 6n im Landkreis Quedlinburg* (Halle Saale: 2006), p.190. Despite Holk's statement that the Via Regia was a sunken or hollow road, Deuticke, *Lützen*, p.58 emphasised that the road had the same height as the surrounding fields, an observation that was neither challenged nor discussed by historians.

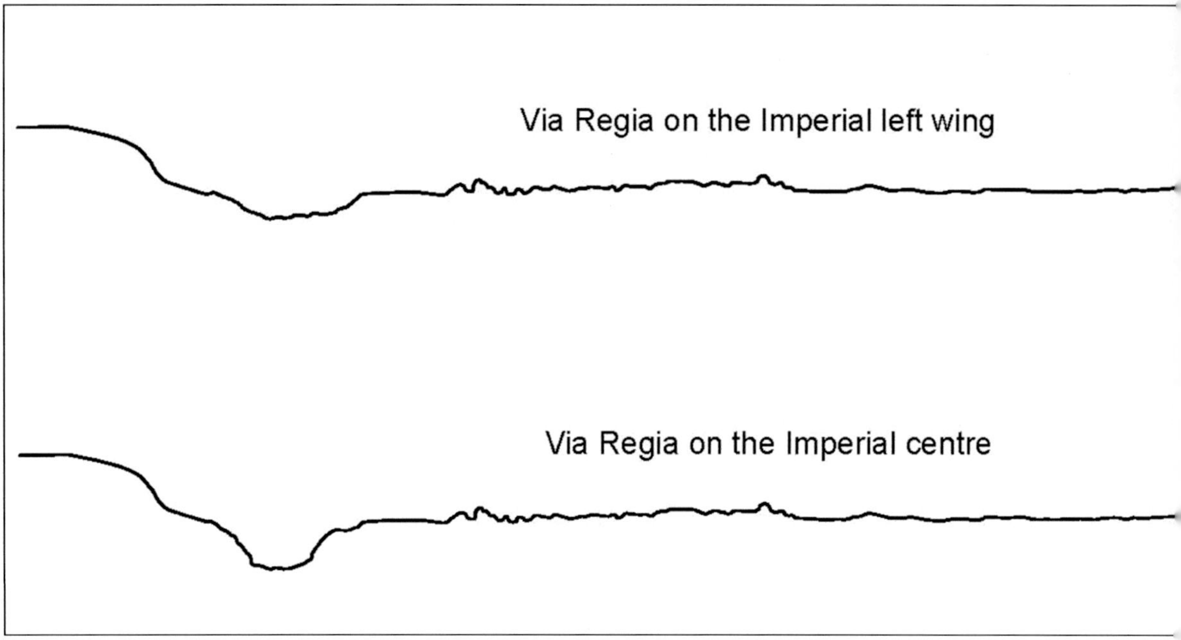

Above: Sectional view of the Via Regia. Section 1: entire Via Regia. Sections 2 and 4: Northern road ditch. (A. Schürger)

Below: Sectional view reconstructing the Via Regia. The missing front (southern) ditch is reconstructed according to the known rear (northern) ditch to illustrate that it is deep enough to provide some cover.

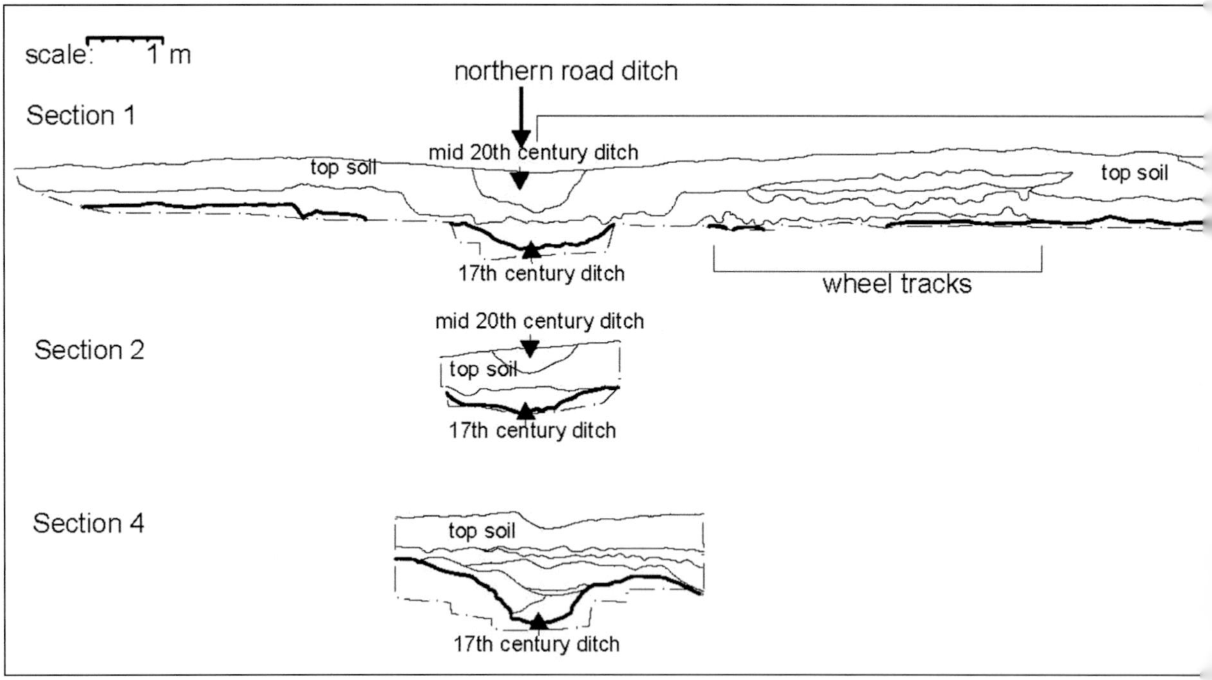

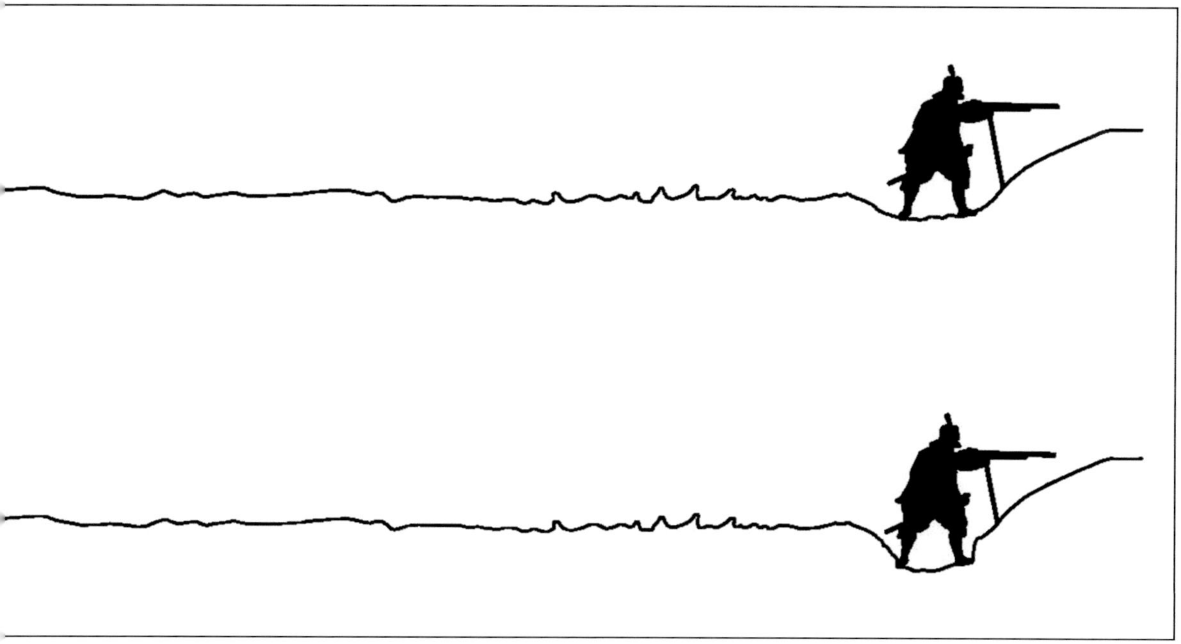

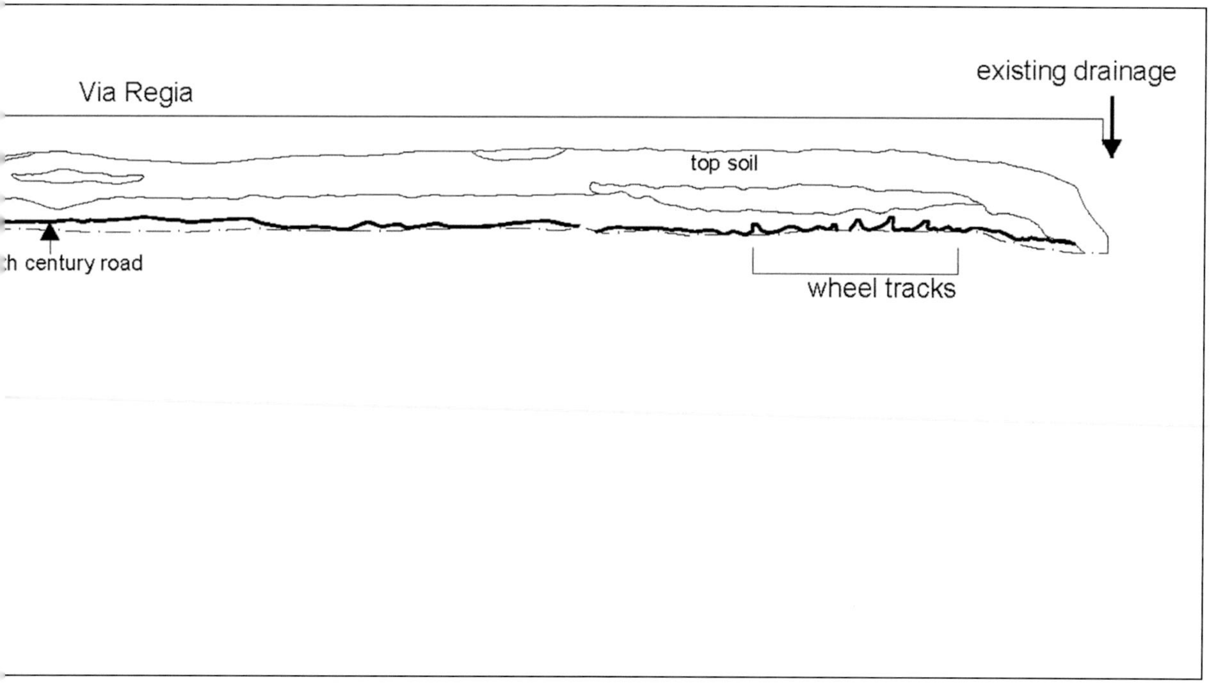

existing drainage
Via Regia
top soil
h century road
wheel tracks

The results from the archaeological excavations show that there was no double trench and additionally demonstrated as well that a second musketeer line on the northern side would have been ineffective, because the Via Regia was a hollow road. Musketeers firing south from such a position would either have the protection of a trench but no line of fire or no protection, but still an ineffective line of fire against the backs of their comrades.

If we assume that the southern road ditch looked similar to the northern, it would have provided average cover, about 0.99 m, from distant fire on the Imperial left wing and good cover of 1.42m in the Imperial centre. Some brush could have provided additional concealment. The ditches, however, would have been insufficient for trench warfare, as is often suggested by historians. Also, it would have been counterproductive to dig the road ditch on the Imperial centre even deeper, because such a trench would have been too deep for musketeers to fire from. The ditches would have provided neither side with an advantage at point-blank range, as Holk mentioned, and it certainly would not have prevented the Swedish cavalry from crossing the Via Regia along the Imperial left wing, where the ditches were shallower than in the centre. Still, the hollow road and the ditches were an obstacle to charging cavalry, as Ottavio Piccolomini described, because cavalry would lose momentum as soon as they reached the road.

Archaeological Sources: Survey

As the southern ditch was probably entirely destroyed by a modern ditch and gas pipeline, a survey was conducted to investigate the fighting at the Via Regia on the Imperial left wing. Imperial musketeers on the Via Regia would have fired southward against the advancing Swedish troops. In an area of three hectares, a maximum of 11 musket bullets were found 40 to 140 metres south of the Via Regia. The widely scattered bullet distribution pattern and distance from the road could suggest there were Imperial musketeers deployed on the road. However, if there were musketeers on the Via Regia, we would expect Swedish troops to have returned fire and there would have been clearly visible bullet distribution patterns south and north of the road. There are almost no bullets near the road reflecting such a combat; in fact, the bullets seem to 'avoid' the road.

Musket bullets south of the road are mixed in with nine pistol bullets. Four show impact damage and one shows firing evidence, confirming that it was a combat situation and not a unit reloading their pistols. The pistol bullets are too far away to be related to any fighting at the Via Regia. Their distribution pattern is similar to patterns 500 metres to the north that can be related to the skirmishes fought by light cavalry and musketeers on open ground. It is, therefore, likely that the bullets south of the road derive from skirmish line firing as well.[67]

Although the bullet distribution pattern is not entirely conclusive, it strongly suggests that there was no heavy fighting along the Via Regia on the Imperial left wing and that it is most unlikely there were any Imperial

67 Schürger, 'Die ersten Minuten', pp.103–120.

musketeers deployed along it. The bullet distribution pattern south of the Via Regia in field IX, however, *is* evidence for an Imperial skirmish line in the road ditches but only in front of the centre.

The Dike

Deuticke claimed that the Via Regia was built on a 1.5 m-high dike near the Flossgraben but without citing any sources or explanation of how he came to this conclusion.[68] In fact, only Fleetwood mentioned a dike on the battlefield, and that was in the context of a breastwork, which was most likely the fortified artillery position.[69] Today, the area where the Via Regia crossed the Flossgraben is completely flat and it is almost impossible that any such extensive earthwork would have vanished without leaving any trace in an area that has never been ploughed. Deuticke, who first created this story, may have been influenced by the modern road, which is built on a 1.5 metre high causeway dating to the late eighteenth century, this is now federal road B81.

The Tactical Value of the Via Regia

Any tactical value of the Via Regia and its ditches for Wallenstein was marginal. It certainly helped Wallenstein's infantry deploy and also in defending the centre by providing a site for harassing the Swedes with skirmishing fire from the road's ditches. On the Imperial left wing, the Via Regia made a turn to the east, in the direction of the Swedish battle line, exposing it to Swedish artillery fire and attacks down its length, making this section of the Via Regia useless to Wallenstein as a defensive position. The fact he chose a defensive battle array with refused wings increasing the distance between Via Regia and his left wing to between 600 m and 1,000 m shows it was tactically useless. Imperial musketeers on the road would have had to retreat this distance across open ground, all the while exposed to pursuing cavalry, before reaching safety with the Imperial cavalry wing. It is most unlikely that Holk, who was in charge of the Imperial deployment, would have wasted his musketeers so casually when he complained that he did not have enough to deploy some in the small wood to his right; and it would certainly have been a waste of time to dig trenches without occupying them.

Conclusion

It is much more difficult to prove that something did not exist than to prove its existence, in particular when it has already influenced research for decades. Despite the numerous illustrations on copperplates and

68 Deuticke, *Lützen*, pp.58 and 65, followed by Mann, *Wallenstein*, pp.847 and 849, Michael Roberts, *Gustavus Adolphus. A History of Sweden. 1611–1632*, Vol. 2 (London, New York: Longmans, Green, 1958), p.765, Generalstaben, *Sveriges Krig*, p.431 and Eriksson, *Lützen*, p.255.

69 Fleetwood, Letter, p.7.

descriptions in secondary sources, archaeology demonstrates there was no double trench and no heavy fighting along the Via Regia on the Imperial left wing. The archaeological results are confirmed by eyewitness accounts, none of which suggest an entrenchment inside the road ditches or any delay the Via Regia might have caused the advancing Swedish right wing. In particular, Holk's silence about any trenches is strong evidence that for their not existing. Excavating a five kilometre-long trench system during one night would have exhausted the Imperial army, while it would have provided only a very limited advantage, particularly on the Imperial left wing. Instead, Wallenstein deployed three Croat regiments as a mobile skirmisher screen in front of the left wing.

According to the historical and archaeological sources, it cannot be ruled out entirely that there was a single trench but only in front of the Imperial centre, as Burgus described it. However, there was no necessity; the road ditch in this area was already deep enough to provide some cover for musketeers. Those musketeers very likely consisted of the first musketeer lines of the five forward infantry squadrons, delivering skirmish fire at the advancing Swedish infantry. They certainly would have retreated behind their lines when the Swedes closed, as there was no tactical advantage in defending the ditches to the last man. It seems as if historians expected Wallenstein to have entrenched his army because he had done so at Dessau Bridge in 1626 and Nurnberg/Alte Veste and 1632, and it became a trope or cliché in printed 'relations'. This new archaeological and historical information changes all former interpretations of the battle and it seriously changes the assessment of secondary sources, written and pictorial.

6

Deployments

The Imperial Battle Array

Probably one of the most debated issues around to the Battle of Lützen over the last 150 years has been the Imperial deployment, at least until Brzezinski published his substantial research in 2001. He re-evaluated all known sources and in addition presented new material that he had located. Since then, a number of publications about the Battle of Lützen have failed to recognise his findings, but simply repeat the out-of-date work from Deuticke in 1917, Generalstaben in 1939 and Seidler in 1954. It is therefore necessary to re-evaluate here all known historical sources and reassess the position of Wallenstein's initial battle lines in combination with the archaeological sources.

Alignment of Wings and Position of the Centre

Historical Sources

There are three crucial eyewitness accounts giving valuable evidence about alignment of the Imperial wings: Vitzthum/Berlepsch, Diodati and Ottavio Piccolomini. Although their accounts were published in the eighteenth and nineteenth centuries, researchers have tended not to take their statements seriously.

Deuticke believed the Imperial battle array was completely aligned with the Via Regia, which he incorrectly reconstructed as an s-turn, thus suggesting some kind of trench warfare. In doing so, he[1] ignored Diodati, the main source in this matter:

> ...the cavalry was deployed equally on the right and left wing in 'stairs' [It.: scala] order, well covering the one and the other flank of the army, advancing when necessary to attack the enemy, joined by the infantry...[2]

1 Deuticke, *Lützen*, p.65, Mann, *Wallenstein*, pp.847–849.

2 Fiedler, 'Diodatis Bericht', pp.561–562.

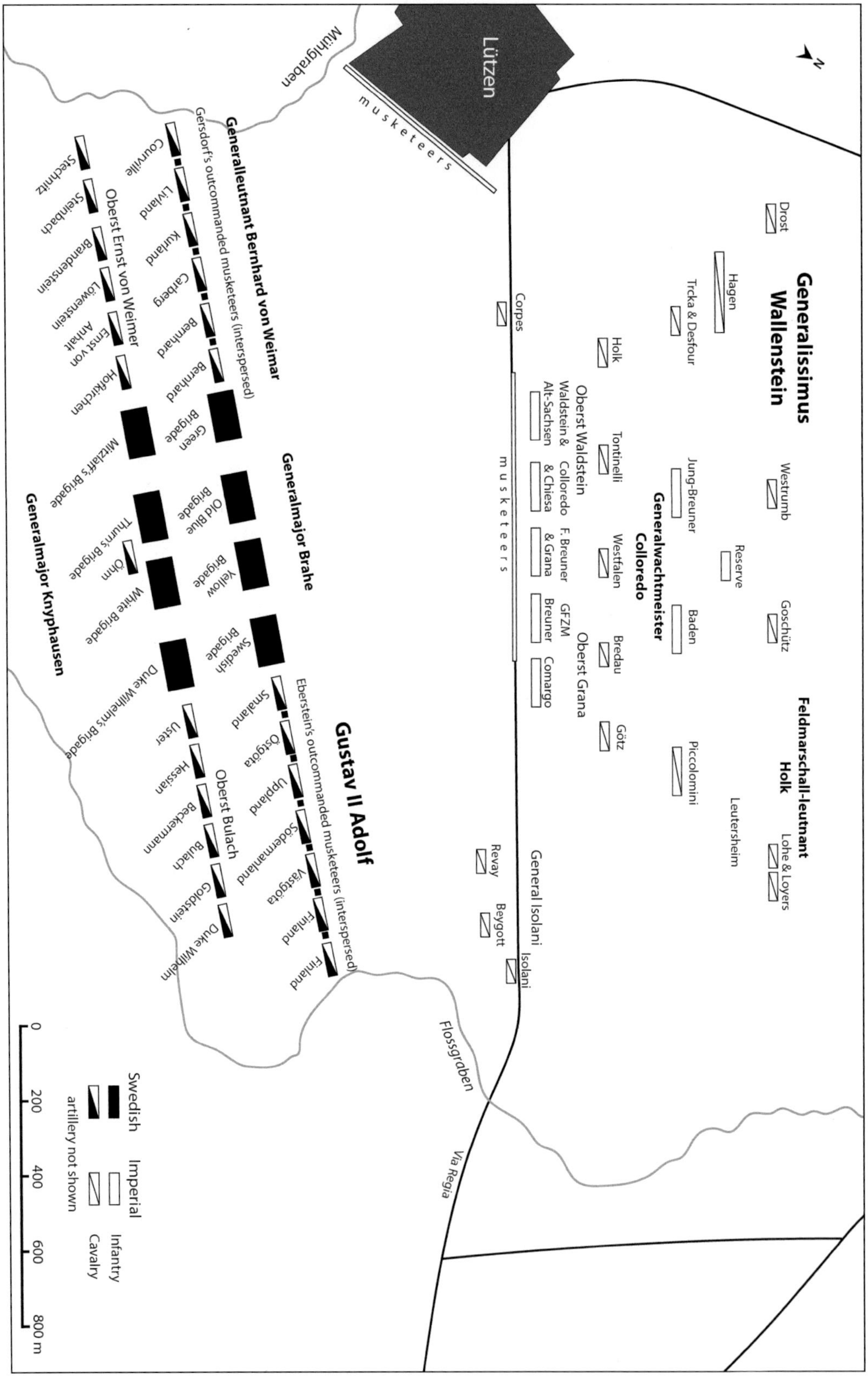

Simplified battle arrays at Lützen (artillery not shown). For detailed arrays of each side, see colour section, plates R and S..

Diodati meant quite literally that the cavalry formations on both flanks were echeloned to the rear like stairs, so that the flanks of the army were covered, but the cavalry had to advance to attack because most of the mounted troops were rearward of the centre's infantry. This is confirmed by Diodati's second statement that the right wing had Lützen to its front,[3] which is only understandable if the right wing was echeloned to the rear, and by Ottavio Piccolomini's account that the Cuirassier Regiment Götz was to his right front from his own point of view.[4]

Although Seidler[5] and Generalstaben[6] recognised Diodati's and Piccolomini's accounts, they did not believe that Wallenstein left a gap between his right wing and Lützen. They therefore concluded that only the left wing was echeloned to the rear, and then only slightly, while the right formed a straight line with the centre, inclining towards the town of Lützen. This still remains the acknowledged view today.[7] To resolve the contradiction between their reconstruction of the Imperial deployment and Diodati's account, Seidler and Generalstaben moved the centre and right wing 230 metres north, away from the Via Regia so that parts of the right wing have Lützen to its front. Even after this adjustment, they still insisted on intensive fighting over the Via Regia's trenches. This would indicate a very serious tactical mistake, because the first line would then have been too far away to effectively support the skirmishers in the ditches.

Brzezinski was the only scholar to recognise what Diodati's account implied. He moved the Imperial centre closer to the Via Regia and reconstructed the alignment of the Imperial wings as angled 45° towards the centre, an interpretation supported by other sources.[8] Vitzthum/Berlepsch reported: '… but finally his Majesty [Gustav II Adolph] advanced the right wing so far that he had almost turned his back towards Ranstädt, with which the encounter on both sides began on horse and foot …'[9]

Ranstädt was a town 3.5 km north-east of the battlefield; from here a straight line would almost align with the Swedish battle array. To have Ranstädt in its rear, the Swedish right wing had to wheel to the left. Since the battle began after this manoeuvre according to Vitzthum/Berlepsch, it must be assumed that the Swedish army had reached the left Imperial wing by this move. If this is so, Vitzthum/Berlepsch implies that the Imperial left wing was refused at an angle of approximately 40° to 50° to the centre, which corresponds with the Diodati and Burgus accounts.[10]

3 Fiedler, 'Diodatis Bericht', p.561.

4 Argang, 'Piccolominis bref', p.89.

5 Seidler, *Untersuchungen*, p.36 initially recognised the Imperial refused wings, but came to the conclusion that the Imperial right wing immediately advanced to the Via Regia at the battle's outset.

6 Generalstaben, *Sveriges Krig*, p.417.

7 Guthrie, *Battles of the Thirty Years' War*, p.203.

8 Brzezinski, *Lützen*, pp.39–55.

9 Glafey, *De Gladio*, p.13.

10 Burgus, *Mars Sveco-Germanicus*, p.317.

Supporting his arguments, Brzezinski presented two previously unknown pictorial representations; an equestrian portrait of Gustav II Adolph by Bianchi and a painting by Snayer.[11] Although copperplates and paintings are usually unreliable, both of these show refused wings, and in addition almost the identical deployment of the Imperial centre that Holk and Diodati described, suggesting the artists had access to Imperial eyewitness accounts.[12]

Archaeological Sources

Bullet distribution on the battlefield also provides some evidence for the Imperial deployment. The densest bullet concentration of the survey is south of field VII; it is oval shaped and runs parallel to the Via Regia. This concentration almost certainly derives from several different fighting episodes, but it clearly indicates the right centre of the Imperial first line, which must have run somewhere through it.

The distribution pattern of 13-bore and 14-bore musket bullets in field VII provides additional evidence to pinpoint the battle line's position. This size of musket bullets was chiefly used by the Imperial army; their bullets are widely scattered across the battlefield except south of field VII, where 15 bullets were scattered in a zone 170 metres long and 70 metres wide parallel to the Via Regia. A distance of 170 metres is only slightly further than the estimated length of an Imperial infantry squadron at Lützen, suggesting these bullets were fired by one unit. Therefore, the north-west end of this concentration very probably marks the first Imperial line as being 70 metres away from the Via Regia, a position that would allow a closer interaction between infantry squadrons and the skirmishers in the road ditches.

The second bullet concentration is located in the south corner of field I. This is not as distinctive as that in field VII, because it is blurred with other distribution patterns to the west (Inf 5). To the north-east this concentration is limited because the bullet distribution pattern thins out, not only marking the end of the Imperial left centre, but also suggesting it is very unlikely that the cavalry was deployed on a straight line with the centre. It also suggests a distance of approximately 70 metres between the first line and the Via Regia. The total length of the Imperial centre, defined by the windmills and the bullet concentration in field I, is approximately 1,035 metres.

The bullet concentration at the Imperial centre's north-eastern (left) end continues spreading northwards (Inf 5). This might indicate the refused left wing's position. Further east in field III, the bullet density diminishes rapidly – this suggests skirmishing rather than full scale combat. The low density bullet distribution in field III definitely rules out Deuticke's reconstruction of the Imperial order of battle. Seidler's and Generalstaben's reconstruction of a first Imperial battle line 230 m north of the Via Regia is also contradicted by the bullet distribution, because their projections would run through low density areas, in particular on the right centre, where most of the fighting took place.

11 Brzezinski, *Lützen*, pp.47 and 55.

12 Brzezinski, *Lützen*, p.46 suggests that Bianchi had information from one of Wallenstein's Italian officers.

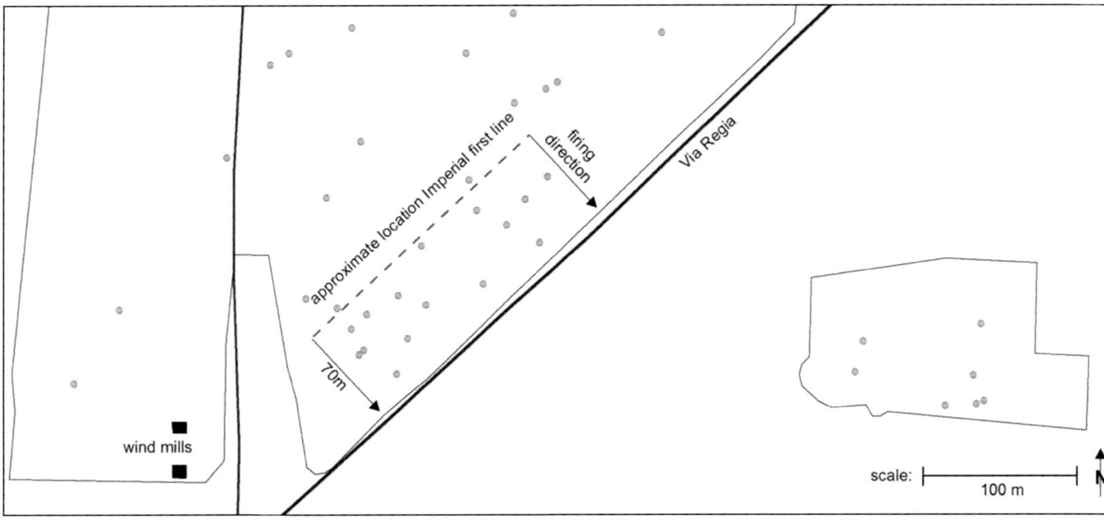

Bullet distribution on the Imperial right centre. Bullets from Imperial 13-bore and 14-bore muskets from Augsburg and Nurnberg (17.3–17.8 mm), possibly mixed with few bullets from 10-bore muskets and a small number of bullets from 14-bore carbines. (A. Schürger)

Additionally, most heavily impacted musket bullets are distributed near the Via Regia, suggesting point-blank musket fire near the road and that the Imperial centre was closer to the road than Seidler and Generalstaben believed.

Thus, the archaeological resources, as well as the eyewitness accounts and pictorial representations, support Brzezinski's thesis of the Imperial battle line with refused wings and a centre in close proximity to the Via Regia.

Battle Array

As we have reliable eyewitness accounts from Holk and Diodati,[13] there is little doubt about the Imperial infantry deployment in eight squadrons: five in the first line, two in the second, and one held as a reserve. According to Holk, each first and second line squadron fielded approximately 1,000 men.[14] However, the reserve squadron consisted of 500 musketeers, not 2,500 as Holk actually stated in error. There are very few hints about the precise positioning of units in the Imperial battle array. The known units are mentioned by their regimental name rather than by squadron composition. Only Diodati gives an approximate position for the infantry regiments; Berthold von Waldstein's on the right centre and Grana's somewhere left of him.[15] There is only one eyewitness account of the centre's cavalry reserve. According to Holk, two cavalry squadrons flanked the reserve infantry squadron, and the second line had either two or three cavalry squadrons, depending on the interpretation of Holk's statement that the two infantry squadrons and the six cavalry companies were mixed two by two.[16] It is not entirely certain if Münchhausen refers to the cavalry reserve when he mentioned the Regiment Bredau, which he probably

13 Wittrock, 'Fyra relationer', p.308, Fiedler, 'Diodatis Bericht', p.561.

14 Wittrock, 'Fyra relationer', p.308.

15 Fiedler, 'Diodatis Bericht', p.565.

16 Wittrock, 'Fyra relationer', p.308.

had seen in action near his Regiment, Comargo.[17]

Five eyewitness accounts[18] concern deployment of the Imperial wings, but they remain relatively vague, allowing historians to come to very different conclusions. Holk's statement, in particular, that the Duke [Wallenstein] fought for two hours against the Swedish infantry with the Cavalry Regiments Holk, Trcka, Piccolomini and Desfour has led historians into erroneously believing that those regiments were initially deployed together on the right wing. However, Holk was actually describing another event that occurred later in battle, when the Imperial cavalry had possibly changed wings.[19]

According to Diodati[20] and Ottavio Piccolomini,[21] the Cavalry regiments Götz and Piccolomini were initially deployed on the left wing adjacent to the infantry centre's left flank.[22] The documents from the court-martial at Prague states that the regiments Hagen and Trcka were initially deployed adjacent to each other somewhere on the right wing but that Hagen later moved to the left near to the Regiment Goschütz, the left wing reserve.[23] Fleetwood reported that 'the crabates haveing the lefte wynge',[24] but some Croats were also deployed on the right wing.[25]

The best sources about the Imperial wings are still the Holk and Diodati accounts. According to Holk, each wing consisted of 36 companies of cavalry with 150 detached musketeers,[26] a statement supported by Diodati, who mentioned an equal deployment of cavalry on both wings.[27] Vitzthum/Berlepsch reported, 'four troops of cavalrymen have shown themselves on the side of the city.'[28]

This statement led Deuticke to conclude that this was the number of cavalry squadrons on the right wing.[29] However, it is more likely that Vitzthum/ Berlepsch was referring to a Croat skirmish screen at the Flossgraben

17 Wittrock, 'Fyra relationer', p.305.

18 Holk, Diodati, Ottavio Piccolomini, court-martial document, and Fleetwood.

19 This part of Holk's account (Wittrock, 'Fyra relationer', p.309) was ignored by Generalstaben, *Sveriges Krig*, p.418, who placed three of these four regiments on the left wing, which would have meant that most of the left wing moved to the right during the battle. It was also misinterpreted by Seidler, *Untersuchungen*, p.38, who believed that all those regiments were initially deployed on the right wing.

20 Fiedler, 'Diodatis Bericht', p.563.

21 Argang, 'Piccolominis bref', p.89.

22 Only Burgus, *Mars Sveco-Germanicus*, p.324 placed Götz incorrectly on the right wing.

23 Seidler, *Untersuchungen*, p.141.

24 Fleetwood, Letter, p.6. This is also mentioned by Gottfried, *Inventarium Sueciae*, p.26, copied by Anonymous, *Wahrhaftige Beschreibung*, Anonymous, *Glaubwürdiger Bericht*, Monro, *His Expedition*, part II, p.164, Abelinum, *Theatrum Europaeum*, p.750 and Chemnitz, *Geschichte*, p.466, which referred to an event in the early afternoon.

25 According to the document of the court-martial the Regiment Hagen was routed by retreating Croats on the right wing (Seidler, *Untersuchungen*, p.141).

26 Wittrock, 'Fyra relationer', p.308.

27 Fiedler, 'Diodatis Bericht', p.561.

28 Glafey, *De Gladio*, p.13.

29 Deuticke, *Lützen*, p.66.

and Mühlgraben before the battle, although each wing did consist of four squadrons (see below).[30]

The discovery of the Trauttmansdorff's list is probably the most important document for reconstructing Imperial deployment. Unlike the accounts, it lists complete squadrons with some consisting of two regiments as they were assembled to provide the necessary troop strength for a battle formation.[31] The squadrons on the list are marked with letters in alphabetical order, in the case of Pappenheim's brigade with symbols, and we can assume that they were marked on a now lost map in a specific order.[32]

In conjunction with eyewitness accounts, the list can be interpreted as follows: Since Waldstein was in the right centre and Grana somewhere left of him, infantry squadrons A to E should be in the first line from right to left. Baden was very likely near Comargo so infantry squadrons F and G were in the second line from left to right and the detached musketeers H formed the reserve. Trcka and Hagen were deployed adjacent to each other on the right wing. Therefore, cavalry squadrons J to M were on the right with Holk's squadron to the front. This deployment almost matches Holk's statement that the Regiments Holk, Trcka and Desfour were on the right, so Piccolomini must have moved from the left to the right during the battle. Götz and Piccolomini flanked the centre on the left, which puts the cavalry squadrons R to V on the left. Bredau was probably in reserve behind Comargo, which makes it likely that cavalry squadrons N to P were the second line reserve from left to right. Isolani's Croats (Q) are listed between the second line reserve and the left wing and could have been deployed anywhere in front of the left wing and moved as circumstances dictated. The cavalry squadrons Westrumb (Y) and Goschütz (X) flanked the musketeer reserve with Goschütz on the left.

Wallenstein detached four musketeer squadrons from his infantry regiments. One squadron of five companies functioned as a reserve. Two 'squadrons'[33] of 150 musketeers each were positioned 'in front of each wing,' probably deployed either as 50-man 'companies' between cavalry squadrons to mimic the Swedish tactics[34] or as one unit, but they were too few to form an effective skirmishing screen in front of the entire wing and were certainly not deployed in the road ditches.[35] One 'squadron' of 400 musketeers was

30 Brzezinski, *Lützen*, p.46.

31 There are eight infantry units marked as A to H on the list, which match the number of infantry squadrons mentioned by Diodati (Fiedler, 'Diodatis Bericht', p.561) and Holk (Wittrock, 'Fyra relationer', p.308).

32 Suggested first by Stadler, *Pappenheim*, pp.891–892 and utilised by Brzezinski, *Lützen*, p.48 to reconstruct the Imperial deployment. Although it was acknowledged by Sennewald, *Das kursächsische Heer*, p.158, he reconstructed the deployment in a mostly confused alphabetical order, by trying to tally it with Generalstaben's incorrect result.

33 The term 'squadron' is not used in historical sources for the musketeers deployed on the wings or in the gardens, but they certainly consisted of more than one company which made them de facto independently operating squadrons.

34 Seidler, *Untersuchungen*, p.34.

35 Suggested by Brzezinski, *Lützen*, p.39 and Sennewald, *Das kursächsische Heer*, p.169.

initially deployed in the city and castle of Lützen,[36] but was redeployed into the Lützen gardens behind a mud wall at the beginning of the battle.[37] The musketeers in the Via Regia road ditch were not independent units, but very likely consisted of one or two ranks sent forward from the front line infantry squadrons, who simply retired to their linear positions after they had performed their duty as skirmishers.

The centre was flanked by two batteries of artillery that were almost certainly in fortified positions. There is evidence for such a fortification at the windmills and some hints about another fortified small Imperial battery. According to Dalbier, the only eyewitness, who gives details for the number of artillery pieces in the smaller, left centre, battery, it consisted of six pieces, four 24-pounders and two 12-pounders,[38] although most secondary sources mentioned seven pieces.[39] There is no historical evidence and no direct archaeological evidence to pinpoint this battery's position. Since the north-east end of the left centre's position is known, the battery must have been deployed close to this location. Secondary sources give a range of different numbers of artillery pieces for the larger battery at the windmills. These numbers range from 9 to 17.[40] If the document from Stralsund is correct, the battery had 17 pieces: five 24-pounders, two 16-pounders, four 12-pounders, one 10-pounder and six 6-pounders.

Regimental guns, probably 8 to 16 pieces, were deployed in the first line between the infantry squadrons. The approximate spacing between the first line infantry squadrons at Lützen can be calculated because a 1,000 strong infantry squadron deployed seven ranks deep had a frontage of 153 metres, assuming five- metre spacing for officers between the bodies of pikemen and musketeers. That would leave a spacing of roughly 67.5 metres between squadrons, since the total length of the centre was approximately 1,035 m. This space was large enough to allow a cavalry squadron to advance through, as was common practice in seventeenth-century warfare, but too small for a second line infantry squadron, as is often claimed for the Imperial army at Lützen.[41] Based on Poyntz and the painting by Snayer, Brzezinski believed that Wallenstein deployed a 'fake' troop at the end of his left wing, consisting of camp followers and baggage train members, to give the impression of a

---

36 Holk (Wittrock, 'Fyra relationer', p.308).

37 Watts, *Swedish Intelligencer*, vol. 3, pp.129, 132 and 149.

38 Dalbier, *Lutzen*, p.252, confirmed by Silvio Piccolomini (Anonymous, *Archivio*, p.240) and Burgus, *Mars Sveco-Germanicus*, p.321.

39 Declaration from 1633 (Droysen, 'Gedruckte Relationen', p.40), Khevenhiller, *Annales Ferdinandei*, p.191 and Gottfried, *Inventarium Sueciae*, p.25, copied by Anonymous, *Wahrhaftige Beschreibung*, Anonymous, *Glaubwürdiger Bericht*, Monro, *His Expedition*, part II, p.164, Abelinum, *Theatrum Europaeum*, pp.749–750 and Chemnitz, *Geschichte*, p.464.

40 Nine pieces: Fleetwood, Letter, p.6, Watts, *Swedish Intelligencer*, vol. 3, p.129. Thirteen pieces: Declaration from 1633 (Droysen, 'Gedruckte Relationen', p.42). 14 pieces: Dalbier, *Lutzen*, p.252, Gottfried, *Inventarium Sueciae*, p.26, Chemnitz, *Geschichte*, p.464. 16 pieces: Burgus, *Mars Sveco-Germanicus*, pp.321 and 327. 17 pieces: Priorato, *Historia dell Guerra*, p.119.

41 Deuticke, *Lützen*, p.66. Generalstaben, *Sveriges Krig*, p.416, Seidler, *Untersuchungen*, p.35.

larger wing.[42] This episode is not mentioned anywhere else and there remains some doubt about it. However, it is possible that Swedish eyewitnesses might not have noticed this 'body', because they ran off before they could have been engaged and Imperial eyewitnesses probably tried to hide such an unworthy military deception in their accounts.

Command Structure

It is curious that so few sources name the Imperial wing commanders and that when they do they contradict each other, leading historians to believe that command changed during the course of the battle, and according to Deuticke, several times.[43] However, it would have been a serious tactical mistake to make changes in command during a battle without reason, and this is not something Wallenstein is believed to have done.

Right Wing

Holk, as second in command, was certainly familiar with the command structure, and stated that Wallenstein commanded the right wing.[44] This is confirmed by the record of the court-martials at Prague, according to which Hofkirchen, when he arrived at the right wing, was guilty of disobeying a direct order from Wallenstein.[45] Therefore, there is no reason to doubt that Wallenstein actually commanded the right wing.[46] Unfortunately, Generalstaben followed Watts' unreliable account that Colloredo commanded the right wing, which makes an impact on even recent research.[47]

Left Wing

Holk, supported by Watts, stated that he commanded the left wing, which has not been doubted since the publication of Holk's letter; indeed, this seems to be one of the few generally accepted facts about the Battle of Lützen.[48]

42 Poyntz, *The Relation*, p.126, Brzezinski, *Lützen*, p.54, Wedgwood, *Der Dreissigjährige Krieg*, p.325.

43 Deuticke, *Lützen*, p.68.

44 Wittrock, 'Fyra relationer', p.308.

45 Seidler, *Untersuchungen*, p.143.

46 See also Seidler, *Untersuchungen*, p.40 and Brzezinski, *Lützen*, p.42.

47 Watts, *Swedish Intelligencer*, vol. 3, pp.129–130. Guthrie, *Battles of the Thirty Years' War*, pp.202–203, Eriksson, *Lützen*, p.239, Wolke, 'Die Schlacht bei Lützen', p.64, Mike Reichel, *Die Schlacht von Lützen vom 6./16. November 1632 und der Tod des schwedischen Königs Gustav II. Adolf*, in Harald Meller (ed.), *Schlachtfeldarchäologie* (Battlefield Archaeology). *1. Mitteldeutscher Archäologentag vom 09. bis 11. Oktober 2008 in Halle (Saale)* (Halle/Saale: 2009), p.129 and Sennewald, *Das kursächsische Heer*, p.169 are the most recent publications to follow Generalstaben's (*Sveriges Krig*, p.417) incorrect assertion.

48 Wittrock, 'Fyra relationer', p.308, Watts, *Swedish Intelligencer*, vol. 3, p.130.

However, it is believed by most historians,[49] following Seidler, that Holk had to hand over command of the left wing to Pappenheim upon the latter's arrival on the field. For some unknown reason, Seidler[50] desperately tried to prove that the unreliable Khevenhiller[51] account was correct in stating that Gustav II Adolph died on the Swedish left instead of the Swedish right wing, a detail contradicting Holk's account among others.[52] To prove his point, Seidler strongly suggested that Pappenheim received an order from Wallenstein on the evening of 15 November to reinforce the left wing upon his arrival, thus taking command from Holk, who in turn was moved to assist Wallenstein on the right. Seidler's assertion is based on the incorrect assumption that the left wing was weaker than the right. His interpretation was based on a flawed translation of Holk's account, and on Watts' and Khevenhiller's unreliable accounts, as well as being influenced by the Weissenfels battle plan, which he believed was some kind of provisional battle plan for Lützen.[53]

Although it is likely, but not certain, that Pappenheim carried the Weissenfels battle plan together with Wallenstein's order with him, both are marred by bloodstains,[54] Wallenstein's Lützen battle order was perfectly symmetrical and Pappenheim's missing units on the left wing, as shown on the plan, were replaced by other units at Lützen. Therefore, there was no need to plan ahead for reinforcements for the left wing. The flaw in his argument is that Wallenstein could not possibly have anticipated the battle's onset before the arrival of Pappenheim's troops. In the end, it remains unconfirmed that Pappenheim carried the Weissenfels battle plan, and the reason for doing so, if he did.

Wallenstein's 15 November written order to Pappenheim states: 'The enemy is marching towards us. Your honour shall drop everything, and route himself hereto with all troops and guns, to be with us tomorrow morning (Fig. 71).'[55] If it was so important for Wallenstein to order Pappenheim to the left wing as early as 15 November, we should have expected him to have included that order in the letter.

Seidler's main argument was that Holk's account states: 'Hertzogen commenderede och förde self den Rette Flügel imod Weimar. Holche, som commenderede I Feldt Marschalls sted, förde den Venstre.'[56] Which he translated: 'The Duke [Wallenstein] commanded and led himself the right

49 Deuticke, *Lützen*, p.68, Generalstaben, *Sveriges Krig*, p.417, Mann, *Wallenstein*, pp.850, 854, Junkelmann, *Gustavus Adolphus*, p.455, Brzezinski, *Lützen*, p.42, Guthrie, *Battles of the Thirty Years' War*, p.203 and Mortimer, *Wallenstein*, p.173 are a few examples.

50 Seidler, *Untersuchungen*, pp.58–77, followed by Diwald, *Wallenstein*, p.500.

51 Khevenhiller, *Annales Ferdinandei*, p.191.

52 Wittrock, 'Fyra relationer', p.309.

53 Seidler, *Untersuchungen*, pp.121–122, ref. 31.

54 Holl, 'Wallensteins angebliche Skizze', p.63. The traces of blood on both papers do not match, which seems to prove that Pappenheim did not receive the battle plan together with the order.

55 Translation by Brzezinski, *Lützen*, p.37, slightly modified by the author.

56 Wittrock, 'Fyra relationer', p.308.

wing against Weimar. Holk, who commanded instead of the Field Marshal, led the left.'

Seidler interpreted this as meaning Holk commanded the left wing *vice* Pappenheim [the Field Marshal] until his arrival.[57] However, there is one mistake in Seidler's argument: He assumed that the second sentence describes one subject. Both sentences consist of a main and a subordinate clause using two different verbs to express command, 'commenderede' and 'förde', which have a slightly different meaning.

'Förde' is used here in context of an actual field command and therefore expresses the commanding of a wing during the battle. The meaning of 'commenderede' is more difficult to comprehend, because the object in the first sentence is missing. In the second sentence 'commenderede' is used in the context of a rank: 'Holk commanded instead of the Field Marshal', which means that Holk was second in command of the army in the absence of Pappenheim, expressing his rank inside the command structure of the army. We can assume the same meaning of 'commenderede' in the first sentence 'Wallenstein commanded', which implies that he commanded the army. Thus, both sentences describe two different subjects at a time: Wallenstein commanded the army AND the right wing; Holk commanded the left wing AND was second in command. It was important to Holk to mention the latter to King Christian IV of Denmark that he, just recently promoted from *Oberst* to *Feldmarschall Leutnant*, now held a high command in the main Imperial field army, even if it was only temporarily, because it was an important career step. There is no connection between 'Holk commanded instead of the Field Marshal' and 'Holk commanded the left wing', as Seidler suggested.[58]

Watts' statement: 'The left wing ... was led by Colonel Hendrick Holck; newly made Lieftenant-Felt-Marshal unto Pappenheim: who but commanded till Felt. Marshal Pappenheim should be comne into Field'[59] has an important similarity to Holk's statement, because the different use of the words 'led,' to express command of a wing, and 'command,' to express his rank in the army, suggests, although not clearly, that Watts had access to Holk's account. However, even if there is no connection and we interpret Watts' statement according to Seidler's basic idea, Watts confused the commanders of the centre and the right wing, leaving his statement about command on the left wing questionable at the very least. A hint on the left wing action is given by Diodati, who wrote that Pappenheim, upon arriving on the battlefield counter-attacked the left wing, 'because there it seemed that the King [Gustav II Adolph] attacked most stubborn.'[60] This is not a description of an attack planned a day ahead.

57 Seidler, *Untersuchungen*, pp.58–59.

58 The author's new interpretation of Holk's account was approved by the Danish Professor Jens Olesen, Institute for Nordic History, University of Greifswald.

59 Watt, *Swedish Intelligencer*, vol. 3, p.130.

60 Fiedler, 'Diodatis Bericht', p.562.

Detail of the equestrian portrait of Gustav II Adolph, by Bianchi.

R
A
S
L
M
L
O
C
D
D
I

There is no hint in the historical sources suggesting a plan for Pappenheim to take command over any wing, nor that there was any plan for the troops under his command to reinforce a specific wing,[61] as no one could possibly have anticipated how the battle would have developed by the time he arrived. As an experienced field officer, it was Pappenheim's decision to counter-attack immediately upon arriving because that was where the crisis developed.

The best fit with the evidence is that Holk retained command of the left wing during the battle. There is no hint in the Silvio or Ottavio Piccolomini accounts, or anywhere else,[62] that Ottavio Piccolomini took command on the left wing after the death of Pappenheim, as Seidler claimed;[63] Ottavio Piccolomini certainly would have mentioned such an important command role in his letter to the Emperor. Since Pappenheim outranked Holk, he would have ordinarily assumed his position as second in command had he not been killed so soon after his arrival.

Centre

Holk did not mention who was in charge of the centre and there is no clear evidence in any other historical source. Diodati wrote that 'Sargente Maggiore di battaglia' Colloredo always assisted the infantry[64] and Silvio Piccolomini mentioned that 'sergente generale di bataglia' Colloredo fought well with the infantry.[65] Although it is not entirely certain that 'bat(t)aglia' should be interpreted as 'centre',[66] both sources demonstrate that Colloredo was in the centre and did not command the right wing as Watts claimed.[67] Diodati's account also suggested that there were some sort of Imperial brigade commanders, Berthold von Waldstein on the right and Grana on the left centre,[68] each leading three infantry squadrons according to the Swedish example, but ordered in a more defensive battle

61 Only Khevenhiller, *Annales Ferdinandei*, pp.190–191 claimed, that Wallenstein gave orders for Pappenheim in the morning before battle to take position where the baggage train stood (i.e. in reserve), which he had sent to Leipzig. Besides the fact that Wallenstein did not send the baggage train away, Khevenhiller's unreliable account is not enough evidence to suggest such an order, although it would have been reasonable to order Pappenheim's corps, which had marched all night, into reserve first.

62 With the exception of Khevenhiller, *Annales Ferdinandei*, p.194, who claimed that Piccolomini rallied the Imperial left wing, because he did not realise that Holk was in command, whom Khevenhiller, *Annales Ferdinandei*, p.187 mentioned only once, when he ordered the Imperial battle array in the night before battle.

63 There is no hint of Piccolomini taking command in the letter of his nephew Silvio Piccolomini (Anonymous, *Archivio*, pp.239–242) as Seidler, *Untersuchungen*, p.59 and rem. 132 claimed.

64 Fiedler, 'Diodatis Bericht', p.565.

65 Anonymous, *Archivio*, p.241.

66 Khevenhiller, *Annales Ferdinandei*, p.195, whose account is based partially on Diodati, interpreted it this way. Also, Monro, *His Expedition*, part II, p.25) used the term 'Battaile' for 'centre' of a Swedish brigade formation.

67 Watts, *Swedish Intelligencer*, vol. 3, p.129.

68 Fiedler, 'Diodatis Bericht', p.565.

array similar to Basta's brigade (two front and one reserve squadrons).[69] Officially, there were no Imperial brigades in 1632 and there is no further evidence apart from Diodati's account, but it seems possible that the wing commanders Wallenstein and Holk extended their commands towards the centre with Waldstein and Grana as local commanders to assist them. Generalfeldzeugmeister Hans Philipp von Breuner as commanding officer of the Imperial artillery, was very likely at the windmill battery.[70]

Conclusion

The Imperial line of battle, with five infantry squadrons in the first line and four cavalry squadrons echeloned to the rear on each wing, is illustrated in the painting by Snayer and the copperplate by Bianchi. Bianchi shows the reserve as consisting of one infantry squadron and seven cavalry squadrons. Snayer shows the reserve according to Holk's account and the Trauttmansdorff list, with the regimental guns between the first line infantry squadrons, making his painting probably the most accurate pictorial representation. The distribution of cavalry on each wing according to the Trauttmansdorff list is also supported by the number of companies: 36 on each wing according to Holk; 37 on the left and 36 on the right according to Brzezinski's calculation. On the other hand, the number of cavalry reserve companies, 15 in the second line and 8 as wing reserve, does not match Holk's account, which lists 6 in the second line and 12 as wing reserve. These discrepancies leave some unanswered questions about the cavalry reserve.

To understand what Wallenstein had in mind with his deployment at the Battle of Lützen a comparison with the plan of Weissenfels is useful as this latter bears some resemblances in the regimental positioning. In comparison with Weissenfels, the first line of the centre at Lützen was reduced by one squadron, likewise the cavalry reserve was reduced by one squadron. However, they were stronger than shown in the Weissenfels plan to compensate for the weaker second line and reserve, comprising only two and one squadrons compared to five and two at Weissenfels. If there was any hint of a plan for Pappenheim's brigade, the weak second line and wing reserves were to be completed by his regiments if they arrived in time to get some rest from their march before being committed to action, as the regiments Tontinelli and Bredau actually did.[71]

It should perhaps be pointed out that Imperial units were probably still arriving during the morning and filtering into the reserve and this could explain the discrepancy between Holk's number and the actual number of reserve cavalry companies. The 6:5:2 infantry deployment at Weissenfels contradicts Generalstaben's suggestion that Wallenstein's infantry was deployed as Basta's brigades, but does not exclude the existence of local commanders. The two rear cavalry squadrons were almost certainly not

69 Generalstaben, *Sveriges Krig*, p.416. See also Brzezinski, *Lützen*, p.42.

70 Khevenhiller, *Annales Ferdinandei*, p.195.

71 Brzezinski, *Lützen*, p.48.

a reserve for the centre but for the wings and could have easily supported either wing from their position at the rear.

In both battle arrays, weak points at the ends of the infantry centre were protected by Wallenstein's veteran troops, the cuirassiers and Piccolomini's harquebusiers, while the less reliable lightly armoured cavalry were deployed at the wings' extremities. It should be noted that Lohe's cuirassiers were deployed at the end of a wing in both battle arrays, possibly because the regiment was recently raised and not yet fully armoured. It has often been argued that the Weissenfels battle plan was not a line of battle, but a square[72] and therefore is nothing more than a stereotype or draft sketch,[73] or an overnight deployment;[74] but with the evidence from Lützen, it seems more likely that it actually shows Wallenstein's defensive battle tactics.[†]

† See PDF download, Plate 18: Weissenfels battle plan from 12 November 1632

The Imperial battle array at Lützen was perfectly balanced, at least as far as possible for such a small army, with a similar number of heavy cavalry on each wing. The Imperial left wing was not weaker than the right and it was not planned that it should be reinforced by Pappenheim's regiments as Seidler, and after him so many others, suggested.[75] Although the right centre had almost three times the number of artillery pieces than the left as well as some 400 musketeers behind the Lützen gardens' mud walls, this was compensated for by many more Croats being on the left. This gave the left wing less firepower but more mobility, a necessity because of the open ground that better allowed for the Croat mobile tactics. The deep deployment would allow for the reinforcing of the most endangered wing, and it was the best tactical solution for a defensive battle line.

A final observation concerns the 70-metre distance between Imperial skirmishers in the road ditches and the Imperial first line, which is not a coincidence. The distance is too far to have allowed the Swedes to effectively fire at the Imperial first line from the cover of the hollow road. At the same

72 Philippi (Holl, 'Wallensteins angebliche Skizze', p.60).

73 Droysen, 'Lützen', p.112. He admitted that the Weissenfels plan has a resemblance with Diodati's description of the refused wings.

74 Guthrie, *Battles of the Thirty Years' War*, pp.202 and 227.

75 Seidler, *Untersuchungen*, p.38, who placed all heavy cavalry except Götz on the right wing and explained his interpretation with reference to the Battle at Nurnberg/Alte Veste, where Gustav II Adolph attacked the most protected location, and he assumed that Wallenstein 'knew' Gustav II Adolph would do the same at Lützen. This notion contradicts all military principles, in particular for a defensive battle array, where a commander has to react to an attack and therefore needs sufficient reserves. Roberts, *Gustavus Adolphus. A History of Sweden*, p.767, Mann, *Wallenstein*, p.850, Holl, 'Wallensteins angebliche Skizze', pp.69–70, Stadler, Pappenheim, p.730, Doughty and Gruber, *Warfare in the Western World*, p.25, Helmut Neuhold, *Der Dreissigjährige Krieg* (Wiesbaden: Marixverlag 2011), p.98 and Mortimer, *Wallenstein*, p.173 followed Seidler's thesis. Generalstaben, *Sveriges Krig*, p.417 placed all heavy cavalry except Desfour on the left wing. Strangely, Junkelmann, *Gustavus Adolphus*, p.454 and Guthrie, *Battles of the Thirty Years' War*, pp.203–204 followed Generalstaben's thesis, but still suggested a weak left wing, which was planned to be reinforced by Pappenheim.

time it seems to have been the optimum musket firing range at which Imperial musketeers usually opened a constant fire.[76]

The Swedish Line of Battle

In contrast to the Imperial battle array, the Swedish deployment is well-documented, although it should be noted that almost all information is based on secondary sources. Nevertheless, there seems to be little doubt about the Swedish battle positions, with some minor exceptions.

Cavalry and Intermixed Musketeers

Most sources state that the Swedish wings each consisted of six first-line and six second-line cavalry squadrons. The squadrons of the right wing first line consisted of the six national Swedish regiments Smaland, Ostgöta, Uppland, Södermanland, Västgöta and Finland, but Fleetwood reported that the Finnish cavalry was divided into two squadrons, which would, technically, have given this wing seven squadrons instead of six.[77]

The question about the number of right wing first line cavalry squadrons is connected to the question about the strength of the commanded musketeers interlined with the first line cavalry squadrons of both wings, which are not mentioned by any eyewitness. According to Khevenhiller[78] and the *Relation from 1633*[79] each of the 10 musketeer companies consisted of 50 men, according to Monro[80] this is the same strength that they had at Breitenfeld in 1631, while Hülshorst[81] and Richelieu[82] give a strength of 200 per company. Most historians assume that musketeers from several regiments formed these detached companies. However Langmann's list suggests that all regiments were at their combat strength on 15 November and it is unlikely they released musketeers before the battle, except possibly as skirmishers to their immediate front. Additionally, the Regiments Löwenstein and Brandenstein, which consisted only of musketeers, were already designated to form these commanded musketeer units.[83] Together, with a total of 798 musketeers,

76 David F. Harding, *Lead Shot of the English Civil War: A Radical Study* (London: Foresight Books, 2012), p.9.

77 Fleetwood, Letter, p.7.

78 Khevenhiller, *Annales Ferdinandei*, p.189 had copied this part from the *Relation from 1633* (Droysen, 'Gedruckte Relationen', pp.24–35).

79 Droysen, 'Gedruckte Relationen', p.29.

80 Monro, *His Expedition*, part II, p.64.

81 Wittrock, 'Fyra relationer', p.303.

82 Richelieu, *Mémoires*, p.257.

83 Brzezinski, *Lützen*, p.22. See also Hülshorst (Wittrock, 'Fyra relationer', p.303), who stated that the commanded companies were formed by the 9th Brigade's Regiments Löwenstein and Brandenstein (Henderson was likely part of the brigade, but formed the 1st line reserve). This would exclude Leslie's Scots, who, according to Monro, *His Expedition*, part II, p.164, formed the musketeer companies on the left wing and charged the Imperial windmill battery (See Brzezinski,

they had the necessary strength and a total of 11 companies. This is exactly the number needed assuming that the left wing's front line consisted of six cavalry squadrons with five musketeer companies, and the right wing of seven squadrons with six companies, averaging a reasonable 72 men each.

Battle Line and Command

The Swedish order of battle array consisted of two almost equally powerful lines,[84] a strong alignment that enabled the Swedish army to attack over a period of 6 hours. Four brigades, and one musketeer squadron in reserve, with a total of 6,170 infantrymen and 16 to 20 regimental guns formed the centre's first line, in theory under command of *Generalmajor* Nils Brahe Greve till Visingborg.[85] It seems that the wing commanders, Gustav II Adolph and Bernhard von Weimar, extended their command over the two centre brigades adjacent to their wings, and also thus effectively commanded the centre's first line.[86] The brigades were not deployed randomly. As Brahe had no cavalry reserve at his disposal, the two centre brigades, the Yellow and the Old Blue, had substantially more pikemen than any other brigade. It was hoped that this would enable them to resist any charge of the Imperial, while the two outer brigades, the Swedish and Green, had fewer pikemen and could have been supported by cavalry from the wings. As it turned out pikemen were not a substitute for a cavalry reserve and of all the Swedish army, the Yellow and Old Blue Brigades suffered the most damage from the combined Imperial infantry-cavalry counter-attack.

Similarly, the centre's second line, commanded by *Generalmajor* Dodo von Innhausen und zu Knyphausen,[87] was formed by four brigades, with one cavalry squadron in reserve, to a strength of 6,512 infantry and 300 cavalry. It is not entirely certain if Knyphausen also had control over the second line wings[88] of six cavalry squadrons each. These cavalry were probably under their

Lützen, p.23, rem. 15). Monro very likely misunderstood a report, probably from Leslie himself. It is almost certain that the Scots charged the battery as part of the Green Brigade, which would have been short of one squadron otherwise. The Scots were in close proximity to the left wing cavalry.

84 This book follows Brzezinski's (*Lützen*, pp.19–23 and 43–49) results, which is largely based on Watts, *Swedish Intelligencer*, vol. 3, pp.128–129 and Gottfried, *Inventarium Sueciae*, pp.27–28 with the copperplate from van Hulsen, copied by Abelinum, *Theatrum Europaeum*, pp.751–752 with the copperplate from Merian, Anonymous, *Wahrhaftige Beschreibung*, Anonymous, *Glaubwürdiger Bericht* and Chemnitz, *Geschichte*, pp.463–464. Lack of information from eyewitnesses prevents verification at the present time.

85 Only confirmed through secondary sources from Chemnitz, *Geschichte*, p.464, Watts, *Swedish Intelligencer*, 129, Abelinum, *Theatrum Europaeum*, p.746 and Khevenhiller, *Annales Ferdinandei*, p.189, who copied the *Relation from 1633* (Droysen, 'Gedruckte Relationen', p.29).

86 The two left brigades, Green and Old Blue, followed the left wing (Fleetwood, Letter, p.7). See also Brzezinski, *Lützen*, p.47.

87 Fleetwood, Letter, p.6, Abelinum, *Theatrum Europaeum*, p.746, Chemnitz, *Geschichte*, p.464, Khevenhiller, *Annales Ferdinandei*, p.189, *Relation from 1633* (Droysen, 'Gedruckte Relationen', p.29).

88 Suggested by Brzezinski, *Lützen*, p.48 according to Watts, *Swedish Intelligencer*, vol. 3, p.132.

local commanders, *Oberst* Ernst von Sachsen-Weimar on the left with 1,430 men, and *Oberst* Claus Conrad Zorn von Bulach with 1,080 on the right.[89]

Six cavalry squadrons with five musketeer companies interlined, with a total strength approximately 1,550 cavalrymen, 423 musketeers and 10 regimental guns, formed the left wing's first line under *Generalleutnant* Bernhard von Sachsen-Weimar[90] with *Oberst* Hans Abraham *Graf* von Gersdorf in field command of the musketeers.[91]

The first line right wing was under King Gustav II Adolph[92], probably with *Överste* Torsten Stalhandske as second in command.[93] This wing consisted of seven squadrons, with six musketeer companies interlined between the cavalry squadrons commanded by *Oberst* Caspar *Graf* von Eberstein.[94] The total strength was 1,850 cavalrymen, 507 musketeers, 12 regimental guns and probably 30 mounted riflemen of the *djurskyttar* company.

With a total of 2,930 horse, 507 foot and 12 regimental guns, the right wing was as strong as the left with a total of 2,980 horse, 423 foot and 10 regimental guns. Gustav II Adolph did not concentrate his forces on one wing and the troop quality was equally high for both wings, with the best units in the first line.[95] The Flossgraben and its narrow bridges most likely delayed the 20 Swedish heavy artillery pieces as, according to Vitzthum/ Berlepsch, Gustav II Adolph opened the battle with only three 24-pounders, probably deployed between the two central brigades.

The deployment of the Swedish army was restricted to a front less than 2,600 metres wide by the Mühlgraben and Lützen to the west and the Flossgraben in the east. The space was barely enough to deploy the army in two lines, if the Swedish cavalry was deployed four ranks deep and the brigades still served with reserve musketeers. If the wings touched the Mühlgraben and the Flossgraben, this linear distance would have left a gap of not much more than 60m between the brigades. A gap this size would have been sufficient space to bring forward reserves or let retreating squadrons through, but not for deploying an entire brigade into the line as

89 Only mentioned by Watts, *Swedish Intelligencer*, vol. 3, p.129.

90 Fleetwood, Letter, p.6, PRO: SP81/39: London: Dalbier, *Lutzen*, p.252 and almost all secondary sources except Hallenus (Mankell, *Arkiv* vol. II, p.662), who incorrectly gave Brahe command of the left wing, and Leubelfing (Murr, *Beyträge*, p.122), who has the entire Swedish command structure completely wrong.

91 Watts, *Swedish Intelligencer*, vol. 3, p.129.

92 Confirmed by all sources except for the account of Leubelfing (see above).

93 Based only on an obscure story of The King personally giving command to Stalhandske at the beginning of the battle (Watts, *Swedish Intelligencer*, vol. 3, p.134; see also Brzezinski, *Lützen*, p.21). Certainly incorrect is Khevenhiller's (*Annales Ferdinandei*, p.191) statement that Fältmarskalk Horn, who took no part in the battle, was second in command of the right wing.

94 Watts, *Swedish Intelligencer*, vol. 3, p.129.

95 A quantitative or qualitative concentration of forces on the right wing is sometimes suggested by historians (Doughty and Gruber, *Warfare in the Western World*, p.25, Brzezinski, *Lützen*, p.53, Seidler, *Untersuchungen*, p.48, Deuticke, *Lützen*, p.70).

has often been suggested.[96] The limited space on the Lützen battlefield is also support for the idea that the Swedish brigades were deployed with reserve musketeers. The baggage train was likely left south of the Flossgraben near Meuchen, where during the battle Croats threatened its capture.[97]

In comparison to Breitenfeld in 1631, where the ratio of first to second lines was 2:1 on the wings and 4:3 in the centre, the Swedish second line at Lützen was much stronger. This strength might have been at least partially the result of the limited space available on the battlefield. Regardless of whether it was planned or not, such a strong and dense reserve needed to be committed as early as possible to prevent both lines from being beaten independently, or the second line from being put to flight because of a routed first line retreating through it. Although there is no historical evidence, it is likely that Gustav II Adolph's tactics were based on the early commitment of the second line. This assumption plays a crucial role in the interpretation of the early stages of the battle.[†]

Tables

Table 17: Trauttmansdorff's list

Trauttmansdorff's list, without Pappenheim's force	Author's notes
A Pertoldt von Waldstein und Alt-Sachsen B Coloredo und Chiesa	
C Grana und Fridrich Breiner	Infantry first line centre
D Alt-Preuner E Comargo	
F Baden G Jung-Breiner	Infantry second line centre
H Comandirte fändl	Infantry reserve centre
J Holckhe K Terzka und des Four L Haagen M Droost	Cavalry right wing

96 Monro (*His Expedition*, part II, p.64) clearly stated that at Breitenfeld the spaces between brigades were large enough to move a cavalry squadron forward, for which a space of 60 metres would be sufficient. A copperplate showing the Battle of Pfaffenhofen, 10 August 1633, actually shows a cavalry squadron filling the space between two brigades (Brzezinski, Hook, *Die Armee Gustav Adolfs*, p.83). It is unclear why Watts, *Swedish Intelligencer*, vol. 3, p.130 believed that this space was large enough to move another brigade between them. This would have meant a space of 120 metres to 150 m, which would have exposed the brigades to flank attacks and the space was not available between Lützen and the Flossgraben. Note: the spacing between Imperial infantry squadrons seem to have been similar to the spacing between Swedish brigades and were very likely common Thirty Years' War practice.

97 According to Swedish HQ (Söltl, *Religionskriege*, p.347). See also Brzezinski, *Lützen*, p.49.

N Breda O Westpfalen P Tontinelli	Cavalry second line reserve
Q Isolani	Cavalry left wing screen
R Göz S Piccolomini V Loyers und Lohe	Cavalry left wing
Y Westromb X Gouschier	Cavalry wing reserve

7

The Battle

Archaeology provides a substantial and valuable addition to the historical sources, but also makes an evaluation of the battle's events even more complicated. Therefore, individual episodes of the battle are discussed below in chronological order; first according to historical sources, and then following archaeological sources. Both sources are then combined to try to reconcile and reconstruct the events. Some important and complex incidents, such as the movement of the Old Blue Brigade, are discussed in several different sections because of this complexity.

The Swedish Approach

The 'Lützen fog'

Most historians believe, based mainly on secondary sources, that fog influenced the battle decisively, by delaying the battle in the morning and around midday concealing the Imperial or Swedish rout.[1] This fog, into which the Swedish King disappeared not to be seen alive again, entered legend as the 'Lützen fog', and is still a local expression for thick fog in autumn.

This fog is a local meteorological phenomenon caused by high humidity. It appears on the plain of Lützen most commonly in November and was observed by the author while coming from Leipzig on a clear day and encountering fog 5 to 7 km from Lützen. Although this is additional evidence, the historical sources and even the eyewitness accounts are inconsistent about the nature and duration of this fog during the battle.

Only two eyewitnesses, Dalbier and the Swedish HQ, reported fog in the morning, but only after it first appeared to be a clear day. According to

1 Deuticke, *Lützen*, pp.68 and 73, Seidler, *Untersuchungen*, pp.44 and 52, Wedgwood, *Der Dreissigjährige Krieg*, p.324, Roberts, *Gustavus Adolphus. A History of Sweden*, p.767, Diwald, *Wallenstein*, p.498, Doughty and Gruber, *Warfare in the Western World*, p.25, Englund, *Die Verwüstung Deutschlands*, p.130, Wolke, 'Die Schlacht bei Lützen', pp.64–65, Neuhold, *Der Dreissigjährige Krieg*, pp.98–99. Although Brzezinski, *Lützen*, pp.43 and 74 suggested fog in the early morning, he had some doubt about returning fog in the afternoon.

Dalbier it lasted until 9:00 a.m., but returned at 10:30 a.m. This contradicts Fleetwood's account, who stated that there was a clear day until 10:00 a.m., just when the battle began, while Diodati and Fabricius reported fog around midday. If the fog was important to the battle as is often claimed, it is unlikely that 13 eyewitnesses just forgot to mention any fog at all![†]

† See PDF download, Plate 19: Typical morning haze on the Lützen battlefield

Despite the differences, all eyewitnesses agree there was no fog at dawn and it is highly unlikely that Gustav II Adolph would have dared to try moving his army in thick fog, or before dawn, without intelligence about an enemy who knew and controlled the terrain with their light cavalry.[2]

Fleetwood, in particular, mentioned no delay of the Swedish army by fog in the early morning 16 November: 'The six of November the Kinge at break of the day marched his army…'[3] and Vitzthum/Berlepsch: 'The other morning, the 6th as soon as it was dawn, one had started to move against the enemy …'[4]

Generally, it seems unlikely that a fog appeared after a clear morning. It is worth noting that this did not happen once during the five years of the Lützen archaeological project, despite many foggy days. There was either fog already in the early morning or there was no fog the whole day, but fog never appeared once the sun was up and fog never reappeared once it was gone.

The most likely scenario is that there was no fog but that there was haze in the morning, something not thought worth mentioning by the eyewitnesses. The first firing and skirmishing, followed by Imperial artillery fire, began long before the battle proper started. The high humidity of the Lützen plain would have caused black powder smoke to remain along the battle line, especially if there was no wind.[5] Then the Imperial forces set Lützen on fire.

A small fire was observed by the author on a calm and hazy November day, when a farmer burnt leaves in his garden. This little fire soon covered a large part of the battlefield with a smoky film – a burning Lützen would have created a massive fire. Very soon after this fire broke out in Lützen, the battle started and the increasing smoke of musket and artillery fire, added to the smoke from the burning town, mixed with the haze and gave the impression of fog building up during the morning, reducing the visibility severely. Due to the unusual circumstances of a combination of high humidity, haze, black powder smoke in a static battle and smoke from a burning town, visibility was reduced more than usual in a battle; the eyewitnesses referred to it as 'fog' or 'mist'.[6] That would also explain the different times given by eyewitnesses about the returning and disappearing fog.

2 Suggested by Seidler, *Untersuchungen*, p.44.

3 Fleetwood, Letter, p.6.

4 Glafey, *De Gladio*, p.12.

5 Lawrence E. Babits, *A Devil of a Whipping: The Battle of Cowpens, Chapel Hill* (Chapel Hill: University of North Carolina Press, 1998), p.80.

6 Brzezinski, *Lützen*, p.52.

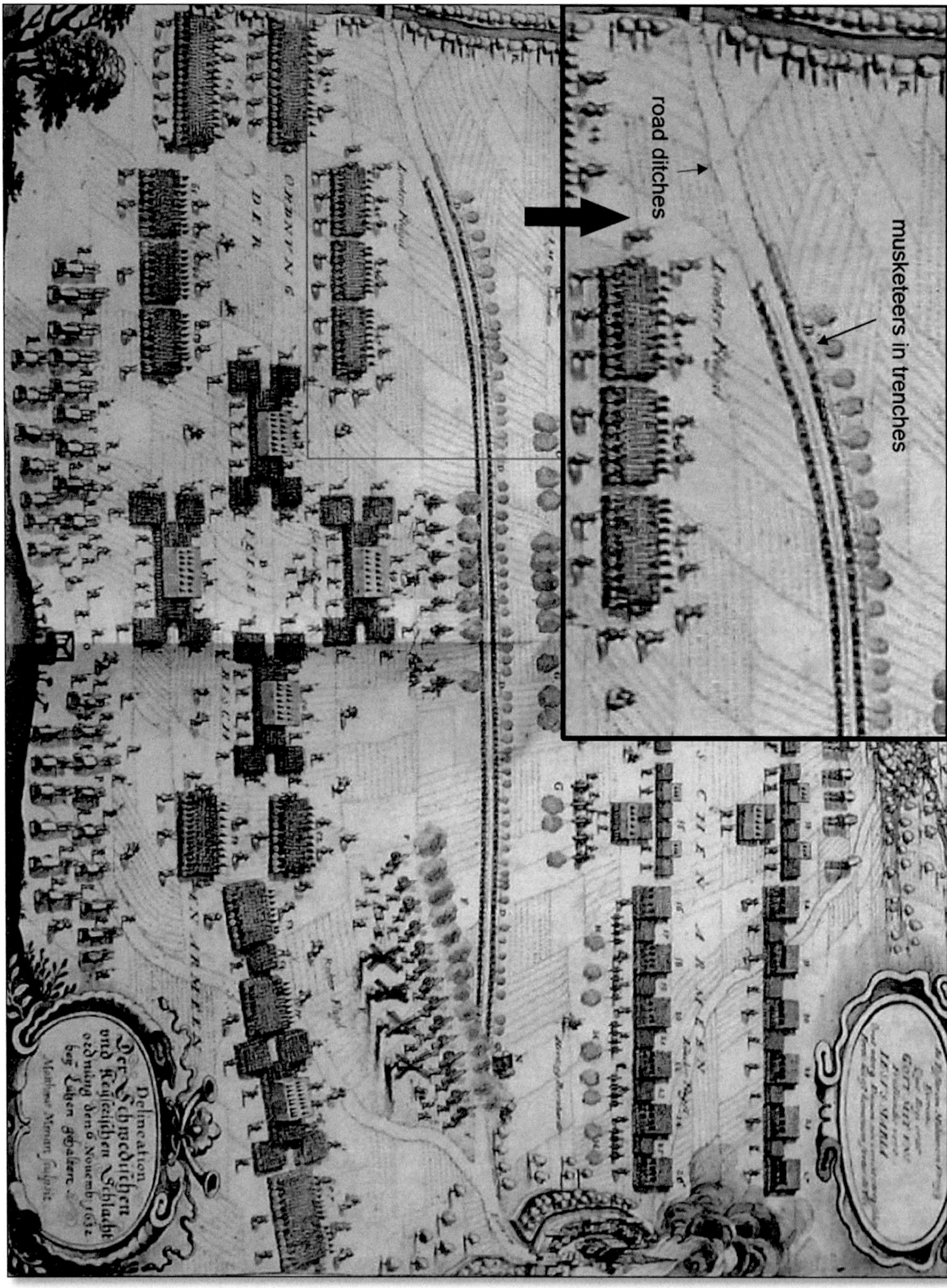

Van Hulsen's most copied copperplate showing a double trench system.

Detail of Merian's copperplate from *Theatrum Europaeum* following van Hulsen's plan. It shows the Swedish right wing crossing the trenches after heavy fighting.

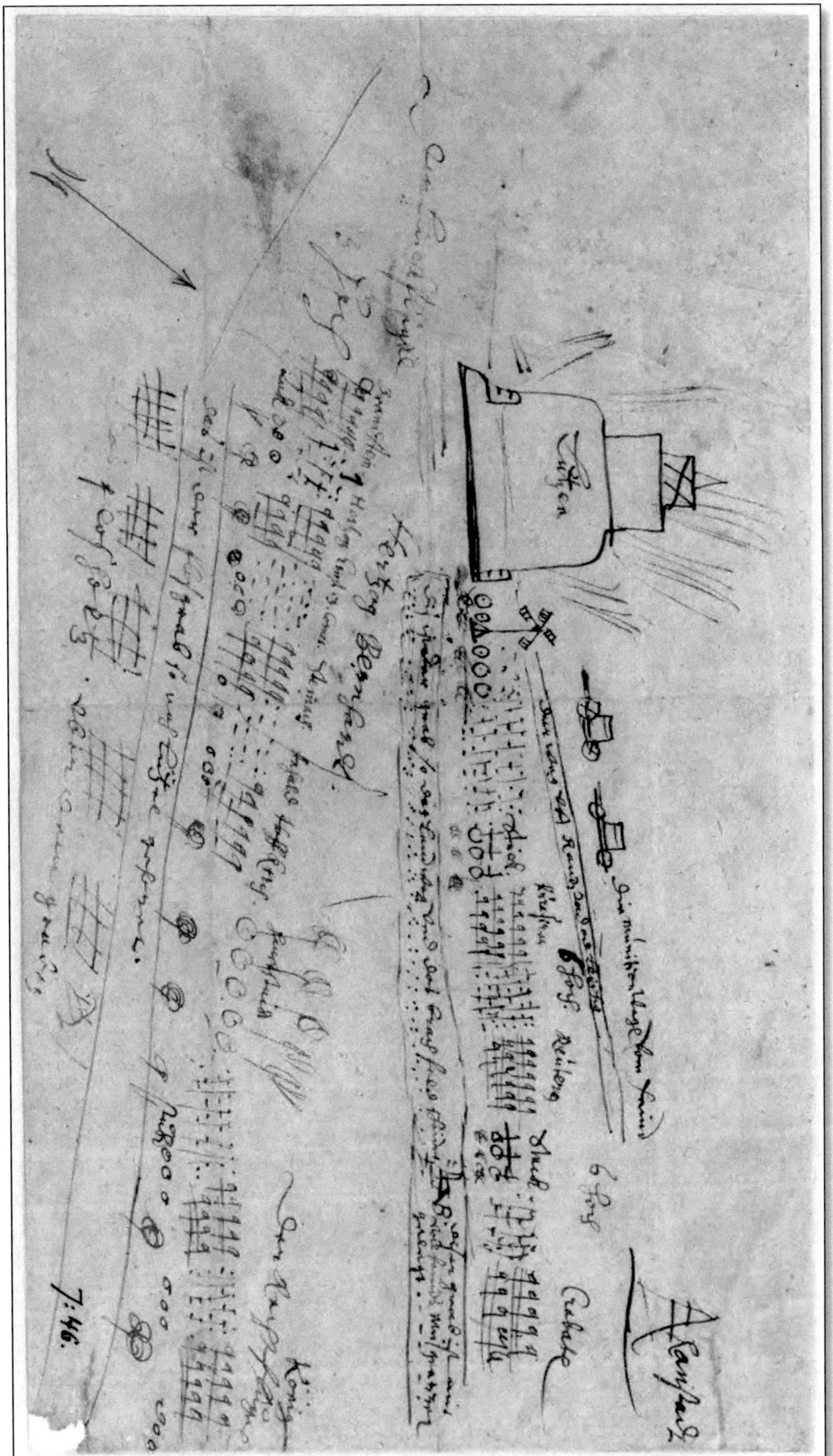

Map of the battle of Lützen, by an unknown Swedish officer participant of the battle. (Krigsarkivet)

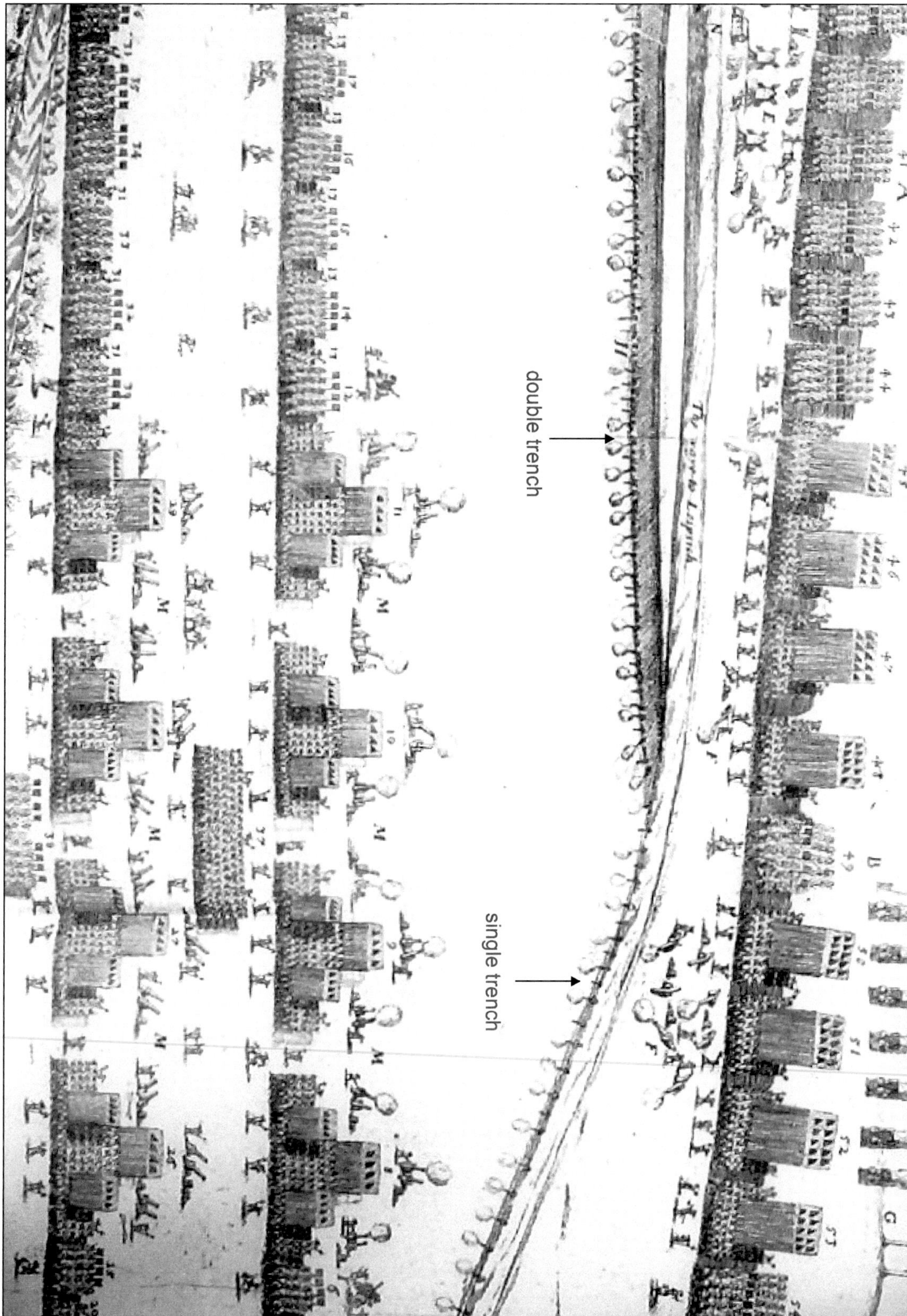

Copperplate from William Watts' *Swedish Intelligencer*.

The first account mentioning an actual delay of the Swedish advance caused by fog in the morning was the *Relation II from Erfurt*, which unfortunately was copied by the *Relation from 1633*, *Inventarium Sueciae*, with its great influence on other sources, Chemnitz and Khevenhiller and it still has a great influence on modern research. However, even in the secondary sources a clear morning is mentioned by the *Declaration from 1633*.

First Skirmishes

Marching 23 km along the Via Regia from Naumburg on 15 November, the Swedish army was delayed at the Rippach by Imperial Croats and Dragoons until nightfall. They camped in full battle order not far from the eastern bank of the stream and only 5 km from the Imperial army's camp at Lützen.[7] Vitzthum/Berlepsch reported that they saw Imperial army watch fires in several villages during the night.[8] As Zöllschen, Kaya and Meuchen cannot be seen from the Swedish camp, the only reasonable explanation is that there were still outposts or scouting parties in Bothfeld and Röcken less than 2 km away, creating a tense situation for the Swedish–German army. This tension would also seem to be the reason why the Swedish army camped in battle order. Well protected against a Swedish surprise attack behind Lützen, Mühlgraben and Flossgraben, Wallenstein sent for Pappenheim and any other forces he could to gather at Lützen after he had declared that 'he would rather die than retreat one foot.'[9]

Reports about the Swedish approach towards Lützen on the morning of 16 November are vague, sparse and largely from non-eyewitnesses. Explaining the Swedish approach is the key to understanding the delay, which proved so fateful for Gustav II Adolph and it seems necessary to understand the events from what little was reported.

After a cold November night on an open plain with probably not much more than a blanket – most of the baggage train had been left in Naumburg to allow faster movement for a surprise attack – the Swedish army was set to march at first light, about 7:00 a.m.,[10] on a hazy and calm day. Knowing that Pappenheim was on his way to reinforce the Imperial army, Gustav II Adolph was in a hurry. With the Imperial army nearby, the Swedish army certainly moved in the battle order in which they had camped, two columns

7 The skirmish at the Rippach is not an issue here. See Brzezinski, *Lützen*, pp.34–38. Fleetwood, Letter, p.6 gave a distance of one English mile between Lützen and the Swedish camp, but that would have meant marching another 4 km in the dark night against an enemy, who was familiar with the terrain. More reliable is Holk's account (Wittrock, 'Fyra relationer', p.308), giving a distance of 'four canon shots', which translates roughly as 6 km.

8 Glafey, *De Gladio*, p.12.

9 Holk (Wittrock, 'Fyra relationer', p.308).

10 At 'daybreak' according to Vitzthum/Berlepsch (Glafey, *De Gladio*, p.12), Fleetwood, Letter, p.6 and Dalbier, *Lutzen*, p.251. All time in this book is given according to our modern standard European time. 7:00 a.m. is the first and 5:00 p.m. the last light on 16 November at Lützen. Time given in historical sources for single events sometimes vary substantially, but it was not possible to establish if both armies used the same or a different time at Lützen.

– the eventual two battle lines – 2 km to 2.3 km long. The right wing was in front, which may have caused some wheeling in the morning, assuming that they camped in battle order, spread across the road to prevent an Imperial surprise attack.

The Imperial scouting parties at Röcken and Bothfeld did not try to resist the advancing Swedes and retreated behind the Flossgraben. The Swedish army advanced 5 km along the Via Regia towards Lützen, blinded by the rising sun at 7:30 a.m., musket fire from the walls of Lützen stopped the advance guard around 8:00 a.m.[11] The approach towards Lützen and the musket fire can be seen as a hint that Gustav II Adolph was not completely familiar with the situation at that time. It took Gustav II Adolph probably another half an hour before he made the decision to move south around Lützen, based on reconnaissance reports that the Mühlgraben to the north had boggy river banks, 'uncomfortable places', and no bridges.[12]

Tontinelli and Bredau had only arrived that morning[13], and they were assigned as a reserve behind the centre to rest from their overnight march. Wallenstein however, still had to wait for the rest of Pappenheim's troops and had to play for time. According to Vitzthum/Berlepsch: 'Four troops of cavalrymen have shown themselves on the side of the city'[14] after the Swedes were fired at from the city walls.

The Swedish HQ reported that when the Swedish army advanced towards Lützen: 'the Imperials had shown and presented themselves there, but did not fire.'[15]

Those troops were very likely Isolani's four Croat regiments deployed as a skirmisher screen at the Flossgraben and Mühlgraben to secure the bridges and delay the Swedish advance.[16] This disposition would agree with Gallas' report[17] of Croats skirmishing during the Swedish advance, which is confirmed by the *Relation from 1633* that reported skirmishes all morning. [18] †

The Croats had already suffered some losses at Rippach on 15 November[19] and were not intended to hold the bridges for any length of time. There were

† See PDF download, Plate 20: Imperial and Swedish camps on the evening of 15 November and Swedish approach in the next morning

11 Vitzthum/Berlepsch (Glafey, *De Gladio*, p.13). Fleetwood, Letter, p.7 reported the first shot at 8:00 a.m. Hallenus (Mankell, *Arkiv* vol. II, p.662) mentioned the Swedish arrival at Lützen at 9:00 a.m., which seems too late in the morning.

12 Mentioned first by the *Relation from 1633* (Droysen, 'Gedruckte Relationen', p.30), copied by Abelinum, *Theatrum Europaeum*, p.748 and Khevenhiller, *Annales Ferdinandei*, p.190.

13 According to Watts, *Swedish Intelligencer*, vol. 3, p.124 'some horse that were Quartered very farre off, being not able to reach up, till 10 a clocke next morning', which probably could have been seen and reported by his eyewitnesses.

14 Glafey, *De Gladio*, p.13.

15 Söltl, *Religionskriege*, p.346.

16 Deuticke, *Lützen*, p.68, Seidler, *Untersuchungen*, p.40, Brzezinski, *Lützen*, p.45.

17 Förster, *Wallenstein's Prozess*, p.95.

18 Droysen, 'Gedruckte Relationen', p.30, copied by Abelinum, *Theatrum Europaeum*, p.749, Chemnitz, *Geschichte*, p.464 and Khevenhiller, *Annales Ferdinandei*, p.190, and was possibly also used by Priorato, *Historia dell Guerra*, p.120.

19 Brzezinski, *Lützen*, p.37.

only two bridges, and possibly a third further south near Kaya, at the first crossing and two at the second, which might have enabled them to delay the Swedish advance for a short while. After clearing the bridges, Gustav II Adolph had to build makeshift bridges from float-wood stored near the Flossgraben, to bring his 18,000 men over as quickly as possible without making the infantry suffer from the cold water by having to wade across.[20] It was this crossing and skirmishing, and not a fog, which was responsible for the considerable delay in the start of the main action and Gustav II Adolph had to break up his battle formation to cross the Flossgraben and then reform it again on the far side.[21]

Archaeology Sources (1): See PDF download

Swedish Deployment and Imperial Artillery Fire

Historical Sources

Some historians have believed that the fog prevented artillery fire before the battle.[22] In fact, it is almost certain that artillery fire was a key factor in actually creating the 'fog' in the first place. In addition, early artillery fire is also reported by eyewitnesses. According to Fleetwood[23] and Münchhausen,[24] it lasted 'a while' before the main battle started.

The artillery fire is described best by Vitzthum/Berlepsch, who reported that:

> ... one [the Swedes] had started to fire several salvos with three half-cannons, which the enemy answered with a battery, which he had cast up [the fortification] at the windmills near the town, and which he continued with the other batteries, he had at the side of Scheiditz [Skölzig] ... and there was heavy firing with pieces but one hour on both sides...'[25]

According to Vitzthum/Berlepsch the Swedes opened fire with only three 24-pounders, almost certainly because the other pieces were delayed crossing the Flossgraben. The commander of the Imperial artillery, *Generalfeldzeugmeister* Breuner, answered first with the windmill battery and later with the smaller left wing battery. This artillery fire went on for an hour. The sequence of fire is an important consideration, because the line of sight from the small battery was blocked by Hill 126 at a distance of about 1,200 metres, suggesting that the

20 Hülshorst (Wittrock, 'Fyra relationer', p.302) reported that the Swedish army could not advance in battle order because of the 'narrow passage', probably meaning the difficulties at the Flossgraben.

21 Brzezinski, *Lützen*, pp.46–47.

22 In particular Seidler, *Untersuchungen*, pp.44–45 and Guthrie, *Battles of the Thirty Years' War*, p.208.

23 Fleetwood, Letter, p.7.

24 Wittrock, 'Fyra relationer', p.304.

25 Glafey, *De Gladio*, p.13.

windmill battery started firing at a greater range and the small battery joined the firing when the Swedes came into sight.

In contradiction to Vitzthum/Berlepsch, the Swedish HQ reported that the Imperial artillery was the first to open fire,[26] which is supported by secondary sources, though of lesser reliability.[27] In particular, Hülshorst[28] and Hallenus[29] mentioned that the Imperial artillery fired during the Swedish deployment. Many eyewitnesses including Diodati and Holk[30] did not report any pre-battle artillery fire, probably because it was such common practice in the early stages of any battle and one that inflicted few casualties, although their lack of reporting of it cannot be seen as evidence that there was no such fire.

Only two secondary sources explicitly state that there was no extensive pre-battle artillery fire. According to the *Relation II from Erfurt*, the Swedish Blue and Yellow Regiments advanced against the trenches, while supported by five rounds from large pieces, which was answered by some 80 rounds.[31] This story can be found changed, but certainly based on the *Relation II from Erfurt*, in the *Declaration from 1633*, which states that the Swedish army fired one round with five 24-pounders and advanced against the trenches, while the Imperial artillery held their fire to acquire better targets.[32] This whole episode is fictitious; there were no trenches, the Blue and Yellow Regiments did not advance first, and four eyewitness and several secondary sources report the pre-battle artillery exchange.

Nevertheless, some historians have given priority to the two second-hand accounts over the eyewitness accounts.[33] Seidler also based his argument on the Swedish HQ account that: 'the Imperials had shown and presented themselves there [Lützen], but did not fire,'[34] which he interpreted as meaning there was no artillery fire, although the account made clear that this event did not occur during the Swedish deployment but earlier during the Swedish advance from Rippach to Lützen.[35]

Although the reports about early artillery fire are not entirely conclusive, there are some facts to consider:

26 Söltl, *Religionskriege*, p.346.

27 Relation from 1632 (Droysen, 'Gedruckte Relationen', pp.7–8) and *Relation from 1633* (Droysen, 'Gedruckte Relationen', p.29), copied by Khevenhiller, *Annales Ferdinandei*, p.189. An early artillery fire, without specifying who fired first, is mentioned by Gottfried, *Inventarium Sueciae*, p.25 (for two hours), copied by Monro, *His Expedition*, part II, pp.163–164, Anonymous, *Wahrhaftige Beschreibung*, Anonymous, *Glaubwürdiger Bericht*, and used by Burgus, *Mars Sveco-Germanicus*, p.321 (one and a half hours) and Abelinum, *Theatrum Europaeum*, p.749 (some time).

28 Wittrock, 'Fyra relationer', p.302.

29 Mankell, *Arkiv*, vol. II, p.662.

30 Fiedler, 'Diodatis Bericht', p.562, Wittrock, 'Fyra relationer', p.308.

31 Droysen, 'Gedruckte Relationen', p.18.

32 Droysen, 'Gedruckte Relationen', p.40.

33 Seidler, *Untersuchungen*, p.45, Brzezinski, *Lützen*, pp.49–50.

34 Söltl, *Religionskriege*, p.346.

35 Seidler, *Untersuchungen*, p.45.

1. The Imperial heavy artillery was already deployed in well-chosen positions, which certainly would have enabled them to fire first if they wished to do so.[36]

2. The main task of heavy artillery in a field engagement was to deliver long range harassing fire either to keep the enemy at distance or force him to quick action, which makes it likely that the Imperial artillery opened fire as soon as the Swedish army came into range. In addition, heavy artillery had a low rate of fire and there was no point in holding fire until the enemy was at close range.

3. Gustav II Adolph could not afford to lose more time with an artillery duel and very likely advanced as soon as his army was deployed.[37]

Under these circumstances, all early Swedish artillery fire was certainly covering fire directed against the Imperial artillery positions while the Swedish army reformed after passing the choke points over the canal.[38] This interpretation is supported by Vitzthum/Berlepsch's statement that only three Swedish pieces opened fire, although they had 20 but which were delayed at the Flossgraben.

The Events

It took the Swedish advance guard until at least 9:00 a.m. to arrive on the battlefield, so they now had the sun at their back.[39] The Imperial windmill battery had a good view of the Swedish army crossing the Flossgraben some 1,750 metres away and a clear line of fire after the Croats had retreated to their designated place in front of the wings. To avoid clustering at the crossing and to be able to form a line between Mühlgraben and Flossgraben, the Swedish army had to advance slowly but steadily as new units arrived on the northern side of the Flossgraben.

Between approximately 9:00 and 9:30[40] as the Swedish lines were slowly forming and advancing, the 12-pounders and 24-pounders at the windmills opened fire with round shot at a distance of less than 1,500 metres.[41] At this range, it was ineffective but it would have unnerved the forming Swedish soldiers, who were still waiting for their own artillery to arrive and return fire.

36 Droysen, 'Lützen', p.119.

37 Dalbier, *Lutzen*, p.251. See also Seidler, *Untersuchungen*, p.44.

38 Firing at the enemy's artillery positions was probably common practice in the Thirty Years' War. The Swedish army used this tactic successfully in the Battle of Rain on the Lech 15 April 1632 (Brzezinski, Hook, *Die Armee Gustav Adolfs*, p.82).

39 According to Pentz (Fiedler, 'Diodatis Bericht', p.570) the whole army arrived at 9:00 a.m. on the battlefield, but that seems too early.

40 There is no reliable information about when the firing started.

41 A maximum firing range for 24- and 12-pounders is estimated at 1,500–2,000 metres, for 6-pounders at 1,150–1,600 metres (Engerisser, *Von Kronach nach Nördlingen*, p.586).

When they reached Hill 126 between 9:30 and 10:00 in the morning, some 1,200 metres south of the Imperial battle line, they came into sight of the small Imperial battery, which now opened fire. Meanwhile, the Swedes had deployed three 24-pounders at a distance of less than 1,000 metres and returned fire, which was even more ineffective than the Imperial fire.[42]

Individual units came over the Flossgraben, reformed under artillery fire, and joined the slowly advancing and growing army, giving the impression of an attack. Diodati reported that the Swedes seemed to be trying to attack the Imperial left and then their right wing, and it must have looked that way to an observer from the Imperial battle line.[43] Fleetwood had also seen that:

'The enimie at first seemed to advance, which soe soone as the Kinge perceaved, he gave presently orders to advance; upon which the enimies they retyred again behinde the dike.'[44]

Which suggests that the Imperial army was not entirely deployed when the Swedish army arrived and that there was a lot of movement on both sides prior to battle?

Although there is no such suggestion in any account, the Imperial artillery fire, regardless of how ineffective it was, might have been at least partially responsible for delaying the Swedish deployment and thus the beginning of the battle; it might also have had a negative influence on morale,[45] at least for the less experienced Swedish-German soldiers.

General Ludwig Johann Hector, *Graf* von Isolani.

The Beginning of the Battle

The time given by eyewitnesses and secondary sources alike for the onset of battle varies between 8:00 and 12:00 a.m. Except for the general observation that time was different in almost every town, not all participants had a clock or watch at hand and sense of time is very personal; this discrepancy can also be explained by the personal opinion of the observer as to what event marks the beginning of the battle; it might have been the first shots from the city walls, the skirmishing, the initial Imperial artillery fire, the final Swedish deployment, their advance, or the first combat at the Imperial battle line.

42 According to Watts, *Swedish Intelligencer*, vol. 3, p.133 the Imperial artillery had the advantage of being deployed already and caused more damage than the Swedish artillery.

43 Fiedler, 'Diodatis Bericht', p.562. Copied by Spanish Relation (Watts, *Swedish Intelligencer*, vol. 3, p.160) and Khevenhiller, *Annales Ferdinandei*, p.191. A manoeuvring Swedish army is also reported by Poyntz, *The Relation*, p.72. However, it is unlikely that Gustavus Adolphus, after being substantially delayed, wasted any time with feint attacks, as it is sometimes claimed (Russel F. Weigley, *Auf der Suche nach der Entscheidungsschlacht. Lützen, 16. November 1632*, in Stieg Förster, Markus Pöhlmann, Dierk Walter (eds), *Schlachten der Weltgeschichte. Von Salamis bis Sinai* (München, dtv 2003) p.140, Wedgwood, *Der Dreissigjährige Krieg*, p.326, Deuticke, Lützen, p.69).

44 Fleetwood, Letter, p.6.

45 Sennewald, *Das kursächsische Heer*, p.168.

Överste Torsten Stalhandske.

Two eyewitnesses referred to this interpretive conundrum when they reported: 'about 8 of the clock, first shott his loouseninge … and the battaile ioyned aboute tenn of the clock' (Fleetwood)[46] and that 'the first salvo was fired at 11:00 a.m.' (Holk).[47]

The 'first shot' might indicate musket fire from the city walls or the first Imperial artillery fire. The 'first salvo' is more likely to mean the first volley of musketry after the Swedish army had already advanced, than it is to mean the first artillery fire. 'the battaile ioyned aboute tenn of the clock' probably means that the Swedish army had deployed and was ready to advance. A beginning at 11:00 a.m.[48] better explains the sequence of events of Pappenheim's arrival and the death of Gustav II Adolph around midday than an earlier beginning would. All this suggests that the Swedish army finished their deployment around 10:30 and was ready to advance, 1.5 to 2 hours later than they would have done if they could have moved in a straight line, rather than making a detour south to cross over the bridges.

As soon as the Swedish army had deployed, Wallenstein ordered Lützen set on fire to avoid the town being taken by the enemy and posing a threat to his right wing. The musketeer garrison, which had fired on the Swedish advance guard from the city walls in the morning, was redeployed into the town's gardens behind a mud wall. Two eyewitnesses, Fleetwood and the Swedish HQ,[49] as well as several secondary sources[50] report this incident. All agree that the fire in Lützen started just before battle.

Gustav II Adolph's plan of a surprise attack had utterly failed the day before at Rippach. Unable to make a quick move on the morning of 16 November, facing unexpected problems, he lost the opportunity to overwhelm the Imperial army before the arrival of Pappenheim's brigade. The distance from Rippach to Lützen is only 5 km, but being forced to make a detour to the south, it became an 8 or 9 km march through an area controlled by Croats, and delayed by the narrow but deep Flossgraben, where makeshift bridges had to be built. When the Swedish army finally arrived on the battlefield, they had to deploy under Imperial artillery fire.†

† See PDF download, Plate 21: Gustav II Adolph: First Swedish attack. Stalhandske's charge 10:30–11:00 a.m.

46 Fleetwood, Letter, p.7.

47 Wittrock, 'Fyra relationer', p.308.

48 11:00 a.m. is the accepted view of the beginning of the battle. See Deuticke, Lützen, p.69, Generalstaben, *Sveriges Krig*, p.430, Seidler, *Untersuchungen*, p.44 and Brzezinski, *Lützen*, p.52.

49 Fleetwood, Letter, p.7, Söltl, *Religionskriege*, p.346.

50 Hallenus (Mankell, *Arkiv*, vol. II, p.662), Relation II from Erfurt (Droysen, 'Gedruckte Relationen', p.19). The latter was copied by Gottfried, *Inventarium Sueciae*, p.25, which in turn was copied by Anonymous, *Wahrhaftige Beschreibung*, Anonymous, *Glaubwürdiger Bericht*, Monro, *His Expedition*, part II, p.163, Abelinum, *Theatrum Europaeum*, p.749 and Chemnitz, *Geschichte*, p.465.

Archaeology Sources (2): See PDF download

Historical Sources

When the Swedish army was deployed at around 10:30 a.m., Gustav II Adolph opened the battle with his right wing.[51] The first action of the battle is reported by Fleetwood:

> … the enimie had ordered the crabates to fall rounde about upon our rere, which the Kinge perceaving gave command to the ffynes [Finns] under the command of Statehomes [Stalhandske] to march upon them, which hee did diligentlie. And haveing eighte companies, hee charged them with fower companies, putting them to flighte; but, upon his retreateing (according to expectation) they charged him soe that they putt him to the worst, till being received by his fower companies (sett for the purpose) hee charged them soe sore that he soe rowted them that the whole day wee were noe more troubled with them.'[52]

Although Fleetwood is imprecise about when this incident occurred, combat between Finns and Croats is reported by the *Relation from 1633* to have occurred at 11:00 during the battle's earliest phases.[53] This is as expected since the Croats were primarily skirmishers and scouts rather than main line battle troops.

The Events

Rather than letting his whole battle line lose cohesion because of the Croat skirmisher screen, Gustav II Adolph sent *Överste* Torsten Stalhandske with two Finnish squadrons and one or two musketeer companies to drive them off. Even against 500 horsemen, 150 infantry and four regimental guns, the approximately 500 Croats did not give up without a fight and made a stand with one regiment positioned 100 metres north of the road, the other near the Leipzig Bridge, where one Croat regiment was possibly cornered and forced to retreat over the bridge.[54] Commanded by the experienced *General* Isolani, it seems unlikely that all three Croat regiments left the battlefield completely as Fleetwood claimed, which certainly would have been an issue during the court-martial at Prague. The more likely scenario is that Stalhandske chased them a good distance, but eventually returned to the battle, while the Croats were rallied somewhere safe and probably returned to the fight with Pappenheim's corps.[55] †

† See PDF download, Plate 22: 10:30–11:00 a.m.: Stalhandske's attack on the Imperial light cavalry screen.

51 It was not Bernhard's left wing that opened the battle, as Richelieu, *Mémoires*, p.258 suggested.

52 Fleetwood, Letter, p.7.

53 Droysen, 'Gedruckte Relationen', p.30. This combat is also reported by Burgus, *Mars Sveco-Germanicus*, p.322 and Khevenhiller, *Annales Ferdinandei*, p.191.

54 Croats have not disrupted their own line on the left wing, which Burgus, *Mars Sveco-Germanicus*, p.322 and Khevenhiller, *Annales Ferdinandei*, p.192 have confused with an event on the right (section 7.2.4).

55 It is a myth that Gustav II Adolph had ordered Stalhandske to charge the cuirassiers, as Watts, *Swedish Intelligencer*, vol. 3, p.134 claimed. The Finns were more light cavalry than the other

After Stalhandske cleared the way, 'Gustavus Adolphus did not lose any time'[56] and advanced at the head of his remaining five right wing cavalry squadrons – Smaland, Ostgöta, Uppland, Södermanland and Västgöta – and two infantry brigades, the Yellow and Swedish, from the centre, probably in echelon, as flank protection.

† See PDF download, Plate 23

Swedish Right Wing Advance, 10:45–11:15 a.m.†

Archaeology Sources (3): See PDF download

Historical Sources

The traditional view, based on secondary sources, is that the Swedish right wing basically advanced in a straight line to the front and, while the Swedish Brigade attacked the small Imperial battery first and then the Imperial infantry, the Swedish cavalry engaged the Imperial cavalry.[57]

This interpretation, however, is contradicted by Ottavio Piccolomini's account:

> … comincio una furiosa salua di moschettate da due Regimenti d'Infanteria et maniche de oschettieri che ogni squadrone de cavalleria conduceva et uno di quelli uenne à occupare un fosso è strada che era auanti li nostri squadroni et cominciando à passare quel fosso è strada si auicinauano à Noi. Io uedendo questo et hauendo tenuto il mio Regimento un quarto d'hora alle descritione di tutte le moschettate di due squadroni, doue mi ammazzorno infinite soldate et officiali, li andai ad inuestiri et ribbutai uno di essi di la dal fosso è strada…[58]

He reported that the battle began with a furious Swedish musket volley from two 'Regimenti d'Infanteria' and the interlined musketeer companies ('maniche de moschettieri', i.e. rabble of musketeers), after which 'one of those' – the demonstrative pronoun 'quelli' relates to 'Regimenti': 'crossed the road [Via Regia] in front of our squadron and approached us [Piccolomini's Regiment].' Piccolomini's Regiment then came under musket fire from two 'squadroni' for a quarter of an hour. The musketry killed many of his officers and men, so he decided to charge one of the opposing squadrons.

Swedish cavalry. As such they were deployed on the outer wing because of their higher mobility. If Gustav II Adolph wanted them to attack the cuirassiers, for which they were not suited, he would have deployed them on the inner wing.

56 Dalbier, *Lutzen*, p.251.

57 Generalstaben, *Sveriges Krig*, p.439, Seidler, *Untersuchungen*, p.47, Brzezinski, *Lützen*, p.55. Relation II from Erfurt (Droysen, 'Gedruckte Relationen', p.19), Burgus, *Mars Sveco-Germanicus*, p.321, Chemnitz, *Geschichte*, p.465, Khevenhiller, *Annales Ferdinandei*, p.191 and Gottfried, *Inventarium Sueciae*, p.25, copied by Anonymous, *Wahrhaftige Beschreibung*, Anonymous, *Glaubwürdiger Bericht*, Monro, *His Expedition*, part II, p.164 and Abelinum, *Theatrum Europaeum*, p.749.

58 Argang, 'Piccolominis bref', p.89.

Ottavio Piccolomini used three different terms to describe types of units; he explained adequately that the 'maniche de moschettieri' are the musketeer companies between the cavalry squadrons. The 'due Regimenti d'Infanteria' in this context means 'two infantry brigades', the Yellow and Swedish brigades, which he could see from his position. One of those units, which could have been only the Swedish Brigade on the right centre, occupied a ditch and a road, which is certainly the Via Regia, and by crossing it the brigade advanced towards Piccolomini's Regiment.

The following musket fire from two 'squadroni' in this context can only describe the squadrons of the Swedish Brigade and not the interlined musketeer companies, as Brzezinski suggested, for several reasons.[59] The musketeer companies are referred to as 'maniche de moschettieri' and there is no reason to believe that Ottavio Piccolomini switched terms. When he described the charge against one of the two 'squadroni', he did not mention any Swedish cavalry being involved and it seems highly unlikely that two Swedish interlined companies of 150 musketeers alone would have been able to pin down Piccolomini's 500 heavily armoured harquebusiers for 15 minutes on open ground and inflict heavy casualties. It is also highly unlikely that Piccolomini would advance 400 metres south to the Via Regia at the start of the battle, as that would have opened a huge gap in the Imperial battle line, and put his regiment in the line of fire of Swedish musketeers in the road ditches, an act that would also contradict his previous statement that the unit in question had already crossed the road.[60] Following the example of Diodati's Imperial infantry 'squadroni', who looked very similar to Swedish infantry squadrons, the two 'squadroni' in Piccolomini's account are very likely two Swedish Brigade squadrons that did not attack the Imperial artillery and infantry but engaged the Imperial cavalry instead.

This incident is reported slightly differently by Silvio Piccolomini:

> And it is certain that we can thank God and Holy Madonna for not all being dead, because basically we were standing a quarter hour at a distance of 20 paces from an infantry squadron, having the colour of this ditch, escaping miraculously and because of the cuirasses of proof, saving the lives of all those, who were spared.[61]

In contradiction to his uncle, Silvio mentioned only one squadron, which is very likely one from the Swedish Brigade, although this is uncertain, because he says in his account that the squadron had the colour of the ditch. No unit with brown colours or uniforms is known to have participated in the battle.

59 Brzezinski, *Lützen*, p.59.

60 Suggested by Brzezinski, *Lützen*, p.59. Silvio Piccolomini's statement (Anonymous, *Archivio*, p.240) that 'the General [Wallenstein] decided to accept battle and we advanced a little to a small ditch, and there we waited' refer to the entire Imperial army, specifically to the infantry, and not to Piccolomini's Regiment.

61 Anonymous, *Archivio*, p.242.

Combat between Swedish and Imperial cavalry. Detail from a portrait by Cornelis Visscher II (1629–1658), 1650. (Rijksmuseum)

'Winckel's Old Blue' and 'Eric Hand's New Blue Regiments' in Historical Sources

A short aside: There is one misconception in the historical sources concerning the New Swedish and the Old Blue brigades, which is deeply embedded in modern research and needs to be clarified. Diodati reported that the yellow casacks[62] ('casacche gialle') were attacked by infantry and the blue casacks ('casacche turchine') were attacked by the regiments Piccolomini and Götz.[63] He is the only Imperial eyewitness who was not speculating about enemy units, but reported what he saw of the uniform colours. The yellow casacks are clearly the Yellow Brigade, while the meaning of 'blue casacks' is unclear, but it was imprecisely translated by Fiedler as 'Blue Regiment'. Both the Old Blue Regiment, which formed the Blue Brigade, as well as Eric Hand's New Blue Regiment, which was operating as part of the Swedish Brigade, had blue uniforms and colours.[64]

Münchhausen, who fought in Comargo's Regiment near Götz and Piccolomini noted in his letter of 19 November that his unit destroyed 'three regiments, which remained in one', which is the description of a Swedish three squadron brigade, and they took 15 colours;[65] while he specified in his 6 December letter that his unit destroyed the Yellow and Old Blue Regiments,

62 A 'casack' (cassock) is a long coat similar in appearance to a sleeved tabard. Brzezinski calls it a 'mysterious garment', by which he means it appearance is uncertain (Brzezinski, *Die Armee Gustav Adolfs*, p.34).

63 Fiedler, 'Diodatis Bericht', p.563.

64 Brzezinski, Hook, *Die Armee Gustav Adolfs*, p.46.

65 Wittrock, 'Fyra relationer', p.305.

taking 14 colours from them.[66] The change between these two letters, only 17 days apart, is clear; in the first letter he stated he fought against one brigade, while in the second he fought two brigades, which are now described as the Yellow and Old Blue Brigades. However, Münchhausen could not have seen the Old Blue Regiment, because it advanced with the Swedish left wing against the windmills. It seems likely that Münchhausen confused the Old Blue with the New Blue, or Swedish, Brigade, which can also be seen in Gallas' account.[67]

That the 'Blue Regiment' in Imperial eyewitness accounts was in fact Eric Hand's New Blue Regiment of the Swedish Brigade becomes clear in Ottavio Piccolomini's account. He described how, after he had pursued one infantry squadron to the Via Regia, the 'Blue Regiment, the king's most vaunted (Regimento torchino [*sic*: turchino] il più stimato dal Re)' advanced against Götz's Regiment to his right. This event happened at the beginning of the battle when Piccolomini's and Götz's Regiments could not possibly have met the Old Blue Regiment. Furthermore, 'the king's most vaunted regiment' is more likely a description of a Swedish national infantry unit than it is of a German unit. Excepting the *Declaration from 1633*, most secondary sources, based on the *Inventarium Sueciae*, seem to have repeated this mistake by reporting that the Swedish, Yellow and Old Blue Brigades advanced together with the Swedish right wing.[68] This scenario is contradicted by results from the archaeological survey. Although eyewitness accounts are unclear about the Swedish right centre, not one explicitly reported that the Swedish Brigade attacked the Imperial battery and left centre.

The Events

While the Finns were very likely still chasing the Croats, five Swedish cavalry squadrons[69] crossed the Via Regia without any difficulties,[70] then wheeled around in a wide outflanking manoeuvre until they took Ranstädt in their rear.[71] They were followed by the Swedish Brigade as left flank protection.

The Yellow Brigade had a more difficult approach as they attacked the small Imperial battery frontally, and were probably being fired on by a

66 BHStA, 2424t194 f. 158: Münchhausen to Maximilian 6 December 1632.

67 Förster, *Wallenstein's Prozess*, p.95.

68 The Declaration from 1633 (Droysen, 'Gedruckte Relationen', p.40) reported the 'Blue Regiment' on the Swedish right centre, aware that it was the Swedish Brigade. It was Gottfried, *Inventarium Sueciae*, p.26, who seems to have confused the two Blue brigades first, reporting both incorrectly to have advanced against the Imperial left centre, which was copied by Anonymous, *Wahrhaftige Beschreibung*, Anonymous, *Glaubwürdiger Bericht*, Monro, *His Expedition*, part II, p.164, Abelinum, *Theatrum Europaeum*, p.750, Chemnitz, *Geschichte*, p.465, and from there entered modern publications. See also Generalstaben, *Sveriges Krig*, p.436.

69 According to Fleetwood, Letter, p.7 Gustav II Adolph attacked with four regiments. Although he reported four instead of five regiments, his statement seems to prove that the Finns were somewhere else at that time.

70 Fabricius (Wittrock, 'Fyra relationer', p.306), Fleetwood, Letter, p.7. However, the latter stated incorrectly that the King was shot at the road as there was no major combat there.

71 Vitzthum/Berlepsch (Glafey, *De Gladio*, p.13).

musketeer detachment of Comargo's Regiment from the road ditches.[72] This total force of 1,350 horse and 3,150 foot advanced 'in the most beautiful order.'[73] The right hand Regiment, Västgöta, had to cover 1,700 metres. For cavalry only, this manoeuvre could have been achieved in a short time, but the musketeer companies pulling regimental guns made for a slower advance, taking approximately 28 minutes.[74]

It is possible that the shift to the right was not deliberate, but resulted from the rightmost Swedish cavalry following the line of least resistance and simply moving too far; the rest had to follow to maintain the line. It seems more likely, however, that it was Gustav II Adolph's plan to occupy the dangerous Imperial armoured cavalry with his infantry, while the Swedish cavalry engaged the harquebusiers.

Although there is no direct evidence, it seems likely that Holk, with only 1,450 horse and 1,150 foot, outnumbered and threatened with being outflanked, reacted by extending his line with reinforcements, probably consisting of the two wing reserve squadrons Goschütz and Westrumb, the latter sent by Wallenstein to assist Holk 'because there all the fury began.'[75] Holk, now had 1,800 horse and had gained cavalry superiority, but was still severely outnumbered by infantry. The Swedish outflanking manoeuvre must have looked so impressive that the Imperial baggage train was relocated to the Imperial right wing to avoid capture.[76] The right wing reserve, Westrumb, moving to the left at the start of the battle is an important indicator of Holk's situation, which would not have been so desperate if he were facing only the Swedish cavalry and musketeer companies, without the Swedish Brigade pinning down his best units – Götz and Piccolomini.

---

72 Münchhausen (BHStA, 2424t194 f. 158: Münchhausen to Maximilian 6 December 1632 and Wittrock, 'Fyra relationer', p.306) of Comargo's Regiment reported that they had fought against the Yellow and Old Blue (*sic*: New Blue) Regiments.

73 Silvio Piccolomini (Anonymous, *Archivio*, p.240).

74 There is no historical evidence on the speed of formations in the seventeenth century. However, it is assumed that seventeenth-century infantry with regimental guns could not move faster than late eighteenth century infantry in common step, which is 60 metres per minute (Babits, *A Devil of a Whipping*, p.114).

75 Holk (Wittrock, 'Fyra relationer', p.308) reported that he was reinforced by five cornets from the right wing at the battle's beginning, which is mostly overlooked by historians. This cavalry was certainly not pulled out of the frontline, which still awaited a Swedish attack, but Wallenstein's right wing reserve squadron Westrumb. Although there is no historical evidence it seems likely that Holk brought in his own reserve too. The commencement of the battle on the left Imperial wing, at the instance when the Swedish right wing had wheeled around is reported by Holk (Wittrock, 'Fyra relationer', p.308) and Vitzthum/Berlepsch (Glafey, *De Gladio*, p.13).

76 Diodati (Fiedler, 'Diodatis Bericht', p.562), copied by the Spanish Relation (Watts, *Swedish Intelligencer*, vol. 3, p.160).

Swedish Right Wing Attack, 11:00 a.m.–12:00 p.m.†

† See PDF download, Plate 24

Archaeology Sources (4): See PDF download

Historical Sources

There is not much historical evidence for the early stages of the Swedish right wing attack. According to Ottavio and Silvio Piccolomini, the Swedish Brigade pinned down their regiment, and very likely that of Götz, by musket fire for 15 minutes.[77] Münchhausen's account started at a later time, when his regiment (Comargo), together with Baden's Regiment of the second line, made a counter-attack, after his *Oberst* was mortally wounded and his *Oberstleutnant* killed.[78] Although he avoided mentioning a retreat, it is quite clear that his regiment was forced to withdraw after taking heavy casualties. Fleetwood stated that the small Imperial battery, deployed in front of Comargo's Regiment, was overrun and its guns spiked.[79] However, there is no historical evidence of the achievements of the Swedish cavalry or of the Imperial harquebusiers.

The Events

Harassed by Imperial skirmishing fire from the road ditches, the Yellow Brigade, commanded by *Generalmajor* Nils Brahe, crossed the Via Regia and advanced against the small Imperial battery of four 24-pounders and two 12-pounders. Seeing Gustav II Adolph's guard in their yellow (Life Regiment) and grey (Lifeguard) uniforms approaching without being greatly affected by their artillery fire,[80] some Imperial gun crews offered little resistance and fled from their guns. That ordnance officers *Hauptmann* Johann Burg and *Hauptmann* Maximilian Kleeblatt were executed a few months later at Prague for desertion may be confirmation of this.[81] After Brahe had taken and spiked the guns,[82] possibly with help from the left squadron of the Swedish Brigade, he turned to the Imperial left centre, where *Oberst* Theodor Comargo commanded one of Wallenstein's most experienced infantry regiments; some of these men had served for 13 years. After a bitter fight in which *Oberst* Comargo was mortally wounded with four shots and the *Oberstleutnant* killed,[83] *Obristwachtmeister*

77 Argang, 'Piccolominis bref', p.89. Anonymous, *Archivio*, p.242

78 Wittrock, 'Fyra relationer', p.305.

79 Fleetwood, Letter, p.7.

80 According to the Spanish Relation (Watts, *Swedish Intelligencer*, vol. 3, p.161) '... our [Imperial] Artillery being never able to disorder it [Swedish infantry] though many a shot was made upon it.'

81 Seidler, *Untersuchungen*, p.56 and Josef Seidler, *Das Prager Blutgericht 1633* (Memmingen: 1962) p.17.

82 The early capture of the small Imperial battery is mentioned by Fleetwood, Letter, p.7, Hallenus (Mankell, *Arkiv*, vol. II, p.662) and Hülshorst (Wittrock, 'Fyra relationer', p.303), but which unit caputred it is not stated.

83 Wittrock, 'Fyra relationer', p.305.

Münchhausen took command[84] and ordered a retreat behind the second line to reform, probably covered by Bredau's cuirassiers.

Meanwhile, *Överstelöjtnant* Gabriel Kyle's Swedish Brigade, possibly assisted by *Överste* Stenbock's Smaland cavalry, arrived in front of Götz' and Piccolomini's Regiments and began delivering volleys of musket fire, which were probably returned by Piccolomini's harquebusiers with their carbines and by one or two Imperial musketeer companies. Only their armour prevented them from being annihilated,[85] but they held the line.[86] While the Swedish Brigade held off the heavily armoured Imperial cavalry, Gustav II Adolph's Swedish National cavalry turned with 950 men on the 900 Imperial harquebusiers of the outer wing. Watts described that the Swedes delivered preparatory fire, first by regimental guns, then by musketeers, and then followed up with a cavalry charge, which was the Swedish standard cavalry tactic.[87] The Imperial harquebusiers were neither equipped nor trained to resist a cavalry charge of this force and many fired their carbines and pistols in the air and fled.[88] Although the Imperial left wing was not entirely beaten, the situation, which Diodati played down as a stalemate,[89] must have become increasingly desperate, particularly if Stalhandske's Finns returned to the battlefield.

† See PDF download, Plate 25

Swedish Left Wing Advance, 11:00 a.m.–12:00 p.m.†

Archaeology Sources (5): See PDF download

Historical Sources

Reports of the events on the Imperial right wing are sparse and short, even in the otherwise more informative secondary sources, and no eyewitnesses reported the cavalry fighting. However, there is one indirect witness account in the form of the death sentence against *Oberst* Johann Nicolaus Hagen von Sauwenbein at the court-martial in Prague. It states that his harquebusier regiment was disordered by routing Croats and as a result he retreated to a safe position, disobeying several orders to return.[90]

Fleetwood's report is crucial to understanding the battle episode in that, 'Hertzoke Bernerds and Winckles regimentes were comaunded upon

84 Münchhausen was still in command of Comargo's Regiment in December 1632 (Hallwich, *Briefe und Akten*, vol. 3, p.617).

85 Silvio Piccolomini (Anonymous, *Archivio*, p.242).

86 Diodati (Fiedler, 'Diodatis Bericht', p.563).

87 Watts, *Swedish Intelligencer*, vol. 3, p.134.

88 Poyntz, *The Relation*, p.74.

89 Diodati contradicts himself by reporting that 'everyone tried to advance to force the enemy from his position' on the Imperial left wing, while stating at the same time that the baggage train was in danger of being cut off and that Pappenheim on his arrival immediately moved to the left wing, where it seemed that the' King charged most stubborn' (Fiedler, 'Diodatis Bericht', p.562).

90 Seidler, *Untersuchungen*, pp.141–142.

the cannons at the mills,'[91] which he could possibly have seen himself. Fleetwood's account contradicts the *Inventarium Sueciae*, and all secondary sources depending on it,[92] with Fleetwood reporting incorrectly that the Old Blue Brigade advanced with the Swedish right wing.

The only report of what happened to the Imperial musketeers in the Lützen gardens is Watts' short note that the gardens were finally taken by Swedish troops before dusk.[93] It seems highly unlikely that von Weimar left them unchallenged and able to deliver flanking fire on his cavalry, which had to advance in close proximity to the mud walls.†

† See PDF download, Plate 26: Detailed musket bullet distribution map, Imperial inner right wing and right centre

The Events

Generalleutnant Bernhard von Weimar faced a difficult situation. Seventeen pieces of artillery and the musketeers in the road ditches to his front and behind a mud wall on his flank made any advance difficult. In addition, there was only a small 150-metre gap guarded by Croats between the fortified artillery position and the Lützen gardens, through which he could advance with his cavalry. While Gustav II Adolph conducted his outflanking manoeuvre, Bernhard von Weimar waited until the Swedish right wing was fully engaged; probably hoping that Wallenstein would commit some of his reserves to the Imperial left.

In order to avoid clustering cavalry immediately in front of the Imperial artillery at point-blank range, it seems likely that Bernhard von Weimar left most of his cavalry behind to advance only when the Green and Old Blue brigades reached the Via Regia and began the attack on the windmill battery. Probably, as Gustav II Adolph did on the right, he sent some cavalry to clear the way. The Croats were easily defeated, but with the limited space and the Swedish cavalry at their heels, the Croats did not retreat around the wing as Wallenstein had planned, but crashed into one of their own regiments, Hagen's harquebusiers, which they put to flight. With his largest regiment gone, a huge hole opened in the Imperial line, and with his reserve of Westrumb's harquebusiers committed to the left, Wallenstein was in an awkward position. Probably at the same time, Bernhard von Weimar ordered *Oberst* Gersdorf to attack the gardens with his five musketeer companies and 10 regimental guns.

Swedish Second Line, 11:00 a.m.–12:00 p.m.†

† See PDF download, Plate 27

With 9,000 men, almost half the army, the Swedish second line was unusually strong. However, the significance of such a large second line is not reflected in the historical sources, which ignore its existence almost completely. Without sufficient reports of when and where the second line troops were

91 Fleetwood, Letter, p.7.

92 Gottfried, *Inventarium Sueciae*, p.25, copied by Monro, *His Expedition*, part II, p.164, Abelinum, *Theatrum Europaeum*, p.750, Chemnitz, *Geschichte*, p.465, Anonymous, *Wahrhaftige Beschreibung* and Anonymous, *Glaubwürdiger Bericht*.

93 Watts, *Swedish Intelligencer*, vol. 3, p.149.

committed, it is almost impossible to understand the battle. It is therefore crucial to develop at least a hypothesis of how the second line might have been used, based on reports from Watts and Dalbier and on the development of the battle during its early stages.

Watts claimed that *Oberst* Bulach was sent with three cavalry squadrons of the second line of the right wing over the Flossgraben further to the right to 'imp out the feathers' immediately after the battle began.[94] Watts' account of the battle has already been shown as generally unreliable and, because there is no other report confirming this incident, there remains some doubt that it actually happened.

After the Finns routed the Croats, there was no immediate threat to the Swedish far right flank and no reason to move units so far away from the central battlefield. In addition, it would have been much easier to deploy the units already there, instead of letting them cross the Flossgraben three times. It would appear that Watts simply made up the story, because he assumed, incorrectly, that the Imperial line of battle was longer than the Swedish.[95] In order to keep the outer right wing from being outflanked, Gustav II Adolph could have easily moved the three cavalry squadrons at the end of the right wing's wheeling manoeuvre. The Swedish HQ reported the Croats as threatening the Swedish baggage train near Meuchen in a later stage of the battle[96] and it seems reasonable to suggest that Swedish second line cavalry intercepted them by moving over the Flossgraben around midday.

Oberst Dalbier reported that *Generalmajor* Knyphausen, his commanding officer, still had two brigades, his own and Duke Wilhelm's, as well as the cavalry reserve Öhm at his disposal, when the Swedish first line collapsed around midday.[97] The other two second-line brigades, Mitzlaff and Thurn, must have been committed some time before midday, indicating that they had advanced during the first Swedish attack together with, or in very close support of, the first line. The newly discovered first-hand account from Dalbier contradicts Watts, who described the same event as the Brigades Mitzlaff and Thurn being released from the reserve at a later time, when the Swedish first line was already in full retreat,[98] a sequence of events most historians agreed on.[99] It even seems possible that Watts had access to Dalbier's account, but did not fully understand it.

The reason for the early commitment of two infantry brigades from the second line becomes clear when the situation of the Swedish army around 11:30 a.m. is considered. In the delayed double outflanking manoeuvre, Gustav

94 Watts, *Swedish Intelligencer*, vol. 3, p.132.

95 Watts, *Swedish Intelligencer*, vol. 3, p.132.

96 Söltl, *Religionskriege*, p.347.

97 Dalbier, *Lutzen*, p.252 reported this event after he made a note on the second Swedish attack in the afternoon. However, he made it clear that those three units were responsible for rallying fleeing soldiers, an event which took place after the collapse of the first line at around midday.

98 Watts, *Swedish Intelligencer*, vol. 3, pp.145–146.

99 Brzezinski, *Lützen*, pp.71 and 75, Seidler, *Untersuchungen*, p.77, Deuticke, *Lützen*, pp.80–81, Generalstaben, *Sveriges Krig*, p.442.

II Adolph's right wing was already engaged in close combat when Bernhard von Weimar's left wing began its advance, creating a gap of about 400 metres in the Swedish centre. At this stage, the battle was certainly going according to Gustav II Adolph's plan and he must have envisioned a separation of his centre, which would have endangered his entire operation, if the gap was not filled. The Brigades Mitzlaff and Thurn did not have to actually attack; their mere presence in close proximity would hold the Imperial centre infantry squadrons, Breuner/Grana and GFZM Breuner, in place.

The entire Swedish troop movement suggests that its main purpose was to play on their advantage of greater numbers, deploying their troops on a spatially limited battlefield, outflanking and outnumbering the Imperial army on its wings, and destroying it with one decisive blow before Pappenheim's corps could arrive and even the odds. This scenario would have been an appropriate strategy in this situation, in particular because Gustav II Adolph was unable to anticipate when Pappenheim's infantry would arrive, thus there was an emphasis on speeding up the Swedish attacks once battle was joined.†

† See PDF download, Plate 28: Swedish army in preparation for a double outflanking or enveloping manoeuvre

Imperial Left Wing: Pappenheim's Arrival, 11:30 a.m.–12:30 p.m.†

† See PDF download, Plate 29

Historical Sources

With eight regiments, a total of 2,400 horse, Pappenheim's cavalry was an impressive force and its arrival marked the turning point of the battle. The exact arrival time is not entirely certain and varies not so much between primary and secondary sources as it does between Swedish and Imperial sources.

Swedish sources give a wide variation for Pappenheim's arrival time; from before the battle to 3:00 p.m., and additionally some sources appear to have confused counterattacks by Imperial reserves with the arrival of Pappenheim's infantry.[100] Imperial sources give a much narrower period in which Pappenheim's cavalry might have arrived – shortly after the battle commenced according to most. Of the Imperial eyewitnesses, only Wallenstein stated that Pappenheim arrived before battle, perhaps trying to hide the fact that he was not able to assemble his entire army in time. For the same reason, Diodati described the circumstances of Pappenheim's arrival so vaguely, apparently on purpose, that some historians were under the false impression he meant the *Feldmarschall* had actually arrived before the battle.[101] Surprisingly, the early Imperial non-eyewitness accounts of Gallas and the *Relation from 1632* agree on an early arrival as reported by Imperial eyewitnesses.

100 Fleetwood, Letter, p.8.

101 Diemar, *Untersuchungen*, p.4. See Seidler, *Untersuchungen*, pp.15 and 49–50 for the interpretation of Diodati's statement.

Feldmarschall Gottfried Heinrich *Graf* von Pappenheim.

Most historians follow Holk's account, since he is the only eyewitness giving a precise time: 12:00 p.m.[102] However, we should not take Holk's precise time too literally, as it should be understood more as a rough timeframe, suggesting that Pappenheim arrived not long after the battle had begun. It is likely that Pappenheim met and rallied at least parts of Isolani's left wing Croats, increasing his force to over 2,800 cavalry. After Isolani's Croats joined Pappenheim, half his cavalry consisted of light cavalry and it seems to be a consensus among historians that Pappenheim divided his force into two columns. All cuirassiers, harquebusiers and dragoons, the heavy and medium cavalry, attacked the Swedish right wing under his own command, while he sent the Croats and Polish Cossacks, the light cavalry, east of the Flossgraben towards the Swedish rear.[103] Although this is a reasonable tactical assessment, and might actually have happened, there is no historical source actually supporting this suggestion directly.

Most secondary sources state that Croats outflanked the Swedish right wing and plundered the baggage train before Pappenheim arrived.[104] This assertion, however, is doubtful for several reasons. Fleetwood, whose statement is supported by the archaeological information (see above), contradicts the early Croat outflanking manoeuvre; the overwhelming Swedish superiority on the right wing would not have allowed it. It is also worth considering that the description of this event in all secondary sources is based on *Relation II from Erfurt*, so that we are actually only dealing with one source, itself not the most reliable.

Only one eyewitness of this event, from the Swedish HQ, mentions that he heard Swedish soldiers shouting that the army was in confusion and Croats were attacking the rear from two sides, after which he got out of danger and returned to Naumburg in the evening.[105] Although this account confirms that

102 Droysen, 'Lützen', p.122. Deuticke, *Lützen*, p.71. Generalstaben, *Sveriges Krig*, p.435. Seidler, *Untersuchungen*, pp.49–50. Brzezinski, *Lützen*, p.58.

103 Deuticke, *Lützen*, p.72. Seidler, *Untersuchungen*, p.57. Generalstaben, *Sveriges Krig*, p.435. Roberts, *Gustavus Adolphus. A History of Sweden*, p.768. Brzezinski, *Lützen*, pp.59 and 73.

104 Relation II from Erfurt (Droysen, 'Gedruckte Relationen', p.19), Watts, *Swedish Intelligencer*, vol. 3, p.135, Gottfried, *Inventarium Sueciae*, p.26, Anonymous, *Wahrhaftige Beschreibung*, Anonymous, *Glaubwürdiger Bericht*, Monro, *His Expedition*, part II, p.164, Abelinum, *Theatrum Europaeum*, p.750, Chemnitz, *Geschichte*, p.466.

105 Söltl, *Religionskriege*, p.347.

Oberst Ottavio Piccolomini di Aragona.

Croats actually did attack the Swedish rear, he puts the event at the end of the battle, which is not an entirely reliable account since the eyewitness might have been trying to hide the fact he left the battlefield well before the fighting ended. The most logical conclusion is that the Croat attack on the Swedish rear occurred when Pappenheim's reinforcement arrived, as most historians believe, but without some additional evidence the time of this event can only be approximated to being around the middle of the battle.

The Events

Feldmarschall Gottfried Heinrich *Graf* von Pappenheim would almost certainly have used the shortest route from Halle to Lützen,[106] allowing his cavalry to arrive behind the Imperial army's position around noon. Here he very likely met and rallied parts of Wallenstein's left wing Croats, increasing the strength of his force. The Croats might have provided intelligence, but even without it, it must have been obvious to Pappenheim that the battle was not going well on the Imperial left, 'where it seemed that the King [Gustav II Adolph] charged most stubborn.'[107]

Probably dividing his forces into one light cavalry flanking force of approximately 1,400 horse, possibly commanded by Isolani, and one equally strong heavy cavalry striking force under his own command, Pappenheim did not waste any time. Although his troops were certainly tired from marching the last two days, he immediately charged at the head of his 'Rennfahne' Lifeguard and Dragoons, followed by Merode's 'Obwacht' Lifeguard and Dragoons, Sparr's cuirassiers, Bönninghausen's harquebusiers and Lamboy's harquebusiers.[108] The Imperial left wing now consisted of 3,200 regular and 1,400 irregular cavalry against 1,800 Swedish troops of the first line. This sudden pressure on the Swedish right must have been immense and certainly restored some stability to the Imperial side,[109] presenting an opportunity for Holk to rally his men, while Piccolomini was able to escape the deadly musket fire by counter-attacking the Swedish Brigade.

106 Brzezinski, *Lützen*, pp.46 and 58.

107 Diodati (Fiedler, 'Diodatis Bericht', p.562).

108 It is a myth, created by Khevenhiller, *Annales Ferdinandei*, p.193 and Poyntz, *The Relation*, p.73, that Pappenheim interrogated Swedish prisoners first to figure out where Gustav II Adolph was, hoping he could challenge the King to a personal duel.

109 Brzezinski, *Lützen*, p.59.

† See PDF download, Plate 30

Imperial Left Wing: Piccolomini's Counter-Attack, 11:30 a.m.–12:30 a.m.†

Archaeology Sources (6): See PDF download

Ottavio Piccolomini, Justus Sustermans (1597–1681). (Nationalmuseum, Stockholm. Photo by Erick Cornelius)

Historical Sources

In their accounts, both Piccolominis referred only to their regiment, which makes it difficult to understand the sequence of events. Diodati stated that Piccolomini's counter-attack took place after the death of Pappenheim,[110] which other sources later repeated.[111] He could certainly have seen Piccolomini's and Pappenheim's troops, but not the death of Pappenheim. However, it does show that Piccolomini's counter-attack took place after Pappenheim's arrival and that would also explain why he stood under musket fire for 15 minutes, after which he attacked. The arrival of reinforcements to support him enabled him to attack without creating a gap in the Imperial line or exposing his flanks to any great extent.

Münchhausen made the strange comment that the Bredau cuirassiers 'took apart' two horse regiments, although Bredau's position behind the left centre would suggest that he fought against infantry.[112] Bredau must have moved to the left wing, possibly supporting Piccolomini in his counter-attack.

The only other eyewitness who recounts Piccolomini's counter-attack is Poyntz. According to his narrative, Piccolomini routed the Finnish cavalry and then attacked a larger infantry formation, but was stopped by a volley of musketry, at which moment the rallied Finns attacked into the rear.[113] Only the latter event shows a similarity to Ottavio Piccolomini's report of a Swedish cavalry counter-attack that caught him in the rear just as he attacked a brigade of infantry. At this point, some soldiers told him that the King had been killed.[114] The Swedish regiment was almost certainly the Smaland cavalry, the last unit to see the King alive, and not the Finns, who were probably fighting Pappenheim's cavalry at the time, and were certainly quite some distance from Piccolomini. Whether Piccolomini first attacked Swedish cavalry before his attack on the infantry squadron is unknown, but

110 Fiedler, 'Diodatis Bericht', p.563.

111 Watts, *Swedish Intelligencer*, vol. 3, p.143, Burgus, *Mars Sveco-Germanicus*, p.324, Khevenhiller, *Annales Ferdinandei*, p.194.

112 Wittrock, 'Fyra relationer', p.305.

113 Poyntz, *The Relation*, p.72.

114 Argang, 'Piccolominis bref', p.89.

it is possible that Poyntz confused Piccolomini's cavalry with another cavalry unit, which could have been either Götz or Bredau.†

† See PDF download, Plate 31: Detailed small-calibre pistol bullet distribution map, Imperial left wing.

The Events

The arrival of Pappenheim's cavalry on the outer left wing might have relieved Piccolomini's harquebusiers and Götz's cuirassiers on the inner left. Probably at the same time, Bredau's cuirassiers, after covering Comargo's retreat, changed their position from the left centre to the left wing. This new situation enabled Piccolomini to charge the right squadron of the Swedish Brigade, which he pursued to the Via Regia,[115] while Götz's cuirassiers attacked and occupied the rest of the brigade. Meanwhile Bredau's cuirassiers possibly protected Piccolomini's left flank, attacking the Smaland and Ostgöta cavalry. By then, the *Överste* of the Smaland cavalry, Fredrik Stenbock, had been shot in the foot and the *Överstelöjtnant* Lennart Nilsson Baat of the Ostgöta cavalry was shot in the head,[116] making it likely that both Swedish regiments had taken heavy casualties.

Swedish Left Wing Attack, 11:30 a.m.–12:30 p.m.†

† See PDF download, Plate 32

Archaeology Sources (7): See PDF download

Historical Sources

Reports about Bernhard von Weimar's attack on the windmill battery are inconsistent. Influenced by the *Inventarium Sueciae*, most secondary sources report that the Swedish attack failed under the Imperial artillery fire that had forced the Green Brigade to find shelter behind the miller's house;[117] this is the accepted modern interpretation.[118] However, this point of view leaves some unanswered questions.

The miller's house is shown in different places along the Via Regia in the battle's imagery; south of the Via Regia on van Hulsen's copperplate, *on* the road in Merian's copperplate, and north of the road in the 1710 field boundary

115 Ottavio Piccolomini (Argang, 'Piccolominis bref', p.89).

116 Hülshorst (Wittrock, 'Fyra relationer', p.303) and Pentz (Fiedler, 'Diodatis Bericht', p.571). At least Stenbock must have been wounded before Gustav II Adolph took command of his regiment around midday (Brzezinski, *Lützen*, p.62).

117 Gottfried, *Inventarium Sueciae*, p.25. Anonymous, *Wahrhaftige Beschreibung*. Anonymous, *Glaubwürdiger Bericht*. Abelinum, *Theatrum Europaeum*, p.750 and Chemnitz, *Geschichte*, p.465. Watts, *Swedish Intelligencer*, vol. 3, p.147 reported that Bernhard von Weimar found shelter and Monro, *His Expedition*, part II, p.164 translated incorrectly from the *Inventarium Sueciae* that the Swedes forced the Imperial guns to find shelter behind the miller's house. Khevenhiller, *Annales Ferdinandei*, p.191 stated that the Swedish left wing was disordered and forced to retreat by Imperial artillery fire.

118 Wedgwood, *Der Dreissigjährige Krieg*, p.326, Generalstaben, *Sveriges Krig*, p.432, Seidler, *Untersuchungen*, p.56. Brzezinski, *Lützen*, p.58 suggests a successful cavalry charge, while the infantry was stopped.

map. If the more reliable 1710 map is correct, the miller's house was located very close to and in front of the Imperial battery, providing almost no cover for the Swedish troops. Even if it was located south of the road, one single building could not have provided sufficient cover for the Green Brigade's 2,000 men.

Holk wrote at the end of his account that:

> The Duke [Wallenstein] ... fought two hours against infantry with four horse regiments, namely Holk, Trcka, Piccolomini and Desfour, and he was encircled completely until Holk sent the cavalry to 'second' him.[119]

Although the timeline in Holk's account is unclear, and he had not seen the event personally, it seems that he is describing the first half of the battle. Bernhard von Weimar eventually achieved a breakthrough by the Swedish left wing that surrounded the Imperial right. Holk then rescued the Imperial right after his success on the left with support from Pappenheim's reinforcements.†

† See PDF download, Plate 33: Detailed musket bullet distribution map, Imperial inner right wing, right centre and rear

This interpretation also corresponds with the troop numbers. After Hagen's rout and the temporary loss of his reserve Westrumb, Wallenstein's right wing was down to 1,000 horse and 150 musketeers with only Tontinelli's 250 horse as a reserve against 1,550 Swedish horse, 423 musketeers and 10 regimental guns of the first line with a second line reserve of 1,400 horse. Despite the 17 Imperial artillery pieces, 400 musketeers behind the garden walls, and the quality of the Imperial cuirassiers, it seems highly unlikely that Wallenstein was able to completely stop Bernhard von Weimar's cavalry charge with his limited force. On the other hand, however, there is no reliable report from any eyewitness about any infantry fighting on the Imperial right centre.†

† See PDF download, Plate 34: 11:30 a.m. to 12:30 p.m.: Pappenheim's arrival and Piccolomini's counter-attack.

The Events

Outnumbered, with 1,500 Swedish horse against 1,000 Imperial, it was only a matter of time, before Wallenstein's right wing collapsed. The situation grew worse when *Oberst* Hagen, who retreated from the front line, but remained on Wallenstein's right, saw Swedish cavalry closing in on him and retreated. His 800 harquebusiers moved from the right to the left wing in full view of Wallenstein, disobeying a direct order, but hoping that it would be quieter there.[120] Only the inner two Imperial squadrons, Holk's and Trcka/Desfours' cuirassiers, stood firm on the Imperial right,[121] and the Swedish cavalry was now able to outflank the much shorter Imperial line, threatening to attack the Imperial army from the rear.

Meanwhile, the Scots and Germans of Bernhard's Green Brigade reached the Via Regia and were about to assault the entrenchments of the windmill battery, commanded by *Generalfeldzeugmeister* Hans Philipp von Breuner. These artillerymen did not give up easily and it is possible that the artillery

119 Wittrock, 'Fyra relationer', p.309.

120 Seidler, *Untersuchungen*, pp.141–142.

121 According to Diodati (Fiedler, 'Diodatis Bericht', p.565) and Holk (Wittrock, 'Fyra relationer', p.309). Holk was referring to the whole combat at the Imperial right wing and Piccolomini was not there at that time.

fire was so severe that some Green Brigade soldiers found cover behind the miller's house. It seems fairly obvious the Swedes needed more than one assault to capture the Imperial battery,[122] which was covered by Wallenstein's nephew, *Oberst* Berthold von Waldstein, who was mortally wounded during the fighting.[123] On its right, the Green Brigade's flank was protected by *Oberst* Winckel's Old Blue Brigade, but the attack lost momentum and was stopped by the squadron Colloredo/Chiesa, probably led by *Oberst* Andreas Matthias Kehraus.

Although there are no clear reports, it seems that *Oberst* Gersdorf's 423 detached musketeers and 10 regimental guns were not successful against the 400 Imperial musketeers behind the garden walls of Lützen.[124] This means the Swedish left flank here was 'in the air'.

Imperial Left Wing: Pappenheim's Death and Imperial 'Fahnenflucht', 12:00–1:00 p.m.†

† See PDF download, Plate 35

Archaeology Sources (8): See PDF download

Historical Sources

The historical sources are inconclusive about the impact Pappenheim's attack might have had, except that when the *Feldmarschall* died at the head of his cavalry, his fall caused the Imperial 'fahnenflucht' (literally 'desertion' but perhaps 'failure' or 'flight' might be a better translation – essentially running away with their colours). Most historians[125] followed Holk's account[126] in stating that Pappenheim's attack was a complete failure. However, the otherwise reliable Holk appears not to have been entirely honest here and was possibly trying to downplay the success of Pappenheim's cavalry in order to enhance his own actions.

122 As with Holk, Vitzthum/Berlepsch (Glafey, *De Gladio*, p.13) reported a whole series of events when he wrote that 'the Imperial wing was pushed back at first, but stood firm then, until the Swedes forced their way into the 'retrangement' and turned the artillery pieces.' Although the meaning of this sentence is not entirely clear, it refers probably, first to the rout of the Croats and Hagen, then to heavy fighting at the windmills and finally the battery's capture. The Spanish Relation (Watts, *Swedish Intelligencer*, vol. 3, p.161) reported a stalemate on the Imperial right.

123 It is not certain when he was wounded. See Holk (Wittrock, 'Fyra relationer', p.309), Diodati (Fiedler, 'Diodatis Bericht', p.565), Fleetwood, Letter, p.10, Hülshorst (Wittrock, 'Fyra relationer', p.303) and Relation from 1632 (Droysen, 'Gedruckte Relationen', p.11).

124 Only Richelieu, *Mémoires*, p.258 reported that the Swedes cleared the gardens at the battle's start, while Watts, *Swedish Intelligencer*, vol. 3, p.149 claimed that the gardens were captured in the afternoon. However, both accounts are unreliable and an exact time cannot be ascertained.

125 Brzezinski, *Lützen*, p.59 believed that Pappenheim's attack stabilised the crumbling Imperial left wing for a while, but was not successful otherwise.

126 Holk exaggerated when he stated that Pappenheim was killed before he could gain a foothold and 3,000 regular cavalry and Croats were routed, which disordered the right wing (Wittrock, 'Fyra relationer', p.309).

Cuirassiers from Pappenheim's command. Artist unknown, post 1632. (Rijksmuseum)

A rout of the Imperial left wing would have been a serious setback, but it contradicts the battle chronology, in particular the Swedish army's collapse an hour later, and the numerical superiority of the Imperial left wing. The main sources of the Imperial 'fahnenflucht' are the court-martial verdicts from Prague, where this incident was examined in detail, when four regiments on the left wing were accused of 'fahnenflucht'. The key to understanding the probable sequence of this episode is Sparr's Cuirassier Regiment, commanded by *Oberst* Albrecht von Hofkirchen, which refused to fight upon their arrival as a part of Pappenheim's force, which in turn caused 'others' to retreat. It is important to note the statement that Hofkirchen's regiment 'caracoled', even when the left wing was victorious, and was caught in the rear by Swedish cavalry.[127] Pappenheim's trumpeter Conrad Ehinger reported that the *Feldmarschall* was wounded and taken prisoner and he (Ehinger) had to rescue him on his own, because Hofkirchen refused to help.[128] Seeing Pappenheim mortally wounded, Hofkirchen left him and moved from the left to the right wing.[129] Hofkirchen's insubordination caused *Oberst* Lothar von Bönninghausen to withdraw his harquebusier regiment.[130] According to this sequence of events, Pappenheim's counter-attack was briefly successful but

127 Verdict vs. Hofkirchen (Seidler, *Untersuchungen*, pp.142–143).

128 Ehinger's testimony (Hallwich, *Briefe und Akten*, vol. 4, p.135).

129 Verdict vs. Hofkirchen (Seidler, *Untersuchungen*, p.143).

130 Ehinger's testimony (Hallwich, *Briefe und Akten*, vol. 4, p.136).

started to fall apart after the *Feldmarschall* was wounded. Swedish sources,[131] as well as the printed 'relations',[132] reported completely different and largely invented stories about Pappenheim's counter-attack; they repeated the circulating rumours, and can be disregarded.

The Events

Given the length of the front line, the Swedish right wing cavalry must have been fully engaged in the fighting, except possibly for Stalhandske's Finns, when Pappenheim's main force hit their flank with 1,400 men. This attack certainly ripped the Swedish outer wing apart,[133] even though Hofkirchen stayed away from the fighting. At the same time, 1,400 Croats outflanked the Swedes even further to their right.

Although there is no evidence, this must have been the point when all 1,200 Swedish cavalry of the right wing's second line were committed, to avoid the total destruction of the wing. While Uslar, the Hessians and Beckermann possibly supported Gustav II Adolph's right wing, it is possible that the squadrons Bulach, Goldstein and Duke Wilhelm, commanded by *Oberst* Claus Conrad Zorn von Bulach, crossed the Flossgraben to counter the Croats, as Watts claimed.[134] However, it is doubtful that fewer than 400 Swedish horse could have stopped 1,400 Croats,[135] so they must have received some reinforcements. It is likely that the three Swedish cavalry squadrons were disordered[136] and suffered heavy casualties, among them *Oberstleutnant* Marx Conrad von Rehlinger, commanding officer of Goldstein's Regiment, who was shot in the arm.[137]

---

131 Poyntz, *The Relation*, p.73: Personal duel between Pappenheim and Gustav II Adolph. Fleetwood, Letter, p.8: Pappenheim was killed in the morning and his corps was commanded by Merode. Hallenus (Mankell, *Arkiv* vol. II, p.663): Pappenheim was killed by Stalhandske.

132 The story of Pappenheim's death in printed accounts originates from the Relation II from Erfurt (Droysen, 'Gedruckte Relationen', p.20) and the *Relation from 1633* (Droysen, 'Gedruckte Relationen', pp.31–32) and was retold by Gottfried, *Inventarium Sueciae*, p.26, Monro, *His Expedition*, part II, pp.164–165, Abelinum, *Theatrum Europaeum*, p.750 and Chemnitz, *Geschichte*, pp.466–467, but not copied as usually done.

133 The Relation II from Erfurt reported that the first Imperial counter-attack 'ruined several (Swedish) cavalry regiments, which had retreated' (Droysen, 'Gedruckte Relationen', p.19), but did not connect this event with Pappenheim's attack.

134 Watts, *Swedish Intelligencer*, vol. 3, p.132.

135 This story was made up by the Relation II from Erfurt (Droysen, 'Gedruckte Relationen', p.19), retold similarly by Gottfried, *Inventarium Sueciae*, p.26 and copied from there by Anonymous, *Wahrhaftige Beschreibung*, Anonymous, *Glaubwürdiger Bericht*, Monro, *His Expedition*, part II, p.164, and Abelinum, *Theatrum Europaeum*, p.750, again retold by Chemnitz, *Geschichte*, p.466.

136 Mentioned only by the Relation II from Erfurt (Droysen, 'Gedruckte Relationen', p.19).

137 However, it is suspicious that this story was first mentioned by Gottfried, *Inventarium Sueciae*, p.26, then copied by Anonymous, *Wahrhaftige Beschreibung*, Anonymous, *Glaubwürdiger Bericht*, Monro, *His Expedition*, part II, p.164, Abelinum, *Theatrum Europaeum*, p.750, and Chemnitz, *Geschichte*, p.466.

Swedish cavalry at Lützen. Detail from the engraving of Gustav II Adolf by Jacob can der Heyden (1573–1645). (Staatliche Kunstsammlungen Dresden)

It would probably not have been long before the Swedish right wing started to fall apart, when Pappenheim was hit, fell from his horse and was taken prisoner. Rescued by his 22-year-old trumpeter Conrad Ehinger, the mortally wounded *Feldmarschall* is reported to have cried: 'Oh brothers, that God has mercy! Is there no one, who fights faithful for the Emperor!'[138] His cry may have been because he saw Bönninghausen's harquebusiers retreating after Sparr's cuirassiers had already fled because they were caught in their rear by a Swedish cavalry attack, after they had fired and retired. Hagen's harquebusiers, realising that the left wing was not as quiet as they first thought, returned to the right.[139] Lohe's cuirassiers did not perform well either; but his *Oberstleutnant*, who was accused of cowardice, escaped execution at Prague due to the intervention of Holk.[140]

138 Ehinger's testimony (Hallwich, *Briefe und Akten*, vol. 4, p.135).

139 Verdict vs. Hagen (Seidler, *Untersuchungen*, p.142).

140 Holk's 8 December 1632 letter to Wallenstein (Hallwich, *Briefe und Akten*, vol. 3, p.588).

Pappenheim's fatal wounding and the confused withdrawal of some Imperial units took some pressure off Gustav II Adolph's right wing. However, he still had to deal with Piccolomini's and Götz's cuirassiers of the Imperial inner left wing, and Isolani's 1,400 Croats behind the Swedish right rear. Holk's wing was far from having disintegrated and still posed a threat.[141]

Imperial Left Wing: Gustav II Adolph's Counter-Attack and His Death, 12:00–1:00 p.m.†

† See PDF download, Plate 36

Historical Sources

The death of Gustav II Adolph is the most discussed event of the Battle of Lützen. Contemporary, as well as modern literature, is thus extensive, diversified, and colourful. At the same time, however, the King's death had

141 Diodati reported that Pappenheim's death 'almost' disordered the left wing (Fiedler, 'Diodatis Bericht', p.563).

surprisingly little impact on the battle; it is, therefore, not necessary to discuss it in any detail to understand the course of the battle. Additionally, no one who saw his death survived to tell the story and any facts have been overlayed by rumour and legend. In particular, it is suspicious that the high-ranking officers, *Herzog* Franz Albrecht von Sachsen-Lauenburg and *Oberstleutnant* Falkenberg, were reported to have been directly involved in the events that led to Gustav II Adolph's death. Very few authors seem to have tried to take advantage of it, like Ottavio Piccolomini, most just embellished their stories to make them more interesting, not believing that Gustav II Adolph was just another casualty.[142]

Gustav II Adolph was last seen taking command of the Smaland cavalry.[143] After that, his whereabouts are unknown until his body was found later.[144]

Ottavio Piccolomini reported that after he retreated from the Via Regia:

> in this moment the Blue Regiment, the king's most vaunted, advanced, and that made it happen that the Regiment Götz, which was to the right in front of me, got damaged by a volley. Hearing this, I immediately charged it, which let down the pikes, but making halve a caracole, I took them from the flank, where I cut it to pieces and took their colours. The king, hearing that this regiment [New Blue] got the 'load', felt the impulse to counter this disorder and crossed my squadron; after I had dispersed this infantry, I attacked again a cavalry regiment and dispersed it and at that time many of my soldiers [i.e. Innecentius Buccela][145] came to me telling me the king is dead ...[146]

Piccolomini could not have known that the King was attacking him. His intention was to get a reward from the Emperor for killing Gustav II Adolph, yet his account is one of the more credible stories that soldiers came to Holk and him showing trophies from the dead King, as Diodati confirmed.[147] A

142 Herzog Franz Albrecht von Sachsen-Lauenburg had defected from the Imperial army to Gustav II Adolph and was suspected of murdering the King (Fleetwood, Letter, p.12, Hülshorst – Wittrock, 'Fyra relationer', p.303). Some reported him as trying to save the King (Dalbier, *Lutzen*, p.251, Extrakt Schreiben aus Berlin – Mankell, *Arkiv* vol. II, p.658, Watts, *Swedish Intelligencer*, vol. 3, p.137, Chemnitz, *Geschichte*, p.466). The Imperial Oberstleutnant Falkenberg was reported to have killed the King (Khevenhiller, *Annales Ferdinandei*, p.192).

143 Fabricius (Wittrock, 'Fyra relationer', p.306) and Hallenus' eyewitnesses (Mankell, *Arkiv* vol. II, p.662) were close enough to have seen this incident. See also Relation I from Grimma (Anonymous, *Studien*, p.51), Watts, *Swedish Intelligencer*, vol. 3, p.137, Richelieu, *Mémoires*, p.259.

144 Even the story of the recovery of the King's body is unclear. According to Hallenus (Mankell, *Arkiv* vol. II, p.662), a boy spotted his horse, while the Relation I from Grimma (Anonymous, *Studien*, p.51) reported that he fell off his horse and was dragged hanging by one stirrup. Certainly unreliable are the stories of Bernhard von Weimar (Fleetwood, Letter, p.8) or Stalhandske (Watts, *Swedish Intelligencer*, vol. 3, p.142) heroically charging the enemy, finding and recovering the King's body.

145 Spanish Relation (Watts, *Swedish Intelligencer*, vol. 3, p.163).

146 Argang, 'Piccolominis bref', p.89.

147 Diodati (Fiedler, 'Diodatis Bericht', p.564).

short while later, Jacobus Fabricius saw the Smaland cavalry returning without the King and shortly thereafter the regiment's chaplain reported to him 'Rex vulneratus est.'[148]

Gustav II Adolph had refused to wear armour at Lützen, because a bullet he received in Poland during the Battle of Dirschau 8 August 1627 was still embedded in his shoulder and wearing armour apparently irritated the wound.[149] The reason for taking personal command of the Smaland Cavalry Regiment and charging the enemy was certainly the immediate necessity to do so, not that it was in the King's nature to take such a risk.[150] It is more likely that he had to, because the Smaland and Ostgöta cavalry's commanders were killed or wounded. Seeing his Swedish infantry dying, he could not wait for reinforcements.

This newer interpretation suggests a timeline for the events, because it must have occurred after the Swedish cavalry took heavy casualties. The heavy casualties place the episode after Pappenheim's arrival and Piccolomini's counter-attack. This scenario agrees with both Piccolomini's account that the King died after Piccolomini attacked the New Blue Regiment, and also with Fabricius' statement that there was not much time between the Smaland cavalry advancing with, and then returning without, the King. In turn, this sequence means that Gustav II Adolph could not have gone very far from his position on the inner right wing.[151] The location of the death of the King on the Imperial left wing is confirmed by Holk[152] and Diodati.[153]

Archaeology Sources (9): See PDF download

148 Wittrock, 'Fyra relationer', p.306. Hülshorst reported that the King was missing for two to three hours (Wittrock, 'Fyra relationer', p.303).

149 Barbo Bursell, *Die Königliche Rüstkammer als Museum – Ein Vermächtnis Gustav Adolfs, Maik Reichel, Inger Schuberth (eds), Gustav Adolf. König von Schweden. Die Kraft der Erinnerung 1632–2007* (Dössel: Verlag Janos Stekovics, 2007), p.95.

150 It is often claimed that Gustav II Adolph attacked the Imperial left wing at the head of his cavalry from the onset of the battle, which seems to be simply another myth about the King: Dalbier, *Lutzen*, p.251, Fleetwood, Letter, p.7, Hülshorst (Wittrock, 'Fyra relationer', p.303), Hallenus (Mankell, *Arkiv* vol. II, p.662). See also Brzezinski, *Lützen*, p.62.

151 This clearly contradicts Seidler, *Untersuchungen*, pp.58–77, who believed, based mostly on Khevenhiller's (*Annales Ferdinandei*, p.191) unreliable account, that the King rode off on a rescue mission for the left wing with only one cavalry regiment. This is a decision which would have left the right wing without strong leadership, would have endangered the success on the right, and would have come too late and with too few forces to change the fate of the left.

152 Wittrock, 'Fyra relationer', p.309. Holk reported that Gustav II Adolph was killed and the battle won 'on this side', which means the left wing commanded by Holk.

153 Fiedler, 'Diodatis Bericht', p.564. Diodati claimed that Holk's trumpeter showed him the King's spurs.

Gustav II Adolf at Lützen. Jan Asselijn (1610–1652), 1635. (Michał Paradowski's archive)

The Events

There is currently little real evidence for the events that led to the King's death. Refusing to wear armour because of the pain caused by a bullet in his shoulder, it was not Gustav II Adolph's intention to personally lead the right wing cavalry into combat. Pappenheim's and Piccolomini's counterattacks caused such serious casualties among the Swedish cavalry and its leadership that, when Gustav II Adolph saw his fellow countrymen being slaughtered on the right centre, he took command of the Smalanders and came to his men's rescue. It seems that he arrived in time to cover the Swedish Brigade's retreat, as it was fighting next to him[154] and because the brigade's pikemen

154 There is little evidence for this interpretation. However, the Swedish Brigade took relatively low casualties of 35 percent in comparison to the 68 percent of the Yellow Brigade (Brzezinski,

were covering the retreat of their musketeers at all costs. When he crashed into Piccolomini's harquebusiers or Götz's cuirassiers before he could reach his Lifeguard, he was separated from his men in the chaos of the melee and the thickening gun smoke and finally he fell somewhere on the Imperial left wing or left centre.[155]

Lützen, pp.87 and 89), except for their pikemen, because they were closer to the Swedish cavalry, according to Watts, *Swedish Intelligencer*, vol. 3, p.145.

155 Under the circumstances that no one had seen the death of Gustav II Adolph, it is almost certainly an invented story that the King was killed by Oberstleutnant Moritz von Falkenberg, commanding officer of Götz's Regiment, as claimed by Khevenhiller, *Annales Ferdinandei*, p.192.

† See PDF download, Plate 37

Imperial Left Wing: Destruction of the Yellow Brigade, 12:00–1:00 p.m.†

Historical Sources

The destruction of Gustav II Adolph's Lifeguard, the Yellow Brigade, was so impressive that most historical sources reported the episode, changing and embellishing it so as to give the King's guard a more heroic end.[156] Although there is a lot of historical evidence, most of it is superficial and the sequence of events is not entirely clear.

The most reliable source is certainly the account from Münchhausen, who was involved in the fight. He reported:

> we [Münchhausen and *Oberstleutnant* Stolper], with the two regiments [Comargo and Baden], had beaten and 'separated' three regiments, which remained in one,[157]

This means three squadrons fighting as one brigade. In another letter Münchhausen stated that the Regiments Comargo and Baden captured 14 colours from the Yellow and Old Blue Brigades, confusing the latter with the Swedish Brigade.[158] This is supported by Diodati, who fought in Grana's Regiment and certainly saw what happened, reporting the Yellow Brigade to have been destroyed by Imperial infantry.[159] Hallenus, whose account is based on two eyewitnesses who fought next to the Yellow Brigade, probably referred to the same event, when he wrote that Brahe was attacked from the flank by an Imperial cuirassier regiment, although Hallenus confused Brahe's command, which was the first line centre and the Yellow Brigade, and not the left wing.[160] The 'cuirassier regiment' in Hallenus' letter could have been Piccolomini's harquebusiers or, more likely, Götz's or Bredau's cuirassiers.†

† See PDF download, Plate 38: Yellow Brigade's attack vector 11:00 a.m. to 1:00 p.m. on musket bullet distribution map

Archaeology Sources (10): See PDF download

156 Originally only noted briefly by Relation from 1632 (Droysen, 'Gedruckte Relationen', p.9), the *Inventarium Sueciae* (Gottfried, *Inventarium Sueciae*, p.25) was the first 'relation' that made up the story of the Yellow Brigade forcing two huge Imperial cuadros (*sic*) to retreat and finally, exhausted from the fighting, was destroyed by two other Imperial cuadros, which would have meant that the Yellow Brigade had fought alone against almost the entire Imperial infantry. This story was copied by Anonymous, *Wahrhaftige Beschreibung*, Anonymous, *Glaubwürdiger Bericht*, Monro, *His Expedition*, part II, p.164, Abelinum, *Theatrum Europaeum*, pp.749–750 and Chemnitz, *Geschichte*, p.465 and retold by Khevenhiller, *Annales Ferdinandei*, pp.191–193.

157 Wittrock, 'Fyra relationer', p.305.

158 BHStA, 2424t194 f. 158: Münchhausen to Maximilian 6 December 1632. Probably based on Münchhausen's report, Gallas noted incorrectly that Comargo had destroyed the Old Blue Brigade (Förster, *Wallenstein's Prozess*, p.95).

159 Fiedler, 'Diodatis Bericht', p.563.

160 Mankell, *Arkiv*, vol. II, p.662.

The Events

After having suffered casualties at the road ditches, the small battery, and the first Imperial line, the Yellow Brigade advanced towards the second line and approached the Regiment Baden; behind which the Regiment Comargo was reforming. Although its left flank was possibly protected by Thurn's Brigade, the Yellow Brigade became more isolated after the Swedish Brigade on its right flank fell back. It appears that *Generalmajor* Nils Brahe was not fully aware of the situation, because the black powder smoke and the Lützen fires had created a dense 'fog'. Less than 1,000 of Gustav II Adolph's guard now faced approximately 1,700 Imperial infantry. The sudden appearance of cuirassiers on their unprotected right flank was even more devastating because their pikemen were engaged in combat against Baden's and Comargo's infantry. Even the Royal Guard veterans had no chance against this combined arms counter-attack.[†]

† See PDF download, Plate 39: 12:00 p.m. to 1:00 p.m.: Gustav II Adolph's and Pappenheim's deaths and destruction of the Yellow Brigade

It was a bloody fight. *Generalmajor* Nils Brahe was shot in the knee and died a few days later;[161] 693 of his 1,017 men were wounded or killed and only 324 men from the Yellow Brigade survived unharmed upon fighting their way back to their own lines.[162] Diodati reported:

> A great body with yellow casacks came up resolutely in formation with pikes covering their musketeers. When they were attacked by our foot they remained completely on the spot, and it was a wonder to see in a moment the body reduced to a mound of corpses.[163]

Gustav II Adolph's Lifeguard and Life Regiment had been effectively wiped out in minutes, although the Imperial army had paid a heavy price. Baden's Regiment took the highest casualties of any Imperial unit at Lützen; the commanding officer, *Oberstleutnant* Stolper, the *Obristwachtmeister* and all the company commanders, except *Hauptmann* Schulder, were killed, and *Obristwachtmeister* Münchhausen of Comargo's Infantry had to take command of both regiments.[164] From Piccolomini's Regiment, the *Oberst* received one musket shot and two sword cuts; *Oberstleutnant* Conte Avogadri was hit by a musket bullet in the right thigh. *Major* Pier Martelini and *Rittmeisters* Baco, Marchese Palavicino and Fesente were killed. *Rittmeister* Crepi was hit in the ear with a pike; *Rittmeister* Silvio Piccolomini, who 'hoped in God and his capable barber', was shot in the thigh and the knee. *Rittmeister* Baron Mattei's horse was killed and a cavalry regiment rode over him. 100 cavalry were killed and another 100 wounded.[165]

---

161 Hülshorst (Wittrock, 'Fyra relationer', p.303), Pentz (Fiedler, 'Diodatis Bericht', p.571), Hallenus (Mankell, *Arkiv* vol. II, p.662).

162 Brzezinski, *Lützen*, p.87.

163 Fiedler, 'Diodatis Bericht', p.563.

164 Münchhausen (Wittrock, 'Fyra relationer', p.305), Relation from 1632 (Droysen, 'Gedruckte Relationen', p.11), Wallenstein's 22 December 1632 letter to Holk (Hallwich, *Briefe und Akten*, vol. 3, p.657).

165 As reported by Silvio Piccolomini (Anonymous, *Archivio*, p.241).

† See PDF download, Plate 40

Imperial Right Wing: Wallenstein's Counter-Attack and Destruction of the Old Blue Brigade, 12:30–1:30 p.m.†

Historical Sources

The Old Blue Brigade is mentioned only once when it advanced along with the Swedish left wing[166] when it appears in the Fleetwood's eyewitness account. All Imperial eyewitnesses and secondary sources have confused the Old Blue Brigade with the Swedish Brigade, because both were wearing, at least in part, blue coats. Because the Green Brigade is also mentioned only sporadically, there are no reliable reports about events on the Swedish left centre around midday. By then the Old Blue Brigade had suffered terrible losses. Of 918 men, excluding officers, only 331 reported shortly after the battle; 63 percent were killed, wounded, or unaccounted for and the commanding officer, *Oberst* Hans Georg aus dem Winckel, was wounded.[167] Even the Green Brigade, which assaulted the fortified Imperial windmill battery frontally, had only 39 percent losses. This suggests that the Old Blue Brigade met a similar fate to the Yellow Brigade.

There is one more question concerning the Imperial right wing: Where was Piccolomini's Regiment? Neither Ottavio nor Silvio Piccolomini mentioned what happened to their regiment after Gustav II Adolph's death. Holk reported:

> The Duke [Wallenstein] … fought two hours against infantry with four horse regiments, namely Holk, Trcka, Piccolomini and Desfour, and he was encircled completely until Holk gave back the cavalry to 'second' him.'[168]

This comment might be the key to understanding what happened on the Imperial right. Holk put this sentence at the end of his account after he had explained the result of the battle, making it difficult to fit into the timeline. The cavalry Holk 'gave back' is certainly that which came from the right as reinforcements, i.e. the Regiment Westrumb. By then the Regiment Piccolomini was already engaged on the right. Both regiments were under Holk's command, at least for a time, and he certainly knew that they left his command, but both regiments could not have been sent to the right wing before Holk was at least partially successful.

It seems that Piccolomini changed to the right wing immediately after his engagement with the Swedish Brigade at around midday, while Westrumb must have followed soon after, possibly after the Swedish right was beaten

166 Fleetwood, Letter, p.7.

167 According to Eberstein, all colonels of the infantry except possibly Mitzlaff and himself, were wounded or killed (Diemar, 'Der Anteil der Hessen', p.348). See also Relation II from Erfurt (Droysen, 'Gedruckte Relationen', p.21), *Relation from 1633* (Droysen, 'Gedruckte Relationen', p.34), Declaration from 1633 (Droysen, 'Gedruckte Relationen', p.44) and Khevenhiller, *Annales Ferdinandei*, p.197.

168 Wittrock, 'Fyra relationer', p.309.

around one o'clock. Piccolomini certainly did not fight two hours on the right before Westrumb arrived, which seems simply to have been one of Holk's generalisations. However, it does not seem likely that the Regiment Piccolomini was responsible for the destruction of the Old Blue Brigade, because he was needed on the right wing to prevent a disaster.[169]

Archaeology Sources (11): See PDF download

The Events

It seems that the arrival of Pappenheim's cavalry on the Imperial left wing, despite the death of the *Feldmarschall* and the Imperial 'Fahnenflucht', had an impact on the whole course of the battle. Once the Swedish attack was stopped by Pappenheim's reinforcements, an Imperial counter-attack punched through the Swedish line between the centre and right wing. Exploiting this success, adjacent units were attacked and beaten freeing Imperial units for other operations; as Holk reported, he sent back the units he had received from the right wing.[170]

With reinforcements from Holk's successful left wing, the Imperial right centre and right wing was stabilised, making it possible to counter-attack the Old Blue Brigade, using Wallenstein's successful combined arms tactics of infantry on their front and cavalry on the flank. Nevertheless, the Swedish infantry still managed to retreat over the Via Regia, albeit closely followed by Imperial units. At some point *Oberst* Hans Georg aus dem Winckel was wounded and the Old Blue Brigade lost cohesion, and then finally broke up. Only 331 out of 918 soldiers made it back to their lines unharmed; Winckel's veteran regiment was in no shape to resume fighting.

Meanwhile, the arrival of Piccolomini's Regiment prevented a disaster on Wallenstein's right, where Bernhard von Weimar was still pressing forward. When the Old Blue Brigade was beaten back, the Green Brigade's right flank was threatened, and *Oberst* Georg Wulf von Wildenstein,[171] who was wounded, could not hold his position. With further reinforcements from Holk, consisting at the very least of Westrumb's harquebusiers, Wallenstein counter-attacked von Weimar's wing and drove it back, and soon almost the entire Swedish army was in retreat.

169 Watts, *Swedish Intelligencer*, vol. 3, p.161 made a comment in the Spanish Relation reporting that Piccolomini destroyed a Swedish regiment, leaving it stretched out on the ground, which Watts, *Swedish Intelligencer*, vol. 3, p.161 said was Winckel's Regiment, which might be one of the sources for the confusion of the Old Blue and the Swedish brigades.

170 Wittrock, 'Fyra relationer', p.309.

171 Monro, *His Expedition*, part II, p.165, Relation II from Erfurt (Droysen, 'Gedruckte Relationen', p.21), *Relation from 1633* (Droysen, 'Gedruckte Relationen', p.34), Declaration from 1633 (Droysen, 'Gedruckte Relationen', p.44), Khevenhiller, *Annales Ferdinandei*, p.197.

Gustav II Adolf at Lützen.
Jan Asselijn (1610–1652), 1634. (National Gallery of Denmark)

Dragoons and Harquebusiers skirmishing. Sebastiaen Vrancx (1573–1647). (Muzeum Narodowe, Warszawa)

Cavalry, perhaps dragoons, in buff coat and with long carbines or dragoon muskets, 1630. Esaias van de Velde. (Rijksmuseum)

Above: Cuirassiers fighting an harquebusier in back and breast and buff coat, 1618. Detail from a painting by Sebastiaen Vrancx (1573–1647). (Staatliche Kunsthalle Karlsruhe)

Right: Dragoon, or possibly an harquebusier. Sebastiaen Vrancx (1573–1647). (Muzeum Narodowe, Warszawa)

Stalemate: Imperial and Swedish Armies at the Brink of Collapse, 1:00–2:00 p.m.

It is impossible to get a clear picture of the situation in the early afternoon. Most accounts from both sides played down the chaos with descriptions such as 'our cavalry was almost disordered.'[172] However, some eyewitnesses give a completely different picture, in particular Gustav II Adolph' Chaplain, Jacobus Fabricius:

> After his Majesty King Gustav II Adolph ..., riding with the Smaland cavalry over a ditch, had engaged the enemy ... it was soon after that, that this regiment returned, and no one wanted to answer my question, where the King was, until a passing by field preacher shouted: 'The king is wounded.' I was shocked about that and turned to the place where I had seen his Royal Majesty moving. But instead I met *Oberst* Ernst von Anhalt-Bernburg, *Oberstleutnant* Winckler and *Oberstleutnant* Rehlinger along with other high-ranking officers, who asked if I have seen their folk ... Two members of the Royal Office rode by and shouted: 'It is a rout.' But I responded: 'Make a stand, our flight provoke all others to flee.' In search for my king I met a lot of fleeing musketeers and cavalrymen and a Livonian nobleman named *Oberstleutnant* Tiesenhausen, whom I ordered to stand. But the more we were shouting the faster they were running, because they thought they were pursued by the enemy, not seeing far because of the thick fog.'[173]

It is a very telling point about the Swedish army's condition that officers were searching for their soldiers. Fleetwood's comment:

> ... for had not our foote stoode like a wall, there had not a man of us come off alive, ... and our horse did but poorely[174]

This is evidence that the Swedish cavalry was even in worse condition than the infantry. *Herzog* Albrecht von Sachsen-Lauenburg fled from the battlefield with 300 horse.[175]

If it seemed that the entire army was about to fall apart, why did Wallenstein not take advantage of the situation? It was certainly not because Fabricius and *Oberst* George Fleetwood began to sing Lutheran songs and so rallied many men.[176] Pursuing Imperial cavalry, which was already moving over the Via Regia to finish off the Swedish army, would have prevented that.†

† See PDF download, Plate 41: 12:30 p.m. to 2:00 p.m.: Destruction of the Old Blue Brigade and retreat of the Swedish army

The answer has to be that the Imperial army was not in a very good shape either. The harquebusier Regiment Hagen had changed wings twice without

172 Diodati (Fiedler, 'Diodatis Bericht', p.563), *Relation from 1633* (Droysen, 'Gedruckte Relationen', p.31).

173 Wittrock, 'Fyra relationer', p.306. The correct names and ranks are given rather than those given by Fabricius.

174 Fleetwood, Letter, p.9.

175 Hülshorst (Wittrock, 'Fyra relationer', p.303).

176 According to Fabricius (Wittrock, 'Fyra relationer', p.306).

fighting and was then waiting behind the right wing, disobeying orders to engage the enemy.[177] Hagen was accompanied by the Cuirassier Regiment Sparr, which had also retreated from the left to the right wing and similarly had refused to fight, until it finally left the battlefield just before the end of the fighting.[178] The worst of all was *Oberst* Lothar von Bönninghausen, whose harquebusiers retreated before they ever engaged, then looted their own baggage train, probably frightening the camp followers who, in turn, cut the wagon horses loose, and fled together with the cavalry.[179] On their way back to Halle they tried to discourage Pappenheim's infantry from reinforcing the Imperial army at Lützen.[180] It was not just the mounted men; the infantry, although holding their ground, had suffered terrible losses and many high-ranking officers were either killed or wounded. In essence, there were too few intact regiments able to pursue the Swedes.

On the Swedish side *Generalmajor* Knyphausen kept his own brigade, the Brigade Duke Wilhelm and the Cavalry Regiment Öhm in reserve.[181] They were holding the line so the routed Swedish regiments could be rallied behind them. The other two second-line brigades, Mitzlaff and Thurn, whose task had probably been to occupy the Imperial centre, but not to break through, had not taken heavy losses[182] and seem to have made an orderly retreat. At this point the battle paused.

Bernhard von Weimar and Knyphausen: the Second Swedish Attack

After the Swedish rout, the battle continued for at least another four hours, but eyewitness accounts are mostly silent about it and secondary sources are inconsistent about what happened in the later stages of the battle. Most seem influenced by the unreliable *Inventarium Sueciae*. Consequently, Deuticke[183] and Brzezinski[184] made only a short mention of any afternoon combat. Seidler reconstructed a completely erroneous scenario based on secondary sources, reporting that the Swedish army attacked in a 'storm of vengeance' created by the death of the King.[185] While Generalstaben suggested a different erroneous account similar to modern warfare with a slowly but steadily

177 Verdict vs. Hagen (Seidler, *Untersuchungen*, p.142).

178 Verdict vs. Hofkirchen (Seidler, *Untersuchungen*, pp.142–143).

179 Watts, *Swedish Intelligencer*, vol. 3, p.142.

180 Verdict vs. officers from Bönninghausen's Regiment (Seidler, *Untersuchungen*, pp.144–145). Bönninghausen himself was too important to be executed. The Imperial 'Fahnenflucht' and plundering the baggage train is also reported by Holk (Wittrock, 'Fyra relationer', p.309) and Münchhausen (Wittrock, 'Fyra relationer', p.305).

181 Dalbier, *Lutzen*, p.252.

182 Brzezinski, *Lützen*, p.87 calculated a total of 38 percent and 15 percent losses during the battle.

183 Deuticke, *Lützen*, pp.79–82.

184 Brzezinski, *Lützen*, pp.79–80.

185 Seidler, *Untersuchungen*, pp.79–83.

advancing front, which completely ignored the Swedish rout.[186]

Of the small number of reliable accounts about the afternoon's events, only Fleetwood and Dalbier provide valuable information, reflecting on the condition of both armies, which were near collapsing, and on the limited visibility due to powder smoke and the burning Lützen. Although it is almost impossible to get a clear picture of the afternoon's events from historical sources alone, additional evidence can be provided by the archaeological survey.

With most soldiers near exhaustion, the nature of engagement in the afternoon is described best by Vitzthum/Berlepsch: 'A fatal earnestness was seen and heard on both sides.'[187] His comment is supported by *Extract Underschiedlicher Schreiben*[188] and *Relation from 1632*[189] reporting that no quarter was given and the Imperial musketeers clubbed Protestants to death with the butt ends of their muskets, demonstrating the brutality of the engagement during its latter stages. The 'storm of vengeance' created by the death of Gustav II Adolph, which is supposed to have turned the tide of battle in favour of the Swedes, is reported by very few sources and seems to be one of the myths associated with the death of the King.[190]

Collapse of the Swedish Command Structure

With Gustav II Adolph's death and the fatal wounding of *Generalmajor* Nils Brahe, the army had lost its overall commander and the right wing and right centre also now lacked a commander. The consequences of the disrupted Swedish command structure have never been subject to research. The most accepted view,[191] that Bernhard von Weimar got Knyphausen to agree to continue the battle, is based only on the unreliable accounts of Siri and Richelieu.[192] This view is very likely a myth, possibly created to justify Bernhard von Weimar taking command of the army a few days after the battle. Although *Generalleutnant* von Weimar outranked *Generalmajor* Knyphausen, and were the only senior officers left, only secondary sources claim that von Weimar actually took command of the Swedish army during the battle,[193] and

186 Generalstaben, *Sveriges Krig*, pp.438–451.

187 Glafey, *De Gladio*, p.14. See also Brzezinski, *Lützen*, p.79.

188 Droysen, 'Gedruckte Relationen', pp.4–5.

189 Droysen, 'Gedruckte Relationen', p.9.

190 Fleetwood, Letter, p.8, Chemnitz, *Geschichte*, p.466. A 'storm of vengeance' is suggested by Seidler, *Untersuchungen*, p.79 and rejected by Brzezinski, *Lützen*, p.9).

191 Deuticke, *Lützen*, p.80, Generalstaben, *Sveriges Krig*, p.447, Seidler, *Untersuchungen*, p.79, Brzezinski, *Lützen*, p.78.

192 Richelieu, *Mémoires*, p.261.

193 Bodo von Bodenhausen (Glafey, *De Gladio*, p.11), 58. Ordentliche Wochentliche Zeitung (Söltl, *Religionskriege*, pp.338–339), Relation II from Erfurt (Droysen, 'Gedruckte Relationen', pp.20–21), *Relation from 1633* (Droysen, 'Gedruckte Relationen', pp.31–32), Declaration from 1633 (Droysen, 'Gedruckte Relationen', p.42), Chemnitz, *Geschichte*, p.467, Abelinum, *Theatrum Europaeum*, pp.749–750, Khevenhiller, *Annales Ferdinandei*, p.196, Richelieu, *Mémoires*, p.260

this is still the accepted view.[194] In fact, two eyewitnesses[195] and four early letters report that von Weimar and Knyphausen shared army command,[196] and Hallenus stated that Bernhard von Weimar only took command in Weissenfels, after the battle.[197]

The command of the right wing and right centre, which was unlikely to have been in the hands of Torsten Stalhandske, who lacked authority as *Överste*, has been completely overlooked by historians. It is likewise improbable that Bernhard von Weimar commanded the entire centre first line and both wings, as Deuticke claimed,[198] because such a command would have been too large to handle. Dalbier reported Knyphausen was connected with the afternoon's events on the right wing and it seems possible, and reasonable, that he took command of that wing,[199] while Bernhard von Weimar kept command of the left wing, sharing command of the centre between them.[200]

Knyphausen's Second Swedish Right Wing Attack, 3:00–6:00 p.m.†

† See PDF download, Plate 42

Archaeology Sources (12): See PDF download

Historical Sources

If we were to believe Holk's account, the battle ended when his wing put the Swedish right wing to flight around midday.[201] The result of the battle, especially with the entire Imperial artillery being captured by the Swedes and the battle going on until darkness fell, are proof that Holk omitted the circumstances surrounding his loss of the small Imperial battery.

---

and Gottfried, *Inventarium Sueciae*, p.26, copied by Monro, *His Expedition*, part II, pp.164–165, Anonymous, *Wahrhaftige Beschreibung* and Anonymous, *Glaubwürdiger Bericht*.

194 Generalstaben, *Sveriges Krig*, p.447, Brzezinski, *Lützen*, p.78. Seidler ignored the question of command.

195 Brandenstein (Glafey, *De Gladio*, p.10), Swedish HQ (Söltl, *Religionskriege*, p.348).

196 Extrakt Schreiben aus Berlin (Mankell, *Arkiv* vol. II, p.658), Copia verträulichen Schreibens (Söltl, *Religionskriege*, p.341), letter from 17 December (Söltl, *Religionskriege*, p.341), Pentz (Fiedler, 'Diodatis Bericht', pp.570–571).

197 Mankell, *Arkiv* vol. II, p.665. The practical problem of taking command of the Swedish main army is also reported by the 19 November letter from an unknown author (Mankell, *Arkiv* vol. II, p.647).

198 Deuticke, *Lützen*, p.79.

199 Dalbier, *Lutzen*, p.252. Knyphausen as commander of the right wing is also noted by Chemnitz, *Geschichte*, p.466.

200 Fleetwood, Letter, p.8, *Relation from 1633* (Droysen, 'Gedruckte Relationen', p.31–32), Chemnitz, *Geschichte*, p.467, Khevenhiller, *Annales Ferdinandei*, p.196 and Gottfried, *Inventarium Sueciae*, p.26, copied by Monro, *His Expedition*, part II, pp.164–165, Anonymous, *Wahrhaftige Beschreibung* and Anonymous, *Glaubwürdiger Bericht*.

201 Wittrock, 'Fyra relationer', p.309.

The second capture of the small Imperial battery is reported by Dalbier[202] in the most detailed part of his account suggesting that he witnessed it. He noted that the Swedes captured the battery and spiked the guns at 2:00 o'clock, but Dalbier's timeline is not always accurate. When he realised that the enemy was not returning, Knyphausen ordered the nails removed and sent ammunition of the correct calibre.[203] After the Swedes had fired the captured artillery for an hour, there was no Imperial unit left on that wing. The absence of Imperial forces here very likely means they were simply out of range. While it sounds as if there was not much resistance from the Imperial side, the battle went on at least another three hours, indicating that details about the fighting around the Imperial battery after it was taken by the Swedes have not survived. A third and fourth attack on the Imperial left wing are mentioned only in secondary sources and it seems likely that those printed accounts were just to fill in the gaps in the knowledge of the narrative.[204]

The Events

At some point in the afternoon it was probably *Generalmajor* Knyphausen who ordered the Swedish right wing to attack with an unknown force. It is likely that the White and Duke Wilhelm's brigades were part of this attack because they were probably the only intact infantry units left in the area. Any other units may have been ad hoc formations created from rallied troops. This attack was at least partially successful as the small Imperial battery was captured and its guns turned against Imperial forces.[205] This episode, in turn, forced Holk's exhausted left wing to retreat beyond firing range. There was certainly a lot of skirmishing until the evening, but no serious action, which would have changed the battle's outcome.†

† See PDF download, Plate 43: 2:00 p.m. to 3:00 p.m.: Second Swedish attack

† See PDF download, Plate 44

The Second Swedish Left Wing Attack, 3:00–6:00 p.m.†

Archaeology Sources (13): See PDF download

Historical Sources

Not much is known about the afternoon's events at the windmills. There is, however, a strange agreement in the historical sources based on the *Relation II from Erfurt* about the late afternoon arrival of Pappenheim's infantry and their subsequent counter-attack against the windmill battery.[206] While more

202 Dalbier, *Lutzen*, pp.252–253.

203 Chemnitz, *Geschichte*, p.466 reported this incident similarly – that Knyphausen's infantry took the guns and turned them on the Imperial army.

204 *Relation from 1633* (Droysen, 'Gedruckte Relationen', p.32), Watts, *Swedish Intelligencer*, vol. 3, p.148, Abelinum, *Theatrum Europaeum*, p.750, Chemnitz, *Geschichte*, p.467 and Gottfried, *Inventarium Sueciae*, p.26, copied by Monro, *His Expedition*, part II, pp.164–165.

205 Chemnitz, *Geschichte*, p.466.

206 Relation II from Erfurt (Droysen, 'Gedruckte Relationen', p.20), copied or retold by *Relation from 1633* (Droysen, 'Gedruckte Relationen', p.31), Declaration from 1633 (Droysen, 'Gedruckte

reliable sources state that the infantry arrived after nightfall, too late for the battle,[207] Fleetwood,[208] incorrectly as Watts stated,[209] believed Bernhard von Weimar was attacked by Pappenheim's infantry in the late afternoon. These Imperial infantry squadrons were more likely rallied, ad hoc assemblies of fragmented units, possibly reinforced by newly arriving companies from nearby garrisons.[210]

According to Fleetwood, the Imperial counter-attack broke down when a high-ranking officer, who he incorrectly believed was Merode, was killed.[211] *Generalfeldzeugmeister* Hans Philipp Breuner and *Oberst* Berthold von Waldstein, both sub-commanders, were also fatally wounded near the windmills, which could have caused a panic among Imperial soldiers in that area.

The Events

After rallying his troops about 3:00 p.m., *Generalleutnant* Bernhard von Weimar faced the same situation as in the morning. He ordered *Oberst* Gersdorf with his commanded musketeers to renew the attack against the Lützen gardens,[212] this time probably supported by additional troops, possibly including Leslie's Scots.[213] The rest of von Weimar's task force is unknown, but very likely consisted of the second line and parts of the first line cavalry, the Green Brigade, and the two left hand second line infantry brigades, Mitzlaff and Thurn.†

† See PDF download, Plate 45: 3:00 p.m. to 4:00 p.m.: Second Imperial counter-attack

Wallenstein appears to have gathered his remaining forces on his right wing at the windmills. These consisted of three infantry squadrons, probably the left hand squadrons Waldstein/Alt-Sachsen, Colloredo/Chiesa and Jung-Breuner, with some cavalry,[214] among them Piccolomini and probably the cuirassier squadrons Holk and Trcka/Desfour.[215]

Relationen', p.42), Gottfried, *Inventarium Sueciae*, p.26, Monro, *His Expedition*, part II, p.164, Anonymous, *Wahrhaftige Beschreibung*, Anonymous, *Glaubwürdiger Bericht*, Abelinum, *Theatrum Europaeum*, p.750, Chemnitz, *Geschichte*, p.467, Khevenhiller, *Annales Ferdinandei*, p.193.

207 In particular Holk (Wittrock, 'Fyra relationer', p.309), Diodati (Fiedler, 'Diodatis Bericht', p.566) and Ottavio Piccolomini (Anonymous, *Archivio*, p.240). See also Burgus, *Mars Sveco-Germanicus*, p.326, Spanish Relation (Watts, *Swedish Intelligencer*, vol. 3, p.163) and Relation from 1632 (Droysen, 'Gedruckte Relationen', p.10).

208 Fleetwood, Letter, p.8.

209 Watts, *Swedish Intelligencer*, vol. 3, p.149.

210 Brzezinski, *Lützen*, p.79.

211 Fleetwood, Letter, p.8.

212 Watts, *Swedish Intelligencer*, vol. 3, p.149 reported that the Swedes finally cleared the gardens in the fourth attack.

213 Monro, *His Expedition*, part II, p.164 stated incorrectly that Gersdorf's musketeers included Leslie's Scots. However, it might be possible that Monro misunderstood an eyewitness and they supported Gersdorf in the second attack.

214 The Relation II from Erfurt (Droysen, 'Gedruckte Relationen', p.20) noted that there were only three Imperial infantry regiments left at the windmills in the afternoon. According to Dalbier, *Lutzen*, p.252 there were two Imperial infantry squadrons and cavalry left at the windmills.

215 Holk (Wittrock, 'Fyra relationer', p.309).

At some point the Green Brigade, now only 50 men strong according to Fleetwood,[216] managed to capture the windmill battery and turned the guns on the Imperial troops.[217] *Oberstleutnant* Albrecht von Hofkirchen finally left the battlefield with Sparr's Regiment.[218] In the end, Wallenstein managed to rally his forces one last time and the infantry recaptured the windmill battery, during which *Generalfeldzeugmeister* Breuner or *Oberst* Berthold von Waldstein were mortally wounded which broke the Imperial morale. It was reported that the Swedish *Rittmeister* Bodo von Bodenhausen managed to get close to the Generalissimus and shot at him but missed.[219] One Swedish brigade, probably Mitzlaff's, pursued the retreating Imperial infantry and engaged them in a last fire fight.

The Battle's End and the Arrival of Pappenheim's Infantry, 6:00–8:00 p.m.

The battle ended with nightfall at around 5:00 p.m. when darkness made it impossible to fight on.[220] The fact that the battle ended at nightfall suggests that it was not over suddenly. Diodati gave a good, although not entirely honest, description of the process:

> Meanwhile the night was near, and the enemy's cavalry left the field in disorder, with the result that the foot had to follow, after that they started again with a

216 Fleetwood, Letter, p.8. The low strength of the Green Brigade cannot be explained with exceptional high losses, but is probably an argument for Leslie's Scots being involved in the afternoon's fight in the Lützen gardens.

217 Fleetwood, Letter, p.8, Vitzthum/Berlepsch (Glafey, *De Gladio*, p.14), Relation from 1632 (Droysen, 'Gedruckte Relationen', p.8), *Relation from 1633* (Droysen, 'Gedruckte Relationen', p.31), Declaration from 1633 (Droysen, 'Gedruckte Relationen', p.42), Gottfried, *Inventarium Sueciae*, p.26, Monro, *His Expedition*, part II, p.164, Anonymous, *Wahrhaftige Beschreibung*, Anonymous, *Glaubwürdiger Bericht*, Abelinum, *Theatrum Europaeum*, p.750 and Richelieu, *Mémoires*, p.261.

218 Seidler, *Untersuchungen*, p.143.

219 Wahrhaftiger Bericht (Diemar, 'Der Anteil der Hessen', p.340).

220 Eyewitnesses and secondary sources agree on the end of the battle. Eyewitnesses: Swedish HQ (Söltl, *Religionskriege*, p.347), Vitzthum/Berlepsch (Glafey, *De Gladio*, p.14), Wallenstein (Lorenz, Quellen zur Geschichte, 256), Silvio Piccolomini (Anonymous, *Archivio*, p.240), Poyntz, *The Relation*, p.73. Secondary sources: Hallenus (Mankell, *Arkiv* vol. II, p.663), Relation from 1632 (Droysen, 'Gedruckte Relationen', p.9), Relation II from Erfurt (Droysen, 'Gedruckte Relationen', p.20), *Relation from 1633* (Droysen, 'Gedruckte Relationen', p.32), Gottfried, *Inventarium Sueciae*, p.26, Monro, *His Expedition*, part II, p.165, Anonymous, *Wahrhaftige Beschreibung*, Anonymous, *Glaubwürdiger Bericht*, Burgus, *Mars Sveco-Germanicus*, p.326, Abelinum, *Theatrum Europaeum*, p.751, Chemnitz, *Geschichte*, p.467 and Richelieu, *Mémoires*, p.261. An exact time is given by Fleetwood, Letter, p.8 and Watts, *Swedish Intelligencer*, vol. 3, p.150 with 5:00 p.m.; by Knyphausen (Anonymous, *Studien*, p.49) and Pentz (Fiedler, 'Diodatis Bericht', p.571) with 6:00 p.m.; by Dalbier, *Lutzen*, p.252 and Holk (Wittrock, 'Fyra relationer', p.309) with 7:00 p.m.; and by Hülshorst (Wittrock, 'Fyra relationer', p.303) with 8:00 p.m., which seems to agree with a battle ending at 'nightfall.'

> heavy artillery fire, concentrated large masses of infantry, and they appeared to attack again, but these were the signs of retreat ...[221]

This illustrates the situation in the evening as the battle ended, with both sides separating. albeit still under artillery fire, after 6 hours of fighting – 'both armies retreated the space of one half English mile.'[222] According to reliable Imperial eyewitnesses, it was after both armies drew apart, after or close to nightfall, that Pappenheim's infantry regiments – Gil de Haes, Goltz, Moriamez-Pallant, Pallant, Reinach and Würzburg, approximately 3,000 men commanded by *Generalwachtmeister* Heinrich *Graf* von Reinach[223] – arrived on the battlefield.[224]

It was dark when Reinach sent the junior officer Augustin von Fritsch and a corporal to gather intelligence about the general situation. He reported that after they had crawled near the windmills, afraid of being caught by Swedish guards, he at first believed he had seen the burning match of muskets:

> I saw, however, that they were only candles which the soldiers were holding as they looted the battlefield or visited the dead. From there I went over to see our big canon, but there was not a single soldier of ours or the enemy's at that place.[225]

Could Wallenstein have continued the battle the next day with Reinach's infantry and perhaps recaptured his artillery? Wallenstein's army had fought for six hours with many fewer reserves, which meant that his soldiers were more often engaged in combat over a longer period than the Swedes, and were exhausted. Poyntz noted:

> wee were scarcely laid downe on the ground to rest and in dead sleep but comes a comaund from the Generall to all Coronells and Sergeant Maiors to give in a Note how strong every Regiment was found to bee, but it seemes finding every Regiment very weake by the Officers Relation, wee had scarcely had one sleep for ourselves & our horses and as little victuals for both.[226]

An additional consideration was that Wallenstein did not know whether any Saxon regiments would arrive the next day to reinforce the Swedish

221 Fiedler, 'Diodatis Bericht', p.566.

222 Poyntz, *The Relation*, p.73.

223 Officially Oberst Jean Graf Merode-Varoux was Pappenheim's second in command, but he was probably somewhere else (Brzezinski, *Lützen*, pp.26 and 81). However, Diodati (Fiedler, 'Diodatis Bericht', p.566) reported Merode in command of Pappenheim's infantry.

224 Holk (Wittrock, 'Fyra relationer', p.309), Diodati (Fiedler, 'Diodatis Bericht', p.566) and Silvio Piccolomini (Anonymous, *Archivio*, p.240), confirmed by the Catholic secondary sources. Relation from 1632 (Droysen, 'Gedruckte Relationen', p.10), Spanish Relation (Watts, *Swedish Intelligencer*, vol. 3, p.163) and Burgus, *Mars Sveco-Germanicus*, p.326, clearly contradicts secondary sources of lesser reliability (section 7.4.3).

225 Brzezinski, *Lützen*, p.81.

226 Poyntz, *The Relation*, p.73.

army. Also in consideration is that Wallenstein's health was not at its best and it seems possible that his will to fight was broken.

After counting his losses,[227] among them many officers, including his nephew *Oberst* Berthold von Waldstein and his brother-in-law *Graf* Harrach, and discussing the situation with his officers,[228] Wallenstein opted to retreat and started an orderly withdrawal from the battlefield between 8:00 and 9:00 p.m.[229] He had to leave his artillery[230] with all their ammunition wagons[231] behind because most of his draft animals had fled when his camp followers had done so.[232] †

† See PDF download, Plate 46: Wallenstein's retreat to Bohemia, 17 November to 4 January.

Except for the second line's reserve, Öhm's cavalry, all Swedish units had been heavily engaged in combat.[233] The Swedes must also have been exhausted, as they made no attempt to pursue the Imperial army that evening or to seize the Imperial artillery. According to Fritsch and Diodati,[234] they withdrew to the positions that they had occupied before the battle, where they camped that night and next day.[235] †

† See PDF download, Plate 47: 4:00 p.m. to 5:00 p.m.: Last operations before dusk

227 Poyntz, *The Relation*, p.73.

228 Holk (Wittrock, 'Fyra relationer', p.309).

229 Two hours after nightfall according to Diodati (Fiedler, 'Diodatis Bericht', p.566), three hours according to the Spanish Relation (Watts, *Swedish Intelligencer*, vol. 3, p.163), 9:00 p.m. according to the Relation II from Erfurt (Droysen, 'Gedruckte Relationen', p.20).

230 There is a conflict in secondary sources about the captured Imperial artillery, made up by the Relation II from Erfurt (Droysen, 'Gedruckte Relationen', p.20), stating that the Imperial army burnt their camp and left three pieces behind. This is changed in *Relation from 1633* (Droysen, 'Gedruckte Relationen', p.32) into 'the Imperial army took three pieces with them'. This was embellished by the Declaration from 1633 (Droysen, 'Gedruckte Relationen', p.42) into 'the Imperial army took three 24-pounders with them.' In turn this was changed again by Gottfried, *Inventarium Sueciae*, p.26 into 'the Imperials burnt their camp and took three pieces with them.' The Anonymous, *Wahrhaftige Beschreibung* and Anonymous, *Glaubwürdiger Bericht* copied the Declaration from 1633 and Abelinum, *Theatrum Europaeum*, p.749 used the Relation II from Erfurt but changed the number of pieces to two. Watts, *Swedish Intelligencer*, vol. 3, p.151 misunderstood the story completely and noted that the Swedes burnt seven pieces, while Monro, *His Expedition*, part II, p.165 claimed that the Imperialists burnt three pieces and took the rest with them. There is no proof from any eyewitness reporting a similar story, which was likely to have simply been made up.

231 Dalbier, *Lutzen*, p.252, Fleetwood, Letter, p.9, Vitzthum/Berlepsch (Glafey, *De Gladio*, p.14) – most ammunition, Hülshorst (Wittrock, 'Fyra relationer', p.303), Pentz (Fiedler, 'Diodatis Bericht', p.571), *Relation from 1633* (Droysen, 'Gedruckte Relationen', p.32).

232 Diodati (Fiedler, 'Diodatis Bericht', p.566), Poyntz, *The Relation*, p.73. Holk (Wittrock, 'Fyra relationer', p.309) noted that they had no horses for towing the artillery.

233 Brzezinski, *Lützen*, p.83.

234 Brzezinski, *Lützen*, p.81, Fiedler, 'Diodatis Bericht', p.566.

235 Dalbier, *Lutzen*, p.252.

Tables

Table 18: The 'Lützen fog' and commencement of battle in historical sources

Eyewitness accounts	Morning, fog before battle (page no.)	Fog during the battle (page no.)	Start of battle (page no.)
Swedish HQ – Söltl, *Religionskriege*	Clear dawn(?) then fog in the morning (346)		11:00 a.m. (346)
Dalbier, *Lutzen*	Clear dawn, then fog until 9:00 a.m. (251)	Fog returns at 10:30 a.m. (251)	9:00 a.m. (251)
Fleetwood, *Letter*	Clear morning (7)	Fog after 10:00 a.m. (8)	8:00 a.m. (first shot) to 10:00 a.m. (7)
Fabricius – Wittrock, 'Fyra relationer'		Fog midday (306)	
Diodati – Fiedler, 'Diodatis Bericht'		Fog midday (563)	
Wallenstein – Lorenz, *Quellen zur Geschichte Wallensteins*			10:00 a.m. (256)
Holk – Wittrock, 'Fyra relationer'			11:00 a.m. first 'salvo' (308)
Knyphausen – Anonymous, *Studien*			10:00 a.m. (49)
S. Piccolomini – Anonymous, *Archivio*			2 hours before midday (240)
Münchhausen – Wittrock, 'Fyra relationer'			9:00 a.m. (304)
Secondary sources, letters			
Hallenus – Mankell, *Arkiv* vol. II	Fog the whole day (662)		After 9:00 a.m. (662)
Pentz – Fiedler, 'Diodatis Bericht'		Fog midday (570)	
Relation I Grimma – Anonymous, *Studien*		Fog 1:00 p.m. (51)	
Hülshorst – Wittrock, 'Fyra relationer'			11:00 a.m.–12:00 p.m. (303)
Gallas – Förster, *Wallenstein's Prozess*			11:00 a.m. (95)
Secondary sources, 'relations'			
Relation II Erfurt – Droysen, 'Gedruckte Relationen'	Fog all morning delayed Swedish advance (18)		9:00 a.m.–10:00 a.m. (19)
Relation 1632 – Droysen, 'Gedruckte Relationen'	Fog the whole day (10)		After 10:00 a.m. (7)

Relation 1633 – Droysen, 'Gedruckte Relationen'	Fog in the morning (30)	Fog 1:00 p.m. (31)	11:00 a.m. (30)
Declaration 1633 – Droysen, 'Gedruckte Relationen'	Clear morning (40)	Smoke and fog midday (41)	Before 10:00 a.m. (40)
Spanish Relation – Watts, *Swedish Intelligencer*, vol. 3		Fog midday (161)	
Watts, *Swedish Intelligencer*, vol. 3	Fog until 8:00 a.m. delayed Swedish advance (126)	Fog after 11:00 a.m. (137) Fog in afternoon until 3:00–4:00 p.m. (147)	9:00 a.m. (132)
Gottfried, *Inventarium Sueciae*	Fog all morning delayed Swedish advance		9:00 a.m.–10:00 a.m. (25)
Burgus, *Mars Sveco-Germanicus*		Fog early afternoon (326)	
Chemnitz, *Geschichte*	Fog all morning delayed Swedish advance (464)	Smoke and fog midday (466)	11:00 a.m. (465)
Khevenhiller, *Annales Ferdinandei*	Fog all morning delayed Swedish advance (188)	Fog midday (194)	11:00 a.m. (190)
Richelieu, *Mémoires*	Clear dawn(?) then fog in the morning until 10:00 a.m. (258)		

Table 19: Pappenheim's arrival according to historical sources

Imperial eyewitness accounts	**Arrival of Pappenheim's cavalry (page no.)**
Wallenstein – Lorenz, *Quellen zur Geschichte Wallensteins*	Shortly before the battle had begun (256)
Holk – Wittrock, 'Fyra relationer'	12:00 a.m., shortly after the battle had begun (309)
Münchhausen – Wittrock, 'Fyra relationer'	Midday (305)
Diodati – Fiedler, 'Diodatis Bericht' = *Spanish Relation* – Watts, *Swedish Intelligencer*, vol. 3	Shortly after the battle had begun (562) (160)
Silvio Piccolomini – Anonymous, *Archivio*	Shortly before the battle had begun (240)
Poyntz, *The Relation*	Shortly after Piccolomini's counter-attack (72)
Protestant eyewitness accounts	
Dalbier, *Lutzen*	Before battle (251)
Fleetwood, *Letter*	2:00 p.m. (6 and 8)
Fabricius – Wittrock, 'Fyra relationer'	After Gustavus Adolphus's death and Swedish rout (307)

<table>
<tr><td>Vitzthum/Berlepsch
- Glafey, De Gladio</td><td>After windmill battery was captured (13)</td></tr>
<tr><td colspan="2">Secondary sources, letters</td></tr>
<tr><td>Gallas
- Förster, Wallenstein's Prozess</td><td>11:00 a.m., shortly after the battle had begun (95)</td></tr>
<tr><td>Hallenus
- Mankell, Arkiv vol. II</td><td>After small battery was captured (662)</td></tr>
<tr><td>Hülshorst
- Wittrock, 'Fyra relationer'</td><td>After Gustavus Adolphus's death (303)</td></tr>
<tr><td>Pentz
'Fiedler, 'Diodatis Bericht'</td><td>3:00 p.m. (571)</td></tr>
<tr><td colspan="2">Secondary sources, 'relations'</td></tr>
<tr><td>Relation II Erfurt
- Droysen, 'Gedruckte Relationen'</td><td>After 3:00 p.m. (20)</td></tr>
<tr><td>Relation 1632
- Droysen, 'Gedruckte Relationen'</td><td>Shortly after the battle had begun (8)</td></tr>
<tr><td>Relation 1633
- Droysen, 'Gedruckte Relationen'</td><td>After 1:00 p.m., when small battery was captured (31)</td></tr>
<tr><td>Declaration 1633
- Droysen, 'Gedruckte Relationen'
= Anonymous, Wahrhaftige Beschreibung</td><td>Cavalry before battle (39)
Infantry after second Swedish attack, afternoon (42)</td></tr>
<tr><td>Gottfried, Inventarium Sueciae
= Monro, His Expedition, part II
= Anonymous, Glaubwürdiger Bericht
= Abelinum, Theatrum Europaeum
= Chemnitz, Geschichte</td><td>Late afternoon
(26)
(164)
(750)
(467)</td></tr>
<tr><td>Burgus, Mars Sveco-Germanicus

= Richelieu, Mémoires</td><td>Before battle (319)

(260)</td></tr>
<tr><td>Khevenhiller, Annales Ferdinandei</td><td>After Gustavus Adolphus' death (193)</td></tr>
<tr><td>Watts, Swedish Intelligencer, vol.3</td><td>2:00 p.m., after second Swedish attack (133)</td></tr>
</table>

8

Aftermath

The Dead

Soon after the battle, both sides began to claim victory based on the casualties, the number of standards and colours captured, and the claim of holding the battlefield. A second battle for the sovereignty of interpretation started. Attempts from the Imperial side to claim that the Swedes left the battlefield first, failed.[1] The Swedes had the captured Imperial guns to display and that settled the question of who could claim possession of the battlefield. However, Corpes' Croats remained three or four days as a rearguard, harassing the Swedes clearing the battlefield and they almost recaptured some Imperial artillery on its way to Naumburg.[2]

According to Diodati, the Imperial army captured 60 colours, of which 36 from the Old Blue and Yellow Regiments were left on the field as no more than bare poles, with the cloth ripped off, however, both units combined had only 32 companies.[3] Münchhausen reported that his regiment, and that of Baden, alone took 14 colours from the New Blue and Yellow Regiments.[4] These numbers correspond with Wallenstein's note that he had captured 30 colours, while he lost only five or six cornets (cavalry colours),[5] or four according to Diodati.[6]

Later, the 'relation' *Glaubwürdiger Bericht* and *Declaration from 1633* claimed that the Swedes captured 28 cornets and 50 colours.[7] There is no

1 Diodati (Fiedler, 'Diodatis Bericht', p.566).

2 Diodati (Fiedler, 'Diodatis Bericht', p.566), Holk (Wittrock, 'Fyra relationer', p.309), Relation from 1632 (Droysen, 'Gedruckte Relationen', p.10).

3 Diodati (Fiedler, 'Diodatis Bericht', p.567), Silvio Piccolomini (Anonymous, *Archivio*, p.240).

4 BHStA, 2424t194 f. 158: Münchhausen to Maximilian 6 December 1632. In his earlier letter he claimed to have taken 15 colours from unknown infantry regiments (Wittrock, 'Fyra relationer', p.305).

5 Droysen, 'Gedruckte Relationen', p.2. Similar numbers are given by three anonymous letters and Relation from 1632 (Droysen, 'Gedruckte Relationen', pp.2–3, 9).

6 Fiedler, 'Diodatis Bericht', p.567.

7 Droysen, 'Gedruckte Relationen', p.43.

confirmation of these numbers from any eyewitness; they were certainly not taken by the Swedes during battle, but perhaps in the pursuit after the battle, as Brzezinski believed, or maybe the number is simply a fabrication.[8]

Few historians have discussed the disproportionate number of captured colours or even wondered why. Most colours were taken from the Old Blue and Yellow Regiments when they were destroyed, but the other 30 colours taken by the Imperial army, show that the Swedish army in general did not perform well. Many colours might have been taken during the collapse and rout of the Swedes around midday by pursuing Imperial cavalry, but the exact circumstances remain uncertain.

Casualties

Generally, the casualties in Lützen are difficult to estimate because only wounded both sides only counted their wounded, probably because these had to be cared for, and cost money. In fact, there are no entirely reliable figures for the number of dead. Not surprisingly, the number of killed was exaggerated, in particular those from the enemy, and constantly increased in accounts and 'relations' in a kind of race for the highest number until it reached a fantastic 18,000 dead according to the *French Relation from 1633*. A good example of how these casualties were estimated is an anonymous and undated letter, which noted that *Oberst* Illow wrote that Holk told him there were 12,000 dead; although Holk himself estimated only 8,000 dead.[9] It seems that the numbers were constantly rounded up a little in most accounts. However, casualties of 25 percent or more are not only suspicious, but also very difficult to achieve as long as the enemy continues to fight and usually applies only to situations where one side breaks and the other pursues as they withdraw and then rout.[10]

Another problematic issue might be the definition of battle casualties. Watts noted that many wounded were frozen to death on the battlefield during the night.[11] The *Declaration from 1633* stated that only 4,000 were killed actually during battle, the lowest number given in any account, but many wounded died over a period of several days and many scattered and lost Imperial soldiers were killed by angry Saxon peasants seeking revenge.[12]

8 Brzezinski, *Lützen*, p.87.

9 Droysen, 'Gedruckte Relationen', p.4, Wittrock, 'Fyra relationer', p.309.

10 Casualties of 9,000 or higher: Hülshorst (Wittrock, 'Fyra relationer', p.309), anonymous letter (Droysen, 'Gedruckte Relationen', p.2), Anonymous, *Wahrhaftige Beschreibung*, Abelinum, *Theatrum Europaeum*, p.751, Khevenhiller, *Annales Ferdinandei*, p.197. The number of 9,000 killed has been suggested by Seidler, *Untersuchungen*, p.95 and has influenced research, but is only a figurative number and too high: Mann, *Wallenstein*, p.861, Neuhold, *Der Dreissigjährige Krieg*, p.101.

11 Watts, *Swedish Intelligencer*, vol. 3, p.152.

12 Droysen, 'Gedruckte Relationen', p.43. The number of 4,000 killed was copied by Anonymous, *Glaubwürdiger Bericht*. Peasants killing Imperial soldiers on their retreat are mentioned by the Declaration from 1633 and a letter from Wallenstein to Arnim (Sennewald, *Das kursächsische*

Overleaf: Looting after the battle. Sebastiaen Vrancx (1573–1647). (Rijksmuseum)

Bas. franck

All of these soldiers died as a result of the battle, but not during the battle itself. However, these second-hand stories are not confirmed by any eyewitnesses.

Shortly after the battle, the Swedish army at Naumburg had an effective strength of approximately 8,000 foot, including Vitzthum's 850-man garrison, and 4,000 horse.[13] The undated casualty listing states that 2,575 infantry[14] were wounded; this would leave approximately 3,300 foot killed or unaccounted for and 2,000 horse killed, wounded or unaccounted for. Some stragglers might have turned up later; many soldiers probably recovered from their wounds, but the Swedish army had lost, at least temporarily, 7,875 men or 40 percent.[15] How many actually died is difficult to tell. Only one 'Swedish' eyewitness, George Fleetwood, mentions a number for those killed, which he estimated as 1,500, but this seems far too low considering that the Swedish army was the attacker in a six hours battle.[16] The number of killed is not usually higher than the number of wounded so the upper limit of killed is less than 3,900 with the most likely figure being around 3,000 to 3,500.[17] Among whom were Gustav II Adolph, *Generalmajor* Brahe, *Oberst* Stenbock, *Oberst* Gersdorf and *Oberstleutnant* Nilsson.[18]

The undated list of Swedish infantry[19] shows the distribution of losses according to regiment. The casualties among pikemen and musketeers in any single regiment are similar, except for two units. The pikemen of the Old Blue Brigade lost 88.0 percent while the musketeers suffered 42.6 percent casualties. With 84.3 percent pikemen and 22.1 percent musketeers, the ratio difference is even more evident in the Swedish Brigade. Swedish pikemen appear to have sacrificed themselves to cover the retreat of their comrades.

The Imperial casualties are more difficult to estimate, because Wallenstein left many wounded behind, both on the field and in Leipzig; not helped by the fact that there are almost no reliable numbers for the Imperial army after the battle. The 'list of damaged' provides an exact number of wounded for seven cavalry regiments, 343 in total, but since we do not have their initial strength

---

Heer, p.180), and was common practice during the Thirty Years' War. This 'other war' between soldiers and peasants is discussed by Herbert Langer, *Hortus Bellicus. Der Dreissigjährige Krieg* (3rd edn, Leipzig: Edition Leipzig, 1982) p.106–111.

13 Pentz (Fiedler, 'Diodatis Bericht', p.572). The number of foot is confirmed by other sources: 7,046 soldiers (Brzezinski, *Lützen*, p.87) with an unknown number of officers and Vitzthum's 850-strong brigade.

14 Mankell, *Arkiv*, vol. III, pp.126–128.

15 Only Deuticke, *Lützen*, pp.53–55 doubted these numbers, because he assumed these men were all dead or badly wounded. See Seidler, *Untersuchungen*, p.43 and Brzezinski, *Lützen*, pp.21–23.

16 Fleetwood, Letter, p.9.

17 Brzezinski, *Lützen*, pp.87–88. Watts, *Swedish Intelligencer*, vol. 3, p.153 estimated 2,000 to 3,000 dead in the Swedish–German army.

18 According to Eberstein (Diemar, 'Der Anteil der Hessen', p.348), Hülshorst (Wittrock, 'Fyra relationer', p.303), Pentz (Fiedler, 'Diodatis Bericht', p.571), Monro, *His Expedition*, part II, p.165, Watts, *Swedish Intelligencer*, vol. 3, p.154, *Relation from 1633* (Droysen, 'Gedruckte Relationen', p.34), Declaration from 1633 (Droysen, 'Gedruckte Relationen', p.44).

19 KiS: GAV u 121a Vol. 32d: Swedish Troop Strength 1628–1632.

it is difficult to estimate a casualty rate.[20] Some cuirassier regiments seem to have taken heavy casualties; Holk had 74 wounded out of approximately 250, which is 30 percent; the total casualty rate may be as high as 50 percent for that regiment. The most reliable sources for the Imperial casualties are Diodati, who suggests that the Imperial army might have lost 3,000 dead or wounded, and Holk, who estimated 3,000 dead.[21]

Considering that the Swedes were the attackers and that two Swedish brigades were destroyed, it seems likely the Swedish army suffered the heaviest casualties, but there is no proof. Imperial casualties may have increased substantially during the retreat because of desertion, stray soldiers being killed by peasants, but also because Wallenstein had to leave most of his wounded on the field.[22] The Imperial army clearly had a much higher rate of higher rank officer casualties compared to the Swedes; *Feldmarschall* Pappenheim, *Generalfeldzeugmeister* Breuner, 4 colonels and 6 lieutenant colonels were all killed and the Generalissimus Wallenstein, four colonels and eight lieutenant colonels were wounded. This fact might be seen as evidence for the extensive use of snipers by the Swedish army, or for the courageous behaviour of Imperial officers who did not flee the field, or for both.

It was an odd coincident that Gustav II Adolph's former Chaplain, Paul Stockmann, was vicar in Lützen. He did not see the battle itself as he was probably imprisoned in the castle or the church together with the townsfolk during the battle, but he visited the battlefield on following days and described what he saw in one of his sermons:

> ...dead, that some missed an arm, the other a leg, the third his head and so forth; some lay there sky blue coloured, broken and crushed by bullet [i.e. roundshot] ... Others lay, 10, 20, or more on a pile, so shot with pieces into pieces, or broken in two that everyone could see the wounded lung, liver, hart and intestines without 'anatomy' ...[23]

The Mass Grave

An Imperial garrison in the castle of Lützen was still present for a few days after both armies left the battlefield,[24] food supply was low and the town was partially destroyed by fire.[25] Thus, the townsfolk were not in a position to clear the battlefield and it took some days before a group of 200 civilians

20 Hallwich, *Briefe und Akten*, vol. 3, pp.596–599.

21 Fiedler, 'Diodatis Bericht', p.567. Wittrock, 'Fyra relationer', p.309.

22 Brzezinski, *Lützen*, pp.87–88.

23 Stockmann, *Lamentatio* (Stöwesand 1927). R. Stöwesand, Magister Paulus Stockmann, *Feld und Schiffsprediger Gustav Adolfs und Senior in Lützen* (Merseburg, 1927) p.90.

24 Stahl, '... die Todten Cörper vf der Wahlstadt begraben', p.258.

25 Lützen was not entirely destroyed (Stahl, '...die Todten Cörper vf der Wahlstadt begraben', p.259), as often claimed (Brzezinski, *Lützen*, p.51. Seidler, *Untersuchungen*, p.47).

from Weissenfels arrived to inter the dead in mass graves.[26] One mass grave was discovered in 2011 in a trial trench sited for the purpose and dug with a 20-ton excavator, after conducting an unsuccessful geomagnetic and aerial photography survey.[27]

The mass grave was located near the Via Regia in an area where the Old Blue Brigade presumably fought. It contained 47 individuals of which the majority, some 31, showed gunshot wounds.[28] Twenty bullets were found in the grave of which seven were in a bone or found inside a skull and therefore 'belonged' to the deceased. Most bullets were too deformed from impact or too corroded to establish their calibre with certainty. Only three bullets probably came from muskets; all others seem to originate from carbines or possibly pistols. These observations agree with reported events surrounding the Old Blue Brigade being destroyed by an Imperial counter-attack by a combined force. However, in the 1645 Alerheim mass grave almost all bullets also derive from pistols or carbines.[29] That might be coincidental, but might be due to some reason unknown today; for example, cavalry using less gunpowder in their pistols and carbines causing these bullets to tend to remain in the body that they struck.

Thirteen individuals showed sharp force trauma; the majority, eleven, inflicted by stabbing and cutting weapons, such as pikes, which is to be expected in infantry combat. The two wounds inflicted by bladed weapons were most likely from cavalry swords.[30] This low number might contain a hint on the nature of the cavalry fighting when compared to the relatively high number of carbine bullets found in the mass grave, suggesting that the cavalry made use of their firearms more often than of their swords in this engagement. In effect, they stayed away from the pikes and engaged them with pistol and carbine fire.[†]

† See PDF download, Plate 48: Bullets from the Lützen and Alerheim mass graves by weight

26 Stahl, '... die Todten Cörper vf der Wahlstadt begraben', pp.258–259.

27 Schürger, *The Archaeology of the Battle of Lützen*, pp.357–360. The mass grave was located by the author from an examination of historical sources and the results of the metal detector survey. It was not found by chance as Nicole Nicklisch, Frank Ramsthaler, Harald Meller, Susanne Friederich and Kurt W. Alt, *The face of war: Trauma analysis of a mass grave from the Battle of Lützen (1632)* (online publication 2017: PLOS ONE 12(5): e0178252: 2017) p.5 stated, inventing a story about illicit excavations to twist the facts of how the mass grave had been found.

28 Nicklisch/Ramsthaler/Meller/Friederich/Alt, The face of war, pp.13–15 and 22.

29 Katrin Misterek, 'Ein Massengrab aus der Schlacht von Alerheim am 3. August 1645', in *Bericht der Bayerischen Bodendenkmalpflege* 53 (Bonn, 2012), p.373.

30 Nicklisch/Ramsthaler/Meller/Friederich/Alt, *The face of war*, pp.12–13 and 21. Few or none of these wounds were likely to be inflicted by halberds simply because halberds were only used by a handful of officers and NCOs at the time.

Romanticised image of Gustav II Adolf's body laid out on a bed. Below the bed, a combat between Swedish horse and Imperial cuirassiers is shown, presumably as a reference to the King's death in battle. (Nordiskamuseet, Stockholm)

Who Won?

Golo Mann once wrote that there is no point in arguing who won the battle because both armies consumed each other.[31] The Swedes did achieve their objective of forcing Wallenstein out of Saxony, thus aiding their ally, which might be seen as a strategic victory. Additionally by holding the battlefield, they gained the spoils of war; all Imperial heavy artillery, parts of the baggage train and many weapons. This victory even had the longer-term effect of preventing Wallenstein from paying his army by looting enemy, Saxon territory, and he was forced to ask Ferdinand II for funds. Furthermore, Wallenstein appeared more concerned about punishing the deserters at Prague. All this may have convinced Ferdinand II to get rid of Wallenstein and he was murdered at Eger on Ferdinand's orders on 25 February 1634.

However, no advantages could outweigh the death of Gustav II Adolph. Even if he was not the brilliant strategist, as is often claimed, he was a charismatic figure and a living legend that held the Protestant alliance together. Even after his death, he was used as a uniting figurehead. 'Der Schwede [i.e. Gustav II Adolph] lebet noch und wird auch ewig leben (The Swede still

31 Mann, *Wallenstein*, p.860. Brzezinski, *Lützen*, p.88.

lives and he will live forever)' claimed a pamphlet in 1633.[32] Nevertheless, the alliance crumbled and Sweden's most important ally, Saxony, along with many other Protestant cities, defected or agreed a peace with Ferdinand II at the treaty of Prague on 30 May 1635. Englund argued that in the long term Lützen was a decisive Swedish defeat.[33]

Pamphlet, *Der Schwedelebetnoch*, celebrating the battle

A Tactical Analysis of the Battle: Consequences on the Development of Seventeenth-Century Warfare

Military historians have often wondered why the same Swedish army, that achieved a decisive victory over Tilly at Breitenfeld, performed so poorly at Lützen. There are several reasons usually given; Wallenstein's fortifications at Lützen, Tilly's clumsy Spanish infantry formation at Breitenfeld, or that Gustav II Adolph had to attack an equally strong army at Lützen – all are incorrect. The Battle of Breitenfeld and Tilly's Spanish-German tactics are not entirely understood, which makes it difficult to understand the differences between Tilly's and Wallenstein's armies, and why the latter was

32 Olaf Mörke, 'Der Schwede lebet noch' – Die Bildformung Gustav Adolfs in Deutschland nach der Schlacht bei Lützen, in Mike Reichel, Inger Schuberth (eds), *Gustav Adolf. König von Schweden. Die Kraft der Erinnerung 1632–2007* (Dössel: Verlag Janos Stekovics, 2006) pp.90–92.

33 Englund, *Die Verwüstung Deutschlands*, p.137.

more successful against the Swedes. The short time between Breitenfeld on 17 September 1631 and Lützen on 16 November 1632, and the fact that both Catholic armies consisted of Imperial and League troops suggest that the armies were not actually that different.

Infantry and Artillery

The Swedish army did not change much between Breitenfeld and Lützen. Its musketeers were not equipped with lighter muskets, providing them with a higher mobility, as often claimed.[34] In fact, musketeers in both armies used similar weapon types at Lützen, and if the Swedes used different types at Breitenfeld, those muskets were more than likely the older, heavier Dutch models.

The Swedish infantry brigade formation was not too complicated to handle and was not responsible for any setbacks during the Battle of Lützen.[35] Otherwise, it would have been abandoned before Nördlingen, two years later. It is very likely that it was only the acceptance of simplicity that led to the disappearance of the Swedish brigade formation by Wittstock in 1636. Wallenstein reduced the number of infantry ranks from Tilly's 10 or 12 deep 'reformed Spanish *esquadron*' to seven ranks and he began equipping his army with three and four-pounder regimental guns that increased his firepower. However, these reforms can hardly be seen as a key reason for his success at Lützen.

What was new was that Wallenstein deployed his infantry in three lines: a skirmish line in the ditches along the road, a five-squadron first line supported by heavy artillery and regimental guns and a two squadron second line. Such a three-line defence can be very effective against an experienced and well-trained enemy, as was demonstrated during the American War of Independence Battle of Cowpens, when it was used by Daniel Morgan against the British forces.[36] This order of battle slowly disrupts morale and formation cohesion, first by the skirmish line firing on officers and then by exhausting the enemy, who have to fight their way through two lines, while the defending units can retreat and reform behind the next line and prepare to counter-attack.

Cavalry

Gustav II Adolph had demonstrated at Werben in July 1631 what a combined arms force of dragoons, light cavalry and musketeers was capable of when he surprised four of Tilly's best cavalry regiments.[37] However, when he pursued the dispersing Imperial army on 15 November 1632, he had no dragoons and was short of light cavalry, he had only of Stalhandske's Finns, to provide intelligence and clear the way at Rippach in time to allow the Swedish army a smooth crossing. Instead, Wallenstein's

34 Jeremy Murray, 'The English-Language Military Historiography of Gustavus Adolphus in the Thirty Years' War, 1900-Present', in *Western Illinois Historical Review*, Vol. V, Spring 2013, p.13.

35 Brzezinski, *Lützen*, p.89.

36 Babits, *A Devil of a Whipping*, p.157.

37 Monro, *His Expedition*, part II, pp.51–52.

Croats and Dragoons, greatly outnumbering the Swedish light cavalry, controlled the entire area of operations, as they did at Nurnberg/Alte Veste as well,[38] preventing Gustav II Adolph from surprising the Imperial army or gathering intelligence. Wallenstein's horse were a constant annoyance during the Swedish deployment on 16 November, and also threatened the Swedish rear during the battle. Although Wallenstein's skirmishing tactics backfired once, when a Croat regiment disrupted his battle line on the right, he proved the point and light cavalry became an important arm in European warfare until the nineteenth century. Gustav II Adolph's lack of light cavalry and dragoons coupled with the interference from the Imperial Croats, caused a very limited knowledge of the terrain for him and which, in turn, cost his army valuable time.

Another decisive factor was the Imperial cuirassiers. Much better armoured than the Swedish cavalry, they protected the vulnerable flanks of the infantry in the centre, and the Swedish cavalry was never able to break them. The poor performance of Sparr's cuirassiers, however, proved that good armour was no guaranty for success when leadership failed. In addition, the insufficiently armoured Imperial harquebusiers almost led to the destruction of Wallenstein's army. Wallenstein tried to upgrade the harquebusiers to cuirassiers, but was unsuccessful, mainly because cuirassiers were too expensive. Cost was probably the main reason why most cavalry remained unamoured across Europe.

Leadership

Although Bernhard von Weimar, Knyphausen and Brahe were good officers, the Swedish army at Lützen lacked some of its best commanders. *Fältmarskalk* Gustav Karlsson Horn *Grevetil* Björneborg, according to Monro one of the best Swedish leaders, commanded a Swedish army in Alsace;[39] General Johan Banér had been wounded at Nurnberg/Alte Veste.[40] In the same battle *Överste* Lennart Thorstenson, who usually commanded Gustav II Adolph's artillery, had been taken prisoner, and succeeded by the inexperienced *Major* Joen Persson Jernlod.[41] Their absence resulted in low-ranking officers, such as *Överste* Thorsten Stalhandske, who was certainly a good officer, but lacked experience as a wing commander, finding themselves in unfamiliar positions of great responsibility when Gustav II Adolph and Nils Brahe were killed. The absence of Gustav II Adolph's best officers, with whom he had achieved the decisive victory at Breitenfeld, certainly led to minor mistakes, such as the delay of his heavy artillery, which in turn, led to the stalemate at Lützen. In essence, the Swedish army's success under Gustav II Adolph was

38 Monro, *His Expedition*, part II, pp.140, 144 & 151 specifically pointed out that Wallenstein's Croats controlled the whole area around Nurnberg, harassing Swedish supply and preventing intelligence gathering.

39 Monro, *His Expedition*, part II, p.58. Engerisser, *Von Kronach nach Nördlingen*, p.133. Murray, 'The English-Language Military Historiography', pp.13–14.

40 Engerisser, *Von Kronach nach Nördlingen*, p.124.

41 Brzezinski, *Lützen*, p.22.

due mainly to its superior leadership.[42]

On the other side, Hofkirchen's and Bönninghausen's cowardly behaviour and flight have distorted our image of Imperial officers. Wallenstein could rely on *FeldmarschallLeutnant* Holk, who demonstrated great prudence in commanding the left wing – the battle would have been lost without him. Many other officers, such as *Oberst* Waldstein, *Oberst* Piccolomini or *Obristwachtmeister* Münchhausen, took the initiative when appropriate, or held the line when necessary, with disregard to their personal safety, and for which the high number of Imperial officer casualties are ample evidence.

Reserve

However, probably the most decisive tactic was Wallenstein's innovation of a cavalry reserve, and here lies the real reason for the success of the Imperial army. While Gustav II Adolph had a very strong second line, his army lacked real reserves, and consisted only of Henderson's musketeers and Öhm's cavalry, and the latter was a last-resort-reserve only. In contrast to the Swedish army, Wallenstein deployed one musketeer and five cavalry squadrons as a reserve. This deployment allowed a more flexible response to the Swedish attacks. The two wing reserve squadrons strengthened the Imperial left wing at the beginning of the battle and prevented an early Swedish breakthrough until Pappenheim arrived to relieve the pressure. Most decisive was the deployment of three cavalry squadrons in reserve behind the centre and the cavalry-infantry combined arms engagements against the Yellow and Old Blue Brigades. If the Battle of Lützen proved anything, it was the value of highly mobile cavalry reserves, which would become an important keystone of European tactics.

Development of the Battle

Unlike at Breitenfeld, at Lützen Gustav II Adolph had to take the initiative and start the action because he could not risk delaying and Pappenheim's force arriving to and reinforce the Imperial army. Without waiting for his heavy artillery, he rushed into action and attacked on both wings in a delayed double outflanking manoeuvre, instead of perhaps attacking on only one wing and watching how the battle developed.

When Pappenheim arrived, the Swedish army's first line was fully committed and unable to react, while the lack of first-class commanders, together with the rivalry between Bernhard von Weimar and Knyphausen, prevented swift action and the moving of the second line cavalry from the left to the right wing. After the Swedish right wing was beaten, the whole army collapsed in a domino effect. The Swedes still had sufficient leadership and an intact second line to avoid total destruction, but from that point, they could not defeat the Imperial army. Still, the Swedish army's cohesion, experience and leadership allowed Bernhard von Weimar to resume the attack and keep the Swedish army in action for a further several hours, when most other armies would have failed.

42 Junkelmann, *Gustav Adolf*, p.351. Michael Kaiser, *Politik und Kriegführung. Maximilian von Bayern, Tilly und die Katholische Liga im Dreissigjährigen Krieg* (Münster, Aschendorff Verlag 1999) p.457. Murray, 'The English-Language Military Historiography', pp.13–14.

The funeral of King Gustav II Adolf in Wolgast in 1633, with his coffin escorted by Royal Drabants. Friedrich van Hulsen, 1634. (Rijksmuseum)

Review and Prospects

Military History

Military history has failed to understand even the basic events of the Battle of Lützen by projecting an incorrectly understood Thirty Years' War military system onto the battle. At the same time, the battle was often used to explain the weapons and tactical development of the period. Additionally, eyewitness testimony has often been discarded in favour of second-hand information simply because it did not fit the received wisdom of the experts. Although eyewitness accounts are often in error, as demonstrated in this study, it needs to be demonstrated as to why a specific statement is incorrect, and on the other hand, every statement from a secondary source has to be proved as correct or based on eyewitness testimony before further consideration.

Once the correct methodology has been applied, historical sources become an indispensable asset for battlefield research, answering the questions of 'who' and 'what happened'.

Battlefield Archaeology

Fieldwork, conducted over five years, stands as the basis of my analytical research. Based on the methodology of previously successful battlefield projects, the Lützen Project aimed towards a more intense small finds collection by using a systematic, full coverage metal detector sweep used for the first time on such a large scale. It provided solid evidence, which is essential for generating meaningful finds distribution maps.

In the future, however, it might be insufficient to use a suitable methodology for single battlefields. There should be only one system or methodology, or at least one for each historical period, to apply on battlefield surveys, allowing a comparison of finds distribution maps for different battles, because they are the key to better understanding the actions. After several decades of battlefield surveys, the best methodology to apply on all pre-modern battlefields is a systematic, all metal, full coverage metal detector survey. This methodology produces a sufficient amount of finds to see beyond bullets and enable an interpretation of non-ammunition artefact distribution maps, something that has not yet been done because buttons, buckles et cetera are usually found in insufficient numbers in systematic surveys.

A similar inconsistent approach concerns the measuring of lead bullets. Calibre graphs of different bullet collections should be comparable. Only if we are able to compare battlefields' calibre graphs and finds distribution maps of ammunition and non-ammunition finds alike, will we better understand the physical evidence of a battle. The recorded calibres should also include a table of other measurements used to denote gun projectiles including weight ranges, number to the pound, including an understanding of weight terminology, and gauge, if appropriate.

An asset to battlefield archaeology lies within its ability to locate combat on the battlefield and as a result answer the question of 'where'. This is particularly effective in showing the orientation and extent of battle lines, as has already been demonstrated for Lützen, where it has been shown that the Imperial wings were echeloned backwards in a 45° angle. Much more challenging was localising single units and events on the battlefield. Most episodes were mixed up with others, which effectively blurred distribution patterns. Those military units, however, which have been located, have changed the interpretation of the battle substantially.

Landscape Reconstruction

One key to understanding a battle is knowing the battle's terrain. Line of sight is as important as cover, concealment, obstacles, ground conditions et cetera to evaluate troop movement, firing range and efficiency, hand-to-hand combat, decisions made according to the visibility of opposing troops and terrain, reliability of eyewitness testimony and so forth. Ideally, this can be achieved by studying a precise historic map created by a reliable source, such as the command staff of an army or by a cartographer of the same period. At Lützen, however, there was no contemporary map available, which is something that applies to most pre-modern battlefields.

Reconstructing a battlefield can be achieved by studying non-contemporary maps, statements of eyewitnesses about terrain, soil study and landscape archaeology and this is an interdisciplinary approach all of its own.

Battlefield Research: an Interdisciplinary Approach

It has been demonstrated throughout this study that the key factor for understanding a battle is a symbiosis between military history, battlefield archaeology and landscape archaeology. In addition, a battle has to be set within a wider context of the tactics and military equipment of the time. Here, 'a similar symbiosis of military history and battlefield archaeology can exist; contemporary military manuals give us an idea of tactics and military equipment during a specific period and how they were meant to be employed, while battlefield archaeology and the eyewitness accounts demonstrate how the weaponry was actually used in a specific event at a specific time. However, there is still an insufficient amount of archaeological data published to enable effective worldwide comparative research, an important step towards an international and interdisciplinary 'battlefield research'. This is the next step for future practitioners.

Tables

Table 20: Swedish casualty listing of wounded from the infantry regiments

	Oberst, Oberstleutnant, Major, Quartiermeister	*Hauptmann*	*Leutnant*	*Fähnrich*	NCO	Soldier
Swedish Brigade	3	5	5	4	20	374
Yellow Brigade						
Yellow Life Regiment	1	5	3	3	0	258
Lifeguard	0	0	1	8	9	15
Blue Brigade	0	5	5	4	18	381
Green Brigade						
Bernhard's Green Life Regiment	1	3	1	3	5	96
Wildenstein's Black	1	2	3	1	7	80
Leslie's Scots	0	0	3	2	7	47
Duke Wilhelm's Brigade						
Duke Wilhelm's Life Regiment	0	2	4	0	7	23
Bose/Pforte	0	0	0	0	3	38
White Brigade	0	3	1	3	5	96
Thurn's Brigade						
Thurn	2	1	0	1	3	3
Isenburg	1	0	0	0	4	10
Wilhelm von Hessen-Kassel	0	0	1	0	2	20
Mitzlaff's Brigade						
Gersdorf	1	1	2	0	12	90
Mitzlaff	1	0	1	1	12	122
Rossow	1	0	1	4	4	45
9th Brigade						
Henderson	0	1	1	1	4	47
Löwenstein	0	1	0	0	4	183

Table 21: Undated list of Swedish infantrymen with losses in percentages. (KiS: GAV u 121a Vol. 32d: Swedish Troop Strength 1628–1632)

	Musket	Pikes	Officers	Total	Musket %	Pikes %	Total %
Swedish Brigade	*832*	*42*	*212*	*1086*	*22.1*	*84.3*	*31.0*
Erik Hand	330	42	96	468	29.0	84.3	43.5
Karl Hard	350	0	96	446	21.7		17.9
Klas Hastfer	152	0	20	172	2.6		15.7
Yellow Brigade	*167 (+40)a*	*82 (+25)a*	*96*	*420*	*68.4*	*70.4*	*65.6*
Blue Brigade	*279*	*52*	*96*	*427*	*42.6*	*88.0*	*61.5*
Winckel's Old Blue	279	52	96	427	42.6	88.0	61.5
Green Brigade	*692 (+79)b*	*200 (+41)b*	*192b*	*1204b*	*37.0*	*28.3*	*40.9*
Bernhard's Green Life Regiment	344 (+44)b	137 (+22)b	96b	643b			
Wildenstein's Black	348 (+35)b	63 (+19)b	96b	561b			
Leslie's Scots	b	b	b	b			
Duke Wilhelm's Brigade							
Wilhelm's Life Regiment	108	60	96	264	60.9	23.1	46.8
Bose	504	120	96	720	6.7	23.1	9.1
Pforte	314c	86c	48c	448c			
White Brigade	*534*	*235*	*96*	*865*	*24.6*	*13.0*	*22.8*
Knyphausen's White	534	235	96	865	24.6	13.0	22.8
Thurn's Brigade	*498*	*234*	*168*	*900*	*13.5*	*31.6*	*28.1*
Thurn	210	126	96	432	12.5	12.5	10.0
Isenburg	96	36	24	156	20.0	33.3	42.2
Wilhelm von Hessen-Kassel	192	72	48	312	11.1	50.0	37.8
Mitzlaff's Brigade	*648*	*282*	*240*	*1170*	*37.6*	*39.0*	*36.2*
Gersdorf	240	48	48	336	27.3	50.0	35.6
Mitzlaff	192	90	96	378	43.9	54.5	44.6
Rossow	216	144	96	456	41.0	14.3	27.6
9th Brigade	*600d*	*0*	*144d*	*744d*	*38.7*		*35.8*
Henderson	d	0	d	d			
Löwenstein	480d	0	96d	576d			
Brandenstein	120d	0	48d	168d			

a Number of unarmed soldiers in parenthesis; suggested distribution of 2:1 to musket/pike.
b As 'a'; the numbers suggest that Leslie's Scots were included in Bernhard's and Wildenstein's Regiments.
c The numbers suggest that parts of Pforte's Regiment were detached somewhere else at Lützen, but were reunited when this list was made.
d The numbers suggest that Henderson's Regiment was included in Löwenstein's and Brandenstein's Regiments.

Table 22: Imperial 'list of damaged' with wounded cavalrymen

	Oberst, Oberstleutnant, Obristwachtmeister, Quartiermeister	*Rittmeister*	*Kapitänleutnant, Leutnant*	Cornet	NCOs	Troopers
Desfour	1	0	2	2	4	52
Holk	0	1	1	1	5	66
Trcka	0	0	0	2	8	58
Götz	1	0	1	0	7	58
Bredau	1	1	0	1	4	7
Loyers	1	0	0	0	3	34
Goschütz	0	0	1	0	0	20

Table 23: Imperial officer casualties

Killed	**Regiment**	**Sources**
Generalfeldzeugmeister Breuner (w)	GFZM Breuner	H, D, B
Oberst Waldstein (w)	Waldstein	H, D, B1, F, Hü
Oberst Comargo (w)	Comargo	H, D1, P, B
Oberst Lohe	Lohe	M, H, D1, B
Oberst Westrumb	Westrumb	M, B
Oberstleutnant Mendj	(u)	M
Oberstleutnant Stolper	Baden	M, B
Oberstleutnant Dauignj/Tauigni (p)	Lamboy	M, D1, B
Oberstleutnant Ehinhaussen (w)	(u)	M
Oberstleutnant Falkenberg	Götz	D1, B
Oberstleutnant (u)	Desfour	D1, B
Oberstleutnant (u)	Comargo	B
Wounded		
Oberst Lamboy	Lamboy	D1, B1
Oberst Colloredo	Colloredo	P, B
Oberst Piccolomini	Piccolomini	B1
Oberst H. G. Breuner	Jung-Breuner	B1
Oberstleutnant (u)	Waldstein	D1, B1
Oberstleutnant Hämmerle	Alt-Sachsen	D1, B1
Oberstleutnant (u)	Jung-Breuner	D1, B1
Oberstleutnant (u)	Friedrich Breuner	B1
Oberstleutnant (u)	Forgatsch	D1, B1
Oberstleutnant Tontinelli	Tontinelli	B1
Oberstleutnant von Rauchhaupt	Trcka	B1
Oberstleutnant Osterhold	(u)	B1

Key:
(w) mortally wounded
(p) prisoner
(u) name unknown
M Münchhausen (Wittrock, 'Fyra relationer', p.305)
F Fleetwood, *Letter*, p.10
Hü Hülshorst (Wittrock, 'Fyra relationer', p.303)
H Holk (Wittrock, 'Fyra relationer', p.309)
D Diodati (Fiedler, *Diodatis Bericht*, p.565), D1 (567)
P Silvio Piccolomini (Anonymous, *Archivio*, p.241)
B *Relation from 1632* (Droysen, *Gedruckte Relationen*, p.11), B1 (12)

Colour Plate Commentaries

By Stephen Ede-Borrett

Plate A. Imperial Cuirassier

Typical of the Imperial cuirassiers, who would all have looked similar. The helmet, of a form today commonly known as 'death's head' from its resemblance to a skull from almost its first appearance *c*.1600, might be replaced with a *zischägge* or 'lobster helmet' or even an open-faced burgonet. His scarf is the only thing that would identify him in the chaos and confusion of battle – red scarves were ubiquitous amongst the Catholic armies.

Plate B. Imperial Croat

The Croats were primarily recruited from along the Habsburg Empire's borders, much in the same way as Pandours would later be, and were not necessarily from 'Croatia', despite the name. The figure carries a war hammer, essentially unchanged in design from its initial appearance in the first century, and more than capable of punching through most armour with ease.

Plate C. Imperial Dragoon

Dragoons were still 'mounted infantry' who would dismount to fight and only fight mounted if no other option presented itself. Although not universal Imperial dragoons were the first to add a sling to their musket, something that spread throughout Europe by the middle of the century. The figure wears a loose coat and a knotted band, which quickly became adopted as the fashionable cravat in France by 1660, his shoes might be replaced by soft leather boots if funds allowed.

Plate D. Imperial Harquebusier

Still called 'harquebusier' or 'arquebusier', this type of cavalry was a development from the 'mounted harquebusier' but had, by the outbreak of the Thirty Years' War, become full-fledged battle cavalry and was swiftly replacing the cuirassier. These troops were cheaper to arm, used lower-cost horses, and were as effective in battle. The buff coat was sometimes worn without the back and breast, and similarly the back and breast could be worn without the buff coat. The older-pattern burgonet might be replaced with a *zischägge* or even a soft hat with our without a 'secrete' beneath. Many Swedish cavalry would have looked near enough identical.

Plate E. Imperial Pikeman

An example of the best equipped of the Imperial pikemen, almost certainly a veteran who had added to his equipment of the years and displays pauldrons, gorget below his back and breast, and a buff coat – almost all of which is probably his own purchase or looted. The use of pauldrons would soon cease (although the French Gardes Suisse are still recorded using them in 1667), and buff coats below the armour was rare except by private purchase or looting. Overall, the man's equipment is already out of date but as it was still serviceable, it would continue to be issued, although burgonet-style helmets would be replaced with the cheaper to produce morion form.

Plate F. Imperial Musketeer

This soldier carries a musket of a newer, lighter form for use without a rest although it still has the older 'fishtail' butt so has probably been 'remade', something that was relatively common. His cassock covers his bandolier, or a bag containing cartridges, either of which would be worn over the top of it in action. The cassock was also common in common use the Swedish army where it often replaced the coat, although this musketeer probably has a short coat and is using the cassock almost as an overcoat. The unusual hat is based on those shown in a number of contemporary paintings, and is also similar to those worn by some of the musketeers of the Gardes Françaises shown in the engravings of *Le Maréchal de Bataille* (Paris 1647).

Plate G. Finnish Cavalry Trooper

Unarmoured and even without a helmet, although he could be wearing a 'secrete' below his hat, this trooper is wearing the longer coat fashionable in the Swedish army and a development of the cassock. His sword is a Polish pattern sabre, which is recorded as being used by Finnish cavalry. The Finnish cavalry had a fearsome reputation and one contemporary writer compared them to the Tartars of the Polish armies.

Plate H. Swedish Yellow Brigade Pikeman

The Yellow Regiment, the senior regiment of The Yellow Brigade, had worn yellow coats since at least the beginning of January 1627, and there was an increasing incidence of coat and breeches being made in the same cloth. The morion and the back and breast – with tassetts, it should be noted – are based on examples in the collection of the Armémuseum in Stockholm.

Plate I. Swedish Blue Brigade Musketeer

The 'lead' regiment of the Blue Brigade certainly wore blue coats, and were frequently albeit not always, issued with similarly coloured breeches. As with other brigades, only the lead regiment of the Blue Brigade can be confirmed as having coats that follow the name of the brigade. The figure carries the usual musket of the army, which still requires a musket rest, and these continued in use for many years after Lützen.

Plate J. Scottish Pikeman

The use of a blue bonnet is noted by many contemporaries and continued to mark out Scots troops into the British Civil Wars and beyond; its use is not recorded outside Scotland at this time. The undyed 'hodden grey' colour of the man's coat is not certain, but documents do refer to the issue of both grey and blue cloth at different times, although grey seems the more common (note, the Scots regiments did not wear or use tartan). The armour was issued by the Swedish Crown and did not come from Scotland or England.

Plate K. Swedish Cavalry Trooper

A well-dressed trooper, although blue was a relatively cheap dye, even if not the cheapest. Note that he wears both a back and breast and a buff coat but no helmet, although it is likely that he has a 'secrete' under the soft hat. Wearing his sword from a waist belt rather than a baldric was commonplace, but fell out of fashion over the following decade. Note the knotted band in place of a collar; although fashionable this also protects the neck again abrasion from the back and breast – Roman Legionaries had worn knotted neck scarves for exactly the same reason at least as early as the 1st century.

Plate L. Saxon Musketeer

The coat is probably centrally supplied but is not, in the true sense, a 'uniform', although it is likely that the majority of his unit would have received coats of a similar colour. The coat is of a fashionable short style that would survive several more years in civilian dress. He has decorated his hat with feathers picked up from somewhere – their cost precludes the likelihood that he actually bought them. He has a matchlock musket, which still needs a rest as many would for another decade, and a good sword carried from a waist belt. His ammunition is carried in bottles hung from his bandolier and his sausage-shaped 'snapsack', slung from the other shoulder, is almost empty.

Plate M. Gustav II Adolph

The Swedish King was unable to wear armour due to a neck wound he received while on campaign in Poland. At Lützen he worn an elk skin sleeved buff coat, which was to be his only protective garb. Having been wounded leading a cavalry counter-attack, the King was being escorted off the field by a small entourage of eight men. Imperial cuirassiers suddenly appeared and either cut down or scattered those around the King; he was shot in the back, and then took several sword cuts and thrusts to his body before a pistol shot to his head finished him off. His body was stripped and looted so completely, that when it was discovered by Swedish troops it was wearing just three shirts. The King's horse, 'Streiff' returned to the Swedish lines heavily wounded and died a short while later. It was later preserved and stuffed and is now displayed at the Royal Armoury Museum, Stockholm, alongside the King's buff coat and other items of clothing worn at Lützen.

Plate N. Imperial Cavalry Cornets

Many cornets and colours taken from the Imperial armies as trophies during the Thirty Years' War are preserved in the Swedish trophy collection in the

Armémuseum in Stockholm. These represent a few, and serve as examples of some of more 'typical' designs – if any can indeed be truly termed 'typical'.

1. Cornet of a cuirassier regiment (inv. no. AMA.0003491)
The obverse depicts an Imperial eagle. The reverse shows, in a circle framed by a laurel wreath, a bird soaring over fire and smoke. Above is the motto: *CONCVSSVS RESVRGO* (literally 'Shocked to Rise', although the meaning of this is unclear).

2. Guidon of a dragoon regiment (inv. no. AMA.0003498)
Dragoon guidons are characterised by their distinctive swallow-tailed shape. They were carried on the same pattern of shaft as cuirassier cornets. The obverse shows an armoured arm holding a sword, emerging from a cloud. On the reverse is an Imperial eagle with a crown above, and above which is the motto: *PRO. CAESARE* ('For the Emperor').

3. Cavalry cornet (inv no. AMA.0003341)
A 'Ragged Cross of Burgundy' on a white field, on the reverse side is a black Imperial eagle under a crown. Both the Burgundian cross and the Imperial eagle are very common devices on regiments in Imperial service.

Plate O. Imperial Infantry Colours

Two colours from infantry regiments of Wallenstein's army, trophies taken by the Swedish army at the battle of Lützen, and preserved in the trophy collection of the Armémuseum in Stockholm. The coloured border on the lower colour is common on Catholic colours of the period, but does not appear on those of Protestant nations. At the end of the seventeenth century, by order of Karl XI, the trophies were ordered to be painted and recorded (these are inv. nos AMA.0003005, AMA.0003006), and it is thanks to this manuscript that we have a record of the original appearance and colours.

Plate P. Swedish/Saxon Cavalry Cornets

1. Cornet of Prince Ernst of Anhalt's Regiment (Saxon)
On the reverse of the cornet is the same style of medallion showing St George slaying the dragon, but the motto above the medallion is the motto *ICH WAGES, GOTT HILFT* ('I Dare, God Helps'), the date 1631 appears below, as here.

Roland Sennewald, *Das Kursächsische Heer im Dreißigjährigen Krieg 1618–1648* (Berlin: Zeughaus Verlag, 2013), p.137

2. Uppland Cavalry Regiment, troop cornet
The regiment carried five red cornets, of which four (possibly all five) were of damask cloth. The device of GARS [Gustavus Adolphus Rex Sueciae] and the three golden crowns, one over two, the Arms of the Kingdom of Sweden, was common on many Swedish cornets and colours.

Michael Fredholm von Essen, *The Lion from the North Volume 1, The Swedish Army of Gustavus Adolphus, 1618–1632* (Warwick: Helion & Co, 2020), pl. 26

3. Lorenz von Hofkirchen's Regiment (Saxon), troop cornet
On the reverse a black patterned cloth, the medallion in the centre carried a different design for each troop, in this example an allegorical image of a crown over a pierced heart, 'Fidelis sum my heart depends on your word'. It is possible that the cloth should be black and the fringe is sometimes shown as mixed black and gold with a black and gold edging to the cloth.

Roland Sennewald, *Das Kursächsische Heer im Dreißigjährigen Krieg 1618–1648* (Berlin: Zeughaus Verlag, 2013) p.130

4. Finnish cavalry company, troop cornet
Lars-Eric Höglund, *Från Karl Knutsson till Kristina Svenska Fälttecken och Beklädnad Från Senmedeltid till Trettioåriga Kriget.* (Stockholm, 2012), p.65

Plate Q. Swedish/Saxon Infantry Colours

1, 2, 3, Duke Wilhelm's Brigade, Regiment Pfordte, company colours
Roland Sennewald, *Das Kursächsische Heer im Dreißigjährigen Krieg 1618–1648* (Zeughaus Verlag, Berlin 2013), p.75.

4. Company colour of the Swedish 'Blue' Infantry Regiment, Blue Brigade
Michael Fredholm von Essen, *The Lion from the North Volume 1, The Swedish Army of Gustavus Adolphus, 1618–1632* (Helion & Co, Warwick, 2020), pl. 9.

5. Company colour of the Swedish 'Green' Infantry Regiment, Duke Bernhard's (Green) Brigade
Michael Fredholm von Essen, *The Lion from the North Volume 1, The Swedish Army of Gustavus Adolphus, 1618–1632* (Helion & Co, Warwick, 2020), pl. 11.

6. Company colour of the Swedish 'Yellow' Infantry Regiment, Yellow Brigade
Michael Fredholm von Essen, *The Lion from the North Volume 1, The Swedish Army of Gustavus Adolphus, 1618–1632* (Helion & Co, Warwick, 2020), pl. 27.

Bibliography

Archives

Public Records Office (PRO): SP81/39: London: 'Dalbier, Johann, *Relation of the Battle of Lutzen* (unknown: 1632)'

Sächsisches Hauptstaatsarchiv Dresden (HSTAD): 11237, III. Abt. Loc. 10826/1 (Artilleriesachen), Bl. 17r: Breitenfeld Battlefield clearing Record October 1631

Krigsarkivet i Stockholm (KiS): GAV u 121a Vol. 32d: Swedish Troop Strength 1628–1632

Landeshauptarchiv Sachsen-Anhalt (LASA) Abteilung Magdeburg/Außenstelle Wernigerode: Rep. D Lützen A XI Nr. 29: Lützen Battlefield clearing Record December 1632

Bayerisches Hauptstaatsarchiv (BHStA) München, Kurbayern Äusseres Archiv, 2424t194 f. 158: Hans von Münchhausen to the Elector Maximilian of Bavaria, Zwickau 6 December 1632

Landesamt für Kultur und Denkmalpflege Landeshauptarchiv Schwerin (LaKD), Feindliche Invasion, vol. XVI, 2.12–2/19 (unknown: 1633)

Pictorial Representations

Bianchi, Giovanni Paolo, *Equestrian portrait of Gustavus Adolphus*

Snayers, Pieter, *Die Schlacht bei Lützen*, Kunsthistorisches Museum Wien, Inv. Nr. GG1820

Unpublished PhD/Masters Theses

Babits, Lawrence E., *The Evolution and Adoption of Firearm Ignition Systems in Eastern North America: An Ethno-Historical Approach* (Master Thesis, University of Maryland 1974)

Deuticke, Karl, *Die Schlacht bei Lützen. 1632* (PhD Thesis, Universität Gießen 1917)

Ferguson, Natasha, *An assessment of the positive contribution and negative impact of hobbyist metal detecting to sites of conflict in the UK* (PhD Thesis, University of Glasgow 2013)

Foard, Glenn, *Integrating Documentary and Archaeological Evidence in the Investigation of Battles: A Case Study from Seventeenth-Century England* (PhD Thesis, University of East Anglia 2008)

Schürger, André, *The Archaeology of the Battle of Lützen: An examination of seventeenth century military material culture* (PhD Thesis, University of Glasgow 2015)

Contemporary and Historical sources

Abelinum, Johann Philipp, *Theatrum Europaeum* (Frankfurt am Main: 1646)

Anonymous, *Archivio Storico Italiano. Serie terza.* XIV (Firenze: 1871), pp.239–243

Anonymous, *The Great and Famous Battel of Lutzen, fought between the renowned King of Sweden, and Walstein* (London: 1633)

Anonymous, *Glaubwürdiger Bericht und Erzehlung* (unknown: 1633)

Anonymous, *Nordalbingische Studien*, vol. 1. part 1 (Kiel: 1844)

Anonymous, *Eigendliche Abbildung und Warhafftige Beschreibung Der grossen und blutigen Schlacht so zwischen Königl. Maj. Zu Schweden und dem Keyserl. General von Wallenstein den*

6. Novembris, Anno 1632. bey dem Städtlein Lützen 2. Meil von Leipzig vorgangen (unknown: 1633)

Anonymous, *Vom 17. Novembris auß dem Kayserlichen Feldtlager bey Leipzig* (unknown: 1632)

Anonymous, 'Ordre op de wapeninghe 1599', in Johannes Bastiaan Kist, Jan Pieter Puype and Robert Balder Frank van de Sloot, *Musket, Roer ende Pistolet* (Den Haag : Gaade 1974), pp.143–144

Anonymous, 'Aus dem dreissigjährigen Kriege', in *Mittheilungen des k. k. Kriegs-Archivs 41* (Wien: 1882), pp.344–347

Antelmi, 'Dispacci Nr. 23 des Residenten Antonio Antelmi an die Signoria in Venedig', in *Archiv für Kunde österreichischer Geschichtsquellen* XXVIII, pp.359–363

Argang, 'Piccolominis bref om slaget vid Lützen', in *Historisk Tidskrift* 14 (1894), pp.87–90

Basta, Giorgio, *Il Governo della cavalleria leggiera. Das ist Bericht von Anführung der leichten Pferde* (Frankfurt: Iohann Theodor de Bry 1614)

Burgus, Petrus Baptista, *Mars Sveco-Germanicus sive rerum a Gustavo Adolfo suecico rege gestarum libri tres* (Cologne: 1641)

Chemnitz, Bogislaus Philipp, *Geschichte des königlich Schwedischen in Teutschland geführten Krieges*, vol. I (Stettin: 1648)

Cruso, John, *Militarie Instructions for the Cavallrie* (Cambridge: University of Cambridge 1632)

Droysen, Gustav, 'Gedruckte Relationen über die Schlacht bei Lützen', in *Materialien zur neueren Geschichte* vol. 1 (Halle: 1880), pp 1–46

Eldred, William, *The Gunners Glasse* (London: T. Forcet, 1646)

Erlach, H. L. von, 'Project und Guttachten. Über die anstellung eines gemeinen Defensionalwercks, so er uff bevelch syner H. Loblichen Statt Bern, etlichen myner Herren allhie zu Jhrem bedencken überreicht, uft den 21. Januarij Anno 1629', in Eugen von Frauenholz (ed.), *Das Heerwesen in der Zeit des Dreissigjährigen Krieges. Zweiter Teil. Die Landesdefension* (München: 1939), pp.107–119

Fiedler, Josef, 'Diodatis Bericht über die Schlacht bei Lützen', in *Forschungen zur Deutschen Geschichte* IV (Osnabrück: 1864), pp.555–572

Fleetwood, George, *Letter from George Fleetwood to his Father* (Stettin: 1632)

Förster, Friedrich, *Albrechts von Wallenstein, des Herzogs von Friedland und Mecklenburg, ungedruckte, eigenhändige, vertrauliche Briefe und Amtliche Schreiben aus den Jahren 1627 bis 1634*, vol. 2 (Berlin: 1829)

Förster, Friedrich, *Wallenstein's Prozeß vor den Schranken des Weltgerichts und des K. K. Fiscus zu Prag* (Leipzig: 1844)

Fronsperger, Leonhardt, *Fünff Bücher, vonn Kriegs Regiment und Ordnung, wie sich ein jeder Kriegssmann inn seinem Ampt und Beuelch halten soll, was zu anfang eines Kriegs zuerwegen unnd zubetrachten sey* (Frankfurt: 1558)

Gheyn, Jan de, *Waffenhandlung von den Röhren, Musquetten und Spiessen* (Gravenhagen: 1608)

Glafey, A. F., *De Gladio quo cum Gustavus Adolphus Rex sveciae in proelio Luzenensi occubuit* (Leipzig 1749)

Gottfried, Johann Ludwig, *Inventarium Sueciae. Appendix Andern Theil Inventarii Sueciae* (Frankfurt am Main: Wolfgang Hofmann, 1633)

Hallwich, Hermann, *Briefe und Akten zur Geschichte Wallensteins 1630–1634*, vol. 3 (*Fontes rerum Austriacarum*. vol. 65) (Wien: A. Hölder, 1912)

Hallwich, Hermann, *Briefe und Akten zur Geschichte Wallensteins 1630–1634*, vol. 4 (*Fontes rerum Austriacarum*. vol. 66) (Wien: A. Hölder, 1912)

Kellie, Thomas, *Pallas Armata* (Edinburgh: The Haires of Andre Hart, 1627)

Khevenhiller, Franz Christoph, *Annales Ferdinandei*, vol. XII (Leipzig: 1726)

Langman, 'Ett par bref om slaget vid Lützen 1632', in *Historisk tidskrift* 12, 1892

Lavater, Hans Conrad, *Kriegs-Büchlein. Das ist grundtliche Anleitung zum Kriegswesen* (Zürich: 1644)

Lorenz, G., *Quellen zur Geschichte Wallensteins. Ausgewählte Quellen zur deutschen Geschichte der Neuzeit*, vol. 20 (Darmstadt: 1987)

Mankell, J., *Arkiv till upplysning om Svenska krigens och krigsinrättningarnes historia* vol. II (Stockholm: 1860)

Mankell, J., *Arkiv till upplysning om Svenska krigens och krigsinrättningarnes historia* vol. III (Stockholm: 1861)

Markham, Francis, *Five Decades of Epistles of Warre* (London: Augustine Matthewes 1622)

Markham, Gervase, *The Souldiers Accidence* (London: W. I. and T. P., 1635)

Melzo, Lodovico, *Kriegs-Regeln von der Reitereij* (Jena: 1625)

Monro, Robert, *His Expedition with the Worthy Scots Regiment levied in August 1626 by Sr. Donald Mac-Key* (London: William Jones, 1637)

Montecuccoli, Raimundo, *Besondere und geheime Kriegs-Nachrichten des Fürsten Raymundi Montecuculi, Röm. Kays. Maj. Generalissimi, Worinnen die Anfangs-Gründe der Kriegs-Kunst sehr deutlich beschrieben sind* (Leipzig: 1736)

Murr, Christoph Gottlieb von, *Beyträge zur Geschichte des dreyßigjährigen Krieges* (Nürnberg: 1790)

Poyntz, Sydnam, *The Relation of Sydnam Poyntz 1624–1636*, in Goodrick, A. T. S., Camden 3rd series, vol. 14 (London: 1908)

Priorato, Galeazzo Gualdo, *Historia dell Guerra di Ferdinando II e Ferdinando III Imperatori e del Re Filippo IV di Spagna contro Gustavo Adolfi Re Svetia e Luigi XIII Re di Francia successe dall'anno 1630 fino all'anno 1636*, vol. 1 (Vienna: 1672)

Richelieu, Armand-Jean du Plessis, *Mémoires Du Cardinal De Richelieu, Sur la Régne De Louis XIII: depuis 1610 jusqu'à 1638.* 7. Années, Livre XXIII, XIV, 1632, 1633 (Paris: 1823)

Schwendi, Lazarus von, *Kriegs Discurs. Von Bestellung deß gantzen Kriegswesens und von den Kriegsämptern* (Frankfurt am Main: 1594)

Siri, Vittorio, *Memorie Recondite di Vittorio Siri dall'anno 1601. fino all' 1641*, vol. 7 (Parigi: Sebastiano Mabre-Cramoisy 1677)

Söltl, *Religionskrieg in Deutschland*, vol. 3 (Hamburg: 1842)

Stöwesand, R., *Magister Paulus Stockmann, Feld und Schiffsprediger Gustav Adolfs und Senior in Lützen* (Merseburg: 1927)

Stockmann, Paul, *Lamentatio Secunda Lützensium seu Epitaphium* (Leipzig: 1633)

Toegel, M., 'Der Schwedische Krieg und Wallensteins Ende', in *Dokumenta Bohemica Bellum Tricennale Illustrantia* V (Prag: 1977)

Turner, James, *Pallas Armata* (London: M. W., 1683)

Vernon, John, *The young Horse-man* (London: 1644)

Wallhausen, Johann Jacob von, *Kriegskunst zu Fuß* (Oppenheim: Iohann Theodor de Bry, 1615)

Wallhausen, Johann Jacob von, *Kriegskunst zu Pferdt* (Frankfurt am Main: Iohann Theodor de Bry, 1616)

Watts, William, *The Swedish Intelligencer*, vol. 3 (London: I. L. 1633)

Wittrock, Georg, 'Fyra relationer om slaget vid Lützen', in *Historisk tidskrift* 52 (1932) pp.299–309

Modern Sources

Ágoston, Gábor, 'Firearms and Military Adaption: The Ottomans and the European Military Revolution, 1450–1800', in *Journal of World History, Volume 25, Number 1* (2014), pp.85–124

Andronov, Svetoslav, *Der Elsterflossgraben. Geschichte und Gestalt eines technischen Denkmals* (Leipzig: Verlag Pro Leipzig, 2006)

Anonymous, *Die Schweriner Waffensammlung: 50 Jahre Verlust und Rückgabe* (Schwerin: Staatliches Museum, 2008)

Babits, Lawrence E., *A Devil of a Whipping: The Battle of Cowpens* (Chapel Hill: University of North Carolina Press, 1998)

Balázs, Polgár, 'Egy török ólomlövedék-típus régészeti perspektívaja', in Hausner Gábor (ed.), *Zrínyi-Újvár emlékezete* (Budapest: 2012), pp.104–109

Brooker, Robert, *Landeszeughaus Graz, Austria. R,dschloss Sammlung* (Graz: Landesmuseum Joanneum, 2007),

Brzezinski, R., 1989, 'Gustavus Adolphus', in *Military Illustrated* 21, pp 53–55

Brzezinski, Richard, *Lützen 1632. Climax of the Thirty Years' War* (Oxford: Osprey, 2001)

Brzezinski, Richard and Richard Hook, *Die Armee Gustav Adolfs. Infanterie und Kavallerie* (Königswinter: Brandenburgisches Verlagshaus, 2006)

Bücker, Hartmut and Dieter Härtig, *Das Gefecht bei Rippach am 1. Mai 1813, Die Schlacht bei Großgörschen am 2. Mai 1813 und der Überfall auf das Lützow'sche Freikorps bei Kitzen am 17. Juni 1813* (Vellberg: 2004)

Bursell, Barbo, 'Die Königliche Rüstkammer als Museum – Ein Vermächtnis Gustav Adolfs', Reichel, Maik, Schuberth, Inger (eds), *Gustav Adolf. König von Schweden. Die Kraft der Erinnerung 1632–2007* (Dößel: Verlag Janos Stekovics, 2007), pp.93–104

Delbrück, Hans, *Geschichte der Kriegskunst im Rahmen der politischen Geschichte*, vol. 1. Neuzeit (Hamburg: Nikol, 2008)

Diemar, Helmut, *Untersuchungen über die Schlacht bei Lützen (16. Nov. 1632)* (Kassel: Döll, 1890)

Diemar, Helmut, 'Der Anteil der Hessen an der Schlacht von Lützen 1632', in *Zeitschrift des Vereins für hessische Geschichte und Landeskunde N.F.* 18 (1893), pp 327–353

Diwald, Helmut, *Wallenstein* (München: Bechtle 1969)

Dolínek, Vladimir and Jan Durdík, *Historische Waffen* (Hanau: Dausien, 1996)

Doughty, Robert Allen and Ira D. Gruber, *Warfare in the Western World. Vol. 1. Military Operations from 1600 to 1871* (Lexington: Cengage Learning 1996)

Droysen, Gustav, 'Die Schlacht bei Lützen 1632', in *Forschungen zur Deutschen Geschichte* vol. 5 (Osnabrück: 1865), pp.69–235

Edwards, Peter, 'Arming and Equipping the Covenanting Armies, 1638–1652', Steve Murdoch and Andrew Mackillop (eds), *Fighting for Identity. Scottish Military Experience c. 1550–1900* (Leiden, Boston, Cologne: Brill, 2002), pp.239–264

Engels, Donald W., *Alexander the Great and Logistics of the Macedonian army* (Berkeley: University of California Press, 1980)

Engerisser, Peter, *Von Kronach nach Nördlingen. Der Dreißigjährige Krieg in Franken, Schwaben und der Oberpfalz 1631–1635* (Weißenstadt: Heinz Späthling, 2007)

Engerisser, Peter and Pavel Hrncirík, *Nördlingen 1634. Die Schlacht bei Nördlingen – Wendepunkt des Dreißigjährigen Krieges* (Weißenstadt: Heinz Späthling, 2009)

Engerisser, Peter, <http://www.engerisser.de/Bewaffnung/Doublehackbut.html> (accessed 24 February 2018)

Englund, Peter, *Die Verwüstung Deutschlands. Eine Geschichte des Dreißigjährigen Krieges* (Stuttgart: Klett-Cotta, 1998)

Eriksson, Bo, *Lützen 1632* (Stockholm: 2006)

Foard, Glenn, 'The investigation of early modern battlefields in England', in Harald Meller (ed.), *Schlachtfeldarchäologie (Battlefield Archaeology). 1. Mitteldeutscher Archäologentag vom 09. bis 11. Oktober 2008 in Halle (Saale)* (Halle Saale: 2009), pp.117–125

Gay, Mary Ann Harris, *Life in Dixe During the War: 1861–1862–1863–1864–1865* (Atlanta: C. P. Byrd, 1897)

Generalstaben, *Sveriges Krig, vol. 6. Fron Lech till Lützen* (Stockholm: 1939)

Guthrie, William P., *Battles of the Thirty Years' War. From White Mountain to Nordlingen 1618–1635* (Westport/Connecticut/London: Greenwood Press, 2002)

Harding, David F., *Lead Shot of the English Civil War: A Radical Study* (London: Foresight Books, 2012)

Holl, Brigitte, 'Wallensteins angebliche Skizze für die Schlacht bei Lützen', in *Schriften des Heeresgeschichtlichen Museums in Wien, vol. 7: Der Dreissigjährige Krieg*, Wien, pp.59–78

Hrncirík, Pavel, 'Prispevek k nálezum munice do rucních palných zbraní v prostoru bojiste Rozvadov 1621', in Vaclav Matousek (ed.), *Zpráva o 1. sezóne systematického archeologického výzkumu bojiste z roku 1621 u Rozvatova, Sborn muzea Ceského lesa v Tachove* (Domazlice: 2011), pp.17–21

Junkelmann, Marcus, *Gustav Adolf. Schwedens Aufstieg zur Großmacht* (Regensburg: Pustet, 1993)

Junkelmann, Marcus, 'Tilly. Eine Karriere im Zeitalter der *Religionskriege* und der Militärischen Revolution', in Marcus Junkelmann (ed.), *Heiliger oder Kriegsverbrecher* (Altötting: Gebr. Geiselberger, 2007), pp.6–51

Kaiser, Michael, *Politik und Kriegführung. Maximilian von Bayern, Tilly und die Katholische Liga im Dreißigjährigen Krieg* (Münster: Aschendorff Verlag 1999)

Knarrström, Bo and Stefan Larsson, *Hans Majestäts Friskyttar av Danmark* (Lund: Riksantikvarieämbetet 2008)

Knarrström, Bo, 'Battlefield Research in Scania, Southern Sweden. Epic battles and small scale skirmishes in the scope of battlefield archaeology', in Harald Meller (ed.), *Schlachtfeldarchäologie (Battlefield Archaeology). 1. Mitteldeutscher Archäologentag vom 09. bis 11. Oktober 2008 in Halle (Saale)* (Halle/Saale: 2009), pp.187–198

Kortus, O., 'Albrecht von Wallenstein zu der Zeit des sächsischen Feldzugs in Böhmen 1631/1632', in Jens E. Olesen (ed.), *Terra felix Mecklenburg – Wallenstein in Nordeuropa* (Greifswald: Druckhaus Panzig, 2010), pp.113–124

Langer, Herbert, *Hortus Bellicus. Der Dreißigjährige Krieg* (3rd edn, Leipzig: Edition Leipzig, 1982)

Larsson, Göran, Nils Erik Villstrand and Lars Ericson Wolke, *Trettioariga kriget. Europa i brand 1618–1648* (Värnamo: 2006)

López, Ignacio and Iván Notario López, *The Spanish Tercios 1536–1704* (Oxford: Osprey, 2012)

Lloyd, Ernest Marsh, *A Review of the History of Infantry* (London: Longmans, Green, and Co, 1908)

Lunyakov, Sascha and Alexander Querengässer, *Feldmarschall Pappenheim und das kaiserlich-ligistische Heerwesen in der ersten Hälfte des Dreißigjährigen Krieges* (Berlin: Zeughaus Verlag, 2010)

Mandzy, Adrian, 'Tartars, Cossacks, and the Polish Army: The Battle of Zboriv', in Douglas D Scott, Lawrence E. Babits, Charles Haecker (eds), *Fields of Conflict. Battlefield Archaeology from the Roman Empire to the Korean War* (Washington: Potomac Books, 2009), pp.193–207

Mann, Golo, *Wallenstein* (Frankfurt am Main: Fischer, 1971)

Martin, Colin, 'Before the battle: undeployed battlefield weaponry from the Spanish Armada, 1588', in Phil W. M. Freeman and Tony Pollard (eds), *Fields of Conflict: Progress and Prospect in Battlefield Archaeology. Proceedings of a conference held in the Department of Archaeology University of Glasgow, April 2000* (Oxford: Archaeopress, 2001), pp.73–85

Misterek, Katrin, 'Ein Massengrab aus der Schlacht von Alerheim am 3. August 1645', in *Bericht der Bayerischen Bodendenkmalpflege* 53 (Bonn: 2012), pp.361–391

Mörke, Olaf, "Der Schwede lebet noch' – Die Bildformung Gustav Adolfs in Deutschland nach der Schlacht bei Lützen', in Mike Reichel and Inger Schubert (eds), *Gustav Adolf. König von Schweden. Die Kraft der Erinnerung 1632–2007* (Dößel: Verlag Janos Stekovics, 2006), pp.83–92

Mortimer, Geoff, *Wallenstein. The Enigma of the Thirty Years' War* (Houndmills, Basingstoke, Hampshire; New York, NY: Palgrave Macmillan, 2010)

Murray, Jeremy, 'The English-Language Military Historiography of Gustavus Adolphus in the Thirty Years' War, 1900-Present', in *Western Illinois Historical Review, Vol. V, Spring 2013*, pp.1–30

Neuhold, Helmut, *Der Dreißigjährige Krieg* (Wiesbaden: Marixverlag, 2011)

Nicklisch, Nicole, Frank Ramsthaler, Harald Meller, Susanne Friederich and Kurt W. Alt, *The face of war: Trauma analysis of a mass grave from the Battle of Lützen (1632)* (online publication 2017: PLOS ONE 12(5): e0178252: 2017), <https://doi.org/10.1371/journal.pone.0178252>

Olesen, Jens E., 'Dänische und schwedische Zusammenarbeit gegen Wallenstein und den Kaiser 1626–1629', in Jens E. Olesen (ed.), *Terra Felix Mecklenburg – Wallenstein in Nordeuropa* (Greifswald: Druckhaus Panzig, 2010) pp.41–57

Parker, Geoffrey, *The Thirty Years' War* (London; Boston: Routledge & Kegan Paul, 1984)

Parrott, David A., 'The Thirty Years' War, 1618–48', in John Andreas Olsen and Colin S. Gray (eds), *The Practice of Strategy: From Alexander the Great to the Present* (Oxford: Oxford University Press, 2011), pp.132–154

Pfaffenbichler, M., 'Waldstein als Kriegsunternehmer', in Eliška Fuciková and Ladislav Cepicka (eds), *Albrecht von Waldstein. Inter arma silent musae?* (Prague: Academia, 2007), pp.263–270

Pirkl, Jürgen, 'Die Handfeuerwaffenmunition des österreichischen Soldaten', in Peter Krenn (ed.), *Die Handfeuerwaffen des österreichischen Soldaten* (Graz: Akademische Druck und Verlags-Anstalt, 1985), pp.27–47

Pollard, Tony, 'Capturing the Moment: The Archaeology of Culloden Battlefield', in Tony Pollard (ed.), *Culloden. The History and Archaeology of the Last Clan Battle* (South Yorkshire: Pen & Sword Books, 2009), pp.130–162

Reichel, Mike, 'Die Schlacht von Lützen vom 6./16. November 1632 und der Tod des schwedischen Königs Gustav II. Adolf', in Harald Meller (ed.), *Schlachtfeldarchäologie (Battlefield Archaeology). 1. Mitteldeutscher Archäologentag vom 09. bis 11. Oktober 2008 in Halle (Saale)* (Halle/Saale: 2009), pp.127–133

Roberts, Michael, *Gustavus Adolphus. A History of Sweden. 1611–1632*. Vol. 2 (London, New York: Longmans, Green, 1958)

Roberts, Michael, 'Gustav Adolf and the Art of War', in Michael Roberts (ed.), *Essays in Swedish History* (London: Weidenfeld & Nicolson, 1967), pp.56–81

Roberts, Keith, *Matchlock Musketeer* (Oxford: Osprey, 2002)

Rost, Achim, 'Alesia, Kalkriese, Little Big Horn. Das neue Forschungsgebiet der Schlachtfeldarchäologie', in *Varusschlacht im Osnabrücker Land. Museum und Park Kalkriese* (Mainz: Verlag Philipp von Zabern, 2009), pp.101–117

Rost, Achim, 'Characteristics of Ancient Battlefields: Battle of Varus (9 AD)', in Douglas D. Scott, Lawrence E. Babits and Charles Haecker (eds), *Fields of Conflict. Battlefield Archaeology from the Roman Empire to the Korean War* (Washington: Potomac Books, 2009), pp.50–57

Schürger, André, Die Entstehung des mittelalterlichen Straßennetzes im Nordharzvorland, in Harald Meller (ed.), *Archäologie in Sachsen-Anhalt. Sonderband 4. Archäologie XXL. Archäologie an der B 6n im Landkreis Quedlinburg* (Halle Saale: 2006), pp.189–191

Schürger, André, 'Die Schlacht von Lützen 1632: Archäologische *Untersuchungen* auf dem linken kaiserlichen Flügel', in Harald Meller (ed.), *Schlachtfeldarchäologie (Battlefield Archaeology). 1. Mitteldeutscher Archäologentag vom 09. bis 11. Oktober 2008 in Halle (Saale)* (Halle Saale: 2009), pp.135–149

Schürger, André, 'Die ersten Minuten der Schlacht von Lützen (16.11.1632): Isolanis Kroaten und Stalhandskes finnische Reiter aus archäologischer Sicht', in Mike Reichel and Inger Schubert (eds), *Leben und Sterben auf dem Schlachtfeld von Lützen* (Lützen/Göteborg: 2011), pp.103–120

Schürger, André, '30 Jahre Schlachtfeldarchäologie: Von Little Big Horn bis Lützen', in Schuberth, Inger, Reichel, Mike (eds), *Die blut'ge Affair' bei Lützen. Wallensteins Wende* (Wettin-Löbejün: Verlag Janos Stekovics 2012), pp.247–253

Schürger, André, 'Theoretical calibre specifications of hackbuts and matchlock muskets in 16th and seventeenth century military handbooks', in Simon Sutherland and Tim Sutherland (eds), *Fields of Conflict Conference Proceedings* (online publication 2019) <http://fieldsofconflict.com/c_conf_papers.php?id=1>

Schwarz, Herbert, *Gefechtsformen der Infanterie in Europa durch 800 Jahre* (München: Schwarz, 1977)

Seidler, Josef, 'Khlevenhüllers Bericht über die Schlacht bei Lützen 1632', in *Zeitschrift für sudetendeutsche Geschichte.* 3/II (Brünn: 1938)

Seidler, Josef, *Untersuchungen über die Schlacht bei Lützen* (Memmingen: self-published, 1954)

Seidler, Josef. *Das Prager Blutgericht 1633* (Memmingen: 1962)

Sennewald, Roland, *Das kursächsische Heer im Dreißigjährigen Krieg* (Berlin: Zeughaus Verlag, 2013)

Sivilich, Daniel M., *Musket ball and small shot identification. A guide* (Norman: University of Oklahoma Press, 2016)

Srbik, Heinrich Ritter von, 'Zur Schlacht von Lützen und zu Gustav Adolfs Tod', in *Mitteilungen des österreichischen Instituts für Geschichtsforschung* 41 (Innsbruck: 1926)

Stadler, Barbara, *Pappenheim und die Zeit des Dreissigjährigen Krieges* (Winterthur: Gemsberg-Verlag, 1991)

Stahl, Andreas, "… die Todten Cörper vf der Wahlstadt begraben' – Das Amt Lützen und die Schlacht', in Inger Schuberth and Mike Reichel (eds), *Die blut'ge Affair' bei Lützen. Wallensteins Wende* (Wettin-Löbejün: Verlag Janos Stekovics 2012), pp.255–261

Kay, Christian, Jane Roberts, Michael Samuel and Irené Roberts (eds), *Historical Thesaurus of the Oxford English Dictionary* (Oxford: University Press, 2009)

Wedgwood, C. V., *Der Dreißigjährige Krieg* (Hamburg: Nikol Verlagsgesellschaft, 2011)

Weigley, Russel F., 'Auf der Suche nach der Entscheidungsschlacht. Lützen, 16. November 1632', in Stieg Förster, Markus Pöhlmann, and Dierk Walter (eds), *Schlachten der Weltgeschichte. Von Salamis bis Sinai* (München: dtv 2003), pp.138–153

Wolke, Lars Ericson, 'Die Schlacht bei Lützen', in Mike Reichel and Inger Schuberth (eds), *Gustav Adolf. König von Schweden. Die Kraft der Erinnerung 1632-2007* (Dößel: Verlag Janos Stekovics, 2006), pp.61–70

Wrede, Alphons, *Geschichte der K. und K. Wehrmacht. Die Regimenter, Corps, Branchen und Anstalten von 1618 bis Ende des 19. Jahrhunderts*, vol. 1 (Wien: L. W. Seidel, 1898)